The Battle of the
POTOMAC

A Century-Long Football Rivalry between the
West Virginia Mountaineers and the Maryland Terrapins

Chip Zimmer, Ph.D.

Contents

1st Quarter: The Rivalry

2nd Quarter: A Look Behind the Curtain

3rd Quarter: Let the Games Begin

4th Quarter: The Future is Bright…Right? 2019-??

Acknowledgements and Dedication

This book is dedicated to those many inspiring friends, mentors and colleagues who over the years have helped to plant this seed of an idea. Having graduated and worked for the athletic departments at both schools, my heart is torn when West Virginia and Maryland play. Couple this with my daughter, Kate, accepting a full athletic scholarship to play volleyball at Maryland, and you'll see my dilemma. I've finally settled into rooting for the Pride of West Virginia Marching Band, whoever is on offense and praying for a tie!

I completed my bachelor's and master's at WVU from 1969-76, was an invited walk-on for the baseball team, served two terms as the elected student representative to the Athletic Council and was selected to be a member of Mountain, WVU's ranking honorary and an honorary member of the Varsity Club. I later served as president of the National Capital Chapter of the WVU Alumni Association. Through these activities, I got to know many of the "who's who" of WVU Athletics over the last half-century. I knew Red Brown and Leland Byrd; Bobby Bowden and Frank Cignetti; Lysander Dudley, Gale Catlett and Fred Schaus. I met Don Nehlen, Jerry West and Sam Huff.

However, the two most impactful men in my journey through the West Virginia Hills have been John Nicholas and Rick Pill. John was my friend and mentor in the Alumni Association. He loved West Virginia with all his blue and gold blood and encouraged and promoted my unsuccessful candidacy to succeed Fred Schaus as Director of Athletics. Rick Pill is a contemporary. We went to school and played intramural sports together. He is a reincarnation of John Nicholas in the Eastern Panhandle, and the most true and dedicated Mountaineer I know. Most importantly, both Rick and John have been loyal friends for a lifetime.

My father-in-law, Hubert Douglas was a hard-scrapple Mountaineer, living his entire life in the hills of Kanawha County, and his wife Lucy. He got his GED after serving in WWII and went right to work in the coal mines and at Carbide. He never missed a Mountaineer game on the radio or TV, many times driving his pick-up truck to the top of a nearby mountain so he could get WCHS Radio and hear Jack Fleming call the game. Every time I watch or listen to the Mounties, I remember him.

Finally, this book is dedicated to my wife's cousin, #84 Bruce Huffman, who played for Bobby Bowden during the mid-70's. A tough kid, tough player and like a brother. Sadly, his life tragically ended in 2006. Rest in Peace, Bruce.

The Washington Capitals gave me my start into "the glamorous world of sports marketing." Special thanks to owner Abe Pollin, general manager Max McNab and director of marketing Andy Dolich.

On the Maryland side of the ledger, I attended grad school there immediately following graduation at WVU, got my Ph.D. in sport and business management and studied and worked there from 1976-82. I was the Assistant Intramural Director and then became the Assistant Athletic Director for Sports Marketing and became an honorary member of the "M Club." Many say that this was the end of the Golden Age in Maryland Athletics.

I worked for three athletic directors: Carl James, who hired me; Jim Kehoe who didn't fire me; and Dick Dull, who befriended me. All strongly impacted my time in Terpland. I got to know Bobby Ross and Jerry Claiborne; Lefty Driesell and Buck Williams; Boomer Esiason and Jack Scarbath; and Renaldo Nehemiah, Ralph Friedgen and Gary Williams.

Terp wrestling coach Sully Krouse, baseball coach Jack Jackson and assistant basketball coach Bill Turner, all took me under their wings and helped me navigate the intrigue of Cole Field House. They also introduced me to the real Maryland—goose hunting on Kent Island and eating freshly caught crabs and oysters with Maryland icons like Jack Faber, Al Heagy, Jack Fletcher and Bosey Berger. They regaled me with Terp stories going back to Bill Cobey and Jim Tatum. Alex Isherwood and Eloise Jones became bosom buddies and life-long friends; while Jack Zane had his thumb on the pulse of Terrapin Nation and helped this new kid on the block.

During my time in the Athletic Department, I had dozens of interns in the Sports Marketing Office, who taught me more than I could ever have taught them. The great triumvirate was Doug Dull (past president and a Hall of Famer in the College Sports Information Directors of America), Manny Rosenberg (restaurant owner in Brisbane, Australia) and Marc Goodman (Advertising Executive ABC, Los Angeles, deceased).

I couldn't have accomplished anything without them! I was especially honored and thrilled when Doug offered to edit this book.

I also had some interns who went on to distinguished careers in athletics: Joe Castiglione (AD at Oklahoma), Jeff Hathaway (former AD at Connecticut and Hofstra), Tom Burman (AD at Wyoming) and Mike Tice (former Head Coach, Minnesota Vikings). I'm proud of them all. Collectively, we kept our sanity thanks to Ruth Richards, my administrative assistant, who was the glue. She didn't even get flustered when she opened the office refrigerator to put in her lunch and out fell a goose that I'd shot the day before… She was the best!

My "Chipper League" buddies stoked enthusiasm for the rivalry, all coming to College Park for the 2011 game. They've all become fans of the rivalry despite their varied loyalties—Randy Hansen (Washington), John Gianotti (Illinois), Dan Andree (Baylor) and the late Joe Sharpless (Penn State). Also, my buds of over 60 years, Sam Schwab and John Cochenour who proofread and encouraged me all along the way.

I also would like to thank my author friends who guided and steered me on this, my maiden voyage—Tony Williams (*Washington and Hamilton*), Dave Ungrady (*Born Ready, the Mixed Legacy of Len Bias*), John Antonik (*The Backyard Brawl*), Walt Atkins (*How to be The Salesman They Remember*), and John Snyder (*Jacob's Bell, A Christmas Story*) and those that helped me through the publishing process: Dave Ungrady, Great Igwe, Doug Dull, Bridget Thoreson, and Lisa DeSpain. Finally, I'd like to dedicate this to my mentors, George Kramer, Zang Auerbach and Bob Guillot. Although they didn't know each other, they each schooled me on sports marketing… but more importantly on friendship, loyalty and life. I'll always remember them.

A special mention to John McNamara who was a reporter for the Annapolis Capital and who started at The Diamondback and then worked for other local papers covering the Terps. Tragically, he was murdered in the terrorist shooting in Annapolis in 2018. God Bless You, Mac.

Most importantly, I dedicate this to my daughter Kate, a Terrapin athlete and graduate, her husband Jon, my folks Bob and June Zimmer, and most importantly, my wife Barb. Barb and I met, married and grew up at WVU; flourished and spread our wings at Maryland. She made me and completes me.

Foreword I

By
Bobby Bowden
West Virginia Coach 1970-75

There are great and historic football rivalries in colleges all across America. It all starts with Army vs. Navy, which is a natural. The biggest in the South is Alabama vs. Auburn—this one is a WAR! Also, there are Southern Cal vs. UCLA and Notre Dame, Ohio State vs. Michigan, Texas vs. Oklahoma, Ole Miss vs. Mississippi State, Florida State vs. Miami and Florida, etc. Most of these are Southern schools that I am familiar with, having been raised in Birmingham, Ala.

The best-kept secret rivalry has been West Virginia University vs. the University of Maryland. It's a battle of border states that really intensified after the 1973 game.

I coached football at WVU from 1966 until 1975. My first years, I was the offensive coordinator, but when Jim Carlen resigned after the 1969 season, I became the head coach for the next six years. It has been over 40 years ago, and I have forgotten many details of those games. But one game stands out from back then.

Jerry Claiborne was head coach at Maryland and, in my opinion, was one of the greatest coaches who ever walked the sidelines. He built his reputation at Virginia Tech and Maryland. In 1976, he finished the regular season undefeated and nationally ranked. I knew him well when he was an assistant at Alabama and I was the head coach at Howard College, 50 miles to the north (now Samford University). He taught me a lot of football when I visited him in Tuscaloosa. Bear Bryant was the Crimson Tide's head coach at that time.

The game I remember most was played at Maryland in 1973. It was one of my team's greatest wins. When we played each other, I really wanted to beat Jerry because I respected him so much.

Maryland had led most of the game, until about five minutes left to play. Then Ade Dillon threw running back Dwayne Woods a 75-yard TD pass to tie the game at 13. With time running out, Maryland had to punt. Jerry said after the game he told his punter not to kick to our All-American safety Danny Buggs. But he did, and Buggs ran it back 69 yards for a TD! We hung on the last eight seconds and won the game.

This is one memory I'll never forget!

Foreword II

By
Bobby Ross
Maryland Coach, 1982-86

Until I got a call from Chip, I had never given much thought to the Maryland vs. West Virginia rivalry after I left Maryland in 1987. But after that call, a lot about our games with West Virginia from 1982 through 1986 started to surface. During those years the Maryland vs. West Virginia game was a BIG one for us, and why not…
- Maryland and West Virginia are neighboring states
- Both are state universities
- Both are Division I-A schools
- The history of their programs touches a number of Hall of Fame Coaches—Bear Bryant, Jim Tatum, Clark Shaughnessy and Jerry Claiborne of Maryland; and Bobby Bowden, Don Nehlen and Alfred "Greasy" Neale of West Virginia

I have never forgotten the time we got peppered with oranges when we took the field at West Virginia and were once delayed by game traffic for about 30 minutes. The West Virginia Police would not let our bus move until I got off the bus and started directing traffic myself!

There was also the time in 1983 when we had our first night game (1983) in the history of Maryland Football. A company from Iowa brought in portable lights and the Mountaineers gave us a 31-21 beating before a record crowd. I think we got all caught up in having lights and forgot about our preparation for the game.

Another important factor to this rivalry was, during our five years of playing the Mountaineers whether at home or at West Virginia, the stadium was packed—always—with fans from both schools.

In my coaching years, I have experienced a number of games which were considered rivalry games:

- Maryland vs. North Carolina
- Georgia Tech vs. Georgia
- Maryland vs. Virginia
- Army vs. Air Force
- Army vs. Navy
- Maryland vs. Clemson
- San Diego Chargers vs. Kansas City Chiefs
- San Diego Chargers vs. Oakland Raiders
- Detroit Lions vs. Chicago Bears
- Detroit Lions vs. Green Bay Packers

And it's my belief that the Maryland vs. West Virginia game, if renewed on a yearly basis, could match any of these for being classified a rivalry. Obviously, with both schools tied to different leagues it may be difficult to schedule. But in most programs, teams have three to four non-league games on their schedule. Perhaps a renewal might fit into this category.

Prologue

Having spent most of my life between College Park and Morgantown with stops in Laurel, Martinsburg, Hagerstown, Cumberland and Deep Creek Lake, I grew up with the Maryland-West Virginia game. Friends went to each school... even my wife and I went to both schools. My junior high buddy was a Terp fan, so, always the contrarian, I became a Mountaineer fan and first cheered them on watching the 1964 Liberty Bowl.

Despite the teams having first met on the gridiron in 1919, they didn't meet again until 1943 and played sporadically throughout the next three decades before the rivalry intensified. Throughout the ages, there are a number of "signature" games that leap out of the sports pages of history...

1919—Signature Game #1, Byrd-McIntire
This first game of the Battle of the Potomac matched two legendary coaches: Maryland's "Curley" Byrd and the Mountaineers' "Tubby" McIntire, who put WVU on the football map. West Virginia shut out the "Old Liners" in this kick-off game, 27-0.

1943—Signature Game #2, Spears-Rodgers
Legendary "Doc" Spears returns to Morgantown as Terp's coach and squared off against his protégé, WVU's legendary "Rat" Rodgers. The Mountaineers prevailed 6-2.

1948—Signature Game #3, Tatum-DeGroot

Featherweight drop-kicker, Gene Simmons, went from goat to hero in this 16-14 Mountaineer victory. He missed an extra point early but redeemed himself with a 22-yard field goal. A key Maryland fumble in the fourth quarter sealed the game for the Mountaineers.

1949—Signature Game #4, Tatum-DeGroot

For the first time, one team came into this rivalry game ranked. The Tatum-led Terps came to Morgantown with a 7-1 record and ranked 15th, on their way to a 9-1 season and a Gator Bowl championship. The Terps won 47-7 in DeGroot's final year at the WVU helm.

1951—Signature Game #5, Tatum-Lewis

Jim Tatum's juggernaut was in full swing as the Terps rolled to an undefeated season, including this 54-7 mauling of the Mountaineers for the 4th-ranked Terps' final regular-season win. Maryland went on to defeat top-ranked Tennessee in the Sugar Bowl, but the final votes had already been cast and the Terps finished No. 3.

*Unfortunately, the rivals didn't meet during their signature **1953** seasons when the Terps under Jim Tatum went to the Orange Bowl and won the national championship, and the Mountaineers under Pappy Lewis went to the Sugar Bowl. Both lost their bowl games, top-ranked Maryland to #4 Oklahoma, 7-0 and 10th-ranked West Virginia to #8 Georgia Tech, 42-19.*

Can you imagine the cast of All-Americans and Hall of Famers 1this game would have pitted against each other? Maryland's "60-Minute Backfield Foursome" of halfback Dick Nolan, fullback Ralph Felton, QB Bernie Faloney and halfback Chester Hanulak vs. West Virginia's guard Sam Huff, QB Fred Wyant, tackle Bruce Bosley and halfback Joe Marconi… Wow, what might have been!

*The **1970's** brought dramatic changes with future College Football Hall of Fame coaches Bobby Bowden taking the reins of the Mountaineers and Jerry Claiborne commanding the Terrapins. They met only once, in 1973 and it was a game for the ages!*

1973—Signature Game #6, Claiborne-Bowden

The Terps led most of the game until Mountaineer quarterback Ade Dillon connected with tailback Dwayne Woods on a 75-yard touchdown pass, tying the game with five minutes to go. It looked like the game would end in a tie until the Terps were forced to punt with just eight seconds to play. The ball sailed to All-American Danny Buggs who, in his patented style, caught the ball at the WVU 31, retreated back to the 15, dodged and deked Terrapin defenders and ran it all the way back for a dramatic touchdown, giving the Mountaineers a 20-13 victory.

By then the series was nearly even with the Terps holding a slight 7-6-2 edge. As Jack Fleming might say, "With Buggs' thrilling touchdown, the battle lines were drawn, teeth bared and weapons primed and ready… **The Battle of the Potomac Rivalry is officially ON!"**

1977—Signature Game #7, Claiborne-Cignetti

This was WVU coach Frank Cignetti's finest hour. Jerry Claiborne's 11th-ranked Terps welcomed the Mountaineers in their home opener after a season-opening win at Clemson. West Virginia surprisingly led 24-0 at the half and held on to win 24-16.

The **1980's** *brought legendary coaches Don Nehlen and Bobby Ross face to face, often led by their quarterbacks Jeff Hostetler and Boomer Esiason.*

1982—Signature Game #8, Ross-Nehlen

No. 17 West Virginia held on to win a 19-18 nail-biter when Terp coach Bobby Ross, upon scoring a TD to get within one, opted to go for the win on the road rather than a tie. The play came down to a mano-a-mano battle between future NFL stars Boomer Esiason of Maryland and Darryl Talley of West Virginia. Talley blitzed and forced Boomer to overthrow, giving the Mountaineers the win. This was even more important than beating Oklahoma the week before, as it proved to the Mountaineers that they could play with anybody.

1983—Signature Game #9, Ross-Nehlen

The rivalry was really heating up. Don Nehlen and Bobby Ross squared off again with both their teams ranked in the Top 20 for the first time.

The game matched star quarterbacks Jeff Hostetler and Boomer Esiason in a classic battle, under the lights for the first time at College Park. The Mountaineers won 31-21.

1984—Signature Game #10, Ross-Nehlen

Coming off two losses to open the season, this was an unlikely "must win" for the Terps in MoTown. The Terps upset the 17-ranked Mountaineers 20-17 on a Jess Atkinson field goal with 21 seconds left. The Terps went on to win eight of their next nine games, including a Sun Bowl win over Tennessee.

In 2001 the stars aligned again with the homecoming of two alumni to College Park and Morgantown. Former Terp and top assistant coach at Georgia Tech, Ralph "The Fridge" Friedgen, returned to his alma mater at the same time that Rich "Rich Rod" Rodriguez came home to the Country Roads after serving as the top assistant at Clemson. It looked like another Lewis-Tatum, Bowden-Claiborne and Nehlen-Ross rivalry in the making. Sadly, it didn't last as long as we had hoped, but it sure gave fans on both sides of the river some thrills!

2002—Signature Game #11, Friedgen-Rodriguez

This proved to be a homecoming party for Terp quarterback Scott McBrien, who had transferred from WVU. He led the Terps to a 28-0 lead in the first quarter with both his arm and his legs for two TD's. Josh Allen took an off-tackle run 70 yards for the third TD of the quarter. Receiver and punt return specialist, speedster Steve Suter, returned a punt 80 yards to end the first quarter and finished the game with eight returns for 142 yards. Maryland won going away, 48-17.

2004 Gator Bowl—Signature Game #12, Friedgen-Rodriguez

Payback. WVU transfer quarterback Scott McBrien smiled all the way to the proverbial bank as he led the Terps to a blowout Gator Bowl win over the Mountaineers. The No. 23 Terps defeated 20th-ranked WVU in a regular-season contest 34-7 and came back to humiliate the Mounties again in Jacksonville's Gator Bowl, 41-7.

2004—Signature Game #13, Friedgen-Rodriguez

After two humiliating losses to Maryland in the Gator Bowl and regular season, this game was a game-changer for the 7th-ranked Mountaineers. It validated Rich Rodriguez' philosophy. This was the game that showed that WVU could once again play with No. 21 Maryland. Since Friedgen and Rodriguez arrived, the Terps had their way with the Mountaineers, winning all four contests by a collective score of 155-51. This game was a nail-biter as the Mountaineers prevailed 19-16.

Fasten your chin straps, tighten your laces and strap in for the Battle of the Potomac… Holy Smokes!

Author's Note: As this is written, West Virginia leads the series by 28-22-2. Since the Terps whupped WVU twice in the 2003 season, West Virginia is on a 9-1 streak.

1st Quarter

The Rivalry

Chapter 1

The Path to the Rivalry

I grew up reading West Virginian Clair Bee's *"Chip Hilton"* novels, which forged my love of football and baseball. Looking back, I realize that reading about Hilton was my first exposure to organized football. I played Pop Warner football in Silver Spring, Md., played on Parkside Elementary School's touch-football team and organized my own neighborhood team, the LaVale Panthers as a 7th-grader in LaVale, Md. I served as a manager for the Allegany High School Campers football team as an 8th-grader and then had a non-descript high school career with Allegany and, after moving to Illinois, with the Herscher High School Tigers.

These formative years in Cumberland exposed me to one of the greatest high school rivalries in the nation: Allegany Campers vs. Fort Hill Sentinels. At that time, it was played on Thanksgiving Day and it seemed that the entire town showed up for the game with overflow crowds of 10,000+ jamming into Greenway Avenue Stadium.

Ironically, in 1948, the WVU freshman team played Maryland at Greenway Stadium in the first college game ever played there. The "Little Terrapins" defeated WVU 26-12 behind future Hall of Famer Ed Modzelewski in front of 4,500 fans.

It became a proving ground for some future collegiate stars on both sides of the river. Tommy Mont, a future Terp QB and head coach, went to Allegany. Spencer (W.Va.) native and WVU grad, Roy

Lester, coached Allegany from 1953-55 and later became the Terp head coach from 1969-71. Charlie Lattimer, a Fort Hill graduate and Terp letterman, played on the Terps' 1953 national championship team, and became a legendary Fort Hill coach from 1959-79. Ironically, he attended WVU for post-graduate work.

Ed Schwarz, 13-year coach of the Allegany Campers played for Bear Bryant and Jim Tatum at Maryland. Mark Manges, a Fort Hill grad, made the cover of *Sports* Illustrated, as he led the Terps to an undefeated 1976 season under Jerry Claiborne. Steve Trimble and Lyle Peck, also from Fort Hill joined Manges. From nearby schools, Wes Ours, a 1996 graduate of Westmar HS, played for Don Nehlen at WVU; Jarrod Harper was a Mountain View grad and a WVU starter. Sean Biser graduated from Keyser (W.Va.) and played for WVU, and Fort Hill grad Ty Johnson played for the Terps.

During this decade of the '60's, my burgeoning love affair with college football was consummated. Beginning with the 1966 "Game of the Century" when No. 2 Michigan State Spartans hosted top-ranked Notre Dame. There was much hype before the game, that I counted the days and hours before I could listen to the game on my transistor radio (both teams had used their allotted television appearances, so ABC decided to show it after it was over on a tape-delayed basis).

I remember a cold November day, passing a football with my buddy in our front yard as we listened. I was enamored with the Spartans barefoot kicker, Dick Kenney. How could he kick barefooted in Michigan weather without breaking a toe? The Irish tied the score at 10 early in the fourth quarter, after which ND Coach Ara Parseghian "took the air out of the ball," opting not to try to score, but settle for a tie. Dan Jenkins of *Sports Illustrated* accused Parseghian attempting to "Tie one for the Gipper." I was hooked!

The first rivalry game I attended was the next year when the 10th-ranked Purdue Boilermakers hosted top-ranked Notre Dame at Ross-Ade Stadium in West Lafayette, Ind., for the Shillelagh Trophy. Purdue won 28-21 before a sellout crowd of over 62,000. All-American Terry Hanratty was outdueled by Purdue QB Mike Phipps and

All-America halfback Leroy Keyes. As we walked out of the stadium, I was amazed to see that newspapers had already been printed with headlines announcing the Purdue upset! How'd they do that?

I was ready for big-time football when I arrived in Morgantown in 1969. I couldn't wait to see the crowds, the stadium, the teams. I quickly learned that Pitt was WVU's primary rival. Penn State was sort of a rival, but you had to win once in a while for it to be a real rivalry (PSU led 27-7-2 as of 1969). West Virginia hadn't beaten them in a long time. Syracuse was probably the next biggest rival then, followed by Virginia Tech or VPI as they were called back then. The Terps weren't on the radar and were considered cupcakes along with Tulane, Richmond, William and Mary and VMI, which still remained from WVU's former Southern Conference schedule.

I missed the first chance I had to attend the Maryland-West Virginia game. I woke up that Saturday morning in 1969 to a deluge of rain. It was going to rain all day. WVU had whupped Cincinnati in its opening game the week before by a score of 57-11. It was Maryland's opening game, but the Terps were awful, coming off a 2-8 season. These factors combined to help me decide to stay dry in my Boreman Hall dorm and listen to Jack Fleming on WAJR Radio. It was a wise decision as the Mounties easily handled the Terps 31-7. It was the only home game I missed in my seven years in MoTown!

It really wasn't much of a rivalry back then. The Terps were languishing. The football program was still clinging to memories of its dominance in the 1950's, while the Mounties were on their way to a 10-1 season, including an upset victory in the Peach Bowl over South Carolina. But that was all about to change.

Bobby Bowden would take over the Mountaineer reins upon Jim Carlen's departure to Texas Tech, while the Terps would suffer three more seasons under Roy Lester (a WVU grad) before bringing in Jerry Claiborne from Virginia Tech to turn the ship around.

Bowden took the Mountaineers to two more Peach Bowls before returning to Florida State to ultimately become a face on the Mount Rushmore of college football. Claiborne, meanwhile, built Maryland into a powerhouse, dominating the Atlantic Coast Conference and taking the Terps to six consecutive bowl games in that decade. This included an undefeated season and trip to the Cotton Bowl in 1976. The two teams only played four times in this decade and Bowden and Claiborne met just once (1973), which effectively began this rivalry.

I came to College Park for grad school in the fall of 1976. I immediately wanted to immerse myself in Terrapin football. As I asked about who the Terps' big rivals were, I received dumbfounded looks and shrugged shoulders.

Maryland had become a "basketball school," and football had become second fiddle. It seemed that whoever was having a good year in the ACC was a football rival, alternating from UNC to NC State to Clemson, but no one consistent. Virginia was kind of a rival, but not really. Penn State? Well, the Terps had a worse record (PSU led 21-1 as of 1976) against the Nittany Lions than even West Virginia did. WVU was the only game that could be expected to sell out at Maryland due to the huge contingent of West Virginians in the D.C. area, coupled with the proximity of the two schools.

So, the rivalry percolated. The Terps were undefeated in 1976. My cousin and I went to the Clemson game late in the season as the Terps were in the midst of pitching three consecutive shutouts against Cincinnati, Clemson and Virginia. But there wasn't the excitement or enthusiasm or fans I had expected and hoped for. But as Claiborne's "three yards and a cloud of dust" football became Bobby Ross's wide-open style and Frank Cignetti handed the WVU reins to Don Nehlen… The rivalry was on!

Until the series temporarily lapsed in 2007, the game was the longest continuously running non-conference game for both schools.

The Maryland–West Virginia rivalry is arguably more competitive than Maryland's other two historically important games—former ACC-rival Virginia and Big Ten-rival Penn State. For West Virginia, it may not be as emotional as the Backyard Brawl, but it is still a vital game. Partially due to the game traditionally being played early in the schedule, both teams have historically viewed the matchup as a good measuring stick for the rest of the year.

West Virginia Rivalry Games:

Pittsburgh (104)	40-61-3	Series began in 1895, last played in 2011
Syracuse (60)	27-33-0	Series began in 1945, last played in 2012
Penn State (59)	9-48-2	Series began in 1904, last played in 1992
Virginia Tech (52)	28-23-1	Series began in 1912, last played in 2017
Maryland (52)	**28-22-2**	**Series began in 1919, last played in 2015**

Maryland Rivalry Games:

Virginia (78)	44-32-2	Series began in 1919, last played in 2013
North Carolina (70)	32-37-1	Series began in 1920, last played in 2012
Clemson (62)	26-32-2	Series began in 1952, last played in 2013
West Virginia (52)	**22-28-2**	**Series began in 1919, last played in 2015**
Penn State (43)	2-40-1	Series began in 1917, last played in 2019
Navy (21)	7-14-0	Series began in 1905, last played in 2010

Penn State is annoyingly mentioned as a rival for both West Virginia and Maryland. However, for a true rivalry to exist, each team should win *some* games. Of teams with more than 40 games against Penn State, Maryland (.060) and West Virginia (.157) have the worst records of any PSU opponents in history. Not much of a rivalry if you lose almost all the time!

Series Data

Record when both teams are ranked: West Virginia leads, 2-1-0
Record when only West Virginia is ranked: West Virginia leads, 10-2-0
Record when only Maryland is ranked: Maryland leads, 4-1-0
Longest winning streak by West Virginia: 7 games (2004-2012)
Longest winning streak by Maryland: 6 games (1949-1966)
Most points scored by West Virginia: 55 (September 19, 1988)
Most points scored by Maryland: 54 (November 24, 1951)
Largest margin of victory by West Virginia: +39 (September 26, 2015)
Largest margin of victory by Maryland: +47 (November 24,1951)

West Virginia began its football program with an 1891 loss to Washington and Jefferson by an inauspicious score of 72-0! The Mountaineers have turned things around since then, and now rank as the 15th-winningest program in NCAA FBS Division (formerly Division I-A) history with 757 wins and a .598 winning percentage (757-502-45). This ranks them higher than such storied programs as Virginia Tech, Pitt, Syracuse, Navy, Washington, Colorado and Michigan State (all have a national championship under their helmet) among others.

The Mountaineers have bounced around the football spectrum with conference affiliation. After playing as an independent for half a century, they joined the Southern Conference in 1953. In 1968, head coach Jim Carlen convinced athletic director Red Brown to move the program out of the Southern Conference and become an eastern independent until 1991, when they became a member of the Big East. In 2012, with the Big East crumbling around them, the Mounties accepted a bid to join the Big 12, after being spurned by the ACC, SEC and Big Ten. Long-time rivalries with Pitt, Penn State, Virginia Tech, Syracuse and Maryland soon disappeared.

Maryland, on the other hand, is tied for 42nd nationally with 652 wins and a .518 winning percentage (652-605-43). The Terrapins, too, rank above some surprising powerhouses who have national championships under their chinstraps: Florida State, Miami, Illinois and UCLA, to name a few.

Maryland began football in 1892 and went scoreless in its only three games that season. The Terps became a charter member of the Southern Conference in 1921 and stayed until becoming a charter member of the newly formed Atlantic Coast Conference in 1953.

In 2014, Maryland shocked its fans by leaving the ACC for greener financial pastures in the Big Ten. Like West Virginia, the Terps' leaving the ACC spelled the end to traditional rivalries as well. Soon gone were Virginia, North Carolina, Clemson, Florida State and West Virginia. The change did, however, allow the annual renewal of the Penn State "rivalry."

Winningest College Football (FBS) Programs (through 1/14/20):

1. Michigan   962
2. Ohio State   924
3. Texas   916
4. Alabama   916
5. Notre Dame   908
6. Oklahoma   908
7. Nebraska   902
8. Penn State   898
9. USC   847
10. Tennessee   846
11. Georgia   831
12. LSU   812
13. Auburn   776
14. Clemson   758
15. **WEST VIRGINIA**   **757**
16. Virginia Tech   752
17. Texas A&M   749
18. Washington   742
19. Georgia Tech   738
20. Florida   735
21. **MARYLAND**   **652**

However, decades of animosity had existed between the two schools, dating back to the 1940's. In 1921, Maryland joined Clemson, North Carolina, NC State, Virginia and Georgia Tech, along with 24 other schools (i.e., Alabama, Auburn, Georgia, Kentucky, Tennessee and Mississippi State) as charter members of the Southern Conference.

Because of the unwieldy size, 13 members withdrew in 1932 to form the Southeastern Conference, leaving the Southern Conference with 10 institutions—Maryland, Virginia, North Carolina, NC State, Clemson, South Carolina, Duke, VMI, Virginia Tech and Washington and Lee.

During this time, West Virginia athletic director Harry Stansbury wanted WVU to focus on aligning with the northeastern football powers rather than looking southward, so the Mountaineers remained independent.

Immediately following WWII, vets flooded college campuses, using the G.I. Bill. Maryland's Bear Bryant coached nearly all older vets in his single season at College Park in 1945, creating some raised eyebrows. West Virginia was caught up in a scandal of their own when it was reported by *The Washington Post* that the school's eligibility requirements differed from others regarding the playing of World War II vets. They were accused of cheating but were eventually exonerated.

It was felt that Maryland's Tatum was the one fanning the flames despite his liberal use of vets at Maryland. Tatum even threatened to cancel the 1947 game in College Park over the controversy but acquiesced and agreed to play at the 11th hour.

In 1948, Maryland was dubbed as one of the Group of "7 Sinners," accused of putting too much emphasis on football and outwardly disobeying the NCAA's "Sanity Code." Tatum blamed West Virginia for spreading this story.

West Virginia joined the Southern Conference in 1950.

In 1951, the conference voted to ban bowl appearances by any member teams without conference approval. Maryland and Clemson ignored the regulation and accepted bids following the '51 season to the Sugar Bowl (Maryland vs. Tennessee) and the Gator Bowl (Clemson vs. Miami).

Longtime WVU reporter Tony Constantine said, "*Jim Tatum was not a fan of West Virginia. The Terps were invited to play in a major bowl (Gator, 1947), and at the time it had to be approved by the other Southern Conference members. WVU refused to approve. Tatum never forgot that.*"

Perhaps as a payback for Tatum's complicity with the "ineligible player" controversy in 1947, West Virginia joined 11 other schools in penalizing Maryland's violation of conference rules.

This vote put Maryland and Clemson on probation for the 1952 season, severely limiting their ability to schedule conference teams, resulting in in the cancellation of Maryland's scheduled 1952 game in Morgantown. Tatum then cancelled all future games with West

Virginia following the one-year probation, eliminating the possibility of the two powerhouses meeting in their heydays (1952-55). Tatum left Maryland after the 1955 season and died in 1959. The rivalry resumed two months after Tatum's passing.

In 1953, with the Southern Conference having grown to 17 schools, seven decided to break away and form the Atlantic Coast Conference. Maryland, along with North Carolina, NC State, Wake Forest, Duke, Clemson and South Carolina, formed this group.

West Virginia was not invited to join, purportedly for using ineligible players after the War, as well as for having poor academic standards, due in part to its adherence to its Land Grant status. Ironically, the four "Tobacco Road" schools—Duke, UNC, NC State and Wake Forest—had all voted for the Maryland/Clemson probation. However, there is little doubt that Maryland's pique with WVU for voting against their participation in the 1952 Sugar Bowl factored into the decision.

West Virginia AD "Legs" Hawley, tried to talk the ACC into taking WVU as the eighth member, but he had supposedly just Maryland and South Carolina supporting WVU. The others said the highways weren't good enough and neither was the air service for easy access to Morgantown.

Instead, Virginia was added as the eighth member. A few months later, North Carolina proposed that Virginia Tech and West Virginia be added as the ninth and tenth members. That proposal died in a 4-4 deadlock, with six votes required to pass. It is suspected that Maryland lobbied against the expansion. As you see, Maryland's Tatum seemed to be playing both sides of the fence.

After being spurned by the ACC, WVU remained in the Southern Conference in order to be a part of an all-sports league which included The Citadel, Davidson, Furman, VMI, George Washington, Richmond, Virginia Tech, Washington & Lee and William & Mary. WVU left the Southern Conference in 1968, at the urging of head coach Jim Carlen, to become an independent. Virginia Tech preceded the Mountaineers by leaving in 1965. In 1991, WVU became a member of the Big East and stayed until it crumbled around them.

Meanwhile, the ACC thrived and eventually added Georgia Tech and Florida State and losing South Carolina before college football was turned upside down as the 21st Century began.

During the 60's and 70's, WVU entered into on-again, off-again discussions with "The Big Four," including Pitt, Syracuse and Penn State, about starting a northeastern conference. But each time discussions got close, one of the schools backed out.

In the mid-1990's, WVU went hat-in-hand to the ACC meetings in Myrtle Beach, S.C., with a check for $1 million, asking for membership to the ACC. They were denied this time due to a small television market, a small library and poor academics. When the ACC expanded in 2005, West Virginia tried again but was similarly denied. In 2012 as the Big East was collapsing, WVU was turned down by the ACC (along with SEC and Big Ten).

In 2015, Mickey Furfari, *Morgantown Dominion Post* writer asked Shane Lyons in his first weeks as the athletic director of West Virginia University about the ACC's unwillingness to add WVU to the conference. Lyons had previously spent 10 years in an administrative position with the ACC. *"I don't think it's a lack of respect; I think that it was just what they were looking at for their footprint for their conference."* Huh?

WVU ultimately went to the Big 12. While Maryland left the ACC for perceived greener pastures with the Big Ten. Was Maryland behind the multiple denials of the ACC to accept West Virginia? We'll never know, but many West Virginians have long memories.

"It's always been a very intense rivalry; a very physical ballgame," former Mountaineer head coach Rich Rodriguez said. *"I think it's been great for both fans because it's so close. It seems like it's always sold out whether we're at their place or they are at our place. I think it's been a great series."*

This rivalry game has recorded five of the top 18 crowds in Maryland Stadium history:

September 17, 1983	54,715 (3rd)	Maryland #17, WVU #20
September 17, 2011	53,627 (5th)	WVU #18
September 13, 2007	53,107 (6th)	WVU #14
September 17, 2005	52,413 (14th)	
September 20, 2003	51,973 (18th)	

No other team has more than one top-10 attendance games at Maryland. The largest crowd ever at Maryland Stadium was against Penn State in a game for the ages. The 9th-ranked Lions edged the No. 13 Terps on Nov. 1, 1975, before a crowd of 58,973.

At Mountaineer Field, eight games have surpassed the 60,000 figure. WVU's record home crowd was 70,222 on Nov. 20, 1993 as No. 9 West Virginia hosted and defeated the No. 4 Miami Hurricanes, 17-13.

Top Maryland crowds at Mountaineer Field:

September 8, 1990	64,950	WVU #25	
September 20, 1986	63,500		
September 17, 1994	62,852		
September 26, 2015	61,174		
September 14, 2006	60,513	WVU #5	
September 18, 2004	60,358	MD #21	WVU#7
September 17, 1988	60,188	WVU #12	
September 18, 2010	60,122	WVU #21	

In 2007, ESPN called this rivalry "One of the country's most underrated rivalries."

Thoughts on the Rivalry... The AD's Chime In

Shane Lyons, WVU AD since 2014: "*The West Virginia and Maryland football series is a classic example of a competitive football border rivalry. The overall series is competitive, and it stands at 28-22-2 in favor of West Virginia, with many great games through the years.*

"I have always thought that this is one border rivalry that was great for both fan bases. The travel was relatively easy and made for great road trips. The stadiums were exciting places to watch college football and playing the game was beneficial to both schools in terms of ticket sales, fan interest and season success.

"There have been some great players involved in the series from both teams. I remember my first West Virginia vs. Maryland football game, as a WVU student, was a rivalry between quarterbacks between Jeff Hostetler and Boomer Esiason. You knew by watching them battle that both would go on to great NFL careers.

Overall, it's a college football series that makes sense. In today's age of conference realignment and long-distance travel, this is a border rivalry that is good for both universities, teams and fan bases. West Virginia and Maryland playing in any sport just makes sense."

Keli Zinn, WVU Interim AD, 2014; WVU Deputy AD, 2010-present (WVU Class of 2010) has a unique perspective, as she served in a similar position at Maryland from 2004-10: *"It's always been a game with good storylines and a long history. It's even more important now with West Virginia in the Big 12 and Maryland in the Big Ten, as it is a big game that fans can get to."*

The two teams were scheduled to play again in 2020 and 2021, but then the next *"window for a WVU-Terps game is in 2029."*

She remembers that when West Virginia came to College Park, she *"always carried a copy of my (U of Maryland) paycheck in my back pocket, to remind me where my loyalties should be!"*

Oliver Luck, WVU AD, 2010-2014: *"It's a very important game, beyond the proximity of the two schools. It's a fun place to play, as the fans can visit the monuments and make a weekend of it. The DMV seems to have as many WVU alums as Western Pennsylvania! I had discussions with Kevin Anderson (former Maryland AD), trying to keep the Terps on the schedule… It was a very meaningful game, especially during the Nehlen years. It was always played early in the season and was a bell-weather game. If we could beat Maryland, we'd go on for a good season."*

Ed Pastilong, WVU AD, 1989-2010: *"This game was outstanding for both teams because of the proximity of the institutions, and the ability for followers to attend was good. West Virginia's large alumni base in the D.C. area was strong and resulted in lots of tickets."*

Dr. Leland Byrd, WVU AD, 1972-1978: *"This was a good rivalry. We played three times while I was there and they all seemed to be close games. Maryland always drew the best crowds with the exception of Pitt games. But for some reason, (former Maryland AD Jim) Kehoe didn't seem very interested in keeping it going. He said their schedule was full."*

Damon Evans, Maryland AD since 2018: *"The Maryland-West Virginia rivalry has been one of the most storied in college football spanning more than 100 years. It features two fervent and passionate fan bases with tremendous affinity for their teams. Being border rivals, separated by 200 miles, allows both fan bases to interact with a short drive between the campuses. There have been some legendary games over the decades and we are excited to renew the rivalry in 2020." (*Now 2021 due to the pandemic).

Debbie Yow, Maryland AD, 1994-2010: *"During my 16-year tenure as AD… the two closest opponents were UVA and WVU… The consistent out-of-conference rival was WVU. The competition mattered, in part, because there were so many recruiting battles for student-athletes and also because a WVU quarterback (Scott McBrien) transferred to Maryland and had considerable success… while WVU landed a Baltimore running back who was an exceptional talent (Tavon Austin). WVU always seemed to be improving their stadium or support services for athletes, and Maryland coaches and administrators took note. There was a considerable amount of respect."*

Dr. Suzanne Tyler, Acting Maryland AD, 1990 & 1994: *"I was acting AD between Lew Perkins and Andy Geiger and then again between Geiger and Debbie Yow, and later became the AD at Maine. West Virginia's AD Ed Pastilong couldn't have been more gracious and helpful. He reached out to me to offer any help or assistance I needed and invited me to a special WVU tailgate party before the WVU-MD game in 1990 in Morgantown.*

Although we were the only ones dressed in red and white, they were very nice and gracious."

Dick Dull, Maryland AD, 1981-1986: *"The West Virginia game was an important rivalry for us. Next to Penn State, of course, we always were on the short end with them. With West Virginia it was very competitive. We usually had a chance to win and had some wonderful games. We had to put up extra temporary bleachers when they came to town.*

I remember Bobby Ross' second game when we went to Morgantown. He went for two to win the game after a late touchdown and didn't make it. We lost something like 19-18, but I knew we had a FOOTBALL coach then!

It's a shame we don't still play them. I know we need to schedule non-conference games that we can win, but we had no business playing Howard."

Thoughts on the Rivalry… AD's with Ties that Bind

Russ Potts (Maryland Class of 1964) Former Assistant AD at Maryland, AD at SMU: *"I wish they played every year! It's horrible scheduling. If you want to play somebody you can move some games around. You can't tell me that playing somebody like Bowling Green is better that playing West Virginia. Even if you have to play the game every year in a neutral site.*

This is a huge rivalry for Maryland because they recruit the same players and recruit the same areas. West Virginia gets some Maryland players and Maryland gets some West Virginia players. It goes all the way back to Jim Tatum who got the best three players off of an undefeated Martinsburg, W.Va., team.

Tom Nugent won a classic game against West Virginia in 1960. Claiborne and Bowden played in 1973 when Buggs ran that damn punt back. It was a heartbreaker. Then Ross and Nehlen had some great matchups with Boomer and Hostetler. Friedgen got things going again. It was awful that he was fired after a nine-win season. He should still be the Maryland coach!

Now more than ever there are so many rivalries that are not played. Texas-Texas A&M don't play anymore, are you kidding me? Maryland-West Virginia, Pitt-Penn State, it's horrible.

College football is doing a horrible job in growing its base. Attendance is down almost everywhere. It needs to go back to basics and get youth groups involved in coming to the games again.

Conference realignment will happen again, but only due to adversity, i.e., money challenges. It just doesn't make sense financially for a school to field so many teams."

Gothard Lane, (Randolph-Macon Class of 1969) Former Assistant AD at Maryland, Former AD at St. Bonaventure. *"The expansion of conferences killed some incredible rivalries, like Maryland-West Virginia. Pitt-Penn State… it's sad. Bowls should grab teams who were traditional rivals and they'd sell them out.*

The Maryland-West Virginia rivalry was incredible. It was a border war, just like Penn State. West Virginia had incredible fans who were extremely loyal. Fans would come by the thousands and fill up the place. Like Texas, you don't mess with West Virginia, they'll fight until the last dog is hung! But rivalries are about playing every year.

"There's talk that the Power 5 conferences are going to consolidate and shrink down to four conferences. The Big 12 would be the odd man out and the other four conferences would divvy up the Big 12 teams, but some would be left out. West Virginia could potentially be reunited with Maryland and Penn State in the Big Ten or with Pitt, Syracuse and Virginia Tech in the ACC."

Jeff Hathaway (Maryland Class of 1981) Former Assistant AD at Maryland, Retired AD, University of Connecticut and Hofstra: *"It's always been an intense rivalry. I remember seeing lines of RV's coming in. West Virginia came in masse… It was a big game on the schedule, usually early in the season. Terp fans were up for it… It was one of two games that they had to bring in 4,000-5,000 temporary bleachers (the other was Penn State).*

Greg Manning (Maryland Class of 1981) Former AD, Georgia State: *"As a Maryland fan, there were always two games you circled on the schedule the moment it was released—West Virginia and Penn State. Each* *one was a fierce border war between non-conference rivals. Over the years, these types of games have increasingly gone away in large part to conference realignment and tremendous pressure to win non-conference games. It sure would be exciting to get back to circling those two dates once again each season. Gas up the RV, hang the Fear the Turtle flag, WVU and PSU here we come!"* And this from a basketball guy!

Gib Romaine (East Stroudsburg, Class of 1964) Former Assistant Football Coach and Assistant Director of Terrapin Club at Maryland, Former AD, Hood College. *"It was quite a rivalry. Both teams were always very competitive. The coaches and players always looked forward to this game. With Morgantown and College Park being pretty close together, it was a natural. I had friends in Morgantown and they always snuck into the old stadium on Friday night and taped bottles of whiskey under the bleacher seats for the game the next day!"*

Rob Mullens, (WVU Class of 1993), Director of Athletics, University of Oregon. *"As a native of Morgantown, a WVU grad and a former employee in the Maryland Athletic Department (1996-2002), I am familiar with the football rivalry. It had lots of energizing elements. Obviously, the proximity as border state and overlap of recruiting territory makes it fun—especially when it's an easy road trip to visiting team fans. It always seemed the game had large, energetic crowds. My biggest recollection was it was an early season measuring stick for both programs which added lots of energy to the game."*

Whit Babcock, (WVU Class of 1996) WVU Executive Dir. of Development; Director of Athletics, Virginia Tech: *"I was employed at WVU from 2002-2007. Those were some great games early in the season. Maryland and WVU were both rolling pretty well those days and the early season matchup certainly set the tone for the season.*

I recall getting beaten pretty badly in College Park and then in the Gator Bowl in 2003-04.… that one was tough. I also remember "getting over the hump" with Maryland and the OT touchdown pass from Rasheed Marshall to Chris Henry in the end zone nearest the Puskar Center in 2004.

WVU kept it rolling for many years after that. It was a good win and psychological victory for WVU in those days… Really sparked the overall momentum.

It should be a tremendous atmosphere when the rivalry renews (same for WVU-Pitt). The dust has seemingly settled with conference realignment. WVU, Maryland, Pitt and Virginia Tech all moved on to new conferences. The landscape seems to have calmed down on that front, thankfully, and scheduling is following suit.

WVU vs. Maryland, WVU vs. VT, and VT vs Maryland. College football needs these strong, regional intra-conference games. Fans and students want to watch them; they are getting more discerning than ever with their entertainment and season-ticket dollars. Players want to play in these amped up energy games on national TV. Alumni enjoy the bragging rights of victory and the on-campus, home-and-home matchups are a nice change of pace to the neutral-site games."

Chapter 2

Hillbillies and City Slickers:
The Rivalry's Cultural Divide

An important aspect of this rivalry is rooted in cultural differences between the two institutions, the citizenries and the history of each.

The University of Maryland is an urban school located inside the Washington Beltway in College Park (elevation 23 feet), almost within sight of the Washington Monument. West Virginia University is located in Morgantown, some four hours (207 miles) west of College Park, nestled among the Appalachian Mountains, just minutes from Cooper's Rock (elevation 2,159 feet). But the eastern-most part of West Virginia is a mere 50 miles from College Park. Conversely, the western-most part of Maryland is only 30 miles from Morgantown. But the differences are as wide as the Shenandoah Valley and deeper than Deep Creek Lake.

Marylanders are sophisticated, cultured and wealthy. They read the world-renowned *Washington Post* every morning and they're connected. Montgomery and Howard counties are two of the top eight wealthiest counties in America. The region is recession-proof, with the Federal Government providing a large percentage of the jobs. But every four years or so, the population turns over with new administrations as housing sales and prices often skyrocket.

Maryland is the wealthiest state in the nation, while West Virginia is near the bottom, leading only Mississippi and Arkansas. Marylanders are crabs, Beemers and Chardonnay; while West Virginians are hot dogs, Ford F-150 trucks and cold beer.

Maryland was a border state with heavy Southern leanings in the Civil War, while West Virginia began as a southern state and seceded from Virginia to join the Union. Maryland is as blue as New York and Massachusetts, while West Virginia is as red as Oklahoma and Alabama.

Marylanders love their sports, but historically have focused more on the Redskins and Orioles and recently the Capitals and Ravens, than college football. In their heydays, the Georgetown Hoyas and Maryland earned attention.

Terrapin basketball teams led the Starbucks' discussions and dominated the headlines. Rarely, however, has the Maryland football team enjoyed this type of support. It did for a few years in the early '50's when the Terps won the National Championship under legendary coach Jim Tatum. Jerry Claiborne lifted them to the national stage in the 70's, while Bobby Ross reignited interest when he arrived in the early '80's and Ralph Friedgen ratcheted it up a notch in the early 2000's. But in a century or more of football, these four instances were merely a blip on the radar screen.

On a sunny, fall afternoon, Maryland football competes with sight-seeing in D.C, a plethora of events and festivals throughout the DMV (D.C., Maryland, Virginia) and of course outdoor activities on the Chesapeake Bay. Consequently, Saturday afternoons at Maryland Stadium are often an afterthought.

Football sellouts are a rarity in College Park, despite the controversial move to the Big Ten, where the likes of Ohio State, Michigan and Penn State, among others, occasionally come to town. Visits from Alabama and Penn State in the '70's remain the two largest crowds ever, and West Virginia games have produced the third (1983), fifth (2011) and sixth (2007) largest crowds. Since 1951, Maryland has hosted West Virginia 23 times. Thirteen of these games were sellouts and 17 produced the largest crowd of that particular season. So, the notion that the WVU game is the one game each year that fills the stadium isn't far-fetched.

Maryland does enjoy and takes advantage of some highly visible alumni—from the late Jim Henson of Muppet fame to CBS' Boomer Esiason, ESPN's SVP (Scott Van Pelt) and Under Armour's Kevin Plank. Collectively these people have helped to improve the Maryland brand and to increase visibility and support. But it hasn't translated to a full Maryland Stadium, except when the Mountaineers venture into town.

Traditionally, it's been very difficult for major cities, especially those with NFL and MLB franchises to embrace and support "big-time" college football on a regular, consistent basis. Maryland, in the shadow of D.C., is no exception.

Look across the nation and see for yourself. Does NYC have a viable college football power supported by sold-out stadiums? Boston? Philly? Pittsburgh? Buffalo? Charlotte? Atlanta? Not even Miami. How about Chicago? New Orleans? Denver, Dallas or LA?

The University of Michigan historically leads the nation in attendance but is located 45 miles from Detroit, thus Ann Arbor can hardly be called a suburb. The Miami Hurricanes, although often a football power, has trouble getting 80 percent capacity in their 65,000-seat Hard Rock Stadium. The Washington Huskies seem to be the closest, averaging some 69,000 in their 72,500-seat building.

Take a look at the top-10 universities in average football home attendance, listed from 2018:

Michigan	Ann Arbor	111,500
Ohio State	Columbus	107,500
Penn State	State College	106,700
Alabama	Tuscaloosa	101,700
Texas A&M	College Station	98,800
LSU	Baton Rouge	98,500
Tennessee	Knoxville	95,700
Texas	Austin	92,700
Georgia	Athens	92,700
Nebraska	Lincoln	89,800

So, you see, those college football programs that thrive and enjoy regular sellouts are generally those in less urban and more rural areas, like… West Virginia!

Aah, West Virginia. Almost Heaven. It's a far different culture and lifestyle. Although WVU joins Maryland as a Carnegie R1 research institution and a Land Grant University, other similarities are few.

West Virginia is a prideful state. Perhaps only behind Texas and maybe Alabama, West Virginians wear their loyalties on their sleeves, chests, hats and pick-up trucks!

The only professional teams in the state are minor league baseball franchises in Charleston, Morgantown, Princeton and Bluefield, thus WVU has become the "state-wide" team. Life in West Virginia pauses during WVU football games, while throngs of RV's and other vehicles can be seen on I-79 and I-68 converging on MoTown as the sun rises on a football Saturday. Every "holler" has the TV or radio tuned in to hear Tony Caridi bring the game into their homes, as internet availability in the hollers is spotty, at best.

West Virginians have been maligned since their birth during the Civil War. It was settled by hard-scrabble Scots-Irish and Italian immigrants who came to carve out a piece of Heaven for their families. They're tough, hard-working, church-going folk who treasure family, country, guns and West "By God" Virginia. Many still work in the coal mines. The chemical plants have thankfully been abandoned. Health-care, WVU, Mylan Pharmaceuticals, Wal-Mart and Kroger seem to be the largest employers. Gardens are plentiful. West Virginians are used to disasters, whether coal-mine collapses or floods, they seem to have lost and endured more than their share.

They view this game, perhaps, as a push-back for all those "West Virginia jokes" they've endured over generations. They've been called hillbillies and rednecks. They've been caricaturized in comics, on television and in Hollywood, as living in trailers with a beat-up truck on cinder blocks and a washing machine on the porch. Their women are all barefoot and pregnant, often with a cousin. These are the slights and insults—the chip on their shoulder—that West Virginians bring to this game. Rightly or wrongly, they may view that winning this game is a vindication of all that they've had to endure, and even wear all of these decades of slights as a badge of honor.

So, when the Mountaineer and the Pride of West Virginia Marching Band leads the team onto Capital One Field at Byrd (sorry, Maryland) Stadium on September 4, 2021 to the chant from the Maryland student section, "*Go Back, Go Back, Go Back Into the Woods*," you'll understand why there is special significance as the firing of the musket echoes across Route 1 and the tune of Country Roads reverberates around the Beltway.

Cultural differences? A ton of them! But through struggles there has grown a mutual respect. It's become a barometer game for both teams. It seems that whoever wins this rivalry game goes on to a successful season and often a bowl. So, there's that.

City Slickers? Hillbillies? Maybe… and proud of it!

Chapter 3:

Rivalries in College Football

The appeal of college football has always been its color, pageantry, traditions and rivalries. Maryland was the nation's leader in promoting its programs, with the hiring of the NCAA's first sports promotions director, Russ Potts, in the mid-70's. I had the honor and challenge of trying to fill his shoes in 1979. Maryland was the first to make a college football Saturday an event with bands, cheerleaders, mascots, balloons, cannons, paratroopers, giveaways, etc. In fact, the Terps were noted in *Sports Illustrated* for their unique season-ticket sales promotion: inserting season-ticket fliers in every Maryland state income tax return in 1981.

But all the hype and excitement cannot match the fervor and enthusiasm that is generated by long-time rivals. Maryland and West Virginia have met 52 times, not the longest rivalry for either of them but one that creates border-state passions.

So, let's look at the true American pastime, and its greatest rivalries, that always seem to take center stage as the turkeys begin looking over their tailfeathers for that "Stanford Axe" (Rivalry game trophy presented to the winner of the Cal-Stanford game since 1899), or that "Sweet Sioux Tomahawk" (Rivalry game trophy presented to the winner of the Northwestern-Illinois game from 1945-2008). College football is vastly different from the NFL. It boasts color and pageantry.

It boasts tradition and loyalty. It boasts "amateurs" and excitement. It's history. It's passion. It's All-American!

As we take a virtual walk through the hallowed halls and visit the ghosts of Rockne, Bryant, Paterno, Camp and Stagg, look closely and you'll experience all the senses of college football.

Walk through the parking lot toward the stadium, as thousands of tailgate parties revel in anticipation. Smell the three-alarm chili, the crispy fried chicken and even that regional favorite, pepperoni rolls! As we stop to sip a mug of steaming apple cider or a cold brew, we hear the marching band from a distance. What song is that? It depends on where your heart is, but it rushes back memories—and goosebumps.

It might be "Hail to the Victors (Michigan)," or "The Eyes of Texas," or "The Notre Dame Victory March," or "Fight On (Southern Cal)," or my personal favorites: "Hail West Virginia" or "The Victory Song (Maryland)." Whatever the song, the band high-steps through the tailgate area, decked out in their colorful splendor, as avid alumni raise a toast and join in with lusty, off-key voices with the memorized words from their student days so many years ago. The band marches into the stadium and plays their favorite memories and forms traditional patterns for the home team to charge out to the roar of nearly 100,000 voices, cheering them on to victory. Cannons are fired, memorable mascots exhort, cheerleaders backflip and balloons are released, as the hopeful victors swarm to their sideline. Wow! Does it get any better than this? These truly are the sights, sounds and traditions of America's sport!

This scenario is repeated hundreds of times throughout the nation each year, whether it's in State College, Tuscaloosa, College Station or Columbus. But these contests take on even greater intensity and stature when the "big game" arrives. These games may or may not have any bearing on the national championship or even the conference title. Much more important, they mean bragging rights and add to the storied traditions of a rivalry.

What defines a classic college football rivalry? First, it should be played regularly, if not annually, for decades. Second, in an ideal world, it would have conference or national significance. Third, it should not be dominated by the same team, year after year. Fourth, it is often an intra-state or border-state rival. Fifth and finally, and most important, it brings out the best in fan loyalty, enthusiasm, excitement and tradition. Throw out the records, the winner of this game enjoys a successful season and basks in the glory of bragging rights until next year!

In 1990, Penn State began changing the face of college football with its membership to the Big Ten (or however many schools it has today). This led to a shuffling of traditional conferences, forever changing the face of college football. The Southwest Conference died, the Big 8 became the Big 12, incorporating much of the SWC, the SEC grabbed others from the SWC, the ACC expanded and the Big East was created and decimated.

The net result for the Nittany Lions was the elimination of such traditional rivalries as Syracuse (68 meetings, beginning in 1922), West Virginia (59 meetings, beginning in 1904) and Pitt (95 meetings, beginning in 1893). In normal circumstances, the Pitt-Penn State game would certainly be included in this discussion of great rivalries, but Penn State's cavalier disregard for these traditional alliances, leaves all of college football dismayed.

Sure, they now can create new rivalries with Michigan and Ohio State, both logical regional rivalries, but they also have added the likes of Minnesota, Iowa and Northwestern to their stable of conference rivals. Penn State did apparently see the error of their decision and occasionally brought Pitt back onto their schedule 10 times in the last in 30 years, but no further contests are scheduled.

With all the conference changes this decade, it's hard to keep track of what team is where. Sadly, this "Great Money Grab" has shot the goose that laid the golden egg—traditional rivalries. Consider the following 50 year-plus traditions that are no longer regularly played:

The Border War: Kansas vs. Missouri (120 meetings)
Texas vs. Texas A&M (118 meetings)
Victory Bell: Missouri vs. Nebraska (104 meetings)
The Backyard Brawl: Pitt vs. West Virginia (104 meetings)

Pitt vs. Penn State (100 meetings)
Tiger-Sooner Peace Pipe: Missouri vs. Oklahoma (96 meetings)
Rice vs. Texas (94 meetings)
Nebraska vs. Oklahoma (86 meetings)
Maryland vs. Virginia (78 meetings)
Penn State vs. Syracuse (71 meetings)
Ben Schwartzwalder Trophy: Syracuse vs. West Virginia (61 meetings)
Penn State vs. West Virginia (59 meetings)
Black Diamond Trophy: Virginia Tech vs. West Virginia (52 meetings)

So, what are the best rivalries left in college football?

We've long passed the idyllic interest in the original "The Game" between Harvard and Yale. Since then, the Army-Navy game has been the ultimate college football rivalry. They've had some classic Heisman winners and contests, but have faded a bit since their hey-day in the 40's and 50's.

To many, Notre Dame is college football. Just consider the movies made about them from "Knute Rockne All-American" staring Pat O'Brien and Ronald Reagan to "Rudy" starring Sean Astin and Ned Beatty. They emit emotions similar to the Patriots or Yankees… you either love 'em or hate 'em. They joined the academies in dominance in the 40's and their rivalry games with them and Michigan were classics. The Notre Dame-Southern Cal rivalry blossomed in the '60's and remains the best inter-sectional rivalry in football.

The Red River Shootout between Oklahoma and Texas dominated the 50's along with Nebraska-Oklahoma.

Rivalries abounded in the 1960's. Army-Navy was still big, but Texas-Texas A&M, Alabama-Auburn, Notre Dame-Southern Cal, and Michigan State-Notre Dame began getting national attention.

"The Game" between Ohio State and Michigan took the mantle in the '70's with classic matchups between coaches Bo (Schembechler) of Michigan and Woody (Hayes) of Ohio State. The Big House and the Horseshoe. Nebraska-Oklahoma cranked out four national championships between them.

The battle of Florida with Bowden's Florida State Seminoles, Steve Spurrier's "the old ball coach," Florida Gators and the Jimmy Johnson-led Miami Hurricanes' battles amongst each other seemed to dominate the 80's and 90's.

We used to think Alabama was a dynasty under Bear Bryant in the 60's and 70's, but Nick Saban has taken the Crimson Tide to a different level. Their rivalry with Auburn has seemingly taken over as the top rivalry in college football.

So, after celebrating last year's 150th anniversary of college football, here is my list of the top national rivalries in college football…today, although some have been temporarily interrupted due to the virus!

1. **The Iron Bowl: Alabama vs. Auburn**
2. **The Game: Ohio State-Michigan**
3. **Army-Navy**
4. **The Red River Shoot Out: Texas-Oklahoma**
5. **Sunshine Showdown: Florida-Florida State**
6. **The Jeweled Shillelagh: Notre Dame-USC**

Once we get past these half-dozen rivalries that generate national interest, the excitement, enthusiasm and passion generated among those of more regional interest are immeasurable and frankly, unrankable. Try to convince a Husky fan dressed in gaudy purple and bright gold that their Apple Cup game isn't as consequential as, for instance, a bright orange-clad alumnus screaming "Punt Tide Punt" as Alabama roars into Neyland Stadium on the Third Saturday in October.

Or that Harvard-Yale is any less important than fighting for Paul Bunyan's Axe (Rivalry trophy for the Wisconsin-Minnesota game). Here are some of the best regional rivalries:

Northeast
- The Game: Harvard-Yale
- The Rivalry: Lehigh-Lafayette

Midwest
- The Shillelagh Trophy: Purdue-Notre Dame
- Paul Bunyan's Axe: Wisconsin-Minnesota

- Land of Lincoln Trophy: Illinois-Northwestern
- The Bedlam Series: Oklahoma-Oklahoma State

Mid-Atlantic

- The Battle of the Potomac: Maryland-West Virginia

Southeast

- The Palmetto Bowl: Clemson-South Carolina
- Third Saturday in October: Tennessee-Alabama
- World's Largest Cocktail Party: Florida-Georgia
- The Florida Cup: Florida State-Miami
- The Egg Bowl: Ole Miss-Mississippi State

West

- Victory Bell: UCLA-USC
- The Big Game: Cal-Stanford
- The Apple Cub: Washington-Washington State
- The TBD (formerly The Civil War): Oregon-Oregon State

Let the debates begin!

Chapter 4:

The Future of This Rivalry

Here is a column I wrote for the *Charleston (W.Va.) Gazette-Mail* on September 4, 2015, regarding the state, and future, of college football:

"What's Next for Mountaineer Football?"

As the Mountaineers kick off their 125th year of college football on Labor Day weekend against powerhouse Georgia… Southern… it seems fitting to both reflect on where they've been as well as where they're headed!

All loyal Mountaineers know the rivalry with Pitt—the late, great Backyard Brawl—was WVU's longest-running rivalry, having knocked helmets 104 times in the 125 years (40-61-3). The Mounties met the Orangemen of Syracuse 60 times (27-33) for the Schwartzwalder Trophy; the Nittany Lions 59 times (9-48-2); and 51 times each against the Terps, in the Battle of the Potomac (27-22-2), and the Hokies for the Black Diamond Trophy (28-22-1).

Alas, these rivalries have faded into distant memories, as the Big East crumbled around the Mounties' ankles and took with it the historic rivalries—the backbone of college football—along for the ride.

Sadly, when the Pride of West Virginia sings the alma mater at the end of the pregame show, no one need scream "Beat the Hell out of Pitt," anymore, as had been done at every game for generations of West

Virginians. For you sentimentalists, Maryland is on the schedule this year and again in 2020 and 2021; Virginia Tech in '17 and '21 and '22; and Penn State in 2023 and 2024. But alas, no Pitt or Syracuse! (Update: Pitt and West Virginia resume the Backyard Brawl in 2023, 2024 and 2025).

The Big 12 is now the Mountaineers' home, as an artificial rivalry has been created with the Cyclones of Iowa State. But "Beat the Hell out of Iowa State" just doesn't have a ring to it.

So, what does the future hold? Will the Big 12 figure out how to count and add two more teams so they REALLY have 12? The commissioner says no and the pickins' are slim. It certainly seems best for the Big 12 to actually have 12 teams, but the most obvious candidates are ones who have already jumped the Big 12 ship (Nebraska, Missouri, Texas A&M and Colorado).

More important, what's in the best interests of WVU? Sure, they get some $20 million a year from the league (to the Big Ten's $24.6; the SEC could hit $27 with a revamped TV contract; the Pac 12 will approach $30 and the ACC about $17), but could they get that or more with a revamped and revitalized "Eastern 12" conference? Think about being able to renew historical rivalries, significantly reduce travel time and costs so student-athletes could actually go to class during the season and allow families and fans to travel to games without mortgaging their home. What a concept!

With a TV package similar to those of the other major conferences, it seems that a new conference could attract the following lineup:

The Doug Flutie/Tony Dorsett Adirondack Division:
- Boston College
- Syracuse
- Connecticut
- Army
- Pitt
- Penn State

The Roger Staubach/Bruce Smith Chesapeake Division:

- West Virginia
- Maryland
- Navy
- Rutgers
- Virginia
- Virginia Tech

These schools would bring in 10 of the top 50 TV markets, including four of the top 10.

This "Eastern 12" would have it all: huge television audiences (i.e., money), natural and traditional rivalries, geographical proximity and, most important of all—and most overlooked in this age of greed—IT MAKES SENSE! Who wouldn't love to see Army-Navy, Pitt-Penn State, West Virginia-Maryland, Virginia-Virginia Tech, Boston College-Syracuse and Connecticut-Rutgers all on Rivalry Weekend and all from the same conference? Add many other long-time rivalries (Maryland-Navy; WVU-Pitt; Syracuse-Penn State, etc.) and you've got a panther by the tail! Whoa Nellie, and don't forget there would still be a conference championship game!

An old friend once told me if it's just a money problem, then it's no problem, money can be found. But to walk away from a $25 million annual payday to create something like this is a huge risk. It can't just be good for WVU but must make sense for the 11 other teams as well as for basketball (men's and women's). It will take a visionary, charismatic leader/salesman with a love of the game and the guts to take a gamble. Anybody out there?

2nd Quarter:

A Look Behind the Curtain

Chapter 5:

The Traditions: Testudo to The Mountaineer

"Fiddler on the Roof's" Tevye famously sang "Tradition," which capsulizes the unique activities, stories, people and memories which make this college football rivalry. Both schools are Land Grant universities and have "grown up" together but each carving its own individual and unique niche in the annals of college football. Here are some of them.

Testudo

Maryland's Testudo is the name of the bronze Chesapeake Bay Diamondback turtle mascot… "an animal known for its ability to bite off the hands and feet of the unwary." The terrapin was suggested as the official mascot by Coach Curley Byrd in 1932, replacing the nickname "The Old-Liners," which had been used since 1916 (from 1892-1916 they were known as the "Aggies"). Terrapins are native to the Chesapeake Bay, and Byrd's hometown of Crisfield, Md., is well-known for its terrapins. Additionally, the school newspaper had been dubbed *The Diamondback* years earlier, so it was a good fit.

The Class of '33 conducted a fund-raiser to have the mascot sculpted in bronze by Rhode Island artist Aristide Cianfarani. Some alumni carried a live turtle to Cianfarani as a model from which to sculpt this "super turtle!" They brought the 300-pound statue back to College Park for a gala unveiling at the May 23, 1933 graduation

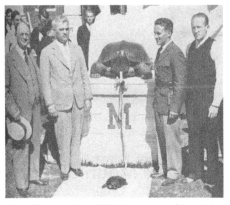

Testudo unveiling, 1933. Courtesy of Special Collections, University of Maryland Libraries, University of Maryland.

ceremony at Ritchie Coliseum. The live turtle model had "two holes drilled through its shell. These were threaded with black and gold ribbons that were tied to a huge cloth. At a prearranged moment, the turtle crawled away from the statue, dragging the cloth and unveiling the replica to the appreciative applause of the assembled dignitaries."

Sadly, Testudo's live turtle model, stressed from its travel (and the holes in its shell), died just two days after unveiling the statue. The turtle is stuffed, mounted on a board and sequestered in a vault in the University Archives. In the event of an emergency, it's understood that the turtle is the first thing to be saved.

Testudo spent his first 15 years mounted in front of Ritchie Coliseum along U.S. Route 1, where it was frequently vandalized by visiting schools. However, in 1947 a group of Johns Hopkins students kidnapped it, resulting in a number of Maryland students rushing to

Photo courtesy of Special Collections, University of Maryland Libraries, University of Maryland.

Baltimore to lay siege on the building where Testudo was incarcerated. 200 police were called, but the siege soon became a party.

Testudo was returned to his Ritchie Coliseum home just to be kidnapped again.

He re-emerged in 1949 when then-President Curley Byrd received a call from a UVa fraternity asking him to "please get Testudo off our lawn!"

Upon his rescue, Testudo was moved to Byrd Stadium, a more secure location in the middle of campus, mounted with steel reinforced rods and filled with 700 pounds of concrete. In 1958 he was mounted on a pedestal in front of McK-eldin Library, overlooking the Quad, where students began to "rub his foot-chomping beak for luck before exams, and also reportedly to ward off parking tickets."

There are five Testudo statues on campus, but the original still overlooks innocent freshman on the Mall, while another is rubbed for luck in Maryland Stadium as the Terps enter the field. This Byrd Stadium version was mounted in 1992 as part of the 100th anniversary of football at Maryland.

Legend has it that when a virgin graduates from the University of Maryland, Testudo leaves his pedestal and flies around the quad. There is another legend that he *has never flown*!

Official & Unofficial Terrapin Logos

Terps and Under Armour: The Oregon of the East

Since 1994, the Oregon Ducks have had Nike. In 2011, the Maryland Terrapins partnered with Under Armour in, what fans perceive, as a battle of uniform one-upmanship.

Oregon is reported to have 384 different football uniform combinations. Nike owner Phil Knight started the relationship with a $27 million donation for renovations for the UO library. He then switched his attention to athletics.

UA founder Kevin Plank played football for the Terps in the mid-80's and, tired of sweaty cotton T-shirts after practice, created a wicking fabric in his parents' garage and Under Armour was born. As their brand grew, Plank donated $25 million to the University of Maryland.

In 2014, Under Armour and Maryland signed a 10-year contract extension that will pay the university nearly $33 million in cash and gear. Under Armour already tests new products on campus, including a new so-called un-grabbable fabric, using athletes as part of its research-and-design process.

Soon, the iconic Cole Field House, overlooking Maryland Stadium, will be home to glassy medical facilities and classrooms, an athletic conditioning center, locker room, two indoor practice fields and one outdoor. *"Maryland is trying to emulate the University of Oregon, riding the largest of a multibillion-dollar apparel company to athletic prominence,"* said the NY Times.

"Our brand, and at some level, our business, has really grown up with Maryland — in Maryland, and with the university around the corner," said Adam Peake, Under Armour's executive vice president for global marketing. *"We've helped each other grow."*

The playbook for such a cozy partnership between a shoe company and a university was written by Nike. Oregon's $95 million Football Performance Center was completed in 2013, courtesy of a gift from Phil and Penny Knight. Nike stirred a revolution in team uniforms by outfitting the Ducks loudly and proudly - in verdant green, neon yellow and charcoal.

"I saw the beginnings of what Nike did with Oregon," said Maryland's then-athletic director Kevin Anderson, who grew up on the West Coast and previously worked at Stanford, Cal and Oregon State. *"And that's been our conversation from Day 1—that we can and do have that kind of relationship."*

Maryland and Under Armour followed with their Maryland Pride uniforms, which feature an almost Cubist deconstruction of the Maryland state flag's taxicab yellow, wavy checkers and clover-capped crosses.

"This project brings together two of my favorite passions, Maryland athletics and entrepreneurship," said Plank. *"The lessons I learned on the football field in College Park continue to fuel my entrepreneurial spirit and shape my professional approach."*

In a 2011 article, ESPN wrote, *"Maryland is—and has for at least 45 years been—a basketball school, with apologies to Boomer Esiason and Bobby Ross. Nationally, Maryland has no football identity, no hook. Plank knows this all too well because he played football at Maryland. The*

Terrapins are rarely in prime-time games or games of national consequence. They haven't been a factor in the BCS picture. The program produces plenty of NFL players but the most famous one is still Esiason, who graduated from Maryland 27 years ago."

In fact, Plank told ESPN of being in a bar at an Eastern Shore beach on a Labor Day weekend, when the Maryland-Cal game was about to kick off. *"It's 8 p.m., the place is packed, and everybody's watching the U.S. Open. I'm thinking people should be in their jerseys saying, 'Our team is playing! Let's watch!'* Instead, he had to talk the folks at the bar to switch to the Terp game!

Plank went on to fortify his company's connections to his home state. The first Under Armour television commercial featured former Maryland defensive end Eric Ogbogu. Maryland was the first college Under Armor signed to an all-school deal.

Maryland is under increased pressure to improve. State financing for Maryland's flagship university has declined recently, forcing the institution to find money elsewhere. The university joined the Big Ten Conference, a financially-driven decision that tested the loyalty of a fan base that cherished longstanding rivalries with Atlantic Coast Conference teams like North Carolina and Duke.

After the move was announced, President Wallace Loh said he required a security detail, but he added, *"In this era of fiscal constraints— meaning, there's less state funding, and so much federal research funding is uncertain—my model is, partner or perish."*

Athletes and coaches seem to support Under Armour's pronounced presence on campus. Former All-American cornerback Will Likely called Maryland *"the school that you want to play for"* because of its uniforms and facilities.

Maryland officials anticipate no immediate changes after Plank stepped down as CEO at the end of 2019, amidst SEC and Justice Department inquiries. Despite two years of significant corporate losses, UA's financial commitments to the athletic department are locked in through 2024. As one prominent donor commented, *"Long-term, they (Under Armour), like Adidas, aren't going anywhere."*

The Mountaineer

The Mountaineer, photo by Randy Litzinger.

The pioneer symbol has served as the WVU mascot since 1934. At that time Mountain Honorary, the school's ranking men's honorary, would select the individual who best personified the spirit of West Virginia.

Early Mountaineers would wear a flannel shirt, bearskin cape and coonskin hat. The traditional buckskin garb the Mountaineer now wears began in the late 1930's. An alumnus donated a number of deerskins to the Honorary with the stipulation that they be made into buckskin outfits for the mascot.

In 1950, the Honorary began a fund-raiser to build a statue of the Mountaineer and mount it in front of the student union, the Mountainlair. Legend has it that the likeness of the Mountaineer Statue is West Virginia's Favorite Son and All-American basketball player Jerry West, from Cabin Creek, W.Va. West is also the likeness used in the NBA's logo. Retired Mountaineers' rifles and costumes are housed in a glass case in the Vandalia lounge of the Mountainlair.

In 1990, Natalie Tennant became the first female Mountaineer and was followed by Rebecca Durst in 2009.

Tennant, who served two terms as West Virginia's Secretary of State, attended WVU for five years. During her final year decided to apply for and try out to be the Mountaineer.

As the first female Mountaineer, she met with opposition but said she received a lot of support from all types of people.

Like Mountaineers before and since, she traveled around the state and beyond for appearances and speaking engagements. When Durst became the second female Mountaineer in 2009, she remembered there being some boos at the time of the announcement but could also tell that attitudes had improved since her own time.

"I just take such pride," in having been the Mountaineer she said.

One of the most iconic mascots in college football, the buck-skin-clad, coonskin hat-wearing, musket-toting Mountaineer leads the team onto the field as the echoes of the discharged musket reverberate through the stadium.

The Flying WV Logo

1980 brought a lot of changes in WVU's football fortunes. After four years of struggles, Don Nehlen was hired to reverse Mountaineer fortunes. Nehlen was Michigan's quarterback coach and the former head coach at his alma mater, Bowling Green.

Coupled with a new coach, West Virginia christened a new stadium. The old 38,000-seat downtown stadium, in use since 1924, was decommissioned and a new 50,000-seat stadium was built on the Evansdale campus between Ruby Memorial Hospital and the WVU Law School, on the site of the University 9-hole golf course.

In order to properly welcome the new coach and stadium, John Denver was given a thunderous welcome as he sang his "Take Me Home, Country Roads" hit during the pregame show.

This game also served as the coming-out party for what is now universally known as the "Flying WV". Nehlen needed to shake-up things and purge the memories of the last four years. When watching game films, he had a tough time telling which team was West Virginia; there was nothing distinctive about the uniform or helmet. So, in talking with equipment manager, Mike Kerin, he said he wanted a dark blue helmet with "WV" on both sides.

Dick Martin was the athletic director at the time and his brother, John, was a renowned graphic designer and illustrator from the Midwest. He had done some work for the Kansas City Chiefs, Atlanta Braves and New York Mets, so having him lend a hand was a no-brainer. WVU sent some ideas and after a few days of sketches, dropping the "U," emphasizing mountain peaks and simplifying the design, he came up with the WV that is so prevalent today. He sent final copies to WVU with an invoice for just $200.

"Had we lost like crazy, maybe the logo wouldn't have caught on so much," Nehlen said. *"That 'WV' became the link between the football team and our fan base. They all wanted it. Now it's on every daggone thing imaginable."*

Sports Illustrated named it a top logo in college sports in one 1980's issue. In 2001, the magazine ranked the WVU football helmet sixth on a top 10 list of helmets.

WVU is one of the top royalty-producing colleges in the country thanks to the sale of officially licensed WVU gear—much of which includes the Flying WV.

"The Flying WV contributes directly, in a financial way, to the well-being of the University through its use on licensed products," says Marsha Malone, WVU's retired director of trademark licensing. *"It's a symbol of a state's pride in its school and a school's pride in its students and graduates. "Seeing the Flying WV is like coming home."*

"There have been three coaches since me (Rich Rodriguez, Bill Stewart, and Dana Holgorsen) and they've kept the logo and helmet," Nehlen said. *"I told Rich when he took over, 'Don't mess with that helmet. That's the thing that sets us apart.'"*

Neal Brown has assumed the reins in Morgantown and has kept the WV flying.

Official & Unofficial Mountaineer Logos

Re-Inventing Maryland Football

If Bill Veeck was the godfather of baseball promotions, Russ Potts was the same for colleges. Maryland track head coach, Jim Kehoe became the athletic director in 1969 with the pledge to revive the moribund football and basketball programs. In six weeks, he hired Lefty Driesell to head the hoops program and shortly thereafter fired former star and future Hall of Famer Bob Ward, and hired a local high school football coach, WVU grad Roy Lester. This didn't work, and in 1972, Jerry Claiborne was hired away from Virginia Tech. During this time, Kehoe hired fund-raiser Tom Fields to head the Terrapin Club, Jack Zane as the sports information director, and Russ Potts as the NCAA's first-ever collegiate sports promoter.

Potts promptly began to re-engineer the image of Maryland Athletics. Recognizing that Maryland was primarily a basketball school, he focused on football. He negotiated television and radio deals to plaster the airwaves in the Baltimore-Washington corridor with Maryland Terp games and news.

Concurrently, he began to promote Maryland to the public like it had never been done before in college sports. Billboards sprouted up across the state. Tens of thousands of pocket schedules were given away in nearly every storefront. Even more "Go Terps Go" red and white bumper stickers adorned vehicles from Cumberland to Ocean City. Deals were made with Giant Foods and Safeway to distribute coupons for discounted tickets. In short, Maryland Football was getting on the map!

Amen Chorus

Lefty Driesell's arrival in 1969 garnered a new era at Maryland. Basketball was moribund, while Terp football fans were still basking in the euphoria of the 1953 national championship and Sugar and Gator Bowl appearances.

But Lefty changed all that. Besides declaring that Maryland could be the "UCLA of the East," he brought excitement, enthusiasm and a jam-packed Cole Field House. He had the Maryland Pep Band break into the Amen Chorus once the game was in hand, sometimes with two minutes left. The crowd loved it and joined in song…" A-amen, A-amen, Amen, Amen."

The tradition carried over to Byrd Stadium where new coach Jerry Claiborne was building his own football legacy.

Maryland Game Day

Maryland Game Day, photo by Randy Litzinger.

With the promotional build-up prior to games, the contest itself needed to become a spectacle. Win or lose, Potts wanted fans to have a good time.

Band Day was expanded, as was being done with many schools across the country. Tailgating was encouraged and exploded among Terrapin Club members. A scoreboard with advertising and running messages was installed. And, like elsewhere, the band, cheerleaders and mascot were prominent on the Byrd Stadium floor.

The Maryland Student Pep Committee was formed and plastered inspirational posters around the inside of the stadium. Revamped printed programs resembled telephone books, filled with ads. Hundreds of multi-colored balloons were released, along with a cannon shot, as the Terps ran onto the field. On occasion, paratroopers dropped in to deliver the game ball to the officials.

A pep committee volunteer ran around the stadium waving an over-sized Maryland state flag. As the game was winding down to the final seconds, the band would break out with "The Amen Chorus." Years later, under the Fridge's regime, the team would jog to the student section in the bowl end of the stadium and sing Maryland's Fight Song to the students.

The idea of giveaways was borrowed from Veeck and baseball. Nearly every home game had a sponsored giveaway item—from 10,000 Coca-Cola cups to team pictures.

I had big shoes to fill when I was hired away from the Washington Capitals to replace Potts who went to SMU as director of athletics. We continued most of what was going on, but tweaked it with some refinements.

BYRD STADIUM ILLUSTRATED

MARYLAND vs VILLANOVA

1979 Program Cover, Special Collections, University of Maryland Libraries, University of Maryland.

Sponsors and/or honorees for the day were recognized with a pregame ceremony on the 50-yard line. Balloons were changed to red, white, black and gold. Snappin' Terp T-shirts were given away, matching the newly designed game program and cover. Terrapin Towels and poster cards were distributed. We initiated a halftime field-goal kicking contest where the winner at season's end got a free trip for two to any location that sponsor, Western Airlines flew.

Finally, we ditched the old green turtle mascot and used Maryland's connection with famous alumnus Jim Henson to create a Muppet-like mascot that is still used today. The new mascot was unveiled by Muppet Sweetums at the 1979 Homecoming Game against Mississippi State. Henson was the Grand Marshal of the Homecoming Parade.

Tobacco-Spitting Contest

With West Virginia coming to College Park in 1981, we pulled out all the stops. Although we had no tickets to sell, we promoted this game like there was no tomorrow, angling for carry-over euphoria with the fans who might return to the rest of our games that year, featuring opponents that were not nearly as attractive.

As an alumnus at both schools, I wanted to play up the rivalry, positioning it as the City Slickers vs. the Hillbillies. This was at the height of the revival of country music. Urban Cowboy was a hit at the box office, starring John Travolta and Debra Winger. Gilley's Bar in Houston became so popular that a half-dozen bars around College Park had mechanical bulls! Ronald Reagan was President and a huge country-music fan, so we felt that the stars had aligned for this type of promotion.

Therefore, we stole a highly successful promotional idea from Minor League Baseball and decided to have a tobacco-spitting contest between WVU and Maryland. We called Levi Garrett Chewing Tobacco and pitched the idea. They loved it and offered to give packs of chewing tobacco to the first 5,000 fans, as well as to sponsor the contest, providing trophies to the winners and hats and T-shirts to both teams.

I called my former boss, Dave Taylor, who ran the Rec-Intramural program at West Virginia and he, too, loved the idea. Each team needed 10 spitters. Dave decided to have a "spit-off" to determine WVU's spitters, in front of the Mountainlair. Some 400 students showed up. The ten winners got free tickets to the game as well as a free bus trip.

That went so well, I called another former boss who ran the Maryland Intramural program. He hated the idea and essentially threw me out of his office! I then remembered that this idea came from baseball, so I called my friend, head baseball coach Jack Jackson, to see if his team would serve as Maryland's 10 spitters. He loved it, so we had our two teams.

We then contacted the *Guinness Book of World Records* to alert them to the event in case a world record was broken, giving us some great publicity. On top of this, we contacted WPKX-KIX Country radio station in D.C. to have them come to the game and do a remote broadcast from the stadium track in front of the student section. They blared out country hits from Charlie Daniels to the Oak Ridge Boys and John Denver to Kenny Rogers. And, they offered the "spit-by-spit" broadcast of the contest. Ultimately, three WVU students were too inebriated to participate, so they had to just grab substitutes from the stands. The Terp Baseball team prevailed and were presented with a 6-foot trophy!

Adding to this excitement was Wild Bill Hagy's Maryland football debut. He was there in all his splendor, complete with his signature cowboy hat and Terps T-shirt, working with the cheerleaders, mascot and radio truck regaling the crowd and radio audience. Naturally, throughout the game he contorted his body to spell "T-E-R-P-S" at key times.

So as not to limit the fun to the student section, we had a Dixieland band playing in the Terrapin Club parking lot and newly designed printed programs were sold.

The game itself lived up to the special hype reserved for big rivals. The music was dueling banjos, but the contest featured dueling quarterbacks: Maryland's Boomer Esiason and West Virginia's Oliver Luck. Ollie and the Mounties won this duel in a 17-13 shootout.

It took the grounds crew a few years to get all the tobacco juice cleaned up from the student section! They probably still haven't forgiven me!

WVU Game Day

Photo courtesy of XOS Digital.

Game day in Morgantown is highlighted by the Pride of West Virginia, the WVU Marching Band. It's been a staple for over 100 years, but "the Pride", took off with the appointment of Dan Wilcox as director in 1971.

He built it from an 88-member all-male band to 280 members by the end of the decade. Both of the University's fight songs, "Fight Mountaineers" and "Hail West Virginia," were arranged for the band by Budd Udell and are, in fact, the same arrangements the band plays today.

Included in the arrangement now are John Denver's iconic "Country Roads" and Aaron Copeland's "Simple Gifts" from "Appalachian Spring," which bring West Virginians worldwide to their feet. As this is played, the band forms the outline of the State of West Virginia, bringing tears to old alums and deafening cheers from the students.

Before moving to the new stadium in 1980, the Pride would triple-time out of the tunnel at the bowl end of Old Mountaineer Field to move into their formations all to the afore-mentioned arrangements. The acoustics of the old field allowed the Pride to conclude the pregame show by singing *a Capella* the Alma Mater, joined by 38,000 off-key voices. Invariably in the final phrase, "*West Virginia Uuuuuuuuuuuuu*" someone, regardless of the opponent, would scream "*Beat the Hell Outta Pitt*!"

In the new stadium, the acoustics are not favorable for a *Capella* singing by the band. But the fans, nonetheless, sing in off-key voices as the band plays.

About 2-1/2 hours prior to kickoff, the team arrives and walks the Mountaineer Mantrap from Don Nehlen Drive through the Blue lot. At the end of this 300-yard march, each WVU player rubs a 350-pound chunk of coal for luck and to memorialize the 29 miners who died in the Upper Big Branch mine in 2010. The coal, mounted on a pedestal, is from the same coal mine.

At game time, after the Pride's famous pregame show, to the public-address announcer's call of "Let's Bring on the Mighty Mountaineers!" the flags and the cheerleaders lead the charge from the "tunnel." Accompanied by the Mountaineer, complete with the firing of his musket, the surrounding Pride plays the West Virginia Fight Song.

At the end of victories, the crowd fills the airwaves with "Country Roads," which has now become one of the official songs of the State of West Virginia… ranked as one of the top traditions in college football!

In Heaven There Is No Beer

In 1956, the song "In Heaven There Is No Beer" was written in Germany by Ralph Marie Siegel and Ernst Neubach. Art Walunus wrote the English lyrics shortly thereafter.

Sometime in the late '50's or early '60's, at Old Mountaineer Stadium, the Mountaineer Marching Band began striking up this polka tune to the joy of the student section. It became a Mountaineer staple, which continues today. But now, instead of the entire band, the tuba section entertains the crowd with it!

Other schools have adopted it as well, including the University of Iowa's "Hawkeye Victory Polka," which has been played since the '60's. The University of Nebraska's "Beer Song," is played as a tuba solo; while Yale, Wyoming and North Dakota State play various renditions. It's unknown which of the schools performed it first, but it was played at WVU during my freshman year in 1969.

In 1922 the Mountaineers, under second-year coach (and future Maryland coach) Clarence Spears, beat Pitt when a "ringer" from Ohio, Armin Mahrt, drop-kicked a 39-yard field goal to win 9-6. In the postgame celebration at the William Penn Hotel, an inebriated Mountaineer fan, upon seeing Coach Spears come into the lobby with the team, blurted out "West by Gawd Virginia." It's unclear whether there's any truth to the rumor that these were the only words he could say before passing out.

Sometime after that, but no later than 1956, the phrase was picked up as a cheer by the cheerleaders and the band. Today it is chanted following the band's singing of the alma mater.

"Sock 'em. Bust 'em! That's our custom, West 'By Gawd' Virginia!"

Mountaineer Week

Every school has Homecoming, but only WVU has Homecoming AND Mountaineer Week! This event marks the time when the leaves are turning and the chill has returned to the air, setting the stage for a celebration of West Virginia and Appalachian culture.

It started in 1947 to generate more school spirit. It started with a pep rally on Friday night and concluded with a dance following the game which required all participants to wear Mountaineer garb. Eventually, an award was given for the best outfits.

The first **beard-growing competition** was held in 1949. The idea for a Mountaineer Mascot Statue was initiated during the 1950 Mountaineer Weekend which ended with a carnival in the Field House, with the proceeds from the various booths being placed in a fund to help pay for a bronze statue of a Mountaineer in front of the Mountainlair.

In 1962, "Mr. and Miss Mountaineer" were named in a halftime ceremony, often with the Governor attending to make the presentation. This prestigious award honors one male and one female student who have a record of academic achievement and extracurricular involvement. Also recognized are the Most Loyal West Virginian, the Most Loyal Alumni Mountaineer, the Most Loyal Faculty Mountaineer, and the Most Loyal Staff Mountaineer for their accomplishments to the state and West Virginia University.

Tradition was always the theme of Mountaineer Week. In 1977, an official quilt pattern was annually adopted. The original "Double Wedding Ring" Quilt is still on display at WVU's Jackson's Mill Conference Center.

Music plays a large role in Mountaineer Week festivities with fiddle contests and clogging exhibitions throughout the week.

With the opening of the PRT (Personal Rapid Transit monorail system), the annual PRT Cram was created in 1975. One specific car has the Mountaineer Week logo painted on it and students see how many can cram into it. The record for the Cram is 97 students in one car by Chi Omega sorority in 2000.

The Voices

Jack Fleming

Jack Fleming, the "Voice of the Mountaineers," served as WVU's football and basketball announcer during the periods of 1947-1959, 1962-1969, and 1974-1996, a total of 42 years. From 1965-93, Fleming was also the play-by-play man for the Pittsburgh Steelers, where his most famous call is that of the Franco Harris' Immaculate Reception in 1972.

He was a seven-time West Virginia Sportscaster of the Year winner, also receiving the 1996 Gene Morehouse Award from the West Virginia Sports Writers Association and the Chris Schenkel Award from the College Football Hall of Fame in 1999. In 1995, he was inducted into West Virginia University's Order of Vandalia, for outstanding service to the state and school. Fleming was inducted into the West Virginia University Sports Hall of Fame in 2001.

He served in WWII as a navigator on a B-17 and was shot down over France.

"Almost every time we'd be on the charter with engines rolling and I'd be at the door waiting for Jack," former West Virginia Athletic Director Ed Pastilong said. *"And then we'd have to figure out a way to get him out of some small towns or whatever and get him to where the Steelers were the next day. He was amazing though, because he loved that existence and thrived on the pressure of getting from place to place, and he never missed a beat on the air. There was a peace about him once the microphone got turned on."*

"There is somewhere close to one million people in West Virginia, and Jack probably touched every one of them in one way or another," Pastilong said. *"Our fans loved him because he was such a homer, but he was very proud of his West Virginia roots and that's who he was. And, truthfully, many West Virginians love the Steelers, and a big reason for that is their familiarity with Jack."*

Fleming, known as the best scene-setter in sports, died in 2001. He famously opened the broadcasts with an opening line beloved by Mountaineers everywhere: *"Wherever you are this afternoon, hoist the battle flag, find a good rock for cover and stay with us, the invaders are here and the hills of West Virginia resound with the sound of Mountaineers in combat and the West Virginia University Mountaineers are on the air!"* Holy Smokes!

Johnny Holliday

Johnny Holliday has been the Voice of the Maryland Terrapins since 1979. The former rock-and-roll DJ was approached by WMAL Radio to join its sports team, which included the famous Redskins trio of Sonny Jurgensen, Sam Huff and Frank Herzog. He did it in hopes of taking over the famous morning drive show by Harden and Weaver. *"Those guys were much older than I was; they're going to retire sooner or later, and maybe in a couple of years I'm just gonna slip in there,"* Holliday remembered to *The Washington Post*. Holliday wasn't new to sports, having broadcast games for Stanford, Cal, GW and Navy.

In the ensuing 40 years, he has broadcast 15 bowl games, the NCAA Men's Basketball Championship, and has seen 10 head football coaches come and go. He called the famous comeback victory in 1984 against the Miami Hurricanes.

The National Football Foundation & College Football Hall of Fame presented Holliday with the Chris Schenkel Award in 2006 for his long and distinguished career broadcasting college football for the University of Maryland. In 2010, *The Maryland Daily Record* named him one of its "60 Influential Marylanders." *Washington Post* columnist Leonard Shapiro named Holliday as his all-time best Washington sports radio broadcaster since 1970. In 2014, Holliday was inducted into the Washington, D.C., Sports Hall of Fame.

"I want them to win every single game—I don't hold that back at all, and I feel very bad when they don't," he said. *"I try to be as honest as I can. We don't sugarcoat it. But any time someone tunes in our broadcast, they will know within a couple of minutes if Maryland is winning or losing by the tone of our broadcast."*

"You could tell he was Maryland's guy without being a homer, which is a fine line," former basketball coach Gary Williams said. *"The thing I liked about Johnny—which is not true of everybody on the business side of things—when we lost, he lost too. He took it just like a coach or just like a player."*

"(Scott) McBrien was the last good quarterback we've had," said Holliday recently. *"Boy was he good!"* With him transferring from West Virginia, the rivalry really intensified.

"It's (WVU game) always tough to win. The fans are so rabid, the Terps have to always bring their 'A' game. It was like a Super Bowl every time we went up there!"

—Johnny Holliday.

Jack Tennant

Tennant began his career in radio at WKNA in Charleston, W.Va. After a stint in Fairmont, he moved to WAJR in Morgantown in 1957, where he served as program director and assisted Voice of the Mountaineers Jack Fleming as color commentator on WVU football and basketball broadcasts.

Tennant spent 13 years at WAJR before accepting a position with WVU Athletics in 1969. He continued as color commentator, produced the statewide Mountaineer Sports Network, hosted the football and basketball coach's weekly television shows and worked as a fundraiser for the Mountaineer

Scholarship Fund (now the MAC), where he developed coaches' caravans, golf outings and other fundraising events around the state.

In 1970 when Jack Fleming left WVU to broadcast Chicago Bulls games, Tennant assumed play-by-play duties as Voice of the Mountaineers for both football and basketball. He served in that role though 1974 and earned the West Virginia Sportscaster of the Year in two of those four years.

He left Morgantown to become assistant athletic director and the play-by-play voice of the University of Louisville Cardinals. He retired after 19 years but continued to assist at Louisville as public address announcer and later as press box announcer. He also wrote for the Louisville Sports Report and appeared frequently on their weekly radio shows. His exclamations were punctuated with *"great day in the morning"* and *"oh my golly!"*

A native of Uniontown, Pa., and a graduate of Waynesburg College, Tennant passed away unexpectedly on May 6, 2002. He was 73.

Tony Caridi

Caridi came to West Virginia in 1984 to work the afternoon news on WAJR-AM in Morgantown. Two years later he became Sport Director of MetroNews upon its creation in 1986. He's been the host of Statewide Sportsline since 1986.

He began working with the Mountaineer Sports Network in 1987 as a television play-by-play announcer. His first WVU basketball game on MSN was on Feb. 20, 1988. He assumed the play-by-play duties in 1997, replacing Jack Fleming.

He holds the unique distinction of broadcasting two WVU games on the same day… on opposite ends of the country. On Dec. 28, 2002, Caridi broadcast the 2002 Continental Tire Bowl against the Virginia Cavaliers from Charlotte, N.C. Immediately following the game, he caught a plane to Las Vegas via Atlanta, to broadcast the WVU men's basketball team game against UNLV. Two WVU games—football and basketball—on the same day, one in the Eastern time zone and one in the Pacific time zone! Wow!

Caridi hosts the Neal Brown and the Bob Huggins statewide radio shows.

His signature line is *"It is a great day to be a Mountaineer, wherever you may be!"*

Hoppy Kercheval

The radio "dean" of West Virginia broadcasters, Hoppy Kercheval joined West Virginia Radio Corporation in 1976. Through the years Hoppy's assignments have spanned the gamut to include news, sports and talk.

A native of Summit Point in Jefferson County, Hoppy began as a news anchor/reporter at WAJR in Morgantown while still attending West Virginia University. After graduating with honors from WVU, Kercheval took over as news director at WAJR and began carving an identity as one of the leading broadcasters in West Virginia.

A founding father of MetroNews, Kercheval served as news director until assuming the role of vice president of operations in 1991. In 1993, he created MetroNews Talkline, which has become a signature program of the network. Hoppy's gift of interviewing has made Talkline a must-listen for lawmakers and anyone interested in state politics and the day's top news.

Kercheval has a master of science in journalism from WVU. He also has an honorary doctorate of humane letters from West Virginia Wesleyan. Kercheval has received a number of honors over the years, including the Mel Burka Award, which is given annually by the West

Virginia Broadcasters Association to the state's top broadcaster. He's served as a sideline reporter, color commentator, expert analyst and a sports talk show host for many WVU broadcasts over his 44 years of broadcasting.

> *"The WVU-Maryland rivalry holds a special place in WVU sports history. As former head coach Don Nehlen famously said about the next opponent after beating Oklahoma in 1982, 'Maryland is the key game!'"*

—Hoppy Kercheval.

Mike Patrick

Mike Patrick is a native of Clarksburg, W.Va., and received a bachelor of arts degree in speech from George Washington University. Despite spending most of his career at the national level, his heart has always remained with his West Virginia roots.

Patrick joined ESPN in 1982, has been the play-by-play voice for many of the network's top events, including college football, NCAA men's basketball and the College World Series.

Patrick was the play-by-play voice on ESPN's *Sunday Night Football* NFL telecasts from 1987 to 2005. In 1998, Paul Maguire joined the booth, and the trio—along with sideline reporter Suzy Kolber—was called by many the best NFL team in the business.

Besides the NFL, Patrick has called NCAA basketball since 1982 and did college football from 1982-1997 when ESPN's NFL schedule expanded to include the entire season. He has also announced ESPN's coverage of the U.S. Olympic Festival (1987 and '90), the College World Series and the British Open (1985 and '86).

Patrick began his broadcasting career in the fall of 1966 at WVSC Radio in Somerset, Pa. In 1970, he was named sports director at WJXT-TV in Jacksonville, Fla., where he provided play-by-play for Jacksonville Sharks' World Football League telecasts (1973-74). He also called Jacksonville University basketball games on both radio and television.

In 1975, Patrick moved to WJLA-TV in Washington, DC, as sports reporter and weekend anchor. In addition to those duties, Patrick called play-by-play for University of Maryland football and basketball (1975-78) and Washington Redskins preseason games (1975-82).

On February 21, 2018, Patrick retired from ESPN after 35 years with the network.

"Don Nehlen has always been my hero for what he was able to accomplish at West Virginia. He got two and three-star players that Pitt and Penn State didn't want… Mark Bulger is a great example and Don coached them up! What a great coaching staff he had!"

—Mike Patrick.

Scott Van Pelt

Scott Van Pelt ("SVP") is native of Brookville, Md., and graduated from the University of Maryland with a bachelor's degree in radio/television and film. He is proud of his Maryland Terrapins sports teams and often attends games as a spectator when his schedule permits.

Van Pelt is host of the midnight edition of *SportsCenter*, bringing his unique perspective to the world of sports since Sept. 7, 2015. The program showcases Van Pelt's passion for sports, with his self-deprecating wit and disposition toward celebrating stars and storylines.

In addition, Van Pelt contributes to ESPN's telecasts of The Masters and The Open, two of professional golf's majors, as both an anchor and hole announcer. He also hosts *SportsCenter* reports and specials from the events.

Van Pelt joined ESPN in early 2001 as the network's lead professional golf reporter, shortly thereafter becoming a *SportsCenter* anchor and later a co-host of "Tirico and Van Pelt" on ESPN Radio each weekday afternoon.

In July 2009, *The Scott Van Pelt Show* made its debut on ESPN Radio and in a simulcast on ESPN2. The show was re-named *SVP & Russillo* in October 2012, and ended in the summer of 2015 when Van Pelt was preparing for the launch of the new midnight *SportsCenter*.

> *"If there is any fan base in America that would stay up until the sun rises to watch its team, it's the fine folks of West "by God" Virginia!"*

> —Scott Van Pelt.

Tim Brant

A 1973 graduate of the University of Maryland with a degree in journalism, Brant was a defensive captain and outstanding linebacker for the Terrapins. He played for the Washington Redskins before a career-ending knee injury.

Between 2008 and 2016, Brant handled play-by-play duties for Raycom Sports' ACC football and basketball telecasts.

The multi-faceted Brant has served many roles at ABC Sports, including host, sideline reporter, expert analyst and play-by-play. He joined ABC Sports as a college football commentator in 1982. After leaving for CBS in 1987, in 1991 Brant returned to ABC in the booth as an analyst and play-by-play man for college football on ABC, a role he held until 2007.

Brant is often best known for his coverage of college football with Keith Jackson. While with ABC, Brant announced three national championship games. While working with Keith Jackson, he was listed as college football's top analyst by numerous publications, including *USA Today*.

In addition to his college football duties for ABC, Brant has also done play-by-play for College Basketball on ABC, Wide World of Sports, the 1984 Winter and Summer Olympics, the Pro Bowl and had a sideline stint on ABC's Monday Night Football.

His first sportscasting job was at WMAL Radio calling Maryland Terrapins football & basketball games with Mal Campbell. He served as vice president, sports at WJLA-TV in Washington through May 2015. He previously served as the station's sports director from 1978 until 1982.

Jay Randolph

Randolph, son of U.S. Senator Jennings Randolph, was born in Cumberland, Md. And grew up in Salem, W.Va., went to George Washington University and got his broadcasting start with WHAR Radio in Clarksburg, announcing high school basketball and football in the Monongahela Valley in the late 1950's.

He got his big break when WHAR outbid WAJR in Morgantown for the Mountaineer radio rights in 1960 and he replaced Jack Fleming, albeit temporarily, as the Voice of the Mountaineers. Two years later WAJR earned back the rights for WVU, reinstating Fleming as the play-by-play announcer. But Randolph's two years doing Mountaineer games gave him a national audience and reputation, as one of the stations carrying the games was WWVA from Wheeling, one of the early "super stations" that had national coverage.

He then did play-by-play stints with the Dallas Cowboys and SMU Mustangs before moving to St. Louis where he became an institution, calling Cardinal games for 21-years, over two stints. He also broadcast golf, NFL, MLB, college football, horse racing and a variety of other sports for NBC throughout the 70's and 80's. In his later years, he broadcast Reds and Marlins games.

He now lives in St. Louis, still dabbling with horse racing at the local Fairmount Park.

The Buildings

Byrd Stadium (aka Maryland Stadium)

Named after the "Father of Maryland Football," Harry "Curley" Byrd, Byrd Stadium has been the home of Maryland football for nearly a century. As the newly named athletic director, Byrd had requested $12,000 for a stadium in 1915 which was finally approved and completed in 1923 with seats for 5,000 spectators and room to expand to 10,000. The final cost of the stadium was $60,000. It was named Byrd Field in his honor.

Home games were played there (also called "Old" Byrd Stadium), across the street from the campus on Baltimore Ave., from 1923-1947 and again in 1949. Home games in 1948 were played at Griffith Stadium in Washington, D.C., while the renovated stadium was being completed.

By the end of WWII, the football program had outgrown "old" Byrd Stadium and a new one was constructed at the cost of $1 million. This "new" Byrd Stadium (capacity 34,680) hosted the biggest crowd to see a football game in D.C.-area history, on Sept. 30, 1950 with a 35-21 win over Navy. An overflow crowd of 45,836 screaming fans jammed into the new stadium. At the dedication, Byrd said, *"I should have double-decked the stadium (to increase the capacity to 92,000), but I was afraid there would be empty seats and it wouldn't look good."* Home games ever since have been played at Byrd Stadium on campus.

Byrd Stadium, 1993. Courtesy of Special Collections, University of Maryland Libraries, University of Maryland.

An expansion in 1976 grew the capacity to 45,000 permanent seats.

The stadium added skybox suites and the Gossett Football Building in 1991. In 1995 the upper deck was added, expanding the capacity to 48,055. Permanent "temporary" bleachers increased the seating to 51,500 in 2002. The stadium capacity is now listed at 54,000.

The record crowd occurred in 1975 as the No. 14 Terps hosted the 9th-ranked Nittany Lions in front of 58,973 fans. This was achieved by the addition of temporary bleachers and some generous crowd estimating. Officials were bound and determined that this crowd would surpass the record-setting Alabama crowd of 54,412 the year before.

In 1983, for the West Virginia game, Maryland shipped in temporary lights from Iowa in what was the first night game in Byrd Stadium history. Permanent lights were installed in 1985.

In 2006, a $50 million expansion project was approved to enlarge Byrd Stadium. This project added luxury suites and increased the capacity to 54,000. In conjunction with this, Maryland sold the naming rights to Chevy Chase Bank (later acquired by Capital One) for $20 million over 25 years. Prior to the start of the 2012 season, the grass field was replaced with FieldTurf.

Ironically, exactly 100 years after requesting the building of a football stadium, the University stripped Curley Byrd's name from it. In December 2015, student groups demanded the renaming of Byrd Stadium due to his segregationist views when he was president of the University from 1936-1954. He resigned from this post to pursue politics where he supported "separate but equal" policies, which were not uncommon in that time.

Maryland's president agreed with the student "recommendations" and endorsed the change to the Board of Regents, which succumbed to political correctness and changed the stadium's name to Maryland Stadium.

During this same era of political upheaval, the State song, "Maryland My Maryland" was banned from being played at official events, including football games, because of its ties to slavery. It was accused of being a pro-Confederacy song and was deemed to be offensive. One would have to be a true student of history to associate the lyrics with slavery. In the nine verses, only in the ninth is there an obvious reference to the Civil War, using the term "northern scum." I dare say that nearly no one knows the lyrics of this song, nor associates it with anything but state pride and "Oh Tannenbaum."

Mountaineer Field

WVU's first game was played on the "baseball grounds" south of Morgantown. From then through 1899, the Mountaineers played only one home game each year on a field where the Mountainlair (student union) now stands.

Mountaineer Field, tabbed the "Jewel of the Mountains," was built in 1924 at a cost of $740,000, which would be about $10 million today. It hosted the likes of Jack Scarbath, Roger Staubach, Jim Brown, Dan Marino, Tony Dorsett and many others before its last game, a loss to Pitt in 1979. It seated 38,000 when it closed. It was nestled in a natural valley on the downtown campus in the shape of a square-cornered horseshoe, with the open end overlooking the Monongahela River.

The stadium seated 30,000 in the 60's, but Garrett Ford, Sr., a former running back and coach, said if they got 15,000 people, they were happy. *"It was such a different atmosphere. Everybody went to the game; they wore shirt and ties."*

The seats were MUCH closer to the field than in the new stadium. *"It was cozy,"* said (legendary) sports writer Micky Furfari.

There were plans to expand the stadium by putting a second tier of seats that would have stretched over Campus Drive. But the plans were abandoned due to infrastructure and its cramped location.

New Mountaineer Field, as it came to be called, opened in 1980 with debut of new head coach Don Nehlen and country music star John Denver christening the new stadium with the singing of "Country Roads."

The stadium's original cost was $22 million. Upon completion it had a seating capacity of 50,000. The stadium was expanded in 1985 with 7,500 seats added to the south end zone for $6.5 million. In 1986, 6,000 seats were added to the north end zone for $650,000. In 2004, the existing north end zone seats were removed, and luxury suites were added at a cost of $13 million.

XOS Digital Photo

The seating area of the facility was renamed "Mountaineer Field at Milan Puskar Stadium" after a $20 million donation to the university by Morgantown resident and founder of Mylan Pharmaceuticals, Inc., Milan Puskar. The most recent expansion actually reduced the seating capacity by 3,500, so the official current capacity is 60,000.

Hoops or Pigskin?

This Battle of the Potomac rivalry carries over to basketball, dating back to 1926. Except for a period when both schools were in the Southern Conference from 1950 to 1953, this has been primarily an out-of-conference rivalry.

From the 1963-64 to 1970-71 seasons, the series was played twice a season on a home-and-home basis. The series was again played annually from the 1983-84 to 1988-89 seasons, then in the 1990-91 to 1992-93 seasons. In December 2003, the two schools played in Washington, D.C., for the BB&T Classic, with West Virginia winning 78–77 in overtime.

In May 2008, West Virginia assistant coach Billy Hahn, who had coached with Gary Williams at Maryland, announced that he and Williams proposed a home-and-home series that would begin after the 2008-09 season. This plan never materialized, but Maryland and West Virginia met again in the third round of the NCAA Tournament on March 22, 2015, with West Virginia winning 69–59.

Both Maryland and West Virginia have long, successful histories in football and basketball. There are very few schools which are consistently good in both sports, whether a result of budgets, facilities, coaching egos, conference affiliation, etc. But West Virginia and Maryland have forged surprisingly similar paths.

Maryland began as a football school with the mighty Curley Byrd calling the shots for decades in a variety of capacities, culminating with the era of Jim Tatum and the 1953 national championship. From that point they declined, and when Lefty Driesell arrived in College Park, excitement and enthusiasm was brought to Cole Field House.

In 1972, Jerry Claiborne came onto the gridiron scene and dramatically increased football's visibility and success. But football always seemed to play second fiddle to the colorful and quotable "Lefthander." Bobby Ross entered the scene in 1982 and re-energized football, making it on par with Lefty's hoopsters.

Then Len Bias died and Maryland Athletics took a swan dive. Lefty was fired and Ross left. It took 15 years before basketball recovered… and recover they did, with a 2002 national championship under Gary Williams and led by Juan Dixon.

Football's recovery nearly coincided with basketball with the homecoming of Ralph Friedgen as head coach. Both sports prospered until The Fridge was fired after the 2010 season and Gary retired a year later.

Football immediately began to flounder again and basketball dropped a few notches and fell even more with the Terps' move to the Big Ten in 2014. As *the Washington Post* said, marking 100 years of Maryland Basketball, *"it's a basketball school playing in a football conference."*

Football, reeling from the death of Jordan McNair in 2018, resulted in the firing of the coach and hiring of Mike Locksley to right the ship. The Maryland ship is out to sea, but it remains to be seen when or if either football or basketball can return to the national prominence they once enjoyed.

West Virginia has similarly moved between dominance on the gridiron as well as on the hardcourt.

Initially, it was a football school, but coaches "Sleepy" Glenn and Dyke Raese dominated the hard-court in the late 30's and early 40's with a prestigious NIT championship in 1942.

Football's initial heyday was in the early 1950's when Pappy Lewis led the Mountaineers to the 1954 Sugar Bowl. Household names like Sam Huff, Freddy Wyant and Bruce Bosley filled the roster.

The end of the decade saw the coming of Jerry West and Hot Rod Hundley and basketball dominance at the Field House on the Monongahela River. WVU went to the NCAA Finals in 1959, losing to California by one.

Neither sport returned to national prominence in the '60's but Jim Carlen and Bobby Bowden got them to three Peach Bowls in the next decade. However, football didn't really come into its own until Nehlen arrived in 1980. WVU became a household name during this era, fielding undefeated seasons in 1988 and 1993.

Meanwhile, Gale Catlett came to the WVU Coliseum and re-energized that program, having one of the nation's winningest programs throughout the '80's. John Beilein and Bob Huggins led the hoopsters to even greater heights and took them to Elite Eight and Final Four finishes.

Football was re-energized with Rich Rodriguez in 2001 until he imploded in 2007. Bill Stewart was essentially a caretaker/cheerleader before controversial Dana Holgorsen came to town and helped the Mountaineers move to their new home in the Big 12 Conference

Huggins is in his 12th year in Morgantown and remains competitive in the Big 12, but the 2010 Final Four appearance seems a distant memory. Neal Brown has taken over the football helm to begin a new era in Mountaineer Football.

With new football coaches at each school, hope springs eternal that they'll bring their respective programs back to national prominence. Both basketball coaches have been competitive but have yet to return the level of the former glory years.

Of course, the Terps have won a national championship in both football (1953) and basketball (2002), while the Mountaineers are still waiting for the fat lady to sing!

Chapter 6:

The Characters:
Wild Bill Hagy to Wild Bob Lowe

The characters in this chapter may never have donned a blue-and-gold or a red-and-white uniform. They may not have impacted the outcome of a single game. They may not have been directly involved with this rivalry. But they are some of the most unique personalities to have touched these programs. They are unique to the Terps or the Mounties and help to make each school special and this rivalry one of the best.

Wild Bill Hagy

I knew Wild Bill Hagy. He was a kind and gentle man who loved Baltimore, the Orioles and the Terps. He became an unofficial cheerleader for the Orioles during their heyday in the late 70's and early 80's and made his debut at Memorial Stadium in 1977 in non-descript Section 34, high in the right-field upper deck. I once asked him why all the way up there. He winked and smiled through his unruly beard and said *"they leave me alone"* up there. Huh? Yeah, he said, *"we can bring in our own beer and, you know, smoke some dope too."* Only Wild Bill.

He would get the entire stadium fired up. Standing in front of the rail in Section 34, he'd wave both arms in a circle and begin a guttural chant *"Heyyyyyyyyyy"* louder and louder until the crowd was sufficiently juiced. Then he would contort his body to spell O-R-I-O-L-E-S as the crowd screamed out each letter with him.

By day he was a professional cab driver in Dundalk, a working-class section of Baltimore. At night, he'd drive up to 33rd Street along with his "boys", a handful of buddies, and settle in to watch the O's. He became a recognizable figure in 1979 when the Orioles lost to the Pirates in the World Series and solidified his spot in Oriole history in 1983 when they beat the Phillies for the championship. During the World Series, the Orioles invited him to the dugout, where he stood on top of it to spell Orioles for a national TV audience. Bob Costas was amazed with Bill's mastery of the crowd and the cameras caught him at every chance.

In the winter of 1980, head basketball coach Lefty Driesell and I met to see what we could do to get the crowd really fired up for an upcoming game with Notre Dame and coach Digger Phelps. We came up with the idea to contact Wild Bill.

Needless to say, he became a fixture at Maryland basketball games that season. One game against Dean Smith's Tar Heels, we gave away 5,000 white "Snappin Terp" towels, courtesy of Safeway and gave a few to Bill. He got out on the court and spelled out T-E-R-P-S to the thrill of the crowd, then waved his towel. The crowd erupted and followed in kind. Cole Field House looked like a blizzard in Buffalo!

Later that spring, I arranged for some Terrapin Club members to fund taking Bill to the ACC Basketball Tournament in Greensboro. Despite Bill's efforts, the Terps lost in the finals to Duke by one point (Buck was fouled!).

During the game, Greensboro experienced a major snowstorm, shutting down the city. It took two hours, but we were finally able to get to the airport to return Bill's rental car. All flights were cancelled. So, we moved Bill's bag into my car and, along with my wife, Barbara, and my intern Doug Dull, we piled into my car and headed to College Park. Six hours and 22 miles later, we stopped at a Holiday Inn in Burlington and got what was, I think, the last vacant room in North Carolina. The four of us were snowed in Saturday night and all-day

Sunday. Finally, on Monday, March 3, we were able to slip and slide home to College Park and take Bill to his apartment in Dundalk.

The next summer, I called Bill and asked if he was a Terp football fan. He said "*I can be!*" He only asked for some beer and three or four tickets for his buddies. Perfect! He came to all our home games that year, spelling out T-E-R-P-S at the 50-yard line and entertaining our sponsors at our advertisers' tailgate party before each game.

Wild Bill is enshrined in the Sport Legend Museum and was inducted in the Orioles' Hall of Fame in 2008. His last appearance was in Cooperstown where he spelled out "O-R-I-O-L-E-S" to an enthused crowd for Cal Ripken's induction. Bill died a month later. R.I.P. Wild Bill.

Kevin Gilson

"Gilley" was a two-sport athlete at the University of Maryland, a swimmer and javelin thrower. He was a 6-foot-5 wild man with a Fu Man Chu mustache. Upon graduation, he became the head swimming and diving coach at WVU and was elected into the WVU Sports Hall of Fame in 2015. But Gilley had a wild side.

Like many athletes, Gilley enjoyed an adult beverage or two. On a Thursday night before the West Virginia game in the mid-60's, he and a few of his swimming and track-team buddies went to Town Hall, a College Park watering hole on Route 1. After a few brews, probably on a bet, Gilley decided to hike up the hill toward UM President Elkins' home on campus. Elkins' daughter loved horses and had one of her own, keeping it in the barn by the President's home. Gilley commandeered the horse and rode it, bareback, back down the hill, across Route 1 and into Town Hall!

Needless-to-say, the Campus, College Park and Prince George's County police were called and captured Gilley and the horse on Route 1. Always quick on his feet, Gilley convinced the authorities that he, in fact, RESCUED the horse. He said he saw it loose on Route 1, so he ran after it and caught it just as the police arrived. They believed him and arranged to take the horse back to Elkins' barn and told the president what happened. He was so grateful, he invited Gilley to dinner as a thank you for rescuing his daughter's horse!

Years later, as a respected member of the WVU coaching staff, Gilley would hold court for athletes and grad students alike—along with baseball coach Dale Ramsburg and soccer coach John McGrath—in their second floor Coliseum offices. They told the stories. They shared the history. Like the Moldy Group, they were the Old Pros. They were the legends.

The Moldy Group: Sully Krouse and Jack Jackson

In the '60's and 70's and into the '80's, a group of athletic department staff, coaches and friends began to gather for food, laughter and goose hunting. This "Moldy Group" was led by long-time wrestling coach Sully Krouse (32 years) and long-time baseball coach Jack Jackson (30 years). Both were Hall of Famers and legends in their fields, but they filled a role much more important… that of Maryland Athletics' "institutional memory."

Often Sully's uproarious laughter would echo through the halls of Cole Field House, as they could often be found gathering in his second-floor Wrestling Office, telling stories, playing gin and, of course, eating. As alumni and former athletes, they had a bond to the university, and to each other, like no others.

Besides Krouse and Jackson, the group included Bosey Berger (All-America basketball player), George Weber (head of Physical Plant), Tom Fields (head of Terrapin Club), his brother Doug and Whitey Miller (both donors and car dealers), among others. "Scrappy" Jack Fletcher became an honorary member as he always brought the food, and it wasn't just cold cuts! Heading up the Food Service for the university, he had access to some mouth-watering victuals. They were the heart of soul of Maryland.

Many a tale was spun in Kent Island's goose blinds—the Manor House and Batts Neck—where stories were told and legends embellished between the goose calling, coffee swilling and tobacco spitting. I luckily, shared a goose blind with many of them.

Sully would host his famous Sunday-morning breakfasts at his home in University Park. It was by invitation only and a sign of acceptance if you were invited to sample his scrapple, pancakes and fried eggs and listen to the retelling of the truth behind the tales of Terrapin history. They knew the Maryland legends first-hand, from Curley Byrd, Jim Tatum, and Bill Cobey to Jack Faber, Al Heagy and Jack Scarbath.

Much like "The Maryland Squad" of a later generation, these guys continued the Maryland legacy. They were the old guard. They told the stories. They were the historians. They were the keepers of the flame.

As the last living member, Jack Jackson told me, "*Maryland has lost the tradition! Who remembers anymore?*"

Super Fan

"Super Fan" Junior Taylor arrived on the Mountaineer stage while still a senior at Morgantown High. This unofficial cheerleader for the Mountaineers came charging down the Coliseum steps during the GW basketball game in 1973. Unknown by the cheerleaders, pep band or the Mountaineer, this chubby, bearded guy ran around the court waving his arms in a successful attempt to get the crowd into the game.

Taylor, like Wild Bill Hagy, was part of the wave of unofficial cheerleaders that spread across the nation in the 70's. From the "Rainbow Man" who proudly wore a rainbow Afro wig and "John 3:16" on his shirt at nearly every major football or basketball game in the country, to Crazy Ray of the Dallas Cowboys to the "Hogettes" of Washington Redskins fame and to the ultimate mascot, "The San Diego Chicken." Each had their own schtick, initially trying to get the crowd fired up, evolving into entertaining the fans. As with many promotional ideas, baseball originated this idea with Max Patkin, the "Crown Prince of Baseball," first hired by Bill Veeck in the 40's. Max later embarked on a 50-year barnstorming career.

Junior had more crowd-appeal than the cheerleaders, "the Buckskin Babes," and the Mountaineer combined, said many West Virginia fans. His enthusiasm, happiness and nerve were all bound up in a gold, extra-large, WVU T-shirt with "Super Fan" on the back.

Taylor's one-man show made its debut at the George Washington basketball game in January of 1973, which resulted in a WVU 63-62 victory. He was an instant success. *"I was really psyched up at that game,"* he recalls. *"A couple of my friends from Morgantown High urged me to go out on the court. I did."*

He didn't miss a Mountaineer home basketball game and later that year debuted at Madison Square Garden in a 77-63 WVU loss to Manhattan.

Taylor was no stranger to WVU sports. A basketball game in 1960 was his initiation to WVU athletics, and he says he has been a faithful Mountaineer fan ever since his late grade-school days.

"Nothing psyches me up more than the Mountaineer song—it almost gives me shivers."

"But there's one thing I'd like to make clear to everyone because I'm always asked about it. I do not drink before games!" insists Taylor.

When asked about becoming the official Mountaineer, Taylor said, *"What greater thing can you be than the symbol of your university? Being the Mountaineer has its advantages, but it has its disadvantages too. I've been thinking a lot about it recently because of all the people encouraging me to try for it."*

But "Super Fan" could lose his special image, and he realized it, if he aimed for Mountaineer.

"Super Fan" took a hiatus during the 1974-75 year to pull on the buckskins of the Mountaineer. He came back after giving up his musket, and Super Fan again charged the Coliseum crowd well into the 80's. He impacted Mountaineer fans for generations.

A precursor to Junior Taylor was **John Borchin,** aka **"Mr. Rainbow,"** a retired barber from nearby Connellsville, Pa. The self-proclaimed "Good Will Ambassador" performed at the student gate at Old Mountaineer Stadium. Clad in red, white and blue, Mr. Rainbow had a small black and white monkey on a chain, Freddy, entertaining the crowd as his sidekick. He drove to Morgantown in a converted school bus, complete with a coffin, electric chair and his former pet dog (now stuffed). Although a Mountaineer fan, he planned to visit every state spreading smiles and good will. By 1973, he had spread his good will to football crowds in 24 states.

Rebel, an unofficial mascot, appeared on the field during the pre-game show and during timeouts for a number of years in the late '60's and early '70's. Sadly, he never caught on like the Vols' Smokey.

Wild Bob Lowe

Bob Lowe was a 6-foot-7 backup center on the WVU basketball team from 1969 to 1971. He averaged 5.3 points and 3.4 rebounds per game in 1970. Lowe started the first nine games of that season, including a 14-point effort in the third game in the WVU Coliseum against top-ranked Kentucky. WVU lost to the Wildcats 106-100 in overtime.

He was benched after those nine games in favor of 7-footer Mike Heitz. Lowe was recruited by Virginia, Maryland, Wake Forest, Davidson, Florida and West Virginia, but chose West Virginia because of the kindness he was shown on his visit.

Lowe became the first former varsity athlete to don the buckskin garb as the Mountaineer in 1972 when he began graduate school. He had a job on campus as a shuttle bus driver, driving campus buses from the downtown WVU Stadium to the Evansdale Campus. This was before the PRT came to town and these buses were the primary means of student transportation between campuses, along with hitch-hiking.

The buses would line up along Stadium Drive and, as they filled, the first bus would pull out and the other busses moved up the queue. Lowe, dressed in the clothes of the day (hippie), sat in the back of his bus. As the bus filled, he began raising a ruckus, yelling *"where's the driver?"* He got the students riled up and finally, he said, *"What the hell, I'll drive,"* ran to the front of the bus and took it to Evansdale to the cheers of the riders. None of them knew that he was actually the real bus driver... Only Wild Bob Lowe!

His devotion to the University inspired him to apply to be the Mountaineer during his first year as a graduate student at WVU. During the selection process, his father's military career worked against him. Because Lowe was not from West Virginia, it was an issue for some members of the selection committee.

"I told them, since I never really had a hometown when I was growing up, I had the opportunity to choose my hometown coming into college," Lowe said. *"Morgantown just seemed different, and it was where I wanted to be."*

Traveling to his first away game as the Mountaineer, he found himself surrounded by 15 Richmond fans as he was leaving the game. Then, just as he thought he was about to be beaten to a buckskin-and-bearded pulp; Mountaineer fans came charging across the parking lot to his rescue.

"It made me realize what a strong following WVU has out of the state," Lowe said. *"Lucky for me, Mountaineer fans travel really well—even back in those days."*

Lefty Driesell

No discussion of Maryland Football traditions would be complete without mention of "The Left-hander." Lefty Driesell arrived on the College Park scene with a bang as he was introduced as the new head basketball coach of the Terrapins in December of 1973. He promptly declared that Maryland could become *"The UCLA of the East,"* a statement that would not only haunt Lefty but also future football coach Bobby Ross.

Lefty was the consummate showman, from his plaid jackets to his "V" gestures after a win to his often-outlandish statements to the media. He was paranoid and driven. His ongoing rivalry or feud with Dean Smith was legendary. And he never met a reporter that he didn't like.

Maryland used to hold year-round weekly press conferences either at Cole Field House or at the Center for Adult Education. Normally in the summer and fall these were focused on football, while the winter and spring conferences were all about hoops. Except…During the dog days of the summer of 1982, Lefty was getting tired of seeing so many articles about the new football coach Bobby Ross and his program and nothing about Lefty and basketball. So, he marched into the press conference, unannounced and promptly held court. His goal was to steal some of the spotlight from Ross, which he promptly did with the announcement that he was no longer "Lefty!" From that point onward, he ordered the media to call him his given name: Charles G. Driesell." This proclamation was the headline in *The Washington Post* the next day, giving the Left-hander his much-needed limelight! Calling him "Charles G." only lasted a few days before all was forgotten and Lefty was once again Lefty!

Rodney Dangerfield

In preparation for the 1981 season, Maryland's advertising agency hired actor/comedian Rodney Dangerfield to do a Maryland football and a Maryland basketball commercial. The feeling was that Maryland was "getting no respect," Dangerfield's catch phrase.

Dangerfield, always the prima donna, arrived hours late, unkempt, unshaved and without his make-up. Finally, he cleaned himself up and, much to our surprise, became the consummate professional as soon as the cameras were turned on.

It was about 95 degrees and Coach Claiborne was beside himself that Dangerfield's lateness was disrupting the scheduling of his summer football camp. However, the real "fun" began when Dangerfield came into Cole Field House to do the basketball spot with Coach Driesell. Lefty considered himself somewhat a comedian and took about an hour exchanging one-liners with Dangerfield. If we weren't so behind schedule, it would have been hilarious. Sadly, the agency spent so much money on the talent, that little was left to air the commercials, so few actually saw them!

Consequently, the average home attendance in 1980 (the year before the commercials) was 36,176, the average following the Dangerfield spots was 31,100.

The following year, not having learned their lesson, the agency hired Susan Anton to cut more Maryland football commercials, with similar results.

Mama Gaga

Cindy (Bissett) Germanotta, a member of the 1974 WVU Cheerleading Squad, is the mother of Lady Gaga! *"My grandma's here tonight,"* Lady Gaga told her fans at a Pittsburgh concert in 2014. *"My grandmother was there with me for one of the hardest times in my life, and she's been there for every other hard time since that one.*

"We have been through a lot together because my grandmother's from West Virginia. She always told me not to give up. She always told me to be myself."

'She'd say 'Oh honey, they will.' I love you, grandma." Mama Gaga is from Glen Dale, home of Brad Paisley, and now lives in NYC.

Brad Paisley

Photo by Dale Sparks Photography and Framing.

Although the country music superstar didn't attend WVU (he's a grad of Belmont in Nashville), his roots are deep in the West Virginia hills! He grew up in Glen Dale and has become a walking billboard for West Virginia in general and WVU in particular. In fact, former Governor Arch Moore, who lived just a few blocks from the Paisleys in Glen Dale, regularly took Brad to campaign stops where he sang "God Bless the USA." He attended a few WVU games at Old Mountaineer Field as a kid with his dad, but wasn't able to join him at the 1980 stadium dedication by John Denver (His dad was in Kingwood for Army Reserve training and couldn't get enough time off to get Brad and go to the game).

But 35 years after Denver's dedication, Paisley made a surprise visit to Morgantown as the Mountaineers hosted the Maryland Terrapins on Sept. 26, 2015. He and his crew left a Hartford, Conn., concert about midnight and drove straight to Morgantown for the pregame show.

WVU athletic director Shane Lyons hinted at something special when he tweeted on Friday afternoon, "*We have a very special moment planned during the pregame show Saturday! Be in your seats by 2:40 p.m. so you don't miss it!*"

Paisley walked onto the field just after The Pride of West Virginia Mountaineer Marching Band finished its traditional pregame show.

The sold-out crowd of 61,174 gold-clad fans was there to watch a border-battle between the Mountaineers and the Terps, but they erupted into cheers when they spotted Paisley, accompanied by a W.Va. State Trooper, walk onto the field wearing a WVU football jersey and his trademark cowboy hat and guitar.

Paisley made his way to a stool near the 50-yard line. Band members, who had formed the outline of the Mountain State, surrounded Paisley then dropped to bended knee just before Paisley took the microphone.

As he began "Almost Heaven…" the crowd inside Mountaineer Field joined in. A chorus of "Country Roads, Take Me Home" echoed throughout the hills of Morgantown and drifted up the Monongahela River.

Once Paisley finished singing, he stood up and waved to the crowd. But before he walked off the field, he leaned back into the mic and shouted, "Let's go!" Fans answered with a resounding "Mountaineers!" Goosebumps!

He left after a halftime radio interview with Tony Caridi, driving to Bristow, Va., for a concert at the Jiffy Lube Center that evening.

Jerry Fishman
On Nov. 7, 1964, Jerry Fishman (#31) made Maryland football history. The Terps were in a very physical game with intrastate rival Navy, led by Roger Staubach. Many personal fouls were called and fights broke out in the stands, the game was that intense.

Navy's Skip Orr returned a punt late in the third quarter and Fishman "creamed" him right in front of press box. The ref threw a flag for unnecessary roughness. "*When I got up, they were booing and yelling at me, so I just flipped them the finger.*" The crowd erupted!

But the coup de gras was late in the game when Terp Ken Ambrusko returned a kickoff 101 yards for a touchdown to give Maryland a 27-22 victory. In celebration, Fishman ran in front of the Navy bench and gave them the bird, again! Navy officials were so incensed that they suspended the series after the 1965 season and didn't resume until 2005, a 40-year hiatus.

On and off over the ensuing four decades, various Terp athletic directors attempted to get Fishman to apologize, but that wasn't in his nature.

"What for? It's a game. It's a silly game. It's football, it's not a diplomatic blunder.

"It's nice to be remembered," Fishman says. *"Most people get their 15 minutes of fame. Me, I got 40 years."*

Fishman, a retired attorney, has never been shy about sharing his opinion and doesn't mind fanning the flames a bit.

In a past interview with the *Annapolis Capital,* he suggested Navy change its mascot from a goat to a chicken. While posing for a photograph to accompany that article, Fishman, wearing a Terps shirt and leaning against his Harley-Davidson motorcycle, gave Navy fans the bird once again. With both hands.

He doesn't think he's to blame for the hiatus, suggesting it was simply a business decision. *"The reason Maryland doesn't play Navy anymore is that, at the time the incident happened, Navy's program was going downhill. They were already getting beat up by Notre Dame, and they didn't need the embarrassment of getting beat by the school down the road."*

But you know how it is said that revenge is best served cold? Fishman practiced law for 16 years in Annapolis.

Years later *"I was in court in Annapolis, waiting for a trial,"* Fishman said. *"And this judge kept calling all these other trials first. All these lawyers were coming in and leaving and I still hadn't been called. Finally, at the end of the day, I'm just fuming. The judge looks around and says, 'That's all for today.' I approach the bench and I say, 'Excuse me, but my trial didn't get called.' "He looks down at me and says, 'What's your name?' and I said, 'Jerry Fishman,'"* Fishman says. *"And the judge smiled at me and said, 'Go Navy.'"*

Lysander Dudley

Lysander Dudley Sr., was the executive director of development for the WVU Foundation. But he was much more than that. It's not an overstatement to say that he was responsible for the most successful run of Mountaineer Athletics.

Prior to the hiring of WVU alumnus Gale Catlett as the Mountaineer basketball coach in 1978, West Virginia could only offer one-year contracts. Catlett had been offered the job a few years earlier but declined because he had a four-year rollover contract at the University of Cincinnati. Although the University couldn't do anything about it, the WVU Foundation could and Lysander did!

Dudley went to work with various donors and was able to put together not only a four-year contract for Catlett in 1978, but also to entice Don Nehlen to become the Mountaineer football coach in 1980.

Catlett recalled that Gov. Jay Rockefeller and Dudley got a group of people together and founded a coaches' annuity fund, which, developed for Catlett and Nehlen, created a deferred compensation package for both coaches if they stayed at least 10 years.

It worked! Despite each having other offers, Nehlen stayed 20 years, is the winningest coach in WVU football history and the 22nd-winningest coach in college football history with 202 wins. Catlett stayed 24 years and won 439 games, probably an unmatchable record in WVU hoops history.

"Both Coach Nehlen and I were offered other jobs, but with that in place we both stayed at WVU," Catlett recalled. *"It was deferred compensation so when you retired you had some money to live on."*

Dudley was not only a proponent of the athletic program but was a tireless promoter for the entire state. He could be called the Godfather of the WVU Band. When they needed money, Dudley found a way and, in fact, coined the name "The Pride of West Virginia," helping the band to become perhaps the most visible ambassadors for the State. Following his dozen years at WVU, he continued to serve and promote the state and helped to launch the fledgling white-water rafting industry. The industry has recognized him by naming a rapids on the New River, "Dudley's Dip!"

Jim Henson

One of Maryland's most famous graduates, Jim Henson is universally beloved for his Muppets.

As a freshman at Maryland in 1954, he was given the opportunity to hone his puppetry skills during a course in the home economics department. His earliest endeavors into television took place immediately before and during his time as an undergraduate.

Following a short-lived morning puppet segment on a local Washington station, he was hired by WRC-TV in 1955 to create a five-minute puppet show that would air twice nightly. Entitled *Sam and Friends*, this program earned Henson his first Emmy in 1958—two years before his graduation from Maryland. For *Sam and Friends*, Henson introduced many of the elements that would become mainstays of his *Muppet Show* aesthetic—music, zany humor, and an early Kermit as a lizard-like creature. During his time at Maryland and WRC-TV, Henson began to develop innovative puppetry skills that made his Muppets life-like and expressive, and that would have a profound effect on the way puppetry would be performed for television and films.

In 1979, Maryland's athletic director, the late Carl James, contacted the Henson group and convinced them to design a new Terrapin mascot. The price-tag was $2,000. It was unveiled during the Mississippi State football pregame show that year. Henson was the Grand Marshal of that year's Homecoming Parade and was presented with the Distinguished Alumni Award.

Chapter 7:

The Fans: Painted, Impassioned and Proud

F ans, a derivative of "fanatics," fuel college football rivalries.

Painted Mountaineer fan at Kansas State game in Morgantown. Photo by Mark Alberti/ICON Sportswire

Kate Zimmer and friends prepping for a Terp night game, courtesy of Zimmer photo collection.

In today's world, buzz phrases like "fan experience" permeate the landscape. How is "fan experience" generated? Does winning do it? It certainly helps, but there's more to it, much like Russ Potts, Don Canham and the pioneers of college sports marketing put it a half a century ago, *"We made it a spectacle, a carnival, a ball,"* Potts remembered Canham as saying. *"Now they come at seven in the morning, go to the game, then go back to their tailgates. We realized early that you can't always be No. 1, and can't advertise that - so we made Saturday an event."*

Since intercollegiate athletic departments are now filled with specialists whose job it is to get "fannies in the seats," let's check with some Terps and Mountaineers who have worked in departments like sports marketing, sports information, event management, fan experience, media relations, digital media, hospitality, ticket sales, Learfield partnerships and others to gather their thoughts about this rivalry game.

Jeff Tennant, Vice President, Learfield Sports (WVU Class of 1978):
"There are a lot of factors that have contributed to the growth of college football over the years. The regional nature of the game was initially dictated by conference member makeup and scheduling opponents in general. This proximity of opponents helped produce great rivalries, many of which have been around for generations. These rivalries are the essence of college football.

I've had the opportunity to attend a lot of great rivalry games—some are intrastate battles like Alabama vs Auburn, Miami vs Florida State, Clemson vs South Carolina or even "cross-town" rivalries like USC vs UCLA or Stanford vs Cal. Others are "border wars" like Ohio State vs Michigan, Georgia vs Florida, Texas vs Oklahoma and yes—WVU vs Pitt.

I grew up in Morgantown in the 60's and 70's and remember WVU leaving the Southern Conference to become an independent. That allowed WVU to keep games with Pitt, Penn State and Syracuse, but with the intent to upgrade the overall schedule. It only seemed natural to look 200 miles east to College Park and the University of Maryland.

Two state schools in contiguous states, and despite the proximity, their teams had met on the football field just 12 times prior to 1969. Since then, they have met 40 times including 27 consecutive years from 1980 to 2007. It was during this time that the WVU—Maryland game truly became a "Rivalry." The games over the past 50 years have created some great memories and featured a lot of outstanding players and coaches from both sides."

John Antonik, WVU Director of Athletics Content and Social Media (WVU Class of 1992): *"It's a big game in the Eastern Panhandle and has always been a barometer game. The rivalry peaked with Rich and the Fridge, a lot of it was around Scott McBrien, who was maybe the last good quarterback Maryland had.*

"The 2004 WVU win in overtime was a big, big win for RichRod. After being badly beaten by Maryland the year before and in the Gator Bowl, people were beginning to question his philosophy. The win changed all that.

"Controversy goes back to 1947 when (Maryland coach) Tatum accused West Virginia of using ineligible players. Gene Corum was one of them."

Chris Boyer, Deputy AD at NC State (WVU Class of 1998) and former Senior Associate AD at Maryland): *"First and foremost, the spirited contempt the schools held for each other related to the gridiron was still near its zenith while I was a student (and working in the athletic department) at both… first as an undergraduate at Maryland, then as a graduate at WVU… and also at the height of my football and college sports fandom.*

"Admittedly, at that time, I would say the game meant more to the significantly smaller and declining passionate Terrapin football fan base simply because the Mountaineers had firmly established themselves as a more successful program and were more consistently competing with teams at a higher level than Maryland, along with its other traditional rivals Pitt and Virginia Tech, while Maryland was in a prolonged downturn.

"That said, the emotions always ran high when the teams did play… and especially again after Maryland re-established itself somewhat under Ralph Friedgen.

"Certainly, while the landscape of college football has changed so much nationally and for those programs since those games and my time at both schools, my love for the institutions has not. So, of course, I would love to see the schools play again (in all sports actually) on a regular basis, as I think it is good for both fan and alumni bases and makes so much sense geographically and from a rivalry standpoint. In fact, in my opinion as someone who has now been fortunate to have an extended career in intercollegiate

athletics administration thanks to my time and mentors at both schools, if college football does not commit itself to restoring and maintaining its fiercest regional rivalries, it will never recapture the magic and passion of days gone by."

Dr. Alex Isherwood, Former Maryland Assistant AD for Sports Marketing (Maryland Class of 1986): *"I was with the Terrapin Club and took a bus to Morgantown for the 1984 game. We stayed at a Holiday Inn in Grantsville, as closer hotels were all sold out. As we were leaving after a victory, driving from the stadium, West Virginia fans began rocking the bus. For a minute, I thought they were going to tip us over. It was scary!*

"It is a healthy rivalry. There's always lots of excitement and anticipation. The size of the crowds are always good and the game is very spirited—from both sides! It always seemed to be close, you never knew who was going to win.

"West Virginia fans would walk through the Terrapin Club parking lot in College Park, chanting 'Turtle Soup… Turtle Soup' and Terrapin Clubbers would respond 'Not this year… Not this year.'"

Walt Atkins, Former Sports Information Director, East Carolina University, ASID, NC State (Maryland Class of '72): *"Rivalry games bring out the best in both schools and build momentum and bragging rights for seasons to come. The Maryland-West Virginia rivalry is a great example and is one of the best in the nation! It may not be as ballyhooed as the Iron Bowl, for example, but it brings ardent fans from Charleston to Baltimore out of the woodwork to usually sold-out stadiums. It builds fan enthusiasm and growing revenue for all sports. In short, it's a sports marketers' dream!*

Playing this rivalry game every year should be a no-brainer! It's important to the schools, the fans and the bottom line!"

The Maryland Squad—I had the unique opportunity to visit with some of the "Maryland Squad," the "institutional memory" of Maryland Athletics, for this book. These ladies have seen Maryland Athletics from the inside, loyal Terp employees since the '70's, having worked with 10 athletic directors and many more head coaches. A total of 150 years in the Terp athletic department… they've seen it all! They are the keepers of the flame, the successors to the Moldy Group.

- **Eloise Jones**, 44-year ticket office employee, retired assistant ticket manager, and her husband Greg, a 55-year Terp fan.
- **Patty Benfield**, 38-year retired operations, tickets and marketing assistant.
- **Debbie Russell**, 46-year employee and current athletics HR director and former ticket manager and her husband Frank, a former Terp player and season-ticket holder for over 40 years.
- **Robin Chiddo**, a 22-year Alumni Association liaison for athletics.

We went to longtime Terp hangout, the original Ledo's in College Park, and over a famous square pizza, they opined on this rivalry.

They collectively viewed this game as a great rivalry, fueled by the closeness of the two schools coupled with the large number of WVU alumni in the D.C. Metro area. It was an easy game for Maryland staff because the WVU alumni group bought blocks of thousands of tickets and managed their distribution.

However, it was felt that WVU students were often nasty, throwing rocks and cans at Maryland buses. "*Going to WVU was scary.*" The drinking got so bad that in the 80's Maryland stopped playing night games against West Virginia in College Park, thus shortening the "tailgate time."

But, generally, tailgating was great! A few bad apples couldn't destroy the party atmosphere in the parking lots where both alumni groups seemed to try to out-do each other.

The "Danny Buggs" game (1973) was viewed as the beginning of the rivalry. Ironically, Frank Russell almost changed the outcome of that game, receiving a cross-field lateral on the kickoff following Buggs' punt return touchdown with eight seconds left. He ran it to the WVU 35-yard line before being tackled out of bounds to end the game. This was nearly a precursor to the Music City Miracle, the 2000 AFC Wild Card Game between the Buffalo Bills and Tennessee Titans, when Terp Alumnus Frank Wycheck threw a cross-field "lateral" on a similar end-of-game kickoff. But in Wycheck's version, the play went for a winning touchdown.

It's been a great rivalry, as both teams were so closely matched. It was a good fit. Generally, they felt that the Penn State game was a bigger rivalry, but acknowledged that for it to be a true rivalry, each team had to win occasionally!

The Maryland Squad, like the Moldy Group before them, have kept the legends of Maryland Athletics alive. But few Terp alumni work there anymore. They haven't had an AD who was a graduate since Dick Dull nearly 40 years ago! And before the Fridge became football coach in 2001, the last Maryland grad to prowl the sidelines was Bob Ward in 1967.

Tailgating

Fans make college football. Whether they're students having a bit too much fun or middle-aged alumni reliving their college years, they're the ones the games are for! They fill up the stands, buy the souvenirs and go to the bowl games. And they tailgate!

Maryland and West Virginia are some of the best tailgaters in the nation, whether you're parked in Maryland's Z lot or WVU's Blue one, the RVs arrive early, the Bloody Mary's and Mint Juleps are flowing and that glorious smell of tailgate food wafts throughout the flags and painted ladies adorning the scene.

If you plan to make a weekend of it, on the way to your tailgate, be sure to stop by these classic sports pubs and restaurants to get a real feel for the homes of the Terps and Mounties:

In Morgantown:

The **Varsity Club** on Willowdale Road. It's only been around since 2008, but it's wall-to-wall memorabilia of WVU sports history!

For you Old Schoolers or Millennials who want a taste of the "good ole days," check out Jerry West's favorite hangout, **Gene's Beer Garden** on Wilson Ave. in South Park, open since 1944. Don't miss their hot dogs! Sorry, but Freddie's is long gone.

If you need to stretch your legs between MoTown and TerpTown, a stop at **Curtis' Coney Island Famous Wieners** is well worth the detour. It has been in Cumberland since 1918. They're Western Maryland's version of West Virginia dogs—without the coleslaw!

In College Park:

R.J. Bentley's on Route 1 is a landmark for Maryland sports fans since 1978. Great Terp memories.

The original **Ledo's** has moved from University Avenue to Knox Road right off of Route 1. It's been "A Terp Tradition since 1955." Don't miss their square pizza at a number of franchises around the DMV.

The Green Turtle, a Maryland hangout since 1976. Check out their nearby Laurel location.

Fans Chime In…

Here's why tailgaters from both sides of the river love this rivalry:

A **Dan Andree (Huntsville, Ala.):** "*I am a fortunate man. I live in Alabama and, every year, get to experience the great 'Bama-Auburn rivalry. For a few years in the '80s, I lived in Lexington, Ky., and got to experience the great basketball rivalries with Louisville, North Carolina and Duke. So, I love the atmosphere of rivalries. When Chip took me to the West Virginia-Maryland game (2011), I found that same atmosphere. Rivalries make or break a year, and you can feel that anticipation in every conversation and every exaggerated gesture. I had no dog in the fight that day, so I went with the home team and soon found myself a Maryland fan. I didn't know the players, but soon picked up the lingo and knew on whose play the game depended. I fell in line and wanted a win almost as much as the alumni. It was a great day! Rivalries take sports to the top and everything is heightened. It's great to be a part of them even when you know the tuba player in the band as well as you know any player on the team.*"

W **Randy Hansen (Everett, Wash.):** "*I bleed purple & gold… a Washington Husky fan since Sonny Sixkiller was throwing a football and James Edwards was dunking one. Being on the west coast, all I knew about Maryland & West Virginia was Jerry West!*

"In 1986, Chip sat me next to Bobby Ross at dinner one night. Did he replace Coach Don James for me? Nope. Did he make an impression? Absolutely. That year, through Chip and the national media, I quietly started sneaking frequent peeks at the Terps & the Mounties. Fast forward to the 2011 UM-WVU game. There I sat, enjoying what college football is all about. The bands, the kids and the rivalry! No matter what stadium you visit, on rivalry Saturday, coast to coast, it's the same. Pure enjoyment!"

WV Rick Pill (Bedington, W.Va.) Founder and president of the Eastern Panhandle Mountaineer Fan Club and EP WVU Alumni Association: *"I haven't missed a WVU-Maryland game since 1973. For the folks in both panhandles, the WVU-Maryland game is more important than any other game on the schedule—including the Backyard Brawl with Pitt! The geography of both state's panhandles makes it interesting among the fan loyalties. Some parts of Jefferson County are closer to Maryland (College Park) than they are to Morgantown... and with so many folks from West Virginia working in Maryland and some Marylanders working in West Virginia, makes this game very interesting!*

"The game I remember the best is the 1973 game when Danny Buggs ran back a 69-yard punt return for a touchdown at the end of the game for a Mountaineer victory. That made this game a rivalry,"

M Fred Frederick (former Terrapin Club President, Laurel, Md.): *"Sorry that it's still not going on. It makes sense from a profitability standpoint. Don't know why they stopped it. It drew big crowds. Every time we went to West Virginia the tickets were limited. And there are a lot of West Virginia people in the Baltimore-Washington area. It drew big crowds!*

"People loved West Virginia's band, even Maryland people. The way they snaked down the hill, single-file, into the stadium, made everyone go crazy! You never see a show like WVU's band!"

WV Aneesh Sompalli (Martinsburg, W.Va.): *"The 2006 season was one where we had high hopes from the beginning. Those hopes were bolstered by Steve Slaton's electric first-half performance against Maryland.*

Slaton had something like 150 yards in the first half and we ended up coasting to a comfortable win.

"2010 was the next time the Terps came to Morgantown. We had JUST come off a thrilling OT win in Huntington against Marshall. We were in the midst of one of the best eras of WVU football. We came out and punched them in the mouth from the get-go. It was great to see Tavon Austin, a Baltimore Dunbar High School product, tear up the Maryland Terps. Although things did get a little more interesting in the second half as our offense sputtered."

M **Ted Ewanciw (Colesville, Md.):** *"My fondest memory was the Terp chant: 'Go back, go back, go back into the woods' that reverberated in Byrd Stadium."*

WV **Bob Rucker (Clendenin, W.Va.):** *"While I attended many of the WVU-MD games my memories are vague. I suppose I had too much 'fun.' I will say the game I seem to remember most was when Danny Buggs returned a punt for a TD to win the game."*

M **Gabe Romano (Bethesda, Md.):** *"This was probably the second biggest rivalry we have only behind Penn State. We aren't competitive with Penn State, but it was more hype and hope, as Penn State always seemed to be ranked in the Top 10. The West Virginia rivalry was more interesting and more competitive than Penn State, but it's died down some since we don't play each other every year.*

"Morgantown was easy for students, alumni and boosters to travel to and it seemed that the game set the tone for the rest of the season for both teams. Both teams were generally strong and evenly matched. Nothing was more obnoxious than hearing the Mountaineer shoot off his musket, but it was a friendly rivalry, no bad blood."

WV **Arch Moore, III (Harper's Ferry, W.Va.):** *"The football rivalry with Maryland was intense, and Maryland was always a tough game. We could ruin their season and they could ruin our season. The Friedgen era was our worst beat-downs in recent memory, particularly the two losses in* *the same year. There was a game in late 60's that I think WV won that was an upset, and of course Boomer was a problem for us. Maryland had the worst football field and the best basketball venue back in the day."*

M Marty Troublefield (Oakland, Md.): *"I remember taking my 13-year-old son to Morgantown for the Maryland game in 2002. Scott McBrien! It felt like we were the only ones in the stadium with red on. I told him not to cheer too loud, especially when Maryland went up 28-0 in the first quarter. But the fans were very nice, what few were left in the stadium at the end!"*

WV Lionel Taylor (Burke, Va.), Treasurer, National Capital Area Chapter of WVU Alumni Association: *"We used to work with the Maryland ticket office and get a block of tickets for our group. We'd sell over 1,000 tickets to games when the Mountaineers came to Byrd Stadium. We generally have a pregame event, usually a tent near the Adult Ed Center. Now it's easier for our alums to buy tickets themselves.*

"I have taken some Maryland graduate friends to Morgantown for their first visit where they spoke of hearing that they would be abused and had batteries thrown at them as has been reported in The Washington Post in the past, but found it quite the opposite. If fact, they expressed envy that the Maryland fans do not support their teams nearly as well unless they are winners. Too many fair-weather football fans for their liking.

"It's an event for West Virginia fans in the DC area to go to the games."

M Jim Klein (Falling Waters, W.Va.): *"I first got my Maryland season tickets in 1992 which I've had consistently since. I would compare the MD-WVU football rivalry to the basketball rivalry between Georgetown and MD. I think it's omnipresent, but the "powers that be" have not consistently scheduled the game which has hurt the development of the combat.*

"Will insults be especially stinging when WVU walks through Lot 1 to the visitor player entrance? Hell yeah. WVU isn't Virginia, WVU is worse. WVU isn't Penn State, because PSU is the nasty older brother that abused Terps fans for years. If WVU would play MD in football more consistently, I can only imagine how that rivalry could grow.

"My favorite season was watching Scott McBrien beat WVU twice in 2003. Bruce Perry was the running back and I can't forget the chant: Bruuuuuuuuuuuuuuuuuuuce."

WV **Aaron Howell (Charles Town, W.Va.):** *"This game is an ongoing battle. I saw the rivalry heat up when Rich Rod chose Rasheed Marshall at QB over Scott McBrien. McBrien left, Rod wouldn't release him at first, finally Nehlen convinced Rod to sign the transfer. That next year the Terps knew exactly what we were going to do. In 2004 Chris Henry caught a two-point conversion in overtime. Great catch!"*

M **Raegon Clutz (Hagerstown, Md.):** *"It's the game I circle on my calendar every year. We have so many WVU alumni from Frederick west. It's for bragging rights. It's always been a real exciting rivalry. There's nothing like going to Morgantown for games. The fans are great, WVU fans in general are nothing but nice, warm-hearted people.*

"The 2003 games were great. No one would have predicted the blowouts. Since then, West Virginia has beaten us every year. It's tough to play them now that we have such tough games as Ohio State, Michigan, Michigan State and Penn State every year. But it's a great rivalry because of the number of fans West Virginia has, especially here in the Panhandle."

WV **Mark Parsons (Nashville, Tenn.):** *"This became a great series after Nehlen arrived. It was a barometer game. If we won that game, we usually won about eight games and went to a bowl. They were always close, defensive battles. My most vivid memories were the night game in '83 in Morgantown with Rob Bennett's clutch catch and the '73 game where Buggs returned a punt for a touchdown at the end of the game."*

M **Steve Rear (Crofton, Md.):** *"I've been attending and working games since the early 80's. This is an intense rivalry! Don Nehlen once said that it is a litmus-test game. But it is a game of streaks for both teams. The only time that it seemed to go back and forth was from 1976 to the early 80's. And it seemed for a while that the visiting team always won! (Maryland's longest streak was six games from 1949-1966. West Virginia's longest streak was seven games from 2004-2012)"*

WV Ron Heymann (Randolph, N.J.): *"Our location set us up to recruiting wars with Pitt and Maryland and, to some extent, Penn State and Virginia Tech. There was tremendous amount of high school talent in the D.C. area that each time we beat Maryland I felt that we would win the recruiting war for the upcoming season and obviously the opposite result when we lost. Do not know if that is factual but that's how important the game was to me as a WVU fan."*

M John Brown (College Park, Md.): *"This has always been an intense game, very aggressive. Beating West Virginia was always big for us. However, the rivalry has become diluted since the teams don't play every year. Our focus is now on Big Ten rivalries. West Virginia fans are not my favorites, but they love their program, I respect that."*

WV Rose Ann Ferrelli McMurray (Fairfax Station, Va.): *"My best story relates to a game my husband and I attended in 1997 at Byrd Stadium. When we took our seats, the guy seated next to me wore a T-shirt that said, 'Beware of the Uncle,' a clear reference to the often-stated (and patently unfair) stereotype of West Virginians being incestuous. I held my tongue, but it didn't make it any easier that the guy was also obnoxious and crass. However, my patience was not unlimited. When he yelled the phrase 'Send the hillbillies back to their trailers,' I calmly reminded him that College Park was, in fact, south of the Mason-Dixon Line and he too, a MD grad, would also be considered a "hillbilly." He looked stricken by this news, stopped cheering and soon after left his seat and didn't return. But the best revenge that day was WVU beating UMD by two touchdowns!"*

M Alex Moyseenko (Hagerstown, Md.): *"I've personally followed this rivalry since 1976. Fans in this area get more geared up for the West Virginia game than any other one. They say that whoever wins this game goes on to have a great season, while the loser usually doesn't do too well, and it seems to hold true.*

"I think that the West Virginia game in 1980, in Morgantown, marked the return of Maryland football. Jess Atkinson kicked a field goal at the end of the game to win 14-11. Maryland Football was back!"

Chapter 8:

The Coaches:
From Byrd & Tatum to Lewis & Nehlen;
With Some Bear and Bobbies Thrown In

Coaches are the heart and soul of college football. Although transient, their names are forever etched in the memories of fans. Who can think of Alabama without immediately thinking about Paul "Bear" Bryant or Nick Saban? What would Notre Dame have been without Rockne, Leahy, Parseghian or Holtz? Can you close your eyes and imagine the Tomahawk Chop without seeing Bobby Bowden prowling the sideline? Or hear that irritating screeching Nittany Lion without JoePa and his horn-rimmed glasses?

The rivalries were just as intense between coaches as they were between the schools. Who can forget the heavyweight knockout brawls between Woody and Bo? How about the Bowden Bowl or Bear and Shug?

Well, this Battle of the Potomac rivalry boasts some unforgettable coaches from both sides of the river! Curley Byrd is credited with perfecting the forward pass at Maryland, while Jim Tatum took the Terps to the national championship in 1953. Even Bear Bryant stopped in Terpland for a season. Jerry Claiborne re-energized the Terps and pioneered the focus on weight training, leaving the rest of the ACC in the dust. Bobby Ross opened up the game and had a plethora of future NFL quarterbacks to his credit. The Fridge came home and, again, re-energized College Park.

Across the river, Pappy Lewis took the Mountaineers to the mountaintop. Jim Carlen stayed a few years, and Bobby Bowden started his famed career in MoTown. Don Nehlen visited the Mountain State and stayed 20 years, providing many Mountaineer memories. RichRod returned home the same season as the Fridge did, promising to make their rivalry gargantuan. Alas he divorced his alma mater in the darkness of the night, much like the Colts did to Baltimore 20 years earlier. The Fridge won, but that wasn't enough and he threatened to tear up his diploma when they fired him.

Once again both schools had new coaches starting in 2019—Neal Brown donned the old gold and blue while Mike Locksley: the red, white, black and gold. Despite being in different conferences, the rivalry continues as the intensity begins to build with the ghosts of Byrd, Tatum, Bear, Nugent and Claiborne roaming the Maryland shores shouting challenges to their cross-river spirits. While the ghosts of the mountain, Rat Rodgers, Sleepy Glenn, Greasy Neal, Stew, and Pappy Lewis exhort their Mountaineers into battle. The Clash of the Titans, 2021 version, is about to begin!

Here's a look at those who roamed the sidelines:

University of Maryland Terrapins
(formerly Aggies and Old Liners) Coaches

Will Skinner	(1892)	0-3-0
Samuel Harding	(1893)	6-0-0
J.G. Bannon	(1894)	4-3-0
Grenville Lewis	(1896-97)	8-6-2
Frank Kenly	(1898)	2-5-1
S.M. Cooke	(1899)	1-4-0
F.H. Peters	(1900)	3-4-1
Emmons Dunbar	(1901)	1-7-0
D. John Markley	(1902-04)	12-13-4
Frank Neilsen	(1905-06)	11-7-0
Charles Melick	(1907)	3-6-0
Bill Lang	(1908)	3-8-0
Bill Lang/E.Larkin	(1909)	2-5-0
Roy Alston	(1910)	4-3-1
Charley Donnlley	(1911)	4-4-2

Curley Byrd (1911-1934: 119-82-15)

Photo courtesy of Special Collections, University of Maryland Libraries, University of Maryland.

0-1 vs. West Virginia

University of Maryland Sports Hall of Fame

Harry C. "Curley" Byrd strode onto the Maryland campus in 1905 full of piss and vinegar. The strapping 138-pound ladies' man was immediately discouraged from playing by Coach Fred Nielson, telling Byrd to *"go play with the kids. Football is a man's game."*

Curley ignored the advice. By the end of the season, he had become the starting quarterback, scoring two touchdowns in the final game against Western Maryland and being named captain. He graduated in 1908 and went to Georgetown, GWU and Western Maryland to study and play football. He came back to Maryland as head coach in 1911 and stayed 41 years, putting Maryland football and the university on his back, serving as football coach, athletic director and eventually president of the university.

He used his popularity to catapult himself into a political career, but lost in a Senate as well as a Congressional race and espoused a number of "separate but equal" policies during the campaigns. He designed the layout of the campus, campaigned for funds to build a stadium, gymnasiums and academic buildings.

As coach, he prowled the sidelines for 24 years. In 1919 he felt that Maryland needed to upgrade its schedule as they had only been playing one major power, Penn State, so Byrd added Yale and West Virginia to the schedule. Maryland lost to the two powers by a collective score of 58-0, but Byrd was undeterred, and the next year he upset powerhouse Syracuse 10-7, on the road.

Byrd had been lobbying for a stadium since 1916, and one was finally built in 1923 across the street from the main campus. It held 5,000 with room to expand to 15,000. He was so beloved that students and alumni petitioned the university to name the stadium after the 34-year-old coach, "an honor usually reserved for those already dead."

Byrd officially retired after the 1932 season but continued to call the shots over a board of coaches headed by Jack "The Hawk" Faber. Byrd had become Assistant VP of the university along with his athletic director and head coaching duties but outside business and politics were tugging at him. 1934 was his last as coach and he went out on another high note, finishing 7-3 with wins over Virginia Tech, Florida, Johns Hopkins and Georgetown. Byrd went through five coaches, including Hall of Famers Doc Spears, Bear Bryant and Clark Shaughnessy before landing Jim Tatum in 1947.

"Dictator, president, athletic director, football coach, comptroller, chief lobbyist and glamour-boy supreme," said sports writer Bob Considine, *"Curley is the most-hated and most-beloved man in Maryland."*

Miller Tydings, a U.S. Senator from Maryland (1927-51) and a Maryland grad, referred to Byrd as *"the father of the University of Maryland,"* while he's been universally hailed as the "father of Maryland Athletics."

Jack "The Hawk" Faber (1935, 1940-41: 12-13-4)

0-0 vs. West Virginia

University of Maryland Sports Hall of Fame

Since Jack never coached against West Virginia, and only coached for Maryland football for a very short time, he's included here because he was perhaps the most versatile coach in either school's history.

Faber served as the Terp lacrosse coach from 1928-1963, during which time he compiled an amazing record of 249-57 with nine national championships. He's in the National Lacrosse Hall of Fame.

Photo courtesy of Special Collections, University of Maryland Libraries, University of Maryland.

In 1930, Faber enticed Bosey Berger, Maryland's first basketball All-American, to join the football team with the promise of free late-night dining hall meals.

In 1933 and 1934, he also served as an assistant football coach under Curley Byrd, and in 1935 when Byrd became the University President, Faber became head coach. *"I was a front for Curley. He was still in charge... he ran the team during the games. He just couldn't devote as much time to it as before."* Faber continued to employ Byrd's pass-oriented "Byrd system" and hired Richmond head coach Frank Dobson as an assistant. Despite facing *"an almost suicidal schedule,"* Faber's veteran team led by back Bill Guckeyson compiled a 7-2-2 record to finish in third place in the Southern Conference.

Faber was succeeded as head football coach by Frank Dobson in 1936, but in turn, replaced him as a co-head coach alongside Al Heagy and Al Woods in 1940 and 1941. Those teams finished with 2-6-1 and 3-5-1 records, respectively, to bring Faber's combined football coaching record to 12-13-4. The coaching trio was subsequently replaced by Clark Shaughnessy.

Faber also spent time as an assistant basketball coach at Maryland, and in 1932, filled in for head baseball coach Burton Shipley, who had fallen ill. Faber served two terms as a president of the ACC.

Frank Dobson (1936-39: 18-21-0)

Clark Shaughnessy (1942,46: 10-8-0)

0-0-0 against West Virginia
College Football Hall of Fame
He was the father of the modern **T-Formation**. While coaching at the University of Chicago (1933-1939), Clark Shaughnessy became intrigued by the pro-T being used by George Halas and the Chicago Bears. He began dreaming of ways to improve the offensive set. Then Chicago dropped football. Shaughnessy was out of work—but not for long. Stanford signed him for the 1940 season and he shocked the collegiate football world with the announcement he planned to install the "T" as his primary formation.

Courtesy of Special Collections, University of Maryland Libraries, University of Maryland.

"If Stanford wins a single game with that crazy formation, you can throw all the football I ever knew into the Pacific Ocean," proclaimed Glenn "Pop" Warner. Stanford went 10-0-0 that year, including a 21-13 victory over Nebraska in the Rose Bowl. Presumably, Pop is still swimming! Shaughnessy earned Coach of the Year honors for his 1940 efforts. Within the next ten years, all but a half-dozen schools had switched to the Shaughnessy "T".

With the threat of Stanford dropping football during WWII, he moved to Maryland for a "lifetime contract," serving not only as head coach, but athletic director and director of physical education.

Shaughnessy introduced a red-and-white color scheme for the Maryland uniforms, which replaced the longstanding combination of black and gold. He installed the "T" formation. He left after one season for Pittsburgh, which he later said was the worst mistake he'd ever made and returned to Maryland in 1946. He wasn't nearly as successful and resigned because he refused to remain as athletic director and quit his consulting position with the Redskins.

He was inducted into the College Football Hall of Fame as a coach in 1968.

The Innovators

Maryland coaches were among the leaders in college-football innovations. In Morris Bealle's 1947 history of the Hoyas, he noted that Curley Byrd's innovation was not the **forward pass** itself, but the use of tactical receivers. Instead of throwing to the fastest man on the team, regardless of needs, Byrd featured a two-receiver option: one end ran longer pass routes, while another ran short routes. This unique offensive scheme was called the "Byrd system", which combined elements of the single-wing and double-wing formations.

Byrd also dealt with a second problem with the play—no one quite knew how to properly throw the ball, which was akin to a rugby ball today. A track athlete as well, Byrd mastered an underhanded, discus-like approach which made his passes more accurate. The passing won appeal after Byrd introduced the pass against Fordham at New York's Hilltop Park in October 1909.

"This was four years before Gus Dorais and Knute Rockne of Notre Dame showed the same thing to Army on the plains of West Point, " Bealle wrote. "The Dorais end-over-end discus throw of 1913 was an exact copy of the pass uncovered by Curley Byrd in 1909, the Notre Damers got the headlines because they had a press agent and Georgetown didn't." It's a shame that Joe Blair and Jack Zane weren't around then!

Clark Shaughnessy was the **Father of the Modern T Formation.** "I don't know of a team that wasn't using either a single-wing or double-wing formations which saw the ball snapped directly to one of the four ballcarriers. The quarterback's role was much different in those days. He was used mostly as a blocking back. It was a power formation, snap the ball and run straight ahead or around the corners. It was boring football with low scoring. Under the T, the quarterback took the ball directly from under center, pivoted and handed up to the running backs or faked a handoff and dropped back to throw a pass," said author Jim Johnson. "Shaughnessy added his own wrinkles, primarily using the man-in-motion and the counter play."

The **I Formation** was the brainchild of Tom Nugent. While a young first-year coach at VMI, Nugent was humiliated in a 54-6 loss to conference power William and Mary in 1946. Vowing revenge, Nugent spent the off-season devising a way to contain W&M's bigger, stronger defensive linemen.

What he created was "dropping the popular Split-T formation in favor of the "I," lining up all three backs "Indian file" behind the quarterback, often sending one in motion. His tailback was lined up six yards off the line of scrimmage—unheard of in those days—and had a better angle to hit the slightest of holes" said the *Orlando Sentinel.*

Nugent unveiled the new formation in 1950, exacting revenge on W&M 28-23 and upsetting Georgia Tech, a four-touchdown favorite by a score of 14-13. The **I Formation** was born. Notre Dame's Frank Leahy sent coaches to learn it. Southern Cal's John McKay, with his abundance of All-America running backs, perfected it. But Tom Nugent invented it!

Not to be outdone, West Virginia contributed to more modern innovations in the game. Bobby Bowden is often referred to as the "Riverboat Gambler" for his penchant for risky trick plays. He is credited with the development of the "**Puntrooski,**" where the ball is snapped to an upback, instead of to the punter, who does his best to sell the play by reaching high over his shoulder as if the ball was snapped over his head. The upback would walk up and place the ball between the legs of a lineman who hesitated and then would run downfield for a hopeful score. This was just one of many exciting "trick plays" that Bowden would utilize at both WVU and later at Florida State.

WVU's Rich Rodriguez was the first coach in the country to run the **spread no-huddle** offense successfully at the major-college level. He was also the first coach to adapt the scheme, staying ahead of defensive adjustments made to try to defend against it. He first developed it at Glenville State and refined it along the way, most notably with WVU's dual-threat quarterback Patrick White and running back Steve Slaton. The strategy features frequent use of the shotgun formation. He is also credited for creating the **zone-read** play run from the shotgun.

Clarence "Doc" Spears (1943-44: 5-12-1)

Courtesy of Special Collections University of Maryland Libraries, University of Maryland.

0-1-1 vs. West Virginia
College Football Hall of Fame

Clarence "Doc" Spears was torn between two loves—football and medicine. As an All-America guard at Dartmouth and later as one of the game's most-respected coaches, Spears left an indelible mark. As a 230-pound guard with unusual strength, he won consensus All-America honors in 1914 and 1915. During those two seasons, Spears helped Dartmouth to a 15-2-1 mark, losing only to Princeton each year.

He began his college career at Knox (Ill.) College. After his playing days, Spears returned to Dartmouth in 1917, serving as the Green's head coach for the next four campaigns and compiling a record of 21-9-1. Along the way, he completed his medical studies at the University of Chicago and Rush Medical School. From Dartmouth, he went on to coach at West Virginia, Minnesota, Oregon, Wisconsin, Toledo and Maryland. His 1927 Minnesota team went unbeaten. Over the years, Spears developed Hall of Fame fullbacks Bronko Nagurski and Herb Joesting. Finally, 30 years after he first played at Dartmouth, Spears surrendered his active participation in football and settled down to practice medicine.

In 1955, he was inducted into the College Football Hall of Fame as a player and a coach.

Paul "Bear" Bryant (1945: 6-2-1)

Courtesy of Special Collections University of Maryland Libraries, University of Maryland.

0-0-1 vs. West Virginia
College Football Hall of Fame

Paul "Bear" Bryant acquired the nickname "Bear" because, as a teenager, he wrestled a circus bear. At Alabama he was an end on the 1933-35 teams. Bryant started his coaching career as an assistant at Alabama (1936-39) and Vanderbilt (1940-41). He was in the U.S. Navy in World War II.

In 1945, the 32-year-old Bryant met Washington Redskins owner George Marshall at a cocktail party hosted by the *Chicago Tribune*, and mentioned that he had turned down offers to be an assistant coach at Alabama and Georgia Tech because he was intent on becoming a head coach. Marshall put him in contact with Harry Clifton "Curley" Byrd, the president and former football coach of the University of Maryland.

After meeting with Byrd, the next day Bryant received the job as head coach of the Maryland Terrapins. In his only season at Maryland, Bryant led the team to a 6-2-1 record, including a 13-13 tie with West Virginia in Morgantown.

However, Bryant and Byrd would come into conflict. In the most prominent incident, while Bryant was on vacation, Byrd reinstated a player who had been suspended by Bryant for a violation of team rules. During the ensuing altercation, Bryant said he had a telegram from Kentucky, offering him the job. He quit and left for the Bluegrass State.

Bryant was head coach at Kentucky eight years (1946-53), Texas A&M four years (1954-57), and Alabama 25 years (1958-82). He had winning records at every stop: Maryland 6-2-1, Kentucky 60-23-5, Texas A&M 25-14-2, Alabama 232-46-9. His career total for 38 years was 323-85-17.

His 1950 Kentucky team won the school's first conference championship and knocked off Oklahoma 13-7 in the Sugar Bowl, ending

Oklahoma's 31-game winning streak. Bryant's 1956 Texas A&M team won the Southwest Conference. Before he became head coach at Alabama, the school had won just four games in three years. Bryant won five games his first year, made a bowl his second year, and was national champion his fourth year. He won six national championships—1961, 1964, 1965, 1973, 1978, 1979.

His Alabama teams played in a bowl 24 straight years. When Alabama beat Auburn 28-17 on Nov. 28,1981, it was his 315th win. This topped Amos Alonzo Stagg's 314 wins and Bryant was saluted as the all-time winningest coach in college football. On Dec. 29, 1982, Alabama beat Illinois 21-15. He previously had announced this would be his last game as a coach. This gave him 323 victories. He died Jan. 26, 1983, in Tuscaloosa, Ala., less than a month after his final game. In 1997 the U.S. Postal Service issued the 32-cent Bear Bryant stamp.

In 1986, he was inducted into the College Football Hall of Fame as a coach.

Jim Tatum (1947-55: 73-15-4)

Courtesy of Special Collections, University of Maryland Libraries, University of Maryland.

4-1-0 vs. West Virginia
College Football Hall of Fame
Big Jim Tatum got his first taste of football with Carl Snavely's North Carolina Tar Heels. He made All-Southern tackle before going on to coach at North Carolina, Oklahoma and Maryland. His overall record for his career stands at 100-35-7.

After graduating from North Carolina, Tatum went to Cornell with Snavely and stayed two seasons as an assistant coach. Tatum then returned to his alma mater as Bear Wolf's assistant, and when Wolf entered the Navy, coached the Tar Heels for one season before he, too, enlisted.

Tatum was assigned to the Iowa Pre-Flight School, where he was an assistant under Don Faurot. It was there that Tatum mastered the Split-T offense, and it was this set (with some variations) that he used so successfully during his later coaching days. After leaving the service, Tatum was named head coach at Oklahoma, posting an 8-3-0 record in 1946. In 1947, Tatum accepted the head coaching job at Maryland and compiled an outstanding 73-15-4 record with the Terps, including one stretch of 19 straight wins. The Terrapins beat top-ranked Tennessee, 23-13, in the 1952 Sugar Bowl, and Tatum was elected Coach of the Year while leading Maryland to the national championship in 1953. He returned to his alma mater in 1956 for three more seasons before his death in 1959.

Byrd told a story on the banquet circuit about how he had breakfast with both Tatum and Bud Wilkinson at a coaches' convention. *"I told them either one could have the (Maryland) job. Tatum wasn't sure he wanted to leave Oklahoma so I said I'd take Wilkinson. We decided they should think about it overnight and decide among themselves who wanted it. Tatum called me the next day and said he did!"* With Tatum's hiring, Byrd made the ultimate commitment to turn over control of the program and the athletic department.

In 1984, Tatum was inducted into the College Football Hall of Fame as a coach.

Tommy Mont (1956-58: 11-18-1)
University of Maryland Sports Hall of Fame

Tom Nugent (1959-65: 36-34-0)

Courtesy of Special Collections,
University of Maryland
Libraries, University of
Maryland.

2-0-0 vs. West Virginia
Florida Sports Hall of Fame
Nugent, from Lawrence, Mass attended Ithaca (N.Y.) College and is a member of their Hall of Fame. Nugent served 17 years as a D-I head coach with stops at VMI, Florida State and Maryland. While at FSU, he also served as the school's athletic director. During World War II, he was a captain in the Army Air Corps, acting as a fitness trainer for officers heading overseas and later as a director of entertainment at a base in Missouri.

In 1959, Maryland hired Nugent, who became one of its most innovative and eccentric coaches of all-time. Nugent was a master promoter and showman, always looking for new ways to draw fans and attention to his Maryland Terrapins. For the 1964 season, one such idea was to turn his kicker into a "human scoreboard." Nugent, who originally asked the ACC if his kicker could wear a question mark instead of a number, hatched the idea when he was told all players would need a number on their jersey. He integrated the Maryland football program and was the first in NCAA history to put player names on the back of their jerseys.

His major contribution to the game of football as a coach was the development of the "I" formation.

Integration in College Park

Darryl Hill took a circuitous route to become Maryland's first black football player. He attended Xavier on a football scholarship,

where he starred as a freshman in 1960. A year later, he received a congressional appointment to the U.S. Naval Academy and was the first black player to play there. He resigned from the Navy after one year and was recruited by Terp assistant Lee Corso, who was encouraged by head coach Tom Nugent to *try to find a black athlete to play for the team."* Hill was reluctant stating *"I'm no Jackie Robinson, I just want to play football."* But he finally acquiesced and enrolled in Maryland in the fall of 1962, becoming the first black athlete to receive an athletic scholarship to play sports for a major university in the South.

Courtesy of Special Collections, University of Maryland Libraries, University of Maryland.

"That first year was damned tough on Darryl," said Jerry Fishman, tailback and star middle linebacker. *"The scout team was raw meat for the varsity, and everyone on it got hit hard, but Darryl got hit a little bit harder. Being the first black athlete, he had something to prove, and some of my redneck teammates had something to prove to him."*

That year Fishman, the team's only Jewish player, and Hill were in the same economics class, a subject Fishman found daunting. *"I said to Darryl, with whom I was already friends, 'You get me through economics, and I'll get [you] through your year on the scout team.' Darryl stuck out his hand and said, 'Deal.' I was kind of his bodyguard, and he got through it."*

The Maryland team was protected by the National Guard when they visited South Carolina for its first road game of the 1963 season.

Fishman had developed a strategy for protecting the increasingly valuable Hill on the field. As one of the co-captains, he would use the coin-toss ceremony to convey a message. *"I'd inform our opponents that if Darryl went out on a bad hit, a cheap shot, their quarterback was going out shortly thereafter, courtesy of me. And I pointed out that losing a quarterback for a flanker was not a good trade... like losing a queen for a bishop."*

Whenever he played in the South that year, Hill found that it was the fans and the coaches, not the opposing players, who were most negative toward him. Meanwhile, his own teammates continued to rally around him. If a hotel or motel refused to admit him, the coaches would take the entire team elsewhere. The same held true for restaurants. The first time Hill was denied service, the others had already been served, but they immediately stopped eating. Fishman—an emotional player who once flashed the finger at the entire Navy cheering section during a game—got so angry he threw his food on the floor, and the team was told to leave.

At Wake Forest late in the season, the Demon Deacons' captain approached Hill at the center of the field. He said, *"I want to apologize for the behavior of my fans,"* then, draping his arm over Hill's shoulder, he began walking him toward the Wake Forest side of the field, where the jeering was at its worst. By the time the two of them reached the middle of the field, the raucous screaming had dropped to near silence. The player's name was Brian Piccolo, who years later would inspire the television movie "Brian's Song."

At the end of that season, the Terps played an away game against Clemson, coached by the legendary Frank Howard. When Maryland announced that Hill was to play, Clemson threatened to leave the conference. Howard vowed that his team would not allow any black to play in their stadium, which was popularly known as "Death Valley" due to the power of their team. They threatened to pull out of the game if Maryland brought Hill.

Hill's mother, Palestine, was refused general entry to the "whites only" stadium, but Clemson President Robert Edwards took Mrs. Hill to his private box. The game went on, and Darryl set the ACC record for pass receptions in a game, a record that stood for many years. But Clemson prevailed 21-6.

Lou Saban (1966: 4-6-0)

1-0-0 vs. West Virginia

Buffalo Sports Hall of Fame

In the early 1960s and again in the 1970s, the Buffalo Bills enjoyed two separate glory eras. The driving force behind both was Lou Saban, whose style of coaching won him the respect, love and loyalty of his players.

A former all-star linebacker with the Cleveland Browns, "Trader Lou" came to Buffalo from Boston as a head coach for the first time in 1962 and set to work building the Bills. In 1964 and 1965 the Bills went

Courtesy of Special Collections, University of Maryland Libraries, University of Maryland.

12-2, and 10-3-1, en route to consecutive AFL championships. He was named Coach of the Year twice, but one week after winning his second title, he "shocked the football world" by suddenly quitting to become head coach at Maryland. He said he was leaving because *"there can be little left to conquer in professional football."* He was given a four-year contract worth nearly $100,000.

He lasted just one year with the Terps, returning to the AFL's Denver Broncos, who gave him a 10-year contract and doubled his annual salary with Maryland. Upon leaving, Saban stated *"I thought they wanted to go big-time. If I had known they were content in the ACC, I wouldn't have taken the job."*

In 1971, Saban returned to Buffalo. inheriting a 1-13 team. During his second stint, he doubled the number of carries per game for O.J. Simpson and assembled the "Electric Company," the offensive line that "turned on the juice." He drafted West Virginia's Jim Braxton as O.J.'s blocking fullback. The Bills improved to 4-9 in 1972 and soared to 9-5 in 1973, the same year Simpson became the first running back to rush for more than 2,000 yards in a season.

Virginia Tech's Jerry Claiborne was offered the job upon Saban's departure, but they couldn't agree on terms. Claiborne, famously, became the Maryland coach a few years later.

Bob Ward (1967-68: 2-17-0)
University of Maryland Sports Hall of Fame

Roy Lester (1969-71: 7-25-0)

Courtesy of Special Collections, University of Maryland Libraries, University of Maryland.

0-2-0 vs. West Virginia
WVU Sports Hall of Fame

Upon being hired as the head football coach at Richard Montgomery High School in 1959, Roy Lester considered himself lucky. For starters, as he looked at prospective members of his team, Lester saw plenty of faces—which was far from the case at his first coaching position, where he had just 14 players on the team. And then, he noted, the team had plenty of talented players, including future NFL linebacker Mike Curtis.

"When I went to Richard Montgomery, they hadn't been winning anything," Lester said. *"I took [former Maryland players Rod] Breedlove and Ronnie Shaffer over with me in the preseason to help me out. They looked things over and said, 'You'll never win here.' But I told them there was a kid there better than any player we had at Maryland—Mike Curtis. That's luck."*

Leaning on Curtis, Richard Montgomery went undefeated in Lester's first two seasons. Curtis went on to Duke University and was selected to the Pro Bowl four times in 14 NFL seasons. But Lester and Richard Montgomery continued their successful ways without their star. In all, Lester guided the Rockets to an 86-10-1 mark with six undefeated seasons before being hired as the head coach at the University of Maryland.

Following three losing seasons in College Park, including two losses to West Virginia, his alma mater, Lester returned to the high-school sidelines. He guided Paint Branch to the 1975 Maryland Class 'B' state championship. He led Magruder to the Class 'B' state championship in 1984 and the Class 'A' state title in 1986.

In 1984, the Touchdown Club of Washington selected Lester as its high school coach of the year. Lester's high-school teams won 260 games. Lester is a member of Maryland Football Coaches Association Hall of Fame and the West Virginia University Sports Hall of Fame. Richard Montgomery named its athletic field Roy Lester Stadium.

"I think I had a good background," Lester said. *"Before I came to Montgomery County, I had coached in a couple impossible situations. I always studied the game close wherever I was and I enjoyed it. I didn't mind working hard to get it."*

I spoke to the 96-year-old Lester for this book. He was sharp as a tack, had a great memory and was quite opinionated toward fellow coaches. Dudley DeGroot was *"great and ahead of his time."* He said Bobby Bowden was *"always very nice."* Rich Rodriguez was *"a great coach, but quit and went to Michigan. That was a great mistake as West Virginians will never forgive him."* Jerry Claiborne was *"a classy guy and asked which of my coaches he should keep."* Don Nehlen came to the 50th Anniversary of the Sun Bowl game and was *"very nice."*

He is unique in this rivalry in that he grew up in West Virginia and played football for WVU, yet coached at Maryland.

Jerry Claiborne (1972-81: 77-37-3)

Courtesy of Special Collections, University of Maryland Libraries, University of Maryland.

2-3-0 vs. West Virginia
College Football Hall of Fame

Jerry Claiborne took over washed-up programs and gave them new life. And he taught his players to be good students. He was a head coach 28 years with a record of 179-122-8. In 1988, the College Football Association gave Kentucky an award for leading the nation in number of football players who graduated on time. Claiborne coached four Academic All-Americans and 87 all-conference academics. His teams were in 11 bowl games. He coached Virginia Tech from 1961-70 with a 69-31-2 record.

Then Maryland called again, having contacted him following the departure of Lou Saban. This time they were able to come to terms. The Terps had won just nine games in five years and athletic director Jim Kehoe needed to give the football program a shot in the arm.

Claiborne came to town and had a winner his second year. Beginning in 1973 his teams made it to six consecutive bowl games, at a time when that actually meant something. In 1974, *The Sporting News* named him the nation's Coach of the Year. His 1976 team went 11-1 and ranked No. 8 in the Associated Press poll. For 10 years at Maryland his record was 77-37-3, including a 2-3 record against WVU.

In 1982, his alma-mater called. Kentucky had endured four straight losing seasons. Claiborne took them to bowl games his second and third years, including a loss in the 1983 Hall of Fame Bowl against West Virginia. He retired after the 1989 season. *Sports Illustrated* said in 1976 his great virtues were "organization, motivation, and hard work."

Claiborne said, *"Coaching is one of the few professions where you can change people and help them to be good citizens and parents."* Claiborne played halfback for Bear Bryant at Kentucky in 1946 and 1948-49. He was a Bryant assistant at Kentucky, Texas A&M, and Alabama before launching a career as a successful head coach. In June of 1999, the Lexington, Ky., chapter of the National Football Foundation was named after Claiborne.

He was inducted into the College Football Hall of Fame as a coach in 1999.

When Maryland Almost "Shocked the Athletic World"

The author, a WVU and Maryland grad and former athletic director at George Washington University, was a member of the senior management team at the University of Maryland athletic department when head football coach Jerry Claiborne left for Kentucky, and athletic director Dick Dull served as a one-man search committee.

Dull shared his plan with his leadership team that nearly "shocked the athletic world" by signing then-Cleveland Browns coach Sam Rutigliano. The deal was signed, but at the 11th hour Browns owner Art Modell made Sam an "offer he couldn't refuse." Upon Sam's withdrawal, Dull called on Bobby Ross to take the Terps' helm. Ross was the quarterback coach with the Kansas City Chiefs and the former head coach of The Citadel.

Bobby Ross (1982-86: 39-19-1)

Courtesy of Special Collections, University of Maryland Libraries, University of Maryland.

3-2-0 vs. West Virginia
Georgia Tech Sports Hall of Fame
Virginia Sports Hall of Fame

Ross was a surprise choice to replace Jerry Claiborne at Maryland. Skeptics criticized athletic director Dick Dull for the choice, but Dull's selection turned out to be spot on. Ross had been an assistant at Maryland during Claiborne's first season (1972) after having been an assistant at VMI, William and Mary and Rice. After his short stint as a Maryland assistant, Ross became head coach at The Citadel. After posting a 25-31 record over five years, he moved to the NFL, serving as the special teams and quarterback coach with the Kansas City Chiefs.

Little in his resume would indicate the success he would bring to College Park, but Dull drew to an inside straight and hit the jackpot!

Ross inherited a 4-6-1 team that had only been to the Tangerine Bowl in the previous three years. But in his inheritance included a left-handed blonde bomber named Norman "Boomer" Esiason, who had languished under Claiborne's emphasis on the ground game. Ross reversed the fortunes in Terpland and had Maryland in the Aloha Bowl in his first season, the first of four straight bowl appearances.

At Ross' inaugural press conference in 1982, he was asked by a wise guy from *The Washington Post* if he intended to make Maryland "the Alabama of the North?" a not-so-subtle reference to basketball coach Lefty Driesell's proclamation a decade earlier that Maryland had the potential to become the "UCLA of the East." Ross had no idea what the reporter was referring to, as the packed press room roared with laughter.

Ross reluctantly left after the 1986 season in the wake of the Len Bias tragedy, to serve as the head coach of Georgia Tech, leading the Rambling Wreck in 1990 to their fourth national championship. He spent five seasons at Tech before returning to the NFL as the head coach of the San Diego Chargers, taking them to their only Super Bowl appearance in 1995. Following the 1996 season, Ross moved to Detroit for a more lucrative contract and, more important, more control over the personnel decisions.

Ross struggled to overcome the "country-club atmosphere" that existed in Detroit. In November 2000, following a home loss to the Miami Dolphins, having had enough of what he called his team's unwillingness to "fight back," he resigned in mid-season. He also had been suffering with blood clots in his legs. After being out of coaching for three seasons, Ross was lured by West Point to turn Army's program around. After three years, he more than doubled the number of wins of the previous three years and retired in 2007.

Ross was named consensus National Coach of the Year in 1990. The Touchdown Club of Richmond has named their annual college football coach of the year award "The Bobby Ross Coach of the Year Award."

The Ross vs. Nehlen contests had Ross winning 3 games to 2 in some classic contests!

Len Bias Fallout

The sudden death of Terp basketball star Len Bias on the night of June 19, 1986 from a drug overdose changed the entire trajectory of the Maryland athletic program, including football. Fallout from that tragedy reverberated for two decades. Seventeen members of the athletic department were fired or reassigned, including athletic director Dick Dull and basketball coach Lefty Driesell. Ultimately, President John Slaughter was forced to resign. The backlash was palpable. New, more stringent academic admission regulations were implemented. Drug testing was implemented for all athletes and higher academic eligibility requirements were implemented.

No sport went unscathed. So many changes were made in recruiting and eligibility that baseball coach Jack Jackson said *"We're playing against kids who we couldn't even talk to, and they're playing for UVA, Duke and Carolina."* The sad irony among insiders was that President Slaughter was trying to make Maryland "The Harvard of the South."

Ultimately, Bobby Ross felt like the situation had become so toxic that he wouldn't be able to sustain the level of success he had built, so he resigned. Initially he accepted a position with the Buffalo Bills, but never went there. Instead, he accepted the head coaching position with Georgia Tech, which he took to the promised land, winning the national championship in 1990 (with future Terp head coach Ralph Friedgen as one of his assistants). He went on to serve as head coach for the San Diego Chargers, taking them to Super Bowl XXIX.

For the next 15 years, future head coaches, beginning with Joe Krivak, grappled with the fallout and reverberations from this tragic night. Revenues dropped dramatically in football and basketball and probably set the stage for the fiscal deficits which caused Maryland to move to the Big Ten Conference some 20 years later.

Joe Krivak (1987-91: 20-34-0)

Courtesy of Special Collections, University of Maryland Libraries, University of Maryland.

2-3-0 vs. West Virginia
Syracuse Sports Hall of Fame

Krivak attended Syracuse University on a football scholarship and earned four varsity letters (three in football and one in baseball), playing on the 1957 Syracuse Cotton Bowl team. He started his career in education at Madonna HS in Weirton, W.Va., in 1960 as a teacher and coach. Over his long career, he came to represent the best of both.

In 1969, Joe faced a crossroads—stay in Weirton as a high school icon or return to his alma mater to pursue his dream of becoming a college football coach. Over the next 27 years, Krivak would build a remarkable resume as one of the outstanding offensive coaches in college football, with stops at Syracuse, Maryland, Navy, back to Maryland where he served as head coach for four years and finally to the University of Virginia.

Krivak was the consummate "quarterback whisperer." He thrived as a quarterback coach and, while at Maryland, directed the development of six future NFL passers. Unfortunately, his niche was as an assistant, not a head coach, at least at Maryland. Despite outstanding quarterbacks, during his five years at the Terp helm, he had only one winning season.

Mark Duffner (1992-96: 20-35-0)
(2-3-0 vs. West Virginia)

Ron Vanderlinden (1997-00: 15-29-0)
(1-3-0 vs. West Virginia)

Ralph Friedgen (2001-10: 75-50-0)

Courtesy of Special Collections, University of Maryland Libraries, University of Maryland.

4-5-0 vs. West Virginia

"The Fridge" served as head football coach of the University of Maryland Terrapins from the 2001 season until 2010. Friedgen originally came to College Park as a player after a standout high school career in Harrison, N.Y., where he played quarterback on his father's team. At Maryland, Friedgen was switched to offensive guard.

After graduating from Maryland in 1970, Friedgen embarked on his coaching career, starting as a graduate assistant with the Terps under Roy Lester. He followed that up with assistant coaching positions at The Citadel, mentored by Bobby Ross, William & Mary, Murray State and then back to Maryland from 1982-86 as offensive coordinator under Ross. The Terps made four bowl games and won three consecutive ACC championships during that time.

He followed Bobby Ross to Georgia Tech as their offensive coordinator and quarterback coach—a stint which included a Yellow Jackets' national title in 1990. Friedgen then moved with Bobby Ross to the NFL's San Diego Chargers. After the 1996 season, Friedgen returned to Georgia Tech for a four-year stint as offensive coordinator.

Maryland fired head coach Ron Vanderlinden in 2000, and athletic director Debbie Yow tapped Friedgen, the 1999 Broyles Award Winner as the top assistant coach in the nation—giving the Terp alumnus his first head-coaching job. During his first year at the helm (2001), Maryland won its first ACC championship since 1985. For that accomplishment, Friedgen was named national Coach of the Year.

"Fridge" brought pride and tradition back to the Terrapin program. Under his tenure, the Terps became the initial face of Under Armor, owned by former Terp football player, Kevin Plank, and created the "Fear the Turtle" campaign. Following each game, his team would run to the front of the student section and sing the fight song. He started out with a bang, bringing in 10-, 11- and 10-win seasons in his first three years.

But two 5-6 seasons brought out the "boo-birds", but they were temporarily quieted with three consecutive bowl seasons. However, with a 2-9 season in 2009, athletic director Debbie Yow named James Franklin as the "coach in waiting," casting a pall of impending doom over the program. Franklin ultimately didn't stick around long enough to take over, and the relationship between Friedgen and Yow, if not good before, became frigid. In 2010, he righted the ship to a 9-4 record with a bowl victory and ACC Coach of the Year honors. Despite this turnaround, new athletic director Kevin Anderson reversed his November support of Friedgen and announced his firing in December.

The Coach in Waiting Fiasco and Intrigue

The "Head Coach in Waiting" was possibly the worst idea to invade NCAA football programs in the last 25 years. It began innocently enough as Wisconsin's Barry Alvarez was set to retire from coaching and move into the athletic director position. Assistant Coach Bret Bielema was identified as the next head coach, or Head Coach in Waiting (HCIW). That 2005 transition was one of the few that went well. As dumb luck would have it, both our rival teams, Maryland and West Virginia, stepped into this HCIW quagmire!

In February 2009, Maryland's then athletic director Debbie Yow, supported by then-president Dan Mote, signed offensive coordinator James Franklin as HCIW. In Franklin's contract was a stipulation that he'd be paid $1 million if he were not named the new Terp head coach by January 2, 2012.

Yow publicly announced that Maryland would NEVER pay the million bucks, throwing down the gauntlet and estranging Coach Ralph Friedgen in the process. This was a long window and the Fridge, although Franklin was loyal to him, wasn't on board and hadn't committed to retiring by then.

Yow resigned in June, 2010, after a controversial 16-year tenure, to move to NC State. At the same time, President Mote announced his retirement, but not before hiring Kevin Anderson as Maryland's new athletic director.

The HCIW scenario never came to be, as Franklin perceived that Anderson had no intention of honoring the HCIW agreement. Vanderbilt beckoned, Franklin left on Dec. 17, 2010, and The Fridge lived to fight another day, barely. A day later, Anderson fired Friedgen despite being named ACC Coach of the Year in 2010.

Maryland has gone through four coaches (plus another A.D. and a president) since then, before settling on Mike Locksley for the 2019 season. Whew! Got all that?

In Morgantown, the HCIW played out much differently and became what can only be described as "coyote ugly!" In a wave of euphoria following WVU's upset of No. 3 Oklahoma in the 2007 Fiesta Bowl, long-time athletic director Ed Pastilong, Board of Governors Chair Steve Goodwin, and then-governor Joe Manchin pressured then-president Mike Garrison, to hire interim head coach Bill Stewart as the full-time coach. Stewart had been named interim head coach following the shocking departure of Rich Rodriguez to Michigan after a season-ending upset loss to Pitt in the Backyard Brawl.

Jim Clements became WVU's president in 2009 and in June, 2010, he named former Mountaineer QB Oliver Luck to replace the retiring Ed Pastilong as athletic director. Following that season, Luck announced that Stewart wasn't the right guy for the job and that Stew's last season would be 2011. He would then be reassigned within the athletic department, and further announced that Dana Holgorsen had been hired from Oklahoma State to serve as the HCIW and Stewart's offensive coordinator.

Essentially, Holgorsen was in charge of the offense and Stewart the defense—resulting, not surprisingly, in creating a toxic atmosphere with the two barely speaking to one another. It didn't take long for the festering situation to erupt. Stewart resigned in June after he was discovered spreading a smear campaign against Holgorsen in the media. Holgorsen was named head coach for the 2011 season.

Gordon Gee returned to WVU as president in 2014, hiring Shane Lyons as the WVU athletic director in 2015. They effectively managed the end of Holgorsen's controversial tenure, ultimately hiring Neal Brown before the 2019 season to lead the Mountaineer gridiron fortunes into the next decade.

Garrison is in private law practice, Clements is president of Clemson, Luck was the CEO of the XFL until the pandemic hit, Holgorsen became head coach at the University of Houston, and Stewart died at the age of 59, many say from a broken heart.

Thankfully, the Head Coach in Waiting has fallen out of favor, leaving turf burns from Capital One Field at Maryland Stadium to Mountaineer Field at Milan Puskar Stadium.

Randy Edsall (2011-15: 22-34-0)

Courtesy of Special Collections, University of Maryland Libraries, University of Maryland.

1-4-0 vs. West Virginia

Randy Edsall's tumultuous tenure at Maryland came to an inevitable end midway through the 2015 season.

"For the majority of his time at Maryland, Edsall was a double-whammy of bad... Edsall signed one of the best recruits in Maryland history, five-star receiver Stefon Diggs in 2012, but never recruited a quarterback who could reliably get Diggs the ball," SB Nation wrote.

After six games, including four blowout losses, Maryland fired Edsall in the middle of his fifth season. He was 22-34 and 0-12 against ranked teams. Maryland was 1-4 against the Mountaineers during his tenure. He was in the fifth year of his original six-year, $10 million contract and received a three-year extension in July 2015, but just $500,000 of the $7.5 million extension was guaranteed.

John Feinstein of The Washington Post predicted this disaster after Edsall's first season. *"He didn't get it a year ago,"* he wrote in 2012. *"He didn't have the class to tell his Connecticut players in person that he was leaving. He didn't get it when he started spouting off about rules as if he had invented the idea of discipline."*

He was never able to replicate the record and culture developed by his predecessor Ralph Friedgen (75-50 and 5-2 in bowl games). Friedgen was 9-4 the season before being fired, much to the chagrin of many Terp players and fans. Thus, Edsall's acceptance was less than enthusiastic, resulting in a disastrous 2-10 season.

The lack of culture notwithstanding, Edsall couldn't seem to recruit. *"His classes were worse after Maryland announced late in 2012 that it would move from the ACC to the Big Ten, which is the opposite of what was supposed to happen,"* wrote SB Nation.

Future Terp head coach Mike Locksley was named interim head coach.

Mike Locksley (2015, 2019-present: 7-22)
0-0 vs. West Virginia

D.J. Durkin (2016-18: 10-15-0)

NCAA photo

0-1 vs. West Virginia

"Just over an hour after the governor of the state laid into the Maryland Board of Regents over their decision to recommend retaining head coach D.J. Durkin, the school has gone in a different direction and bowed to public pressure by firing the embattled coach," NBC Sports reported on Oct. 31, 2018.

Durkin completed his once-promising tenure at Maryland with just a 10-15 record and 5-13 in Big Ten play over just two seasons on the sidelines. His tenure took a deadly turn when the tragic death of offensive lineman Jordan McNair occurred at a campus workout in May 2018, resulting in Durkin's indefinite suspension. Despite the suspension, he maintained his job amidst growing controversy and investigations into both McNair's tragic death as well as the overall culture of the football program.

The resulting reports intensified calls for Durkin's firing, but the chairman of the Board of Regents stood behind the coach and recommended his immediate re-instatement. In a bizarre twist 24 hours later, the University president fired Durkin without cause.

"Since returning to campus after yesterday's press conference, I have met with the leadership of the Student Government Association speaking on behalf of numerous student organizations, the Senate Executive Committee, Deans, department chairs and campus leadership. The overwhelming majority of stakeholders expressed serious concerns about Coach D.J. Durkin returning to the campus," UMD President Wallace Loh wrote in a letter announcing the move.

"The chair of the Board of Regents has publicly acknowledged that I had previously raised serious concerns about Coach Durkin's return. This is not at all a reflection of my opinion of Coach Durkin as a person. However, a departure is in the best interest of the University, and this afternoon, Coach Durkin was informed that the University will part ways.

"This is a difficult decision, but it is the right one for our entire University. I will devote the remaining months of my presidency to advancing the needed reforms in our Athletic Department that prioritize the safety and well-being of our student-athletes."

According to *USA Today*, Durkin was owed a buyout of just over $5 million if he were to be fired this season.

Interim coach Matt Canada continued in this role throughout the remainder of the season.

Matt Canada (2018: 5-7-0)
0-0 vs. West Virginia

Talent Raiding

College football rivalries wouldn't be what they are without some intrigue or skullduggery. *"It was really competitive because of the fact that they would sometimes come to Maryland and recruit our players, and we would try to go to West Virginia and recruit some of them,"* said Lee Corso, an ESPN college football analyst who participated in the rivalry as a Terrapins assistant coach in the 1960s. *"That adds to the rivalry."*

Talent raiding between the two rivals has been a staple of the programs. In 1953, Joe Marconi, a future No. 1 draft choice of the L.A. Rams, accepted an athletic scholarship at Maryland. He enrolled but didn't like the school and instead wound up at WVU.

The talent raiding has continued since those glorious 50's and '60's! In 2007 Terp fullback Cory Jackson, who was born and raised in Morgantown, stood in the lobby of the Gossett Football Team House the week of the game wearing a bright red T-shirt that read 'Beat WVU.'

Doug Harbert grew up in Lumberport, W.Va., (population 876) and was a Mountaineer fan through and through. He attended many WVU home games with his dad and went to the WVU football camp numerous times. There was no doubt that he'd play football in Morgantown. Garrett Ford recruited him and Harbert committed to WVU his junior year. But Maryland came calling. He decided to visit College Park, to the chagrin of Ford and Bobby Bowden, and fell in love with the team and coaches. Bowden and Ford put the full-court press on him, but he ended up playing for Jerry Claiborne's Terps and had a huge interception of a Danny Kendra pass, returning it 66 yards for a touchdown in the 1976 game.

Mike Beasley was a starting running back for Joe Krivak at Maryland in 1988. He gained 588 yards and scored five touchdowns but decided to transfer to West Virginia due to a disagreement with Krivak over redshirting. Beasley wanted to focus on grades during his redshirt spring and not go to practice, but Krivak refused. Beasley subsequently requested a release by Krivak so he could transfer to West Virginia. Krivak refused to release him because WVU was an opponent. Beasley left anyway and was forced to pay WVU tuition and sit out one year. In 1990 he led the Mountaineers in rushing with 607 yards and was moved to flanker in 1991. He played every game for WVU in 1990 and 1991.

Perhaps most impactful, former Terrapin quarterback Scott McBrien started his college career at West Virginia, but after falling in the depth chart and becoming disenfranchised with new coach Rich Rodriguez, he requested a transfer. Rodriguez refused until former coach Don Nehlen (who recruited McBrien) asked him to sign the forms. McBrien, bitter with the way he felt he was treated at WVU, played them like a banshee and led the Terps to three straight victories over his former team, including a Gator Bowl thrashing in 2004. All told, the McBrien-led Terps outscored the Mountaineers 123-31!

But the knife cuts both ways. In 2005, WVU's All American, Steve Slaton originally had committed to Maryland. But when the Terrapins found themselves short of scholarships, they rescinded Slaton's offer. Slaton made the trip west to Morgantown and All-America status.

Similarly, WVU starting fullback Owen Schmitt, who played at Fairfax (Va.) High School, dreamed of playing for the Terps. When Maryland showed no interest, he drove to Morgantown and earned a tryout as a walk-on. Dunbar (Baltimore) superstar Tavon Austin spurned the Terps in 2009 to head to Morgantown, despite having to change positions from running back to receiver. He became a two-time All-American and opened the door for WVU in Baltimore.

West Virginia Mountaineer (formerly "Snakers") Coaches

Frederick Emory	(1891)	0-1-0
William Rane	(1893-94)	4-3-0
Harry McCrory	(1895)	5-1-0
Thomas Trenchard	(1896)	3-7-2
George Krebs	(1897)	5-4-1
Harry Anderson	(1898)	6-1-0
Louis Yeager	(1899, 1901-02)	12-9-0
John Hill	(1900)	4-3-0
Harry Trout	(1903)	7-1-0
Anthony Chez	(1904)	6-3-0
Carl Forkum	(1905-06)	13-6-0
Clarence Russell	(1907)	6-4-0
Charles Lueder	(1908-11)	17-13-3
William Edmunds	(1912)	6-3-0
Edwin Sweetland	(1913)	3-4-2
Sol Metzger	(1914-15)	10-6-1

Mont "Tubby" McIntire (1916-20: 24-11-4)

Courtesy of West Virginia and Regional History Center, WVU Libraries.

1-0-0 against Maryland

"Tubby" McIntire was the 17th head football coach at WVU. He coached from 1916 to 1920, playing Maryland in the first "Battle of the Potomac" in 1919. He compiled a record of 24-11-4. Due to World War I, WVU did not field a team in 1918.

He put the Mountaineers on the football map, defeating football power Washington and Jefferson twice. He is also credited with the development of the forward pass with a win over Princeton in 1910.

Despite some campus rumblings, it was a shock that McIntire left for "other fields." As it turned out he coached a Phillips University in Oklahoma in the 1921 season. The Haymakers were a regional southwestern power who had recently joined the Southwest Conference.

Clarence "Doc" Spears (1921-24: 30-6-3)

Courtesy of Special Collections, University of Maryland Libraries, University of Maryland.

College Football Hall of Fame

"Doc" Spears owns the highest winning percentage of any Mountaineer football coach with at least a four-year tenure. During his years at WVU from 1921-24, Spears compiled a record of 30-6-3, good for a winning percentage of .808.

Born in DeWitt, Ark., Spears had the distinction of coaching three All-Americans in Russ Meredith, Fred Graham and Red Mahan and also had four second team All-America picks.

He led West Virginia to its first bowl game in 1922, San Diego's East-West Game, where the Mountaineers defeated Gonzaga 21-13 to cap a 10-0-1 season and post the first undefeated season in school history.

The 1922 team racked up victories against Pitt, Rutgers, Cincinnati, Indiana, Virginia and Ohio, among others. The only blemish that season was a 12-12 tie versus Washington & Lee. Spears' charges outscored the opposition 267-34 in 1922 and posted seven shutouts.

His WVU teams showed records of 5-4-1, 10-0-1, 7-1-1 and 8-1, respectively. His 1924 squad was the first to play at Old Mountaineer Field, christening the facility with a 21-6 victory against West Virginia Wesleyan on Sept. 27 of that year.

Spears' football roots trace back to Kewanee (Ill.) High School. After a solid prep career, the 230-pound Spears went on to earn consensus All-America honors as a guard at Dartmouth in 1914 and 1915 for legendary coach Frank Cavanaugh. The Big Green posted a 16-2-1 mark those two years.

His alma mater was his first coaching stop, leading Dartmouth to a 21-9-1 record in four years, including a 28-7 win at Washington to give the Big Green their first-ever West Coast victory. Spears then went on to coach at West Virginia, Minnesota, Oregon, Wisconsin, Toledo and Maryland. Led by the great Bronko Nagurski, Spears' 1927 Minnesota team went undefeated. His battles with Notre Dame's Knute Rockne are legendary in Midwestern football lore.

During his tenure at Dartmouth, Spears found the time to finish his medical degree from the University of Chicago and Rush Medical School. In fact, "Doc" Spears maintained a surgical practice during his time in Morgantown.

After a 30-year football career, Spears finally retired from coaching in 1945 to practice medicine on a full-time basis in Ypsilanti, Mich. He also served in either a scouting or medical capacity for several NFL teams, including the Green Bay Packers, Washington Redskins and Detroit Lions.

He was inducted into the College Football Hall of Fame as a coach and player in 1955. He died Feb. 1, 1964, at Jupiter, Fla. at the age of 69.

He was an inaugural member of WVU's Mountaineer Legends Society in 2016.

Over the River and Through the Woods

Three coaches, **Doc Spears, Roy Lester and Joe Krivak** crossed the river to coach on both sides.

The oft-traveled Spears didn't stay in one place too long. He was an All-America guard at Dartmouth and two years after graduating, became the Indians' head coach. He stayed just four years (21-9-1) before moving to West Virginia (30-6-3), Minnesota (28-9-3), Oregon (13-4-2), Wisconsin (13-17-2), Toledo (38-26-2) and Maryland (5-12-1). He averaged about three years per school, with his longest tenure being seven years at Toledo. It seemed that despite induction to the College Football Hall of Fame, his first love was medicine, to which he returned after his final, unsuccessful stint at Maryland in 1943-44.

Lester grew up in rural Spencer, W.Va., and attended WVU, where he was a three-sport letterman. He began as a high school coach in Walton, W.Va., and then moved to Allegany HS in Cumberland, Md., where he met future Terp head coach Tommy Mont. Mont recruited him to College Park, where he served as an assistant from 1955-58. But his love was high school football, and he accepted the head-coaching position at Richard Montgomery HS for 10 years, compiling an unbelievable record of 86-10-1. Maryland A.D. Jim Kehoe, trying to find the Terps' fourth head coach in five years, turned to Lester to bring the Terps back from their lowest point in history.

Alas, Lester was not the man for the job. He was a great recruiter and nearly added Penn State's Lydell Mitchell and Franco Harris to his list of future Terps, along with Randy White and Paul Vellano. But he didn't have the time to enjoy their contributions. His three-year tenure at Maryland resulted in 3-7, 2-9 and 2-9 records with dwindling crowds and revenue, causing Kehoe to fire him. Lester returned to a highly successful high-school career, coaching at Paint Branch and Magruder before retiring.

Krivak grew up in Southwestern Pa., and became a three-year letterman at Syracuse. He began his coaching career at West Virginia's Weirton Madonna HS in the Northern Panhandle in 1960 as an assistant coach and became head coach after three years. During his 11 years at Madonna, Krivak became an icon in West Virginia high-school football circles. In his eight years as the head coach, he compiled a record of 50-24 and won a Catholic State HS championship.

In 1969 he faced a career-altering decision… continue to build on his success as an outstanding educator and football coach, or pursue his dream to become a college coach. He decided to "go for it" and became an assistant coach at his alma mater, where he stayed five seasons. This was followed by stints at Maryland, Navy and Maryland again, where he developed a reputation as a "quarterback whisperer." At the age of 51, the patient Krivak got his shot when Bobby Ross left the Terps for Georgia Tech. Krivak commented, *"This is my shot, I'm either going to get retired out of this job or fired out of it."*

He stayed five years, compiling a 20-34-2 record and resigned following a 2-9 season in 1991. He served as an assistant for two more years at Virginia before retiring from coaching.

Ira "Rat" Rodgers (1925-30, 1943-45: 41-31-8)

Courtesy of West Virginia and Regional History Center, WVU Libraries.

1-0-2 vs. Maryland

College Football Hall of Fame

From Bethany, W.Va., All American Ira Rodgers became a physical education instructor and assistant WVU football coach for Clarence Spears in 1921, and four years later was named the school's head coach when Spears left for Minnesota after the 1924 season. Rogers coached the Mountaineers for six years, leading the Mountaineers to an 8-1 record in 1925 and an 8-2 mark in 1928 that included the school's only victory over Pitt's Jock Sutherland.

Rodgers also coached a team of civilians during the war years in 1943, 1944 and 1945 when regular coach Bill Kern was commissioned in the Navy Pre-Flight program. In addition, Rodgers oversaw the baseball and golf programs while continuing to serve on the physical education staff until a year before his death on Feb. 22, 1963.

He compiled a 41-31-8 record in football and a 204-208-3 mark in baseball. Rodgers was elected into the College Football Hall of Fame in 1953. He is also a member of the WVU Sports Hall of Fame.

Alfred "Greasy" Neale (1931-33: 12-16-3)

Courtesy of West Virginia and Regional History Center WVU Libraries.

College Football Hall of Fame

As a member of the College Football Hall of Fame, it would have been impossible to omit Greasy Neale from this section. A native of Parkersburg and the WVU coach for two seasons, Neale made his mark outside of Morgantown. He was one of the greatest athletes from the Mountain State and was a star end at West Virginia Wesleyan (Class of 1914), he also excelled in baseball and basketball, and once reached the semifinals of the West Virginia Amateur Golf Tournament, He was even an accomplished bridge player. In a 1912 football game with arch-rival West Virginia, Neale caught 14 straight passes and sparked Wesleyan to its first-ever victory over the Mountaineers, 19-14.

Neale went on to combine two careers. For eight seasons he was a major-league baseball player, and in the fall, he coached college football. In the infamous 1919 World Series, he was the leading hitter for the Cincinnati Reds with a .357 average. He then coached football at Marietta and lost just one game. In 1921, he again played with the Reds and then coached Washington & Jefferson to an unbeaten season and a trip to the Rose Bowl. Between 1915 and 1933, he also coached Virginia, West Virginia Wesleyan and Muskingum, finishing at WVU. In 1934, he moved to Yale as an assistant under Ducky Pond, and in 1941, he became head coach of the Philadelphia Eagles. He led them to NFL Championships in 1948-49.

Neale was inducted into the College Football Hall of Fame in 1967 and was the first man to be elected to both the College and Pro Football Hall of Fame as a coach.

Charles Tallman (1934-36: 15-12-2)

Marshall "Little Sleepy" Glenn (1937-39: 14-12-3)

Courtesy of West Virginia and Regional History Center, WVU Libraries.

WVU Sports Hall of Fame

The hiring of Marshall "Little Sleepy" Glenn to coach the WVU football team in 1937 followed roughly the same pattern athletic director Harry Stansbury had intentionally or unintentionally fallen into since Doc Spears left to take the Minnesota job in the summer of 1925—interview coaches with some sort of West Virginia tie who were willing to work for a modest salary. Hmm, sound familiar?

Glenn, the school's basketball coach who also doubled as the freshman football coach, certainly fit the bill.

He was offered $6,000 for his seven-month stint as the school's football/basketball coach, with part of his arrangement including the continuation of his studies at Rush College to complete a medical degree.

Glenn was offered the football job in 1937, succeeding Charles "Trusty" Tallman when he resigned to accept an appointment to head the West Virginia state police. Glenn inherited a strong team from Tallman and used a couple of visits with Chicago Bears coach George Halas while in Chicago attending medical school to learn Halas' famous 'T' offense, which he used at West Virginia.

In 1937, Glenn had the players at West Virginia to make the 'T' successful, namely speedy backs Harry "Flash" Clarke, David Isaac and Sam Pinion, a powerful, straight-ahead runner in Sam Audia, and a capable passer in Kelly Moan.

With the exception of a 20-0 loss to undefeated Pitt (the Panthers' only blemish was a scoreless tie against Fordham) and 6-6 tie to George-town, Glenn's Mountaineers ran the table against a somewhat weak schedule that included victories over West Virginia Wesleyan, Washington & Lee, Xavier, Western Maryland and George Washington.

However, an impressive 34-0 home win over Clarence Spears' strong Toledo team got the attention of the Sun Bowl, which extended an invitation to West Virginia following its 26-0 home victory over George Washington to conclude the regular season.

It was just the school's second-ever bowl appearance, the first coming 15 years earlier in 1922.

Glenn's record slipped to 4-5-1 the next season as the schedule became more difficult and his off-season medical studies were requiring more of his time.

He canceled spring football practice in 1938 so he could get an early start on his medical schoolwork, and the team's decline continued in 1939 with a 2-6-1 record. WVU scored just 26 points over its remaining eight games, as it became apparent that Glenn was going to resign his post at the conclusion of the season and team morale sank. He made it official in a letter to the Board of Governors after West

Virginia's season-ending loss to George Washington, 13-0, leaving Glenn's three-year record at 14-12-3.

"Wild" Bill Kern (1940-42, 46-47: 24-23-1)

Courtesy of West Virginia and Regional History Center, WVU Libraries.

0-1-0 vs. Maryland
WVU Sports Hall of Fame

"Wild" Bill Kern, an All-America tackle at Pitt, served as the Mountaineer head coach from 1940-42 and 1946-47, compiling a record of 24-23-1. His tenure was interrupted by three years during WWII, when he served as a Naval Commander.

Upon his return, WVU went 5-5 in 1946. Immediately following the season, criticism was directed toward Kern and other members of the athletic department, resulting in an athletic department-wide investigation which suggested retention of Kern but the creation of a stronger athletic council.

WVU began 1947 with a 4-0 record, followed by four straight losses. They ended the losing streak by shutting out Temple, giving WVU a 5-4 record before heading into the Backyard Brawl with Pitt. That week, prior to the Pitt game, Kern announced his resignation to come following the game, citing that "it was best for all concerned."

Prior to coming to WVU, Kern coached Carnegie Tech from 1937-39, compiling a 12-12-1 record, and taking them to a No. 6 ranking and to the 1938 Sugar Bowl. He played for the Green Bay Packers in 1929 and 1930.

Dudley DeGroot (1948-49: 13-9-1)
1-0-0 vs. Maryland

Art "Pappy" Lewis (1950-59: 58-38-2)

0-3-0 vs. Maryland

WVU Sports Hall of Fame

Art "Pappy" Lewis will always be remembered as one of West Virginia University's most colorful and successful football coaches. His association with football spanned four decades, and Lewis left his mark everywhere he went.

Born Feb. 18, 1911, in Pityme, Ohio, Lewis was a standout tackle at Middleport (Ohio) High School. It was as a 21-year-old freshman at Ohio University in 1932 when Lewis first acquired the nickname "Pappy" and it stuck wherever he went. Earning Little All-America honors at tackle, Lewis played in the 1935 East-West Shrine Game and was later drafted in the first round by the New York Giants (the Giants' first-ever draft selection). He played one season with the Giants.

Courtesy of West Virginia and Regional History Center, WVU Libraries.

After coaching one year at Ohio Wesleyan College, Lewis joined the Cleveland Rams in 1938 as an assistant coach, and a year later he assumed the head-coaching duties on an interim basis in the middle of the 1939 season at age 27—the youngest head coach in NFL history. One of his greatest moments as a coach came during that season when his Rams defeated the great Chicago Bears twice.

Following a stint in the Navy from 1942-45, Lewis became the head football coach at Washington & Lee University. Though going just 11-17, Lewis found his niche as a recruiter (several of his recruits were from West Virginia) and turned the school into a formidable opponent.

After one year as line coach at Mississippi State, Lewis was appointed head football coach at West Virginia University in 1950, a job he said he had always wanted. After guiding West Virginia to two lackluster seasons in 1950 and 1951, he steered WVU to a 7-2 record in 1952, including victories over nationally ranked Pitt and South Carolina. The Pitt win was the school's first ever against a nationally ranked team.

The reason for the turnaround was simple—Lewis assembled the greatest collection of football players in school history. Sam Huff, Bruce Bosley, Fred Wyant, Joe Marconi, Chuck Howley, Tommy All-man, Larry Krutko, Gene "Beef" Lamone and Bobby Moss were just a handful of the great players Lewis brought to Morgantown.

In 1956, *The Saturday Evening Post* spent a week on the recruiting trail with Lewis to describe his tactics: "With a safety lamp on his cap, he'll go into the belly of a mine to talk to a coal-digging father about a football son. He'll drink straight vodka with an immigrant mother, go trout fishing at dawn with a boy who loves the rod, or seek out a prospect deep in the backwoods where modern transportation couldn't budge. It's not for nothing that Lewis is referred to in some quarters as 'America's No. 1 football recruiter.'"

Lewis was also an outstanding fundamentals coach who wanted his football players big and tough. That formula led West Virginia to its first-ever major bowl appearance against Georgia Tech in the 1954 Sugar Bowl. The greatest win that season was a 19-14 win over Penn State, a team led by future NFL stars Lenny Moore and Roosevelt Grier.

Lewis led West Virginia to another outstanding season in 1955 with an 8-2 record, but late losses against Pitt and Syracuse kept the Mountaineers from a return trip to a bowl game.

When Huff, Bosley, Wyant and then Howley graduated, Lewis' teams began to decline in the late 1950s. In 1960, he resigned his coaching position to accept a scouting job with the Pittsburgh Steelers.

Lewis held that post until his death of a heart attack on June 13, 1962. Winning 58 games as a Mountaineer coach, including a 30-game Southern Conference winning streak, his win total was a WVU record that lasted 28 years. He was inducted into the West Virginia Sports Hall of Fame in 1966.

Gene Corum (1960-65: 29-30-2)

0-1-0 vs. Maryland

WVU Sports Hall of Fame

Born May 29, 1921, in Huntington, W.Va., "Gentleman Gene" Corum was an all-state guard at Huntington High School before accepting a scholarship from Bill Kern to play for WVU in 1940. An undersized lineman, Corum immediately displayed an intense desire to play the game and became a starter in just his sophomore season.

Courtesy of West Virginia and Regional History Center, WVU Libraries.

Interrupting his college career to participate in the war effort, Corum, who barely weighed 185 pounds, rejoined the Mountaineers in 1947 and was nominated team captain. He played a key role in the Mountaineers' memorable 17-2 upset of Pitt, blocking a punt and returning it for what he thought was a touchdown. However, the field was covered with snow and he pounced on the ball at the 10-yard line thinking he was at the goal line. Since he could have run with the ball, he was denied his only opportunity to score a touchdown.

Earning a bachelor's degree in 1948, Corum went on to finish work on a master's degree that same year. After receiving his degree, he was hired as the football coach at Point Marion High School where he led the team to a 9-1 record in his first season, including a win over rival Masontown High School.

Coaching one more year with Point Marion, Corum rejoined the Mountaineers as the freshman coach in 1950 under Art "Pappy" Lewis. After a year of guiding the plebes, the freshman rule was abolished and Corum was moved up to the varsity, where he coached the ends.

He soon developed into one of Lewis' top assistants, helping the Mountaineers reach the 1954 Sugar Bowl. Corum remained on the Mountaineer staff until Lewis resigned in 1960. In the spring of that year, he was appointed by the West Virginia University Athletic Council as the University's 26th football coach.

Taking the job right before spring football practice, Corum endured a difficult first year as coach of the Mountaineers. Things picked up in 1961 and, in just his third season, Corum guided the Mountaineers to an 8-2 record, his best as a Mountaineer coach. He integrated WVU football and the Southern Conference with his signing of Dick Leftridge and Roger Alford in 1963. His greatest season came in 1964, when he guided the Mountaineers to a 7-3 regular-season record and a berth in the 1964 Liberty Bowl, the first bowl game played indoors.

Corum coached one more year before handing over the reins to Jim Carlen. During his last year as a head coach, Corum defeated Pitt 63-48 in what is considered one of the greatest offensive shows in West Virginia history.

A long-time instructor in the School of Physical Education, Corum also served a stint on the Morgantown city council. He was inducted into the West Virginia Sports Hall of Fame in 1984.

Integration in MoTown

Dick Leftridge (#31) and Roger Alford (#66), courtesy of West Virginia and Regional History Center, WVU Libraries.

The recruitment and signing of Dick Leftridge accompanied by the subsequent signing of another black player Roger Alford, represented a shift in the culture at WVU. Despite being from Hinton, W.Va., the in-state option was not his first choice... he wanted to play for Woody Hayes at Ohio State. But he bowed to pressure from boosters and politicians who wanted him to stay home and play. Even the local NAACP chapter encouraged Leftridge to attend WVU and be the one to break the color barrier.

In 1963, the 100th Anniversary of the State of West Virginia, Leftridge and Alford became the first black football players at WVU as well as in the entire Southern Conference.

Leftridge was the top rusher in 1963, gaining 393 yards with an average of five yards per carry. He caught 10 passes and scored seven touchdowns his sophomore year. His best game was 79 yards and two touchdowns against George Washington. He made the All-Southern Conference second team, the first African-American to be named to such honor. In 1964 (junior year) he rushed 125 times for 534 yards with a 4.3 average. He was the team's leading rusher in 1963 and 1964 and considered a pioneer, a hitter and a performer.

Roger Alford joined Leftridge as the first black student-athletes to receive an athletic scholarship at West Virginia. Alford was a three-year letter winner and an outstanding offensive lineman. He was part of the 63-48 win over Pitt in 1965 and the 28-27 upset win over No. 9 Syracuse in 1964 that propelled the Mountaineers into the Liberty Bowl against Utah.

He was named to the WVU football all-time team from 1960-69. Alford was inducted into the School of Physical Education Hall of Fame in 1996 and into the West Virginia University Sports Hall of Fame in 1999.

Jim Carlen (1966-69: 25-13-3)

Courtesy of West Virginia and Regional History Center, WVU Libraries.

1-1-0 vs. Maryland

University of South Carolina Athletic Hall of Fame

Carlen came to West Virginia after eight years as a Georgia Tech assistant and coached the Mountaineers to a record of 25-13-3 from 1966-1969. He transformed football at WVU.

His first year in Morgantown he traveled the state and gave 367 talks in 365 days. He recruited some of WVU's greatest players—Carl Crennel, Jim Braxton, Mike Sherwood, Bob Gresham and Oscar Patrick, all big-time recruits and players. He ran a tight ship and, as one of the original members of Fellowship of Christian Athletes, required his team to go church on Sunday.

Carlen announced his resignation immediately after upsetting South Carolina in the Peach Bowl, accepting the head coaching position at Texas Tech.

At Tech he was named Southwest Conference Coach of the Year in 1970 and 1973, leading the Red Raiders to an 11-1 record and a Gator Bowl win over Tennessee—taking Tech to four bowls in five years.

From 1975 until 1981, he coached the Gamecocks of South Carolina, where he coached Heisman running back George Rogers, compiling a 45-36 record.

The Birth of a Riverboat Gambler

"My whole system was run the veer and the wishbone and run the ball all the time. I had just never been around the throwing game," remarked Jim Carlen.

That's the main reason he hired Bobby Bowden to run his offense at West Virginia. Carlen may have hired Bowden to throw the ball, but he rarely let him do it the way Bowden wanted. During one game WVU was comfortably winning, Bowden wanted to call a halfback pass, but Carlen got on the headsets and ordered no more passes. When Carlen got off, Bowden decided to call the play anyway in open defiance of his head coach. It was only after objections from the rest of the offensive coaches that Bowden stopped the play from going in.

Carlen let Bowden open up the offense in 1968, and quarterback Mike Sherwood threw for 1,998 yards and 12 touchdowns, setting the school single-game passing record with 416 yards in a big 38-15 win at Pitt. Carlen's departure after the 1969 season enabled Bowden to develop his "riverboat gambler" reputation, complete with experimental trick plays, which Bowden would make into an artform.

In 1972, Bernie Galiffa became the first quarterback in school history to pass for more than 2,000 yards in a season (2,496 yards) and lead the sixth-best passing attack in the country. West Virginia won eight games in '72, and with exciting players such as Danny Buggs, Marshall Mills, Nate Stephens and Kerry Marbury frequently scoring touchdowns, Mountaineer fans were always on the edge of their seats.

"Because of the offense that we ran, we weren't out of any game," explained Galiffa.

Offensive coordinator Frank Cignetti could sense Bowden's irritation whenever he called too many running plays in a row.

"He was the kind of guy who liked it wide-open," Cignetti recalled. *"Man, if you didn't have 21 points on the board in the first four or five minutes... I'll never forget one day we were out there and we were running the ball against Miami and he gets on the phone and he says, 'Frank, don't you have faith in your quarterback? Let him throw the football!'"*

Bobby Bowden (1970-75: 42-26-0)

2-0-0 vs. Maryland
College Football Hall of Fame

Bobby Bowden began his career as the coach of his alma mater Howard College (later Samford University). His first two teams each lost only one game as he posted a 31-6 record in four seasons. After seven seasons as an assistant at Florida State and West Virginia, he became the Mountaineers head coach in 1970.

Courtesy of West Virginia and Regional History Center, WVU Libraries.

As head coach at West Virginia, he guided them to Peach Bowls in 1972 and 1975, with his 1975 team finishing No. 20 in the nation. Bowden posted a 42-26 record at WVU from 1970-75 and developed three first-team All-Americans in Jim Braxton, Dale Farley and Danny Buggs, along with numerous NFL Draft selections.

Bowden was the first coach to lead WVU to multiple bowl games, and his 1972 team was ranked fourth in the nation in scoring (36.5) and sixth in passing yards (227.8).

His success at WVU led him back to Tallahassee, where he became the head coach in 1976. Prior to his arrival, the Seminoles won only four games over three years. His success over the next 30-plus seasons was remarkable. His second team went 10-2 and, in his fourth year, he had a team that contended for the national title.

Bowden is the only coach in NCAA Division I to lead his team to 15 consecutive New Year's Day bowl games (1991-2005), the only Division I coach to win 11 consecutive bowl games (1985-95), the only Division I coach with 14 straight bowl trips without a loss (1982-95), the only coach in Division I to compile 14 straight 10-win seasons (1987-2000), the only coach to take his team to 28 consecutive bowl games and the only coach in Division I history to compile 14 straight top-five finishes in the AP poll (1987-2000).

Perhaps the most notable of his records is that for 14 consecutive years, the 'Noles finished the season as one of the nation's top-five teams. He compiled a 315-98-4 record at FSU from 1976-2009.

Bowden received the National Football Foundation's highest award—the Gold Medal—in 2006. He was the Bobby Dodd Coach of the Year in 1980, the Walter Camp Coach of the Year in 1991 and won the Amos Alonzo Stagg Award in 2011.

In addition to two national championships, Bowden led Florida State to 12 Atlantic Coast Conference titles. In 2004, Doak Campbell Stadium at Florida State was named Bobby Bowden Field and a bronze statue of Bowden was unveiled. Among the awards named in honor of Bobby Bowden are the Bobby Bowden National Coach of the Year Award, presented by The Mountain Touchdown Club of Birmingham and the Bobby Bowden Athlete of the Year Award, presented by the Fellowship of Christian Athletes.

He was an inaugural member of WVU's Mountaineer Legends Society in 2016. He was inducted into the College Football Hall of Fame, as a coach, in 2006.

Perhaps fittingly, his final game was in the 2010 Gator Bowl, a 34-21 victory over the West Virginia Mountaineers.

We Are Marshall

On November 14, 1970, the Marshall University football team's plane crashed just two miles from home, returning from a loss at East Carolina. There were no survivors.

This was Bobby Bowden's first year as head coach at WVU. Bowden asked NCAA permission to wear Marshall jerseys and play Marshall's final game of the 1970 season against Ohio, but was denied.

In memory of the victims of the crash, Mountaineers players put green crosses and the initials "MU" on their helmets. Bowden allowed Marshall's new head coach Jack Lengyel and his assistants access to game film and playbooks to acquaint themselves with the veer offense, a variation of the option offense which aids teams with weak offensive lines. Lengyel credits Bowden with helping the young Thundering Herd recover. Bowden reportedly became emotional while viewing the movie "*We Are Marshall*", and ironically, had been offered the head coaching job at Marshall a few years earlier. He could have been on that plane.

Perhaps as a "tip of the hat" to Marshall, WVU scheduled them in 1997, but controversy ensued regarding an agreement or lack thereof, about continued games. They didn't play again until the Friends of Coal Bowl series was brokered by then-Governor Joe Manchin, resulting in the teams playing for seven straight years from 2006-12. There are no plans for future contests.

Frank Cignetti (1976-79: 17-27-0)

Courtesy of Special Collections, Pennsylvania Sports HOF.

1-1-0 vs. Maryland
College Football Hall of Fame
Cignetti was the logical successor to Bowden, having spent six years as his assistant with similar styles, philosophies and beliefs. However, the cupboard was nearly bare.

In his first year, Cignetti redshirted nearly the entire incoming freshman class. They had a difficult year (5-6, including a loss to No. 10 Maryland), but he started WVU on a path for long-term improvement. Unfortunately, something happened which nobody saw coming… Cignetti got a rare form of cancer. He ultimately beat it, but reluctantly gave up the reins of the football program and became assistant athletic director. This gave him a position with stature, an income and mostly a source of health insurance.

In 1986 he returned to his alma mater as head coach. The most successful head coach in Indiana University of Pennsylvania (IUP) history, Cignetti led the Hawks to unprecedented success during his

20-year tenure. Under his coaching, IUP ranked in the Division II Top 20 each season from 1986-2004, achieving undefeated regular seasons in 1991 and 1993. Cignetti's teams received the Lambert Cup 10 times as the top Division II team in the East. He was named the PSAC West Coach of the Year five times and the Kodak College Division Regional Coach of the Year three times en route to earning Chevrolet Division II National Coach of the Year honors in 1991. He was inducted into the College Football Hall of Fame as a coach in 2013.

Don Nehlen (1980-2000: 149-93-4)

12-9-0 vs. Maryland
College Football Hall of Fame

Don Nehlen came to Morgantown for a visit and stayed 20 years. He was a reluctant recruit. His boss, Bo Schembechler, told him not to take the job. He took the job anyway.

West Virginia, suffering through four straight losing seasons, declining fan support and poor morale, desperately needed a football coach capable of injecting some passion and enthusiasm into the program

Courtesy of Special Collections, University of Maryland Libraries, University of Maryland.

and its new stadium. Nehlen turned out to be the right man at the right time for Mountaineer football.

When the Canton, Ohio, native came to West Virginia in 1980 after three years as a Michigan assistant coach, he changed everything. The veer offense that West Virginia had used since the Jim Carlen days was scrapped in favor of the more modern I-formation and pro-offense. The defense was going to attack and blitz more often. His guys were going to live in the weight room and build themselves up physically and mentally. He changed the uniforms because he couldn't tell which team West Virginia was from the film he watched, demanding a look that was simple and identifiable.

Most of the changes Nehlen made looked a lot like Bo Schembechler's Michigan program, the exception being a simple W and V for the team's new logo—the flying WV that has become so popular today.

Nehlen's first season in 1980 wasn't a winning one, but it wasn't a losing one either. A strong 4-1 start turned into a 4-5 record after a tough mid-season stretch brought losses against Hawaii, Pitt, Penn State and Virginia Tech. But the Mounties recovered to win two of their last three to finish with a 6-6 record.

The second season saw West Virginia win eight of 11 regular-season games to earn a bid to play Florida in the 1981 Peach Bowl. The Gators were regarded as heavy favorites. A popular sports guy predicted a Gator win as "the mortal lock of the century!"

Everyone knew Nehlen's name after the Mountaineers won, 26-6. Nine months later, he produced an even more stunning victory when West Virginia, led by QB Jeff Hostetler went to Norman, Okla., and defeated the ninth-ranked Sooners 41-27.

It was probably the most important nine-month stretch in school history. The Oklahoma victory gave the team the self-confidence it needed to beat a motivated Maryland team, which was coming off a heart-breaking loss to Penn State; and to defeat Pitt in 1983, breaking a seven-game losing streak to the Panthers. After that came wins over fourth-ranked Boston College and Doug Flutie in 1984, and finally, Penn State a week later. The victory over the Nittany Lions ended 29 years of frustration and validated Nehlen's status as one of college football's great coaches.

When Nehlen entertained other job offers, seemingly every year following his team's stunning upset victory over Florida in the 1981 Peach Bowl, Merry Ann would subtly remind her husband that their son Danny and daughter Vicky were all together here in Morgantown.

Then, when Ohio State opted to hire John Cooper instead of Nehlen following the 1987 season, Merry Ann made her desires clear.

"Don, that's enough," she told him. "This is our home."

The next two seasons, Nehlen's teams hit a wall while he searched for another good quarterback, finally coming up with an outstanding one in Pittsburgh's Major Harris.

Harris and a veteran cast of players Nehlen had assembled around him got West Virginia to the pinnacle of college football in 1988 when the Mountaineers won all 11 regular-season games, reached No. 3 in the national polls and faced Notre Dame in the de facto national championship game in the Sunkist Fiesta Bowl in Tempe, Ariz. WVU lost after Harris suffered a separated shoulder on the game's third play.

Late in the 2000 season, Nehlen decided that 20 years at WVU and 34 total years as a college football coach, was enough.

Nehlen won his final game—a 49-38 victory over Ole Miss in the Music City Bowl and walked off into the sunset with a 149-93-4 overall record at WVU, easily the most victories in school history. He was named the Walter Camp, Bobby Dodd and AFCA coach of the year in 1988, and was the Kodak Coach of the Year in 1993.

He took 13 teams to bowl games (4-9 record), produced 17 winning seasons, coached 15 first team All-Americans, 82 all-conference players, six first-team Academic All-Americans and 80 players who went on to play professional football.

Five years after his retirement in 2005, he was inducted into the College Football Hall of Fame, the only coach with WVU ties to be enshrined based solely on his record at West Virginia.

Bobby Bowden, who spent six years coaching the Mountaineers from 1970-75, understood better than anyone what Don Nehlen was able to accomplish at West Virginia University.

"Don did an amazing job," Bowden said. *"No. 1, he had that Michigan background. He used to coach at Michigan when he was an assistant coach, and he was used to being big-time all the way. So, when he comes to West Virginia, he just assumes he's going to do the same thing here. He changed the uniforms to even look like Michigan. Don is one of the best coaches ever, in my opinion."*

He was named an inaugural member of WVU's Mountaineer Legends Society in 2016. His daughter, a former WVU cheerleader is married to former WVU quarterback and NFL star, Jeff Hostetler.

Rich Rodriguez (2001-07: 60-26-0)

4-4-0 vs. Maryland

Glenville State Athletics Hall of Fame

Rich Rodriguez, a native of Grant Town in Marion County, succeeded his former coach Don Nehlen to take over the Mountaineer reins in 2001. He had developed a reputation of fast-paced, no-huddle offenses while head coach at Glenville State, taking them to four consecutive WVIAC Championships and runner-up in the NAIA Division II National Championship.

Photo by Randy Litzinger.

Rodriguez left Glenville State at the end of the 1996 season to serve as assistant coach, offensive coordinator and quarterback coach for Tulane University from 1997 to 1998, under head coach Tommy Bowden. Rodriguez knew Bowden's father Bobby, having worked at his summer camps.

In Rodriguez's first year as offensive coordinator, his innovative offense succeeded, as Tulane went 7-4 and had their best season since 1980. Rodriguez was part of Tulane's success the next year, posting an undefeated season and finishing No. 7 in the nation after a win in the Liberty Bowl over BYU. Bowden then left for Clemson, bringing Rodriguez along with his spread offense. The success continued, with the Tigers playing in consecutive Peach Bowls.

WVU came calling and Rodriguez succeeded Mountaineer legend Don Nehlen in 2001. After a rough start (3-8), he righted the Mountaineer ship and led WVU to the Continental Tire Bowl and a 9-4 season in 2002. Two eight-win seasons followed with losses at the Gator Bowl, before future All-Americans Steve Slaton and Patrick White took the Mountaineer offense to new heights and 32 wins in the next three seasons. The stretch included three Top-10 finishes and wins in the Bowl Championship Series' Sugar Bowl over Georgia and a subsequent Gator Bowl win over Georgia Tech.

Everything blew up for Rodriguez in the 2007 season. He was rumored to have accepted the Alabama job and, although ranked No. 5, lost for the second year in a row to South Florida. They climbed back and were ranked No. 1 and No. 2 as they hosted the 4-7 Pitt Panthers in the 100th Backyard Brawl. Pitt scored the biggest upset of the series, winning 13-9.

Throughout the season, Rodriguez had become more and more disillusioned. He and his agent reportedly had conflicts with the WVU president and negotiations over a $4 million buyout clause. Immediately following the Pitt loss, it was reported that he met with Michigan and visited recruits encouraging them to wait to commit until his move to Michigan was announced. Two weeks of fan anger followed and he announced his departure for Michigan on December 16. After escalating fan uproar, two days later he stated his resignation was effective at midnight and that he would not be coaching the Mountaineers in their forthcoming BCS matchup with Oklahoma.

In July 2008, Rodriguez and WVU settled their lawsuit around the $4 million buyout. Michigan paid $2.5 million, while Rodriguez paid the remaining $1.5 million in three installments. Five years later, a Public Policy Poll found that Mountaineer faithful had a 47% unfavorable opinion of RichRod, while only 11% were favorable. Mountaineers have long memories!

After three tumultuous seasons (15-22) wrought with controversy and NCAA violations in Ann Arbor, he was let go. He spent a year away from the sidelines before taking the head-coaching position at Arizona, but self-inflicted troubles continued to haunt him. He was fired in 2018 amid sexual misconduct allegations from a former administrative assistant. In 2019, Rodriguez served as the offensive coordinator at Ole Miss. He is currently the Offensive Coordinator and Associate Head Coach at the University of Louisiana at Monroe, under former WVU alum, Terry Bowden.

Bill Stewart (2007-10: 28-12-0)

2008 Fiesta Bowl victory, photo by Dale Sparks Photography and Framing.

1-0-0 vs. Maryland
Wetzel County Hall of Fame

"Stew" was a tragic figure in the WVU athletic department's Shakespearian tragedy. He was born in Grafton, W.Va., and bled old gold and blue his entire life. He was a three-year letterman at Fairmont State and for his first 20 years, moved from assistant to assistant position before finally becoming head coach at VMI in 1994. He stayed three years and compiled an 8-25 record, eventually resigning after using a racial slur.

He coached in Canada for two years before Don Nehlen called him to come to Morgantown. When Rich Rodriguez was hired in 2001, Stew was retained as an assistant coach. Upon Rodriguez' sudden flame-out, Stew found himself coaching the 9th-ranked Mountaineers against No. 3 Oklahoma in the Fiesta Bowl. WVU pulled an amazing upset, 38-28 and Stewart was named permanent head coach the next day.

He was the guy you'd want your son to play for… honest, loyal, kind, but sadly, he was in over his head at the helm. He did, however, lead WVU to three consecutive 9-4 seasons. But after an embarrassing loss to NC State in the Champs Sports Bowl, new athletic director Oliver Luck made another controversial decision—announcing that Stewart would coach the 2011 season but would then step down to take a position in the athletic department.

Meanwhile, Dana Holgorsen was hired from Oklahoma State to be the "coach in waiting" while serving as Stewart's offensive coordinator. This arrangement was doomed to fail, and in June 2011, Stewart resigned among allegations that he was attempting to dig up dirt on Holgorsen and leak it to the media.

Tragically, less than a year later, the 59-year old Stewart died playing golf. Officially, he died of a heart attack, but most believe that he died of a broken heart.

U.S. Sen. Joe Manchin, who was governor at the time Stewart became head coach, said Stewart was a longtime friend who *"leaves behind a lifetime of memories and love for our state... Bill was a proud West Virginian in every sense of the word, and he was the best cheerleader this state ever had."*

Dana Holgorsen (2011-18: 45-30-0)

Special Collections, UM Libraries

4-1-0 vs. Maryland

Dana Holgorsen's tenure in Morgantown was fraught with controversy. On Dec. 22, 2010, Holgorsen was hired by athletic director Oliver Luck as offensive coordinator and, in effect the co-coach. The prevailing wisdom was that Holgorsen would replace Bill Stewart as head coach in 2012, with Luck saying that he didn't think Stewart was capable of leading the Mountaineers to a national championship.

Needless to say, this "coach-in-waiting" idea was doomed from the start, with the two "co-coaches" barely speaking to one another. Seemingly Luck anticipated (some say orchestrated) and built pro-rated salary increases into Holgorsen's contract should this scenario play out.

According to news reports, to make matters worse, an intoxicated Holgorsen was escorted out of the Mardi Gras Casino in Cross Lanes, W.Va., on May 18. No charges were filed but the tone was set. Shortly thereafter, Stewart resigned amid some skullduggery.

Holgorsen coached the Mountaineers to a share of the Big East Championship in his first season at WVU and a BCS berth in the 2012 Orange Bowl against Clemson. WVU won 70-33 and it looked like WVU was going places, including to the Big 12. The successful season triggered $225,000 worth of bonuses for Holgorsen, $100,000 for a 10-win season, $75,000 for a BCS appearance and $50,000 for a BCS win.

In August 2012, Holgorsen received a new six-year contract. He received $2.3 million in the first year of the pact, with raises bringing his salary to $2.9 million at the end of the contract. He also was eligible for up to $600,000 in bonuses each year. The deal brought Holgorsen's compensation in line with other Big 12 coaches. In only his second year as a head coach, he ranked seventh in the 10-school conference in salary. Alas, things got bumpier in the ensuing years.

But Holgorsen was never a good fit in Mountaineer Nation. He was never a great leader and shunned the PR side of coaching, preferring to do things his way—public reaction be damned. He refused to wear blue and gold and wore silver and black instead, a slap in the face to Mountaineer fans everywhere, but he just didn't care. He wore their distain like a badge of honor and never embraced the Mountaineer spirit.

He was an average recruiter—a difficult job being located nearly a thousand miles from WVU's nearest conference mate.

The highlight of his tenure at West Virginia was his first season's Orange Bowl demolition of 3.5-point favorite and 14th-ranked Clemson, 70-33, culminating a 10-3 season and a Big 12 Conference championship.

Neal Brown (2019-present: 11-11)
0-0-0 vs. Maryland

Sweet Home Alabama

Did you know that two of the most successful coaches in history once coached for each of these rivals and have ties to this rivalry game? None other than Paul "Bear" Bryant coached at Maryland for the 1945 season, while Alabaman Bobby Bowden coached the Mountaineers from 1970-76.

There seems to be an unofficial connection to the Alabama Crimson Tide with both programs. Obviously, Bear Bryant completed his illustrious coaching career at Alabama, but Bobby Bowden was from Alabama and had been recruited to move there from Florida State after the 1982 season. Bowden was a freshman QB at Alabama but finished his playing career at Samford.

Jerry Claiborne, on the other hand, followed Bear from Kentucky to Texas A&M to Alabama as Bryant's assistant throughout the '50's! WVU's Rich Rodriguez was offered the Alabama head-coaching job after the 2006 season but turned it down.

To add to the intrigue, Nick Saban accepted the Tide job when RichRod turned it down. Incidentally, Saban is from West Virginia and Michael Locksley, Maryland's new head coach, moved back to the Terps after serving as offensive coordinator for Saban at 'Bama.

Butch Jones, currently the assistant head coach at Maryland (Tennessee head coach, 2013-17), served under Saban as an analyst (2018) and was wide receivers Coach at WVU from 2006-08. Finally, Lou Saban, the Terps' head coach for the 1966 season, is a distant cousin of Nick!

Besides Nick Saban, did you know the following head coaches called West Virginia and/or WVU home? Fielding "Hurry Up" Yost (Michigan, 1901-26), Ben Schwartzwalder (Syracuse, 1949-73), Jimbo Fisher (Texas A&M, 2018-present), Curt Cignetti (2019-present, James Madison), John McKay (Southern Cal, 1960-75), Lou Holtz (Notre Dame, 1986-96), Rich Rodriguez (WVU, 2001-07), Don Nehlen (WVU, 1980-2000), Doc Holliday (Marshall, 2010-2020), Tommy Bowden (Clemson, 1999-08) and Terry Bowden (Auburn, 1993-98).

One of the most famous rivalries in college football is the Iron Bowl—Alabama vs. Auburn. Legend has it that once, when Bear Bryant faced Shug Jordan in the Iron Bowl, Alabama was winning by less than a touchdown and Bear ordered QB Ken Stabler to run out the clock at about the Auburn 20. Stabler decided to pass and it was intercepted by an Auburn cornerback who raced down the sideline for an apparent winning TD. But out of nowhere, the gimpy Stabler ran him down and tackled him out of bounds as the game ended. At the postgame press conference, Shug, in his deep Alabama drawl asked Bear, *"How is it that my boy who is an All-SEC sprinter got caught by your boy from behind?"*

Bear replied, *"Shug, that's easy. Your boy was only running for a touchdown… my boy was running for his life!"* I don't know if it's true or not, but it sure adds to the color of college football rivalries!

NCAA Winningest Division I Coaches

1.	Joe Paterno	Penn State	409
2.	**Bobby Bowden**	**West Virginia,** FSU	**377**
3.	**Bear Bryant**	**Maryland,** Alabama	**323**
4.	Pop Warner	Stanford, Pitt	319
5.	Amos Alonzo Stagg	Chicago	314
6.	Frank Beamer	Virginia Tech	280
7.	Mack Brown	UNC, Texas	259
8.	Lavell Edwards	BYU	257
9.	Andy Talley	Villanova	257
10.	Nick Saban	Alabama, LSU	256
11.	Tom Osborne	Nebraska	255
12.	Lou Holtz	Notre Dame, S. Carolina	249
13.	Jimmy Laycock	William & Mary	249
14.	Jerry Moore	Texas Tech, App. State	242
15.	Woody Hayes	Ohio State	238
16.	Bo Schembechler	Michigan	234
17.	Chris Ault	Nevada	234
18.	Hayden Fry	Iowa	232
19.	Jim Tressel	Ohio State	229
20.	Steve Spurrier	Florida, S. Carolina	228
21.	Bill Snyder	Kansas State	215
22.	**Don Nehlen**	**West Virginia,** Bowl. Green	**202**

3rd Quarter

Let the Games Begin!

Once again, the Terps and Mounties are near mirror images. The Maryland Aggies/Terrapins have fielded five undefeated teams, while the West Virginia Snakers/Mountaineers have fielded three and the series is nearly even. Both have disputed national championships.

There are a variety of vignettes scattered throughout the next six chapters. Each game is presented, using a news reports of the day along with "Game Notes" to put the game in perspective. Actual newspaper articles from Maryland and West Virginia were used to set the stage for the thirteen "Signature Games," when possible. Featured player writeups are often taken from their various hall of fame biographies.

The Undefeateds

1893 Maryland Aggies, 3-0 or 6-0
Head Coach Samuel Harding

Maryland began this "run" in 1893 with a 6-0 record, sort of. In just their second year; after losing all three of their games in 1892 by a collective score of 128-0, they regrouped and defeated two high school teams and a club team along with three college teams. The Maryland media guide lists them as 6-0 and District of Columbia Champions. The St. John's (Annapolis) game provided some fireworks, as St. John's walked off the field in the second half after protesting a referee's call. One report indicated that the Aggies were aided by "half the student body" in scoring the Aggies' only touchdown. St. John's walked off the field in protest!

1922 West Virginia Mountaineers, 10-0-1, Unofficial National Champions
Head Coach Clarence Spears

In front of 20,000 fans at Forbes Field, the Mountaineers eked by Pitt in the inaugural edition of the Backyard Brawl with a 9-6 score. The following week, they tied Washington and Lee 12-12. Following the tie, the angry Mountaineers reeled off six straight shutouts to finish the regular season 9-0-1, earning an invitation to their first postseason bowl game, the San Diego East-West Christmas Classic versus Gonzaga. Although WVU expected a Rose Bowl bid, they came to San Diego with something to prove. Amazingly, only 19 players made the trip. WVU started strong, leading 21-0, led by Russ Meredith's 80-yard "Pick Six." The Mounties held on to win 21-13. WVU outscored their opponents 267-34, including seven shutouts. There were five undefeated teams and it was widely criticized that WVU didn't get their share of the national championship.

1951 Maryland Terrapins, 10-0,
Unofficial National Champions
Head Coach Jim Tatum

The 1951 season was spectacular yet proved a bitter pill to swallow. The Terps were coached by Jim Tatum and led by junior quarterback and future All-American and Heisman runner-up Jack Scarbath. Other stalwarts on that team are recognizable names in Terp lore: Bernie Faloney was the sophomore backup quarterback, fullback Ed Modzelewski (Big Mo), future All-American Bob Ward at guard, and Ed's "little" brother Dick Modzelewski at tackle. Tommy Mont was the backfield coach.

They ran roughshod over opponents, sweeping their nine regular-season games by a collective score of 353-61. This included a 54-7 shellacking of West Virginia in their final regular-season game.

In those days, the final poll was conducted following the regular season. Although the Terps were 9-0, there were two other teams which finished undefeated—Tennessee at 10-0 and Michigan State at 9-0. The Terps were voted third behind the Vols and Spartans. However, the final chapter had yet to be written.

The Terps were invited to the Sugar Bowl in New Orleans to face the heavily favored Vols from Rocky Top. Before a crowd of 82,271, the largest to watch a Maryland football game, they promptly proved the voters wrong by defeating top-ranked Tennessee 28-13, earning bragging rights but not the official national championship! Ed Modzelewski rushed for 153 yards and was named the game's outstanding player. He finished the year with 825 yards and averaging 7.3 yards a carry.

1953 Maryland Terrapins, 10-0 (Regular Season), National Champions
Head Coach Jim Tatum

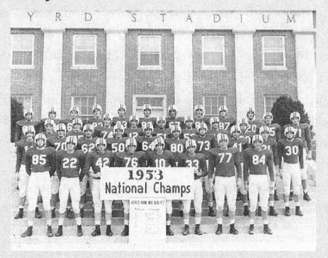

Courtesy of Special Collections, University of Maryland Libraries, University of Maryland.

The tables were turned on the Terps two years after their bittersweet season of '51. In their inaugural season in the ACC, they finished the regular season 10-0 by outscoring their opponents 298-38 with six shutouts.

This time it was the Terps who benefited from the polling prior to bowl games. The Terps finished the regular season ranked No. 1 in virtually all the polls, and were crowned national champions.

They met the 4th-ranked 8-1-1 Oklahoma Sooners in the Orange Bowl but lost 7-0 in front of 68,640 fans. Coach Jim Tatum continued to direct the Terps, having lost many of the stars from the '51 team. Bob Ward was now on the coaching staff. Jack Scarbath and Dick Modzelewski were playing for the Washington Redskins. Ed Modzelewski was playing for the Pittsburgh Steelers. But Bernie Faloney led the charge at quarterback and finished fourth in the Heisman voting.

1955 Maryland Terrapins, 10-0 (Regular Season)
Head Coach Jim Tatum

In a spectacular run, Maryland opened the 1955 season on a five-game winning streak from the 10th-ranked 1954 team. Tatum predicted during the preseason that the Terps could be better than both the 1951 and 1953 teams, *"better than any of them. We have more talent than any team I've coached. We could be very good."*

For Tatum "very good" meant another undefeated season! They struggled at Missouri in their opener but eked out a 13-12 win. They then beat top-ranked UCLA 7-0 in front of a rare sellout crowd at Byrd Stadium. The Terps then ran off eight straight easy wins to finish 10-0 and earn a No. 2 ranking. Tatum faced old friend Bud Wilkinson's top-ranked Oklahoma Sooners in the Orange Bowl. Wilkinson had a record of 83-8-3 since 1947, while Tatum wasn't far behind with a 73-14-4 record in the same time period.

Oklahoma simply had too much speed and prevailed 20-6, marking the end of the Tatum era.

1976 Maryland Terrapins, 11-0 (Regular Season)
Head Coach Jerry Claiborne

The Terps rolled through the regular season, with only a 17-15 win over Wake Forest being close. Their final three games against Clemson, Cincinnati and Virginia were all shutouts with a collective score of 69-0. They started the season ranked 12th in the nation and swept their ACC opponents along with non-conference challengers Richmond, West Virginia, Syracuse, Villanova, Kentucky and Cincinnati. A scheduling quirk caused the Terps not to play North Carolina this year, the only ACC team to be ranked during the season. By the time they met Houston in the Cotton Bowl, they had risen to No. 4 in the polls. Alas No. 6 Houston ended the Terps' magical run with a 30-21 defeat.

1988 West Virginia Mountaineers, 11-0 (Regular Season)
Head Coach Don Nehlen

This was the high-water mark for Coach Don Nehlen. Major Harris came on the scene as a redshirt freshman and took the Mountain State and the nation by storm. They had a favorable schedule, with Pitt being the only challenging road game.

Their first challenge was the rival Maryland Terps. After falling behind 14-0, the Mounties stormed back to win going away, 55-24. Three of their next four games were rivalry games—Pitt, Virginia Tech and Boston College—before culminating with the Goliath in Penn State.

WVU easily disposed of them and welcomed the 7th-ranked Nittany Lions. The Mounties hadn't beaten Penn State since 1955. Although the Nitts were having a down year, they always seemed to have WVU's number. They were 4-3 coming into the game after a tough 8-3 loss to Bear Bryant in Birmingham. Harris outgained the entire Penn State team, 301-292, and produced the school's most exciting run ever in the first quarter of that game. The rout was on and the Mountaineers won 51-30 in front of a CBS national audience. He was Michael Vick before there was a Michael Vick. The scoreboard fittingly said it all, simply: "FINALLY"!

West Virginia steamrolled the remaining opponents to finish with an 11-0 record, a No. 3 ranking and an invitation to the Fiesta Bowl to face top-ranked Notre Dame for the national championship. Alas, the magical season was over when, on the third play of the game, Harris suffered a separated shoulder. The Irish won 34-21.

1993 West Virginia Mountaineers, 11-0 (Regular Season)
Head Coach Don Nehlen

There never was a more unlikely run to the national championship than the 1993 version of the Mountaineers. Since Major Harris left a year early, the Mounties averaged just five wins in each of the ensuing three years (1990-92) and nothing seemed to make 1993 any different. Nehlen had three quarterbacks who alternated. It was not a season for the weak of heart. Five games were won by a total of 15 points, including Maryland, Virginia Tech, No. 17 Louisville and No. 11 BC. Yet they had blowout wins over Missouri, Syracuse, Rutgers and Temple.

Surprisingly, WVU was ranked ninth when they hosted and defeated the 4th-ranked Miami Hurricanes, 17-14, in front of a still-record Mountaineer Stadium crowd of over 70,000 in one of the biggest wins in West Virginia history!

QB Jake Kelchner was out with an injured shoulder, so Darren Studstill took the reins for the upcoming bowl game. The No. 2 Mounties were hoping for an Orange Bowl contest with the only two undefeated teams (Nebraska and W.VA.) and alternatively were pulling for a Cotton Bowl matchup with 7th-ranked Texas A&M. But money talked, and WVU ended up in the Sugar Bowl with a faster No. 8 Florida team. It was never a contest, with the Gators whupping the Mountaineers, 41-7—a defeat which carried over to an embarrassing 31-0 loss to Nebraska in the Kickoff Classic that opened the 1994 season.

Chapter 9:

The Early Years 1919-1960

Maryland's Ascension to the Mountain Top

The first game of this rivalry occurred in 1919. In order to put this game in historical perspective, in 1919:

- The Chicago Black Sox threw the World Series to the Cincinnati Reds.
- President Woodrow Wilson declared Armistice Day signifying the end of WWI. It was announced on the 11th hour of the 11th day of the 11th month. This later became Veteran's Day.
- The Russian Civil War was in full swing as the Red Army's Bolsheviks, led by Lenin, faced and ultimately defeated the White Army.
- The Spanish Flu pandemic was in full swing.
- Pancho Villa was running wild in Mexico.
- Prohibition was passed by the U.S. Congress.
- Babe Ruth was sold to the N.Y. Yankees by the Boston Red Sox for $125,000.

And....

- The Battle of the Potomac was born.

Game I
Signature Game #1
West Virginia 27, Maryland 0
West Virginia leads series 1-0-0

October 18, 1919

Athletic Field, Morgantown, W.Va.

Attendance: Unknown

West Virginia Head Coach: Mont McIntire (4th year)

Maryland Head Coach: "Curley" Byrd (9th year)

Barometer: West Virginia finished 8-2, while Maryland finished 5-4.

Game Notes: The first meeting of this fledgling rivalry took place at Athletic Field in Morgantown. The Maryland "Aggies" were in their ninth season under the tutelage of legendary Hall of Famer Curley Byrd. They finished 5-4 that season but lost to the Mountaineers by a score of 27-0. Maryland came into this game surprisingly highly regarded, not the "breather" that was expected when the game was scheduled.

The Mountaineers were led by future Hall of Famer and 1919 All-America fullback Ira Rogers. George Hill ran for 108 yards. A number of WVU records were set in that game, including:

Fewest plays by an opponent: Maryland 12

Fewest opponent yards: 14

Fewest opponent rushes: 12

Fewest opponent pass attempts: 0

Joe Harrick blocked 3 Maryland punts

This initial Battle of the Potomac occurred five years to the day before Grantland Rice penned the "most famous football lead of all time," in the New York Herald Tribune:

"Outlined against a blue-gray October sky, the Four Horsemen rode again. In dramatic lore their names are Death, Destruction, Pestilence and Famine. But those are aliases. Their real names are: Stuhldreher, Crowley, Miller and Layden. They formed the crest of the South Bend cyclone before which another fighting Army team was swept over the precipice at the Polo Grounds this afternoon, as 55,000 spectators peered down upon the bewildering panorama spread out upon the green plain below."

Mountaineers Have Easy Time with Maryland State
Pittsburgh (Pa.) Daily Post

MORGANTOWN—Though the Maryland State College eleven came here highly touted and with a victory over the University of Virginia and a close score with Swarthmore, West Virginia had no trouble in walloping the visitors in the mud to the tune of 27-0.

West Virginia consistently pushed the visitors back and scored a touchdown in each quarter. At no time was Maryland in serious scoring distance. Not until practically all the West Virginia regulars had been withdrawn in the fourth quarter and two punts were fumbled and blocked respectively, did the Marylanders get in the Mountaineers' territory. Then it was at the 35-yard line and the ball too heavy to attempt a field goal there was no worry on the part of West Virginia. Not once in the course of the game did the visitors make a first down and no gain of any consequence whatever was recorded.

The visitors' line held fairly well at the start with Mackert doing spectacular work on backing it up, but West Virginia was only forced to punt on three occasions, so it can be seen that her offense was consistent.

West Virginia had to work hard to get the first touchdown, but after two exchanges of kicks, West Virginia got the ball on the West Virginia 45-yard line. Hill made six yards, Rodgers six, Hite made three, King again passed to Rodgers for 12 yards and then Rodgers ran the end for 13 yards to the 2-yard line, from where Hite went over. Rodgers kicked the goal. Just before the first quarter ended, Harrick blocked and recovered a Maryland punt on the 18-yard line.

On the first play in the second quarter, King passed to Hagar for a touchdown. Rodgers again kicked goal. The rest of the second quarter, West Virginia was held fairly safe by Maryland, but just as the whistle blew the Mountaineers had a first down on the Maryland eight-yard line.

Soon after the third quarter passed, Herrick blocked another Maryland kick and himself recovered on the Maryland 30-yard line. On the first play, Hill ran end for 20 yards; Hite made six and Rodgers punched it over. Twice more in this quarter, West Virginia threatened to score but two fumbles prevented.

As the fourth quarter opened, Maryland had been shoved back to her 10-yard line. Knode punted to Rodgers on the 40-yard line who made a magnificent return to the visitor's 18-yard line. Neale, who had been substituted for King, ran the end twice, carrying the ball to the one-yard line, but here Maryland braced and held for downs. When Knode attempted to kick, he partially missed the ball, the oval running to the four-yard line, where Mills recovered. On the first play, Rodgers went over for a touchdown and later kicked goal. Then it was that Maryland got into West Virginia's territory. Twice Martin's kicks were blocked by his own inexperienced backs stepping immediately in front of him and both times Maryland got the ball. Her offense was negligible however, and the 30-yard line was her closest point to West Virginia's goal.

Next to the great running of Hill, Harrick's magnificent work in blocking and recovering Maryland's punts was the feature. No less than three times did the big tackle pull this stunt, and on three other occasions a whole flock of West Virginia tacklers helped to break up Knode's attempts. Only three times in the whole game did the visiting captain get his kicks away.

Rodgers ran the team like an old hand at the job and there was a noticeable increase in the quality of generalship. Rodgers, too, was no slouch with the ball, as is his custom he tore off a number of big gains, three rushes of his netting more than 20 yards and four times he was on the receiving end of passes that netted more than 10 yards. Mills played a brilliant game at end and followed the ball like a greyhound, while Hagger's tackling was ferocious. Neale did well when he got in the game in the fourth quarter and West Virginia's whole line did notable service in turning back the Maryland attacks.

Featured Player: Ira Errett" Rat" Rodgers, West Virginia

Played Maryland in 1919
Consensus All-American
College Football Hall of Fame

Ira Errett Rodgers is recognized as the school's greatest all-around athlete of the first half-century. Born and raised in Bethany, W.Va., Rodgers played high school sports at Bethany College because there were no high schools in the area for him to attend.

At age 12 and penniless, he hopped a freight train to see Jim Thorpe and the Car-lisle Indians play Washington & Jefferson in

Courtesy of West Virginia and Regional History Center. WVU Libraries.

Washington, Pa. It was from that moment that the young farm boy became hooked on sports.

At WVU he accounted for more touchdowns (66) with runs and passes than any other player in school history at the time to become the school's first-ever consensus All-America selection in 1919. His statistics likely would have been even more impressive if more complete records were kept when he played.

As a senior in 1919, Rodgers led the nation in scoring with 147 points on 19 touchdowns and 33 extra points. His 313 points scored were a school record that lasted nearly 60 years, a testament to his lasting greatness. He also threw 11 touchdown passes, which was a rare feat for that era and a WVU record until 1949.

Rodgers could throw a football farther than just about anybody, could out-run most, had legs as "thick as tree trunks" and was a shifty, elusive open-field runner. He could easily throw a football 50 yards in the air, which at the time was considered a phenomenal distance considering the size and the weight of the ball used back then.

He was also famous for fending off tacklers with his left arm while he scanned the field for open receivers. *"The only way opponents could grab him was low,"* wrote NEA sportswriter Harry Grayson in 1943. The problem with that was Rodgers only stood 5-feet-10, which made it nearly impossible to get lower than him.

Rodgers had some of his best games against the top teams in the country. He passed for 162 yards and three touchdowns in a 25-0 upset win over Princeton in 1919. Walter Camp, considered the game's leading authority of that period, was so overcome by Rodgers' performance that he asked the team manager if he could meet him after the game. The manager excitedly went into the locker room to retrieve Rodgers, knowing full well what the attention would mean to his career.

"Come out right away, Walter Camp is here to see you!" the manager yelled.

Rodgers continued to slowly get dressed. *"I'll be out after a while,"* he said. *"Them alumni are always bothering me."*

When Rodgers finally came out to meet Camp, the sportswriter left impressed. *"It would have taken a team of supermen to beat West Virginia because of the great leadership and skill shown by Rodgers,"* Camp wrote.

None other than Grantland Rice, another football authority, wrote of Rodgers, *"There may be a greater all-around football player in America than Rodgers of West Virginia, but no one has uncovered his name as November slides briskly along the autumnal trail. And it is likely no one ever will."*

During his junior year in 1917, Rodgers also led West Virginia to a stunning 7-0 upset victory over Navy, giving Mids coach Gil Dobie his first loss in 12 years of coaching. Dobie took the loss especially hard; he could be seen crying on the field after the game.

Before Rodgers came to West Virginia, the Mountaineers had beaten Washington & Jefferson just twice in 15 meetings. But with Rodgers in the lineup, WVU defeated the Prexies twice and tied them a third. All three scores against W&J came from Rodgers, including the one that won the 1919 game in Morgantown. Afterward, WVU students, in Rudy-like fashion, carried Rodgers off the field on their shoulders.

His jersey No. 21 was the second of three retired football numbers at WVU (joining Sam Huff and Bruce Bosley), and the road leading to West Virginia's football complex is named Ira Errett Rodgers Drive. He was named an inaugural member of WVU's Mountaineer Legends Society in 2016.

As a testament to his lasting greatness, during the centennial celebration year of college football in 1969, the Newspaper Enterprise Association (NEA) named Rodgers to its 22-member All-Time All-America Football team.

Featured Player: Russ Bailey, West Virginia

Courtesy of West Virginia and Regional History Center. WVU Libraries.

Played against Maryland in 1919
Consensus All-American
WVU Sports Hall of Fame

Russ Bailey was one of the finest offensive linemen ever to wear the Gold and Blue. Born Sept. 3, 1899, in Weston, W.Va., Bailey came to Morgantown with Ira "Rat" Rodgers and Andrew "Rip" King in 1915. That trio helped the Mountaineers to 24 victories over the next five years, including an 8-2 record in 1919.

Paving the way for Rodgers and King, Bailey was an agile center on offense whose crushing blocks and intelligent play earned him rave reviews from some of the most notable people in football.

According to John Heisman in 1928, for whom the Heisman Trophy was later named, *"Russ Bailey had the unusual knack of being able to snap the ball without watching back between his legs; he could snap accurately while keeping his eyes fastened on the man opposite. This enabled him to charge into the opponent much more quickly and effectively than most centers; and at the same time, he had a good idea, as he snapped the ball, of the layout of the enemy forces. Thus, when he snapped, he simultaneously lunged into his man, checked him for a bare instant—long enough to give his back time to be gone—then knifing right through the line, again got ahead of his runner."*

Standing 6-feet tall and weighing a solid 180 pounds, Bailey was a fierce tackler on defense as well. He earned first team All-America honors from the *Chicago Tribune, Pittsburgh Sun, Pittsburgh Press, New York Evening Journal*, Frank G. Menke and A.M. r in 1917. After WVU canceled football for the 1918 season because of an outbreak of influenza, Bailey again was accorded first team All-America honors from the *Sioux City Tribune* and the *Philadelphia Press* in 1919.

Following his stellar career at WVU, Bailey joined Mountaineer assistant coach Elgie Tobin and former teammates Rip King and Harry Harris with the Akron Pros in 1920. Playing in the American Professional Football Association, the precursor to the NFL, Bailey helped the Pros to a 6-0-3 record and the first professional football championship. He played one more season with the Pros in 1921 before giving up football to pursue a career in medicine.

After graduating from West Virginia, he went on to complete his degree in medicine at Cincinnati in 1922. Following his internship at Long Island College, he returned to West Virginia and became a member of the surgical staff at the Wheeling Clinic.

Keenly interested in the treatment of cancer, Bailey was president of the West Virginia Cancer Society, and shortly before his death was named director of the American Cancer Society. The crowning event of his career came in August 1949, when he was named president of the West Virginia State Medical Association, a post he held less than a month. He suffered a heart attack and died in Wheeling on Sept. 15, 1949.

He was named an inaugural member of WVU's Mountaineer Legends Society in 2016.

Following a 24-year hiatus, the series resumed in 1943 and missed only one year in the next seven.

Game II
Signature Game #2
West Virginia 6, Maryland 2
West Virginia leads series 2-0-0

October 16, 1943
Mountaineer Field, Morgantown, W.Va.
Attendance: 3,621
West Virginia Head Coach: Ira Errett Rodgers (7th year)
Maryland Head Coach: Dr. Clarence Spears (1st year)
Barometer: Maryland finished 4-5, West Virginia 4-3

Game Notes: West Virginia lost their first two games to Pitt and Virginia, being shut out in both contests, while Maryland came in with a 2-1 record. With rosters decimated by the War and schedules changing at nearly every turn, this game came on the schedule just as the season began. Maryland, in fact, played four military teams in the course of their 4-5 season. West Virginia played "regular" college teams, rather than military teams, in compiling a 4-5 record.

Mountaineers Winner of Maryland
Pike Runs 55 Yards as Old Liners are Beaten 6-2
Morgantown (W.Va.) Dominion Post

MORGANTOWN—Last Saturday's affair with Maryland, the first game of the season at Mountaineer Field, found Errett Rodgers' boys breaking into the scoring column for the first time, as they splashed their way to a 6-2 victory before a slim turnout of 3,261 spectators, including some 1,200 Army Air Cadets and engineers.

Saturday's 6-2 triumph over Maryland's Old Liners was a bitter pill for Terrapin coach Dr. Clarence W. Spears to swallow. It marked the second defeat at the stadium in recent years for the man who coached West Virginia grid teams in what has since been called "the golden era" of football here. In 1937 while coaching at Toledo, Spears was defeated by Dr. Marshall Glenn's Sun Bowl championship eleven. Returning last Saturday with a highly favored Maryland aggregation, Spears had hoped to square accounts with the Mountaineers.

While taking nothing from the Gold and Blue's victory, the sloppy condition of the field proved a greater handicap to the Old Liners than it did to Rogers' Mountaineers, whose boys are not particularly fast. But, the home-boys displayed plenty of defensive pluck in holding the liners several times in scoring position.

The lone touchdown in the game came in the second period when Buddy Pike, a freshman end from Northfork, scooped a fumble off Joe Makar's shoestrings and ran it back into payoff territory.

Makar fumbled while attempting to pass and Pike grabbed up the ball like a baseball shortstop and galloped 55 yards for the first West

Virginia touchdown of the season. Tom Jochum's try for the extra point failed as the muddy ball went low.

The Maryland safety was posted after the Mountaineers had held the Old Liners on their strongest scoring threat of the game. Makar got off a 76-yard punt that put the Mountaineers in the hole at their own 17. With Fryer out of the game for a few minutes, Bob Dutton took over the punting and got off a poor kick into the wind. Dick Tushak returned it to the Mountaineer 10 to set the stage for what appeared to be a certain Maryland touchdown. But the Mountaineers threw up a tough defense to hold three-line plays and finally break up an attempted pass and take possession of the ball.

Fryer fumbled the slippery ball and recovered before giving up the two points to the Liners. On the next play, standing in his own end zone to punt, the Mountaineer captain fumbled again and Maryland registered the safety.

Game III
West Virginia 6, Maryland 6 (tie)
West Virginia leads series 2-0-1

October 14, 1944
Byrd Stadium, College Park, Md.
Attendance: 5,600
West Virginia Head Coach: Ira Errett Rodgers (8th year)
Maryland Head Coach: Dr. Clarence Spears (2nd year)
Barometer: West Virginia finished 5-3-1, while Maryland was 1-7-1.
Game Notes: This turned out to be a tough year for future Hall of Fame coach Clarence Spears. After losing to Hampton-Sydney and Wake Forest by a collective score of 51-0, his weary Terps hosted West Virginia and, surprisingly, came from behind to tie the game. The luckless Terps wouldn't win a game until the season's finale at VMI, 8-6, finishing with a 1-7-1 record. West Virginia came into the game with a 1-2 record, having lost to Pitt and Virginia. This game seemed to be the turning point to the season, as the Mountaineers went on a four-game win streak, beating Penn State by one point and shutting out Bethany,

Temple and Lehigh by a collective score of 97-0. WVU ended their season with a 40-9 loss at Kentucky.

Maryland Ties Mountaineers in a Game of Punts and Miscues

COLLEGE PARK—West Virginia came to Byrd Stadium to face Maryland in what was to become a rough-and-tumble 6-6 deadlock. Maryland came from behind to tie the score late in the third period.

West Virginia opened the scoring following an opening quarter that featured exchanges of punts interspersed with nice runs. James Walthall took the opening kickoff 50 yards to the Maryland 40, only to be thwarted by the Maryland defense at the 19.

Again, punt exchanges prevailed in the second quarter, but WVU broke through when Walthall threw a 37-yard touchdown pass to Gene Crookshank to break the scoreless tie. The extra point failed as the pass from center was bad and Robert Haman was unable to attempt the kick.

The Marylanders opened the second half with three straight first downs to the West Virginia 16, with Robert Troll and Love doing the heavy work. Love ran to the 9 and fumbled with Walter Mott recovering for WVU on the 7. A holding penalty pushed the Mountaineers back to their 1.

Walthall's punt only went to his own 35 and was returned to the 22. Love hit the line three times before gaining a Maryland first down at the 11. Troll passed to Jones for another first down at the 1, then Troll dove to the center for the Terrapin touchdown. Frank Doory's placement was wide and the score remained knotted at 6 apiece.

The momentum had definitely shifted in favor of the Marylanders. Walthall fumbled Troll's kick at the West Virginia 10, and Patrick Moran recovered for the Terps at the 6. The Mountaineers held as Troll and Petroiff punched the ball to the West Virginia 1-yard line, where the Mountaineers held on downs.

Following another short WVU punt, Troll returned it to the 28. Morris came in to kick the field goal, but it was blocked by the Mountaineer interior line and recovered by Clifford Cooper on the Mountaineer 38.

Game IV
West Virginia 13, Maryland 13 (tie)
West Virginia leads series 2-0-2

October 27, 1945
Mountaineer Field, Morgantown, W.Va.
Attendance: 12,000
West Virginia Head Coach: Ira Errett Rodgers (9ᵗʰ year)
Maryland Head Coach: Paul "Bear" Bryant (1ˢᵗ year)
Barometer: Maryland finished 6-2-1 in Bear Bryant's only season, while West Virginia was 2-6-1
Game Notes: The ECAC and WVU counted eligibility differently than some other conferences and schools regarding returning WWII vets. This prompted WVU to look at the Southern Conference for clarification. Maryland claimed WVU and Penn State were using ineligible WWII vets. Future WVU head coach Gene Corum was one of the players in question.

Mountaineers Rally to Tie Terrapins
MORGANTOWN—The well-balanced and favored Maryland Terrapin team came to Morgantown expecting to push the Mountaineers into the Monongahela River. But instead, the Terps squandered a 13-point lead and had to return to College Park with a 13-13 tie.

The Marylanders dominated from the opening kickoff. In just four minutes, the Terrapins, under new coach Paul 'Bear" Bryant, had moved to the West Virginia 15-yard line. A few plays later, halfback Bill Poling went over for the touchdown and then converted the extra point, giving the Terrapins an early 7-0 lead.

The Old Liners showed no letup as they continued to push the home team up and down the field. Late in the second quarter, Maryland halfback Sam Behr galloped to the West Virginia 7-yard line. Poling dove across on the next play making the score 13-0. He failed to convert the extra point.

It appeared as if the teams exchanged uniforms in the second half, as West Virginia began to dominate. They got their first break when left end John Pozega crashed into the backfield to block Poling's punt and recovered it on the Maryland 10. Quarterback Harold McKibben passed to Dick Maylander for the Mountaineers' first score. Tom Jochum missed the extra point, making the score 13-6.

Maryland then stiffened and held the West Virginians scoreless for the rest of the third quarter. But late in the game, the Mountaineer air game came alive and, much like Doolittle's Raid, halfback Vic Bonfili tossed an apparent touchdown to Maylander. But the speedy end dropped the ball as he crossed the goal line and it was recovered by Maryland for a touchback.

The WVU defense again stiffened and forced a Maryland punt. West Virginia took over on their own 44-yard line and scattered passes all over the field, moving to the Terrapin 1, where McKibben tossed to Bonfili for the West Virginia touchdown making the score 13-12 in favor of the Marylanders. This time, however, Jochum converted the kick to tie the score.

Game V
Maryland 27, West Virginia 0
West Virginia leads series 2-1-2

November 1, 1947
Byrd Stadium, College Park, Md.
Attendance: 16,500
Maryland Head Coach: Jim Tatum (1ˢᵗ year)
West Virginia Head Coach: Bill Kern (5ᵗʰ year)
Barometer: Maryland was 7-2-2 including a Gator Bowl tie with Georgia in Jim Tatum's first season, while West Virginia finished 6-4.
Game Notes: The largest crowd in Byrd Stadium history turned out for this perfect football afternoon. It was not without controversy, as Maryland's Jim Tatum had stated to *The Washington Post* three days earlier that WVU was using five players in "their fifth year of intercollegiate football and consequently were ineligible this year. However, on Friday, Tatum changed positions and, in a telephone call with Morgantown reporter Tony Constantine, said he was *"satisfied that these*

players had met their requirements." The players in question had played on service teams during the war and Tatum felt that this constituted collegiate eligibility.

West Virginia was favored by two touchdowns to ruin Maryland's Homecoming.

Gambino Leads Terps to Homecoming Shutout

COLLEGE PARK—Led by Lu Gambino, the Southern Conference's leading scorer, Maryland whipped West Virginia 27-0, for the first time in the border rivalry in front of a sold-out Homecoming crowd at Byrd Stadium.

Maryland scored early as quarterback Vic Turyn engineered a 71-yard game-opening drive. The Logan, W.Va., quarterback capped off the drive with a 9-yard touchdown pass to end Elmer Wingate. Freshman Tom McHugh kicked the bonus point.

Maryland held the Mountaineers and immediately drove toward the WVU goal line as fullback Harry Bonk ripped through the center of the Mountie line for 12 yards to the WVU 43. Fireplug halfback Gambino then scored the first of his three touchdowns with a spectacular 43-yard broken-field run.

It looked as if the score would end at 14-0, as Maryland dominated all aspects of the game, keeping the Mounties on their end of the field for the entire first half and most of the second.

But the Terrapins broke it open in the fourth quarter when Vernon Siebert intercepted a Jimmy Walthall pass and, with a penalty, the ball rested at the WVU 44. Bonk slammed for a dozen before Turyn took a deep drop and threw a bomb to Gambino, who caught it on the dead run for another TD.

Another interception ended the scoring. With the Terp offense sputtering, Gambino was called from the bench. Backup quarterback Joe Tucker fired the ball toward the end zone where Gambino made a spectacular catch to end the scoring.

Game VI
Signature Game #3
West Virginia 16, Maryland 14
West Virginia leads series 3-1-2

November 22, 1948
Mountaineer Stadium, Morgantown, W.Va.
Attendance: 20,000
West Virginia Head Coach: Dudley DeGroot (1st year)
Maryland Head Coach: Jim Tatum (2nd year)
Barometer: West Virginia finished 9-3 including a Sun Bowl victory over Texas Mines, Maryland finished 6-4.
Game Notes: Tatum brought his 6-3 Terps to Morgantown as favorites to defeat the Mountaineers despite WVU's 7-3 record. With the impressive upset win over Maryland under their belt, Dudley DeGroot's gridders were invited to the Sun Bowl, where they defeated Texas Mines, 21-12. The Terps' 6-4 finish was Tatum's poorest record during his nine-year tenure in College Park.

Future Maryland coach and WVU player Roy Lester said that DeGroot *"was great and way ahead of other coaches. Bill Kern (Former WVU Coach)called us his 'Hamburger Squad'… Well, the 'Hamburger Squad' went on to win nine games the year after Kern left and went to the Sun Bowl!"*

Field Goal, Costly Terp Fumble
Give Mounties 16-14 Win over Maryland
Beckley (W.Va.) Sunday Register
MORGANTOWN—The toe of a 147-pound dropkicker and a costly Maryland fumble in the fourth quarter gave West Virginia University a close 16-14 decision in the season wind-up yesterday. A crowd of 20,000 at Mountaineer Stadium saw Maryland gain a 7-0 advantage within minutes of the start of the game and then stay ahead until the last five minutes of play. Young Gene Simmons, feather-weight dropkicker, who has made himself a hero this year, was first the goat of the game by missing a point after touchdown, but then he put his team

back in the ball game in the third quarter with a field goal that cut the Maryland lead to 14-9.

It was a hammer and tongs contest throughout with the issue always in doubt, as the Mountaineers several times threatened but failed to get over. The first score of the game came on a 30-yard pass from Maryland's Joe Tucker to Jim Larue in the endzone. It had been set up after halfback John Idzik had intercepted a pass from Jimmy Walthall of West Virginia. Guard Bob Dean kicked the point.

The Mountaineers started a comeback minutes later in the first period and halfback Jimmy Devonshire, closing out his regular-season football career, made the first of two touchdowns he scored during the day. He found a hole at right tackle at the Maryland 19 and scampered through and over.

The hometown folks sighed in unison when Simmons' kick was blocked and left the Mountaineers one point behind.

The second Maryland score came 26 seconds after the second half started when veteran halfback Vic Turyn of Logan, W.Va., threw a pitchout to Hubert Werner.

Werner caught it on the 18 and shook off the whole Mountaineer team for an 82-yard run and a touchdown. He was aided by end Elmer Wingate, who took out the last potential tackler at midfield. Dean kicked the extra point and it looked as if the Terrapins had the game on ice. In spite of two previous defeats, they had been favored to win today.

Simmons made himself the man of the hour in the third quarter after fullback Pete Zinaich and halfback Vic Bonfilli had worked the ball down to the Maryland 7-yard line. Three plays failed to get anywhere and the "Little Toe" with number 15 on his back went in. Simmons, who previously this season had made 25 conversions in 31 tries and had booted one field goal, made his second three-pointer of the year.

That led to West Virginia's big chance in the fourth quarter, Hellas had punted out of bounds at the Maryland 26-yard line. Fullback Harry Bonk got three yards, but on the next play Werner fumbled and end Frank Remo recovered for the Mountaineers.

Devonshire and Bonfilli went to work and got the ball within inches of the goal line. It took three plays there before Devonshire dived across and scored. Simmons made the point.

Today's game, in addition to giving West Virginia revenge for last year's 27-0 shellacking at College Park, Md., made it eight victories and three defeats for the first season under coach Dudley Sargent DeGroot. West Virginia had already accepted a bid to play against Texas Mines in the Sun Bowl in El Paso.

Just Kick Me!

Lou Groza, namesake of the award for college's best kicker once said: *"Old place-kickers never die, they just keep missing the point!"*

Kickers, like left-handed pitchers, seem to be wired a bit differently than the rest of us. Often ostracized by announcers, coaches and teammates, they develop an "us-against-them" bunker mentality. Mountaineer and Terrapin kickers are no different.

Coach Don Nehlen once commented, *"**Paul Woodside** was my first one. He was the team clown. I mean, he was a clown. He was funny, unbelievably funny.*

*"(Later) I had **Todd Sauerbrun** and **Mike Vanderjagt** on the same team."*

Perhaps Nehlen should have known this was going to be a circus, as he recruited Sauerbrun as a place-kicker and he later became the greatest punter in WVU history. He recruited Vanderjagt as a punter and he wound up being one of the top place-kickers. Each went on to solid NFL careers. *"They both marched to their own drummer,"* said Nehlen.

Take the Terps' **Bernardo "Chili Bean" Branson**, who was at Maryland on a soccer scholarship but gave it up after one month to focus on football. From Santiago, Chile, he was also nicknamed the "the human scoreboard," changing his jersey number with every point he scored! He finished the 1964 season with 44 points

(9 field goals and 17 PAT's). This was a Maryland record at the time and third-best in the nation.

Both the Mounties and Terps have been blessed over the years with outstanding kickers along with a few classic head-to-head matchups:

October 27, 1945—Tom Jochum, after missing an earlier conversion, hit his second attempt with little time left to earn West Virginia a 13-13 tie against the Bear Bryant-led Terrapins in 1945. It was a contest between two future College Football Hall of Famers—Bryant and Coach Ira "Rat" Rogers for WVU.

November 27, 1948—The toe of a 147-pound drop-kicker, **Gene Simmons**, and a costly Maryland fumble in the fourth quarter gave WVU a close 16-14 decision in the season finale. Simmons made himself the "man of the hour" in the third quarter after the Mountaineers worked the ball down to the Maryland 7-yard line. Simmons, who had made 25 conversions in 31 tries this season and had already booted one field goal, made his second three-pointer of the year.

September 19, 1959—Maryland sprung a pass-crazy quarterback and the torrid toe of **Vince Scott** at West Virginia and sent the Mountaineers down to a 27-7 defeat before 28,000. Scott kicked three "radar-guided" boots of 38, 41 and 48-yard field goals "with the aplomb of a pro." These were the only field goals he kicked in the entire season!

September 18, 1982—All-Americans **Paul "Woody" Woodside** and **Jess Atkinson** had matched up in what turned out to be a battle of quarterbacks—Boomer Esiason and Jeff Hostetler—but the kickers made their mark as well. Woody hit four field goals, three of them over 40 yards, while Jess boomed a 49-yarder, as the Mountaineers won after stopping a Terps' two-point conversion attempt for the 19-18 win. Woodside ranks fourth in WVU history with 323 points, while Atkinson is second in Maryland history with 308 points.

September 22, 1984—Two years later, **Paul Woodside** again teed it up against the Terps' **Jess Atkinson** in Morgantown. Atkinson's 20-yarder with 21 seconds to go lifted the Terps to a 20-17 upset of the No. 18 Mountaineers. Both Atkinson and Woodside had 30+ yard field goals earlier in the contest. Woody had missed one earlier in the game.

September 18, 2004—Another classic see-saw battle took place in Morgantown in 2004. Fresh off two blowout losses to the Terps the previous year, Rich Rodriguez's tenure was on the line. Both teams had a chance to win the game in regulation. Maryland's **Nick Novak** hit two FG's during the game but missed a 49-yard potential game-winner with just 1:15 left. West Virginia marched down the field and **Brad Cooper**, who also had two field goals, had a 39-yarder blocked with only five seconds left, forcing OT. In the overtime, **Novak** hit a 33-yarder to take the lead, but WVU's much-maligned quarterback, Rasheed Marshall tossed a 7-yard TD for the 19-16 win.

Novak is Maryland's all-time leading scorer with 393 points, while Cooper is 10th at WVU with 149. Woodside, a good friend and mentor of Novak, was on the sideline during the game and wandered over to the Maryland side during the OT period. When Novak hit his 33-yarder, Woody was captured on film jumping and cheering for his Terp protege, much to the chagrin of WVU's coach and former WVU teammate Rich Rodriguez!

September 13, 2014—This promised to be a showdown, with the Terps' All-American Lou Groza winner **Brad Craddock** at home in College Park to match kicks with WVU's Groza runner-up **Josh Lambert**.

Craddock made three field goals, but Lambert had the final say, kicking a 47-yarder as time ran out to give the Mounties a 40-37 road win. This was after having one blocked just a minute earlier, and it was one of two last-second winning field goals by Lambert—the other a 55-yarder against Texas Tech. He recorded an NCAA record of 16 field goals of 40+ yards and five longer than 50!

Craddock is the Terps' most accurate place-kicker in history with an 81.4%. He owns the longest FG in Terp history with a 57-yarder against Ohio State. He also hit a game-winner against the Nittany Lions. Lambert is third in WVU scoring history with 337 points, while Craddock is third at Maryland with 297 points.

September 26, 2015—looked to be a repeat of the previous year's kicking duel, with the nation's two best kickers teeing it up in Morgantown. Alas, it turned out to be a WVU blowout win where the kickers had little impact.

Other Kickers of Note

West Virginia

Tyler Betancourt, ranks second in WVU history with 357 points between 2009-12, with a long kick of 52 yards.

Pat McAfee, a 2008 CBS First Team All-American, is the WVU career leader in kick scoring with 384 points. He had an eight-year NFL career with the Indianapolis Colts.

Bill McKenzie, WVU's last straight-on kicker, is best known for his clutch 38-yarder against Pitt in the 1975 Backyard Brawl to win the game. He's ninth in all-time WVU scoring with 152 points.

Todd Sauerbrun, was a 1994 Consensus All-American as a punter but did kick field goals for WVU during the 1993 season, scoring 114 points. He had a 13-year NFL career with six teams.

Mike Vanderjagt, a transfer from Michigan State, punted and place-kicked for the 1991-92 seasons. He is 13th in WVU history with 114 points. After his nine years in the NFL, he retired as the most accurate NFL kicker in history.

Maryland

Dale Castro was a 1980 Consensus All-American after starting as a walk-on. He set an NCAA-record 16 straight field goals and finished 12th in Terp history with 121 points in just two years. He was drafted by the Dallas Cowboys and was released, then spent one year in the USFL and another in the Arena Football League.

Brian Kopka, a 1999 honorable mention All-American. Kopka ranks fifth on Maryland's all-time scoring list with 218 points. A Lou Groza Award candidate, he had a two-FG game against WVU in 1998 and repeated it in 1999. He had a tryout with the Baltimore Ravens.

Steve Mick-Mayer, 1974 Sporting News First Team All-American. He kicked a 54-yard field goal and scored 203 points, sixth in Terp history. He had a six-year NFL career with four teams.

Dan Plocki kicked a 20-yard game-winning FG with six seconds left for a 31-30 win in a 1985 matchup at Death Valley in Clemson. He is fourth on Maryland's all-time scoring list with 233 points. He was an 11th-round draft pick of the Cleveland Browns but was released.

Featured Player: Ray Krouse, Maryland

Courtesy of Special Collections, University of Maryland Libraries, University of Maryland.

Played WVU in 1948 and 1949
All-American
Maryland Athletic Hall of Fame

Ray Krouse a graduate of Western High School in Washington, D.C., was an All-American & All-Southern Conference football tackle in '48 & '49. He won the 1949 D.C. Touchdown Club Award as "Outstanding Collegiate Player." He was a three-time All-Pro in the NFL and played on three NFL championship teams: Detroit in 1957; Baltimore in 1958 and 1959. He was an offensive lineman for the Baltimore Colts in "The Greatest Game Ever Played," the NFL Championship Game on Dec. 28, 1958, against the N.Y. Giants. It was the first game to go into sudden-death overtime, won by the Colts 23-17. Playing defense for the Giants was former WVU All-American Sam Huff.

Krouse's coach Jim Tatum called him *the best tackle I've ever coached or seen.*

His brother was the late William E. "Sully" Krouse, who lettered in wrestling and football at Maryland and coached the Terp wrestling team for 32 years. Both brothers are members of the Maryland Athletics Hall of Fame.

Game VII
Signature Game #4
Maryland 47, West Virginia 7
West Virginia leads series 3-2-2

November 24, 1949
Byrd Stadium, College Park, Md.
Attendance 16,117
Maryland Head Coach: Jim Tatum (3rd year)
West Virginia Head Coach: Dudley DeGroot (2nd year)
Barometer: Maryland finished 9-1 with a Gator Bowl win, West Virginia finished 4-6-1.
Game Notes: For the first time in this rivalry, one of the teams was ranked. Maryland welcomed West Virginia to Byrd Stadium with a No. 15 ranking and a 7-1 record.

Maryland, led by All-American Ray Krouse, came to this Thanksgiving Day game with a chip on their shoulder. WVU coach Dudley DeGroot provided the Terps blackboard fodder by stating, after getting thrashed by Boston U., 52-20, that *BU will annihilate Maryland.*

Maryland edged BU 14-13 and coach Jim Tatum didn't let his Terps forget DeGroot's comment.

Following this Maryland win, the Terps improved to 8-1 to help their case for an eventual berth in the 1950 Gator Bowl. The Terrapins extended their season scoring total to 233 points, the most in school history. This was the start of the Tatum juggernaut in College Park. It stretched for seven years, including two undefeated seasons, and began with this year's nine-win season.

Maryland's Vincent Scott kicked a then-Byrd Stadium record 48-yard field goal.

Maryland Crushes West Virginia Outfit
By Dick Kelly
Hagerstown (Md.) Daily Mail

COLLEGE PARK—"It's impossible for anybody to be utterly annihilated."

These words were spoken nearly 300 years ago by the great English Philosopher, Sir Francis Bacon.

"Boston University will annihilate Maryland."

These words were spoken not too many weeks ago by the coach of the West Virginia University football team, Dud DeGroot.

Yesterday afternoon at College Park, Jim Tatum's great University of Maryland football team proved that Mr. Bacon was not entirely right—that Mr. DeGroot was entirely wrong.

According to Webster's International Dictionary, anything that is annihilated is reduced to nothing or put out of existence. West Virginia University may not have been entirely annihilated in the 47-7 rout at the hands of the Terps, but it was the neatest job of near-annihilation we've seen in a long time.

Coach DeGroot, one-time mentor of the Washington Redskins, made the biggest mistake of his long coaching career when he went overboard in predicting a Boston U. landslide victory over the Old Liners. He sent his own Mountaineers to the slaughter on Thanksgiving Day.

The 16,117 fans on hand at Byrd Stadium either cheered wildly or sat back in stupefied amazement as the powerful Maryland team completely outclassed the unfortunates from Morgantown. You could even sense the revengeful glee on the Terps' bench as Jim Tatum's boys rolled mercilessly over the West Virginians.

Tatum, who usually goes easy on any outclassed opponents, really poured it on yesterday. He even added insult to injury by playing every member of the large Maryland squad, including the three Hagerstown representatives—Bob Roulette, Buck Early and Dave Cianelli. The Terps had everybody in the game but the water boy when the Mountaineers scored their only TD in the final period.

In rolling up 47 points, the Old Liners set a new season's scoring mark for a University of Maryland team. They have now tallied 233 points, two more than the old mark of 231, established in 1930 during a 12-game schedule. And they still have another game against Miami in the Orange Bowl next Friday night.

Very few fans can now doubt that the University of Maryland is one of the finest teams in the nation… a team that justly deserves a bid to one of the big postseason bowl games.

Featured Player: Ed "Big Mo" Modzelewski, Maryland

Courtesy of Special Collections, University of Maryland Libraries, University of Maryland.

Played WVU in 1949, 1950, 1951
All-American
Maryland Athletic Hall of Fame

"Big Mo," grew up in West Natrona, Pa., a Pittsburgh suburb, was one of six children, and a three-sport high school athlete. He accepted a football scholarship at Maryland, where he became a three-year starter.

He played with his brother Dick on the undefeated 1951 Sugar Bowl Champion team, where he rushed for 153 yards and was named Sugar Bowl MVP.

After leaving Maryland, he played six years with the NFL Cleveland Browns.

Like the Krouse brothers, he joined his brother Dick, "Little Mo," in the Maryland Athletic Hall of Fame.

The Iron Maul

The rivalry was building. Since fledgling series resumed in 1943, West Virginia had won one game, Maryland had won one and two were tied going into the 1948 season. But it now looked as if they'd play each other every year… forever.

In 1948, the Junior Chamber of Commerce (Jaycees) of both Maryland and West Virginia decided to sponsor a trophy for the winning team each year.

Like the "Old Oaken Bucket" awarded to the winner of the Purdue-Indiana game each year or the "Little Brown Jug" for the Michigan-Minnesota rivalry, "The Iron Maul" was conceived to be the Mountie and Terp version, essentially consummating this rivalry.

Two trophies were awarded—the Iron Maul and a standard trophy with a gold football player and a ball. It was set up that the standard trophy had to be won three times before it became the permanent possession of the school. The Iron Maul would continue to be a traveling trophy, awarded each year to the winning team.

Dave Kauffmann, then-president of the Maryland Jaycees explained, *"A maul is a hammer… It has a head of iron and is used to drive wedges or spikes."* Kauffman was joined in the inaugural 1948 presentation by Bill Jones, president of the WV Jaycees, at a halftime presentation made to Irwin Stewart, president of WVU and Dean Ben Robinson, substituting for Maryland president Curly Byrd.

The Jaycees conceived this trophy as a symbol of industrial development of the two states. The traveling trophy was an exact replica of the maul or sledgehammer used to drive the first spikes in the first B&O railroad track linking Maryland and West Virginia.

An exact replica of the first maul was manufactured and donated by B&O.

West Virginia upset Maryland for the inaugural Iron Maul in 1948. The Terps shellacked the Mounties in 1949, 1950 and 1951, giving them permanent possession of the standard trophy, while the actual Iron Maul was to remain a traveling trophy.

But a funny thing happened on the way to the 1952 Sugar Bowl. Maryland was placed on probation for violating Southern Conference rules prohibiting schools from participating in bowl games. Maryland went anyway. West Virginia voted for Maryland's probation, and Maryland suddenly cancelled all future games between the two institutions.

The teams didn't play again until 1959 and it didn't become an annual contest again until 1980. The annual series lasted until 2008 when some politics put the game on hold for two years, resuming again from 2010 through 2015. Now, due to conflicting conference affiliations, they simply play sporadically and are only scheduled for 2020 and 2021 meetings, coronavirus permitting.

As of this writing, neither the Maryland nor the West Virginia departments of intercollegiate athletics had ever heard of this trophy. Sadly, the Iron Maul's whereabouts are lost in the annals of gridiron history.

Game VIII
Maryland 41, West Virginia 0
Series tied, 3-3-2

November 18, 1950
Mountaineer Field, Morgantown, W.Va.
Attendance: 16,000
Head Maryland Coach: Jim Tatum (4th year)
West Virginia Head Coach: Art "Pappy" Lewis (1st year)
Barometer: Maryland finished 9-2-1, while West Virginia was 2-8.
Game Notes: This was in the midst of Tatum's seven-year stretch of unmatched excellence at Maryland. They finished 7-2-1 this year and won 60 games over those seven years.

Maryland came into the game as 20-point favorites. But Pappy Lewis' Mountaineers were in great shape, causing Jim Tatum even more concern since his Liners had never won in their four meetings on the Monongahela River. After a disappointing tie at North Carolina the previous week, Maryland dropped out of the Top 20 coming into this game.

WVU operated a modified "T" which features flankers, giving the Mounties a chance against Maryland's questionable pass defense. Future All-American Paul Bishoff had already hauled in 27 passes for 475 yards.

Maryland Steamrolls West Virginia in Easy Victory

MORGANTOWN—Led by speedy end Bob Shemonski, Maryland dominated the day with a 41-0 Southern Conference victory over West Virginia in front of 16,000 fans in Morgantown. The outcome could have been worse, as Maryland recovered five of seven WVU fumbles and intercepted six of 26 Mountaineer passes.

Shemonski scored three times, including a circus catch of a Jack Scarbath pass that bounced of a WVU defender's arms in the back of the endzone. Ed "Big Mo" Modzelewski scored two more, while Ed Fullerton smashed in for the Terrapins' sixth touchdown.

Mountaineer miscues ruled the day as every one of Maryland scores came off a turnover or other West Virginia mistakes.

Maryland dominated from the opening gun as Shemonski intercepted a William Allen pass on the WVU 28-yard line. "Big Mo" threw and ran it in for the first score.

Maryland's magnificent guard, Bob Ward, anchored the Maryland line that kept West Virginia in its own territory most of the game. Four times, Jack Targarona's punts were downed inside the WVU 8-yard line. West Virginia, which didn't record a first down in the first half, only got as far at the Maryland 31-yard line.

Maryland scored three touchdowns in an action-filled second quarter including two by Shemonski and another by "Big Mo."

The Terps also dominated the box score, gaining 227 yards to West Virginia's 148. This was the first time Maryland had beaten the Mountaineers in Morgantown and deadlocked the series 3-3-2, dating back to 1919.

Coach Jim Tatum cleared his bench, playing everyone on the squad in the fourth quarter, but the Mountaineers were still unable to mount any type of threat.

Featured Player: Jack Scarbath, Maryland

Played WVU in 1950 and 1951

Consensus All-American

College Football Hall of Fame

This local Maryland boy made very good with Jim Tatum's Split-T in the early 1950s. Jack Scarbath was born in Baltimore and played football at Baltimore Poly, where he was noticed by Dr. Harry C. Byrd, former Maryland coach turned University president. Byrd recruited Scarbath, and the youngster accepted a full four-year scholarship and made Maryland football history.

Courtesy of Special Collections, University of Maryland Libraries, University of Maryland.

One historic event was Maryland's 28-13 upset of national champion Tennessee in the 1951 Sugar Bowl. Another was Maryland's undefeated streak of 22 games while Scarbath was calling signals for the Terps. In 1951, AP and UP polls named Scarbath to honorable mention All-America citations. In 1952, he was honored with unanimous first-team All-America honors and was runner-up for the Heisman Trophy to Oklahoma halfback Billy Vessels. Scarbath was also Southern Conference Player of the Year and the South's Most Valuable Player in the North-South Game in Miami.

After graduation, Scarbath played in the NFL with the Washington Redskins and Pittsburgh Steelers, and coached at South Carolina before going into business in Maryland.

Featured Player: Bob Ward, Maryland

Played WVU in 1948-51

Consensus All-American

College Football Hall of Fame

Bob Ward became Maryland's first All-America player in 1950 as a defensive middle guard. He displayed his tremendous versatility the next season, being named a unanimous All-American as an offensive guard. He helped spark Jim Tatum's Terrapins to a perfect 10-0 season and the national championship in 1951, climaxed by a 28-13 conquest of Tennessee in the Sugar Bowl. Tatum called Bob Ward, *"the greatest football player I've seen ounce-for-ounce, and the best I've ever coached."*

Courtesy of Special Collections, University of Maryland Libraries, University of Maryland.

Despite his two-time All-America acclaim, he cherished another honor even more; he was voted the Terps' Most Valuable Player four straight years. Ward served as assistant football coach at Maryland, Oklahoma, Iowa State and Army, and as head coach at Maryland 1967-68. When he was inducted into the College Football Hall of Fame in 1980, the ceremony at New York's Waldorf-Astoria was witnessed by 12 of Ward's relatives, 16 former teammates and his 84-year-old father. His jersey number, 28, was the first to be retired by Maryland.

Player: Dick "Little Mo" Modzelewski, Maryland

Played WVU in 1950 and 1951

Consensus All-American, Outland Trophy Winner

College Football Hall of Fame

Dick Modzelewski was one of three brothers who played football at the University of Maryland. The first was Ed, a fullback who made All-American in 1951. Since he was first, he was called "Big Mo." Dick came a year later, a 6-foot, 235-pound tackle. Since he followed his

Courtesy of Special Collections, University of Maryland Libraries, University of Maryland.

older brother, he was called "Little Mo." The next Modzelewski, who was third and last, was called "No Mo."

In Dick Modzelewski's three varsity years, Maryland's record was 24-4-1, including a 22-game unbeaten streak. In 1951, Maryland was ranked third in the nation and knocked off top-ranked Tennessee in the Sugar Bowl, 28-13. (In those days, bowl games did not count in final rankings.) In 1952, Dick was a consensus All-American at tackle, won the Outland Trophy as the nation's best interior lineman, and was named Lineman of the Year by the Washington Touchdown Club.

He had a 14-year NFL career as a tackle with the Redskins, Steelers, Giants and Browns from 1953-1966. He was in eight league championship games and on two championship teams (Giants 1956, Browns 1964). He was assistant coach of the Browns (1968-1977), Giants (1978), and Cincinnati Bengals (1979-1983).

Game IX
Signature Game #5
Maryland 54, West Virginia 7
Maryland leads series 4-3-2

November 24, 1951
Byrd Stadium, College Park, Md.
Attendance: 14,385
Maryland Head Coach: Jim Tatum (5th year)
West Virginia Head Coach: Art "Pappy" Lewis (2nd year)
Barometer: Maryland finished with an 11-0 record including a victory in the Sugar Bowl and a No. 3 ranking, while West Virginia finished 5-5
Game Notes: The Terrapins were in the midst of their juggernaut, ranked fourth and coming off a 53-0 shellacking of NC State at Byrd Stadium and accepted an invitation to the Sugar Bowl. They enter the game as a whopping 40-point favorite over the Mountaineers! This would be Jim Tatum's 50th game as the Terrapin head coach, then sporting a record of 37-9-3.

Maryland has already scored a record 299 points and needed only 70 yards to set the all-time rushing record. They're ranked 8th in the nation in rushing and 9th in overall offense.

On the bright side for West Virginia, they rank 8th in total defense. The Mountaineers rank 10th in rushing defense to Maryland's No. 4 ranking. West Virginia is expected to go to an aerial game, while the Terps are expected to grind it out on the ground.

The gamed marked the farewell of two great Maryland stars—guard Bob Ward and fullback Ed "Mighty Mo" Modzelewski. Ward was recognized as the greatest player ever to wear a Maryland uniform. Meanwhile, Mo has been called the best "offensive fullback in the nation."

Maryland Mauls Mountaineers 54-7

COLLEGE PARK—This wasn't much of a tune-up for the Terrapins, as they crushed a young West Virginia team in their final regular-season game, 54-7, giving Maryland its first undefeated season in 57 years. Despite having mauled West Virginia, the best team in Maryland history will still have to share the Southern Conference title with VMI. Both are undefeated in conference play and didn't meet on the gridiron this year.

Thirteen Terrapin players played their final game in College Park. Two scouts from the University of Tennessee Volunteers, the Terps' upcoming Sugar Bowl opponent, were in the crowd. So, no one expected Coach Jim Tatum to reveal too much of his sophisticated split-T offense with spies in the stands.

West Virginia won the opening toss and, somewhat surprisingly, engineered a drive to the Maryland 24 before quarterback Gerald Fisher was sacked on a fourth-down attempt. Passes to All-America end Paul Bischoff and to Dick Luciani highlighted the drive.

Maryland's flashy backup quarterback Bernie Faloney responded with a 24-yard gain on a fake punt, taking the ball to the Mountaineer 32. Then fullback, Ed "Mighty Mo" Modzelewski took over, scoring the game's first touchdown on a 16-yard rumble.

Surprisingly, the young Mountaineers responded. On the ensuing drive, Fisher's arm led WVU from their own 28 to the Maryland 17 before the Terrapin defense stiffened. All-America quarterback Jack Scarbath led the charge and hit Ridgeley, W.Va., native Paul Lindsey on a 42-yard score to make it 14-0.

The flashy Faloney later intercepted a Fisher pass on the Mountaineer 34 and returned it all the way down to the WVU 2-yard line, where "Mo" took it in for a 21-0 first-quarter lead.

"Mighty Mo" and quarterback Jack Scarbath led the charge in the first half. "Mo" carried the ball 14 times for 131 yards and two touchdowns, outgaining the entire Mountaineer offense.

Maryland had six first-half possessions and scored on five of them—three touchdown passes by Scarbath and two by "Mo."

After a 27-yard TD pass from Scarbath to Lou Weidensaul, Fisher led the Mounties on yet another drive, this time resulting in what would be West Virginia's sole touchdown of the game.

Maryland's Tatum took it easy on West Virginia in the second half, playing mostly substitutes after his starters racked up a 35-7 halftime lead.

In the second half, Maryland's subs drove 76 yards to score early in the fourth quarter. The payoff came on perhaps the game's most exciting play, a 25-yard run by Faloney who then lateraled to fullback Caney Scioscia for the last 13 yards. Freshman Joe Horning added a 77-yard touchdown run for the Terps.

WVU quarterback Gerald Fisher threw for all but one of the Mountaineer first downs, completing 19 of 57 attempts including their lone touchdown, a 5-yarder to end Bill Marker.

The win in this border rivalry gave Maryland permanent possession of the first "Iron Maul" trophy.

Featured Player: Bernie Faloney, Maryland

Played West Virginia in 1951
1st Team All-American
Maryland Athletics Hall of Fame

B.J. "Bernie" Faloney played high school football in Carnegie, Pa., prior to attending the University of Maryland. As the backup quarterback to Jack Scarbath, he helped the Terps reach the Sugar Bowl after the 1951 undefeated season. In his senior season of 1953, Faloney quarterbacked Maryland to be NCAA Division I-A national football champions and into the 1954

Courtesy of Special Collections, University of Maryland Libraries, University of Maryland.

Orange Bowl. At season's end, Faloney finished fourth in the balloting for the 1953 Heisman Trophy (won by Notre Dame's Johnny Lattner) and was named the ACC Player of the Year. *Sporting News* and the *International News* both named him a First Team All-American. He also lettered in baseball.

He was a first-round pick of the San Francisco 49ers, but instead took a bigger paycheck to play for the Edmonton Eskimos in the CFL, leading them to the 1954 Grey Cup. After spending two years in the U.S. Air Force, he returned to Canada to play for the Hamilton Tiger-Cats, leading them to two Grey Cup championships. He was a five3-time all-star and, in 1961, the CFL's Most Outstanding Player. He's in the Canadian Football and the Canadian Sports halls of fame.

Character Counts

Although the game was a blowout, the West Virginia Mountaineers could take some consolation in the fact that they were rated equal to the Terrapins in character by the Pop Warner Foundation in Philadelphia.

John D. Scott, President of the Northwest Philadelphia Junior Chamber of Commerce and Bud Dudley, the former President of the Notre Dame Alumni Association, observed how the players and fans behaved, seemingly based on Grantland Rice's famous quote: "It's not whether you win or lose, but how you play the game."

Using a 50-point scoring system, each team were scored 45. This was the second time the Foundation had "character-scored" an intercollegiate football game. The previous week, they rated Swarthmore a 45-43 winner over Haverford.

Scott said, "both were excellent in general character. Maryland excelled in alertness. West Virginia earned points on its courage and will to compete. If what they portrayed today carried through in later life, they undoubtedly will amount to something."

He visited the Maryland dressing room after the game and "was impressed with the great respect the players had for Coach Jim Tatum."

Prior to the game, Secretary of the Foundation Albert W. Zackey hinted that the Terps might be penalized on the character rating if they ran up the score.

But Tatum began liberal substitutions after getting a 28-0 lead in the second quarter, eventually using every player on the team.

Featured Player: Paul Bischoff, West Virginia

Ebay Photo

Played Maryland in 1951
1st Team All-American
WVU Sports Hall of Fame
Paul Bischoff lettered at end for Coach Pappy Lewis' teams from 1950-52, earning All-America honors as a senior.

WVU's career receiving leader at the time with 96 catches for 1,349 yards, he set three other records for receiving as well. Bischoff served as team captain in 1952. An outstanding blocker and defensive player, he earned All-Southern Conference honors. He was also an Academic All-American and served as WVU student body president.

Bischoff played a vital role in West Virginia's first-ever victory over a nationally ranked team—a 16-0 win at Pitt in 1952—with a 23-yard touchdown reception to give the Mountaineers a 7-0 lead.

An admiring teammate described Bischoff as not only the best pass-receiver but also the best tackler, blocker and pass-defender, and as smart and as good as anybody else on the squad.

Pittsburgh Press sports editor Chester Smith picked an all-time WVU football team in 1960 and listed Bischoff as one of the squad's four ends.

He played professionally for the CFL's Hamilton Tiger-Cats and later coached football at Geneva College and the high school level.

He was named an inaugural member of WVU's Mountaineer Legends Society in 2016.

Featured Player: Stan Jones, Maryland

Played WVU in 1951

Consensus All-American

College Football Hall of Fame

Stan Jones played offensive and defensive tackle for Maryland and was a unanimous All-American in 1953. Maryland posted a 10-0 record in 1951 and was ranked third in the nation. The Terps were 7-2 in 1952 and ranked 13th. In 1953, they were 10-1 and national champions.

Courtesy of Special Collections, University of Maryland Libraries, University of Maryland.

Jones, playing under coach Jim Tatum, was at Maryland when it was a big winner in different leagues. The Terps were co-champions with Virginia Military Institute in 1951 in the Southern Conference. In 1953 they played in the Atlantic Coast Conference and were co-champs with Duke. During the 1951 regular season, Maryland outscored its opponents 353-62. In 1953, the margin was 298-31.

In 1953, the school gave Jones the Anthony Nardo Award as the team's best lineman. He won the Knute Rockne Award as the nation's best lineman and was later inducted into the College Football Hall of Fame.

Honors were heaped on Jones after his playing days ended. In 1977, he made the Atlantic Coast Conference 25-year team. A native of Lemoyne, Pa., he was named to the Pennsylvania Sports Hall of Fame. Then he was elected to the Pro Football Hall of Fame. His pro playing days covered 13 years—from 1954-66 with the Chicago Bears and Washington Redskins. He served as assistant coach with Denver and Buffalo from 1967-77.

The Queen's Game

On Oct. 19, 1957, Jim Tatum returned to Byrd Stadium in front of a sellout crowd of 43,000, returning for the first time since leaving Maryland following the 1955 season. Coincidentally, this was also the game that Queen Elizabeth II and Prince Phillip (the Duke of Edinburgh) attended to see their first "American football" game, on the invitation of University President Wilson Elkins and Governor Theodore McKeldin.

Queen Elizabeth with players from both teams.
Courtesy of Special Collections, University of
Maryland Libraries, University of Maryland.

The campus was giddy. A special box was constructed on the press-box side of the stadium so the Queen could see the card section which formed the Union Jack, a Golden M and the Queen's crest, as well as the Stars and Stripes. Not insignificantly, the UNC side of the field was also selected, according to the SGA "because alcohol consumption at Maryland football games was considered "a major sport in the 1950s."

At halftime, both bands took the field, with the Carolina band forming a huge banjo to the tune of "Dixie." Both bands formed the words "USA-Brit" as they played "God Save the Queen" and "The Star-Spangled Banner."

Students were schooled as to how to address the Queen and Duke. President Elkins, upon addressing the possibility of any 'unfortunate events' occurring during the Queen's visit, warned students: *"If there is any question, one ought not to do it!"*

Each team's captains then presented the Queen and Prince Philip with an autographed football and a replica of the coin used in the game's coin toss. Prince Philip, "humbly accepting" the autographed football said, "I feel like kicking it myself!"

According to SGA President Howard Miller's account of the Queen's Game, with a few minutes left in the fourth quarter, the announcer at Byrd Stadium asked the crowd to remain in their seats so the Queen and Prince Philip could leave first to attend dinner with President Eisenhower. The Queen's motorcade entered the stadium and the Queen left before "a full house broke for the exits." Miller recalled *"never had so many Marylanders showed so much courtesy."*

Maryland upset the 14th-ranked Tar Heels, 21-7, in Tatum's homecoming. Despite the huge Terp victory, the game will always be known as "The Queen's Game." Across town at Griffith Stadium, West Virginia defeated GW, 34-14, in front of only 9,000 fans.

Game X
Maryland 27, West Virginia 7
Maryland leads series 5-3-2

September 19, 1959
Byrd Stadium, College Park, Md.
Attendance: 30,000
Maryland Head Coach: Tom Nugent (1st year)
West Virginia Head Coach: Art "Pappy" Lewis (10th year)
Barometer: Maryland finished 5-5 under new coach Tom Nugent, while West Virginia finished 3-7.
Game Notes: Tom Nugent became Maryland's new coach and had a member of the team, lineman Charles "Sonny" Lohr, die from heat

exhaustion—an eerie premonition of Jordan McNair's passing 59 years later, also of heat exhaustion.

Pappy Lewis introduced his "green as grass" team, his least-experienced club since taking over the team 10 years earlier. With only 10 lettermen on the team, it looked to be a tough day for the Mountaineers. He said, "*we have a pretty fair first team, but after that the pickin's are a bit slim.*"

Coach Pappy Lewis felt that if West Virginia could beat Maryland on this opening game that the Mountaineers might have a pretty good year. This was the first reference to this rivalry becoming a "barometer" game, scheduled for early in the season.

Afterwards, it was generally felt that this loss to the Terps led to the "ultimate deterioration" of the WVU season.

Terps Pass and Kick to 27-7 Win Over WVU

COLLEGE PARK—Between the arm of quarterback Dick Novak and the foot of Vince Scott, Maryland sent the Mountaineers down to a 27-7 defeat in front of 30,000 in College Park. This was the Terps' fourth straight win over the Mountaineers.

Maryland, not billed as a passing team, surprised West Virginia with sophomore Novak's gunslinger attack. The Terrapins hung up 232 yards through the air with 18 completions in 34 tries. Novak himself completed 11 of 18 attempts. He also dazzled the field with his feet, as he had a 38-yard run to set up a Maryland field goal.

Scott added three booming field goals of 38, 41 and 48-yard*s*.

West Virginia had three good shots at the scoreboard but cashed in only once. But by that time the speedy Terrapins were off to a 18-0 lead.

Maryland got off to a 6-0 lead with Novak's 9-yard pitch to Tony Scotti, climaxing a quick 33-yard drive set up by a Mountaineer fumble. Then Scott produced the 9-0 lead at halftime with the first of his "radar-guided" boots.

Novak started the second half with four passes eating up 66 yards, the last one going to end Gary Collins for a touchdown.

Scott, whose three field goals in one game set a Maryland record, then kicked the Terrapins to an 18-0 lead with a placement from the 41—a boot fired directly into a brisk wind.

West Virginia showed some grit as second-string quarterback Carmen Pomponio scored on a 3-yard keeper that climaxed a 66-yard march in the third.

But the Terps broke the game wide open in the final quarter with the Novak-Scott combination exploding again. Novak added six more points on a 40-yard heave to Jim Davidson, who made a sensational catch at the goal line. Scott then kicked his final field goal, a gargantuan boot of 48 yards that broke the Maryland record of 47 set by Dick Bielski in 1953 against Mississippi.

Featured Player: Gary Collins, Maryland

Courtesy of Special Collections, University of Maryland Libraries, University of Maryland.

Played WVU in 1959 and 1960
Consensus All-American
Maryland Athletic Hall of Fame

Collins, a two-way end and punter, carried Maryland on his back. Week after week, he found ways to win games for the underdog Terps, who went 18-12 during his three varsity years (1959-61).

Against North Carolina, Collins made three straight tackles in a goal-line stand and then, with one-minute left, caught the game-winning touchdown. Against Wake Forest he blocked a field goal and, at the finish, intercepted a Norm Snead pass in the end zone to preserve Maryland's one-point victory.

The Terps' Tom Nugent called Collins, *"the finest player I've ever coached. He produces in the clutch and has never failed me whenever I asked him to do something special."*

Against NC State, Collins picked off a Roman Gabriel pass; landed a punt six inches from the goal line; and blocked an enemy punt that a Maryland teammate fell on in the end zone for a score. And in a 22-21 upset of Syracuse, Collins made a spectacular catch of a two-point conversion to win it. Earlier, on defense, he'd twice stopped All-American Ernie Davis on consecutive plunges at the Terps' 1-yard line.

Though violently ill against Penn State, Collins responded by leading Maryland to a 21-17 win in 1961, the Terps' only triumph in their 37-game series. Double-teamed all day, he had six receptions, including one on which he dragged defenders for three yards to the end zone. On defense, he saved a Penn State score by running down a ballcarrier from behind. Collins also punted six times against the top-rated team in the East for a lusty 46.5-yard average.

A native of Williamstown, Pa., Collins wore No. 82 in college—a nod to his role model, the Colts' Raymond Berry.

In 1961, he was 8th in Heisman Trophy balloting and was the fourth player selected in the 1962 NFL Draft.

Game XI
Maryland 31, West Virginia 8
Maryland leads series 6-3-2

September 17, 1960
Mountaineer Field, Morgantown, W.Va.
Attendance: 18,000
Maryland Head Coach: Tom Nugent (2nd year)
West Virginia Head Coach: Gene Corum (1st year)
Barometer: Maryland finished 6-4, while West Virginia was 0-8-2.
Game Notes: This was the season-opening game for the Mounties, as they introduced former WVU lineman Gene Corum as head coach giving him the reins of the Mountaineers following the departure of legendary Art Lewis.

Containing the Terps' passing game would be the Mountaineers' biggest task, but *"another may be the toe of Terrapins' end Vince Scott. Scott kicked field goals of 31, 41 and 49 yards against the Mountaineers last season, the only field goals he kicked last year."* wrote the *Weirton Daily Times*.

West Virginia Drops Season-Opener to Maryland 31-8
MORGANTOWN—West Virginia started fast, taking the opening kick all the way down to the Maryland 13 on a mix of short passes and slicing drives. Ominously, the Mountaineers fumbled the ball three

times on this drive, recovering all but the last one—which stopped the drive and turned the momentum.

The Terrapins quickly recovered to bury the Mountaineers 31-8 in front of 18,000 West Virginia faithful in both teams' season-opener.

Maryland looked much like former coach Jim Tatum's juggernaut of a few years earlier in winning their fourth straight game of the season. It was West Virginia's sixth straight loss, spoiling rookie head coach Gene Corum's debut.

After their initial hiccup, the Terrapin line dominated the bigger West Virginia front, carving gaping holes in the Mountaineer front wall. Quarterback Dick Novak mixed it up with short passes, keeping the WVU defense on their heels.

Second-year Maryland coach Tom Nugent used his celebrated "I" formation only about half the time, but it was highly effective.

Maryland gained 339 total yards, 229 in the air; while West Virginia gained 126 on the ground and 97 in the air. The Terps earned 15 first downs to West Virginia's six.

A light rain beginning at halftime did little to slow the Terrapins. Their four touchdowns came on a 19-yard pass from Novak to Gary Collins and a rushing touchdown each by Pat Drass, Dale Betty and Ken Smith. Vince Scott booted a 30-yard field goal to finish the scoring.

West Virginia's lone score came in the second quarter as they drove from their 35 to the Maryland 24. After a third-down completion from Dale Evans to Bob Timmerman to the 15, Evans ran to the 3 before Bob Bence bounced outside for the score.

Chapter 10

1966-1979:
Saban and Claiborne to Carlen and Bowden

The turbulent '60s found the rivalry catching steam. Both programs took a nose-dive after their heyday in the early '50's. Big-name coaches made their way to both College Park and Morgantown. The game that brought it all together seemed to be the 1973 contest at Byrd Stadium. Claiborne vs. Bowden, both Hall of Fame coaches, squared off in a game for the ages. This game, along with the 1976 and 1977 games, combined to create the beginning of the West Virginia-Maryland rivalry—a dramatic WVU win in 1973, a Maryland undefeated season in 1976, and a West Virginia upset of No. 11 Maryland in 1977 set the rivalry in motion.

Game XII
Maryland 28, West Virginia 9
Maryland leads series 7-3-2

October 15, 1966
Byrd Stadium, College Park, Md.
Attendance: 28,800
Maryland Head Coach: Lou Saban (1st year)
West Virginia Head Coach: Jim Carlen (1st year)
Barometer: Maryland finished 4-6, while West Virginia was 3-5-2.
Game Notes: West Virginia was 1-2-1 when they visited the Terps and finished 3-5-2 under new coach Jim Carlen. Maryland suffered a similar record, 4-6, under their new coach Lou Saban, who was most recently from the Buffalo Bills. Maryland came into the game with a 2-2 record, winning both home contests with nice wins over Wake Forest and Duke.

The Mountaineers were led by D.C. area product Garrett Ford… one who got away, having played at nearby DeMatha. Ford was the 6th-leading rusher in the nation with 430 yards and three touchdowns, averaging 4.7 yards per carry.

The Terps outsized the Mountaineers across both lines and hoped that this would negate Ford, who lined up as the tailback from the "I" formation.

"*Even when I played, it was a big rivalry,*" said Ralph Friedgen, Maryland player from 1966-68 and future assistant and head Terp coach.

Terps Overpower Mountaineers 28-9
COLLEGE PARK—Maryland used a balanced attack to gain a relatively easy 28-9 victory over the West Virginia Mountaineers in front of 28,800 at Byrd Stadium.

West Virginia's "new breed" couldn't cope with the seasoned Terps, led by quarterback Alan Pastrana.

Two of Pastrana's six completions in nine throws went for touchdowns, as he passed for 130 yards.

The Terps' ground game did the heavy lifting, led by halfback Bill Lovett with 141 yards on 27 carries. Washington, D.C., product Garrett Ford led the Mountaineer attack with 138 yards on 25 carries.

The Mountaineers drew first blood, sort of, when Johnny Mallory ran 67 yards for an apparent touchdown, only to be nullified by a clipping penalty.

Maryland took advantage when end Ron Pearson deflected Tom Digon's jump pass at the Terp 35. It bounced into the arms of end Dick Abshire, who ran it back to the WVU 46. West Virginia couldn't stop the Terps, as they scored in just four plays. Pastrana tossed to halfback Billy Van Heusen for a 15-yard touchdown. Bernardo "Chili Bean" Bramson added the extra point with under three minutes left in the half.

Maryland struck again just 47 seconds later, covering 66 yards in just two plays with Pastrana hitting Rick Carlson on a 44-yard bomb for the touchdown. Bramson added the extra point with 10 seconds left in the half, taking the starch out of the Mountaineers.

WVU's only real threat came in the third quarter when Ford recovered a fumbled punt on the Maryland 42, ultimately settling for a 22-yard Carl Kinder field goal.

Maryland got a little sloppy in scoring two second-half touchdowns. They drove 76 yards in nine plays before John Mallory intercepted a Pastrana pass at the Mountaineer 2.

The Terrapin defense held, forcing Kinder to punt from deep in his end zone. It only went to the 25 and then bounced backwards, allowing Maryland to recover at the WVU 18. Pastrana took it in for the touchdown and soccer-style kicker Bramson made it 21-9.

In their final drive, Maryland recovered two of their own fumbles along the way to score. In the final two minutes, the Mountaineers scored a late touchdown, highlighted by Ford's 62 yards on three carries in the drive.

Game XIII
West Virginia 31, Maryland 7
Maryland leads series 7-4-2

September 20, 1969
Mountaineer Field, Morgantown, W.Va.
Attendance: 31,000
West Virginia Head Coach: Jim Carlen (4th year)
Maryland Head Coach: Roy Lester (1st year)
Barometer: West Virginia finished 10-1 with a Peach Bowl victory and No. 17 ranking, while Maryland finished 3-7.

Game Notes: The Terps came to Morgantown with seemingly a hopeless task of upsetting the heavily favored Mountaineers. Maryland had not had a winning season since 1962. New head coach Roy Lester, a member of the WVU 1954 Sun Bowl team, hadn't been back to Morgantown since 1949 and wasn't relishing the reunion. The Terps had a 2-17 record over the past two years and were heavy underdogs.

"Nobody thinks we can throw the ball; it will be to our advantage," Lester said. *"When Dennis (O'Hara) completes a pass, the other team may go into shock."*

In a downpour, the passing game was severely limited. Coach Roy Lester had recruited greats like Randy White, Bob Avellini, Tony Greene... 15 NFL players. But they weren't ready for West Virginia in this, Lester's first game.

Lester, in a classic understatement, said, *"We were outclassed a little bit."*

West Virginia Romps Terps 31-7
MORGANTOWN—Legendary John Henry has nothing on West Virginia's pile-driving fullback Jim Braxton. Braxton pounded the Terp defense for two touchdowns and 161 yards on 32 carries in front of 31,000 rain-soaked fans in Mountaineer Stadium. The newly installed Astroturf prevented the game from becoming a quagmire.

West Virginia jumped to a 21-0 first-quarter lead, spoiling Maryland's new head coach and former Mountaineer player Roy Lester's debut.

Maryland's only score came in the second quarter on a 19-yard double-reverse by senior wingback Paul Fitzpatrick.

The Mountaineer drives were engineered by junior quarterback Mike Sherwood, who kept the Terrapin defense guessing.

But the Terp defense stiffened in the second quarter and held the Mountaineers scoreless for the period. West Virginia led at halftime 21-7.

Starting the second half, Sherwood hit Oscar Patrick for a 12-yard touchdown pass. Braxton not only battered the Terp defense, he also booted four extra points and a field goal, giving him 19 points for the day. Tom Miller led the Terps with 47 yards on 12 carries, while Fitzpatrick went for 36 yards on 11 tries.

Featured Player: Jim Braxton, West Virginia

Courtesy of West Virginia and Regional History Center. WVU Libraries.

Played Maryland in 1969 and 1970
First Team All-American
WVU Sports Hall of Fame
A physically imposing athlete on the field, fullback Jim Braxton was a soft-spoken, gentle person off it. Entering WVU in 1967 after a stellar high school career at Connellsville High School, it took the Vanderbilt, Pa., native just one year before becoming a regular for WVU in 1968.

The Mountaineers' second-leading rusher as a sophomore with 272 yards on 83 carries, he also snared 18 passes for 276 yards and two touchdowns. As a junior, he rushed for a team-best 843 yards on 199 carries while scoring 13 touchdowns for the 10-1 Peach Bowl champions. Equally talented as a kicker, Braxton booted three field goals and converted 26 of 30 PAT's to finish eighth in the country in scoring with 113 points.

Converted to tight end as a senior, Braxton snagged 27 passes for 565 yards and eight touchdowns. He also ran the football 51 times for 347 yards and one score. For his efforts, he was honored by the Associated Press as a first team All-American at tight end. All told, Braxton accumulated 1,462 yards rushing and 906 yards receiving in a brilliant Mountaineer career.

As a professional, he would take on a different role. Drafted in the third round by the Buffalo Bills, Braxton no longer was the team's main offensive weapon. Instead, he found a niche as the blocking back for O.J. Simpson.

Standing 6-foot-1 and weighing nearly 250 pounds, Braxton was certainly suited for the task. Built like a tank, Braxton was also quick and agile, which enabled Simpson to get many of his 11,236 career rushing yards. A good runner in his own right, Braxton's best year came in 1975 when he rushed for 823 yards on 186 carries for nine touchdowns. During one game that season against the St. Louis Cardinals, Braxton plowed his way to a career-best 160 yards on 34 carries.

Injuring his knee in the first game of the 1976 season, he played one more year with the Bills before finishing out his NFL career in 1978 with the Miami Dolphins. In eight years, he gained 2,890 yards rushing, while catching 141 passes for 1,473 yards. He accounted for 31 touchdowns as a rusher and receiver.

After his playing career, Braxton, nicknamed "Bubby or Bubba," was involved in many community and civic organizations while serving as a manager of the Hilltop complexes in Buffalo.

Braxton, a 1990 inductee into the West Virginia Sports Hall of Fame, succumbed to cancer on July 28, 1986, at the age of 37. He was an inaugural member of WVU's Mountaineer Legends Society in 2016.

Featured Player: Carl Crennel, West Virginia

Played Maryland in 1969
First Team All American
WVU Sports Hall of Fame

Carl Crennel was a three-year starter at middle guard from 1967-69. He captained the 1969 team that defeated South Carolina 14-3 in the Peach Bowl, winning MVP honors by anchoring a defense that did not yield a touchdown to the Gamecocks.

For the season, the Mountaineer defense limited opponents to just 10 points per game.

Courtesy of Special Collections, University of Maryland Libraries, University of Maryland.

The 1969 team finished 10-1 and ranked 20th in the final polls. Under Coach Jim Carlen, the Mountaineers posted records of 5-4-1 (1967), 7-3 (1968) and 10-1 (1969) for a 22-8-1 mark during Crennel's career.

The Lynchburg, Va., native (who did not play organized football until his junior year of high school) was named a first team All-American by *Playboy* magazine in 1969, second team by the Associated Press in 1967 and 1969, and third team by the AP in 1968.

He played in the 1970 Hula Bowl. Crennel is a member of the WVU football all-time team and was the 1969 John Russell Award winner.

Selected by Pittsburgh in the ninth round of the 1970 NFL draft, he played one season with the Steelers before embarking on a successful career in the Canadian Football League.

He played 11 years in the CFL with the Winnipeg Bombers, Montreal Alouettes, Edmonton Eskimos, Hamilton Tiger-Cats and Saskatchewan Roughriders. He played on three Grey Cup teams and was an Eastern all-star in 1973, 1978 and 1979.

Former Buffalo Bills Coach Marv Levy, who coached Crennel in Montreal, said recently, *"He was a terrific linebacker, very coachable. Quite a gentleman."*

Ali and Bubba

In November of 1969, heavyweight champion Muhammad Ali visited Morgantown to speak during his three-year ban from boxing. During the course of the talk to a sellout crowd at the Mountainlair Student Union, Ali asked who the toughest guy on campus was. The crowd chanted "Bubba" and All-America fullback Jim Braxton climbed onto the stage. Ali promptly shadow-boxed with Braxton to the joy of the crowd!

O.J. Simpson offered these goodbye words to Braxton: *"I've lost a teammate; I've lost a dear friend. Bubba was my protector on the field, my companion off it. What he meant to my career is impossible to calculate, but I know many of the things I achieved wouldn't have been possible without him."*

Game XIV
West Virginia 20, Maryland 10
Maryland leads series 7-5-2

November 28, 1970
Byrd Stadium, College Park, Md.
Attendance 12,821
West Virginia Head Coach: Bobby Bowden (1ˢᵗ year)
Maryland Head Coach: Roy Lester (2ⁿᵈ year)
Barometer: West Virginia finished 8-3 in Bobby Bowden's inaugural season at WVU, while Maryland was 2-9.
Game Notes: This was Bobby Bowden's first season at the helm of the Mountaineer ship and came into this rare late-season game with the Terps with a 7-3 record, while the Terps were a dismal 2-8.

This was the first game after the Marshall University football plane crash. Bowden had equipment manager Carl Roberts put green crosses on each WVU helmet in memory of the victims.

Bowden had requested the NCAA allow WVU to play Marshall's last game that season against Ohio U. He also requested to wear Marshall's jerseys. The NCAA declined both. Ironically, two years earlier, Bowden had been offered the Marshall job and turned it down.

Miscues Abound but Mountaineers Hold On to a 20-10 Win

COLLEGE PARK—In recent years the breaks have seemed to fall in the Mountaineers' favor. Today they were pretty even, but the Terps were still unable to take advantage of them, as they lost their ninth game in 11 starts this season.

"I'm just glad to win," Mountaineer coach Bobby Bowden said after the Mountaineers won 20-10 despite miscues which wiped out three touchdowns and stalled other drives.

"We made a whole lot of mistakes, untimely mistakes," Bowden said. *"We kept hurting ourselves like on the missed field goal, the fumble and the penalty. We weren't as sharp as we have been, but I'm not making any alibis. 8-3 is not a bad record."*

Both teams were sloppy, as Maryland gave away three interceptions and a third-quarter fumble which led to a WVU touchdown, putting the Mounties ahead 17-7. West Virginia lost three fumbles as well, one of which led to the Terps' only touchdown. But the others were wasted.

The Mountaineers set the tone on the first play from scrimmage as quarterback Mike Sherwood connected with tight end Nate Stephens for a 65-yard gain, before Stephens fumbled at the Maryland 15.

The Mountaineers bungled two more touchdown chances in the fourth quarter when flanker Wayne Porter dropped a halfback pass in the end zone from Jim Braxton. In a later series, halfback Bob Gresham fumbled at the Maryland 1 as he went in for an apparent touchdown. Earlier West Virginia missed a 26-yard field goal.

Terp coach Roy Lester felt the turning point of the game came early when the Terps were down only 3-0. They had a 22-yard pass to the WVU 46 called back on an illegal-motion penalty, forcing them to punt. Leon Jenkins returned it 23 yards to the Maryland 40. Eighteen seconds later, Sherwood connected with Braxton for a 24-yard touchdown, expanding the Mountaineer lead to 10-0.

"We had a first down and then were forced to punt," Lester said. *"The first thing you know, they had 10 points."*

Game XV
Signature Game #6
West Virginia 20, Maryland 13
Maryland leads the series 7-6-2

September 15, 1973
Byrd Stadium, College Park, Md.
Attendance: 35,112
West Virginia Head Coach: Bobby Bowden (4th year)
Maryland Head Coach: Jerry Claiborne (2nd year)
Barometer: West Virginia finished 6-5, while Maryland was 8-4 with a loss in the Peach Bowl and a No. 18 ranking.
Game Notes: Bud Johnson of Morgantown recalls heading to the game the night before: *"We stopped for gas at a country store/gas station*

somewhere around Bruceton Mills—this was before the interstate. I went in the store to pay and get a six-pack. The old boy running the store asked where we were headed. I said the Baltimore area. His reply was classic! "Hail, ya cain't get to Balmer on a six pack of beeer!"

This game was the season-opener for both teams. *The Annapolis Capital* predicted that Ken Wagenheim, a walk-on kicker for the Terps, could hold the key to the game. Little did they know! He had never played in a football game before and was charged with trying to pin the Mountaineers as far back as possible before their explosive offense took over. *"Wagenheim will have to boot the ball high enough to allow proper coverage and prevent Danny "Lightning" Buggs from running away from the Terps."* The year before, Buggs returned 12 punts for 170 yards and two touchdowns.

Wagenheim met Terp coach Jerry Claiborne at a banquet and convinced the coach to give him a try-out. He was a graduate of Montgomery Junior College.

Over 30,000 fans were expected at Byrd Stadium, the largest crowd in years. The Terps were six-point favorites.

"We didn't think of this game as a rivalry yet," said Jonathan Claiborne, a Terp starter and son of head coach Jerry Claiborne. *"We hadn't played that much, and we weren't sure how good we were going to be."*

WVU's "Lightning" Buggs Burns Terps 20-13
By A.E. "Shorty" Hardman
Charleston (W.Va.) Gazette-Mail

COLLEGE PARK—A sensational 69-yard punt return by West Virginia's All-American candidate Danny Buggs, with only 32 seconds left on the clock, brought the Mountaineers a thrilling 20-13 victory over the Terps of Maryland here Saturday afternoon, in their 1973 opener.

A crowd of 35,112 screaming fans, the largest to file into Byrd Stadium since 1966—was just recovering from a 75-yard touchdown pass from WVU's Ade Dillon to Dwayne Woods, which had tied the score at 13-all with 5:14 left in the game when Buggs did his thing.

He grabbed Phil Wagenheim's kick at the 31-yard line as a horde of Maryland players moved in on him. He stepped back a couple of yards then ran to his left a stride or two then reversed his field to go all the way up the right sideline.

It wasn't even close after he got started, although wingback Kim Hoover had gotten his fingers on Danny's jersey just before he reversed his field.

It had been a day filled with frustration for the Mountaineers who had to settle for two first-half field goals by gifted Frank Nester when touchdown opportunities had been forfeited to the strong Maryland defense, best in the Atlantic Coast Conference a year ago.

But the Terps got a good dose of the WVU defense too, as the game wore on and they also had to settle for matching field goals off the toe of soccer-style kicker Steve Mike-Mayer.

Nester put a couple through the uprights from 35 and 33 yards out in the first half, then Mick-Mayer came back to get both of his in the third quarter from distances of 48 and 43 yards.

West Virginia's five fumbles, four of which were lost to Maryland weighed down its running attack and put great pressure on its defensive unit headed by Ron Brown, Jeff Merrow, Tree Adams and Tom Zakowski.

Then, when it appeared that the game was strictly headed for a 6-6 conclusion, WVU's center Wib Newton's snap to punter Chuck Brooks went sailing over his head and rolled to the one-foot line.

It took the Terps three hard slugs at the West Virginia line to get the ball over. But back Louis Carter finally went airborne to jump high over the line to score the touchdown that certainly seemed to be the decisive one.

But the Maryland lead was to be of only 20-seconds in duration. On the first play after the next kickoff with the ball at the WVU 25, Dillon drifted back and sent a wobbly pass to Woods, who took the ball in at the 38-yard line and simply ran off and left the Maryland defense for a 75-yard touchdown dash. When Nester booted the point, it was another deadlocked score, 13-13.

The Terps had the ball for 11 plays after the final kick off, moving it from the 20 to the 45. But the WVU defense, simply terrific all day, started to move in, Brown and Merrow making jarring tackles that set the Terps back to their 29, fourth down and 26.

Weinheim's punt went sailing to 31 and Buggs was there to take it in. It was a good example why rival coaches, including Maryland's Jerry Claiborne, call him the most sensational runner in this football era.

Although the Mountaineers led 6-0 at halftime, that entire period was loaded with despair for West Virginia. After Johnny Harcharic blocked Weinheim's punt and Merrow had recovered on the Terp 26, West Virginia's offense was tested by the vaunted Maryland defense which let the Mountaineers get no closer than the 19.

Then on fourth down, Nester booted a 35-yarder for first blood.

Harcharic intercepted an Avellini pass later in the period to set the Mountaineers up in business on the WVU 45-yard line. But Dwayne Woods fumbled the ball right back to the Terps.

Maryland offered WVU another opportunity in the early part of the second quarter when Dick Jennings fumbled at the Terp 23 and Jack Eastwood recovered for the Mountaineers.

But a Dillon pass was a wild pitch with Danny Buggs in the clear and then two running plays netted only six yards.

So, Nester was back to kick again in lieu of a much-desired touchdown. He sent it through the prongs from 33 yards out.

Zakowski intercepted a Ben Kinard pass at the 35 midway in the second quarter and the Mountaineer attack seemed to catch fire. Woods got eight yards and Dillon passed to Dave Jadgmann for nine and then hit Buggs for 17 and a first at the 14.

But then Dillon fumbled and Kevin Ward recovered for the Terps at the Maryland 37.

Near the end of the quarter when Wegenheim went back to punt, he bobbled the ball momentarily and had to run. But he only got as far as the seven where WVU took the ball.

Once again, the Maryland defense clamped down on the Mountaineers. Dillion being tossed for a 13-yard loss by Randy White and a third try for a field goal was in order on fourth and 19. But Nester's kick, this time from 35 yards, was wide and the Terps had once again stymied the Mountaineers.

And so, the Mountaineers are off to a good start toward another fine season under Bobby Bowden, whose teams had won 23 and lost 11 in the three seasons before this one.

The victory, third in a row West Virginia has scored over Maryland, reduced the Terps' margin in the series to 7-6-2.

It was West Virginia's first away-from-home opener since 1966 when it lost to Duke.

Featured Player: Danny Buggs, West Virginia

Buggs receiving Player of the Year Award from author and WVU Athletic Council student representative, Chip Zimmer, courtesy of Zimmer photo collection.

Played Maryland in 1973
First Team All-American
WVU Sports Hall of Fame

Danny Buggs, a 1973 Kodak first team All-America wide receiver from Atlanta, Ga., may be best remembered for his blazing speed, which baffled Mountaineer football opponents from 1972-74. His 96-yard touchdown reception from Ben Williams against Penn State in 1973 was the longest pass play from scrimmage in WVU history.

Buggs' expertise was his ability to make the big play on the gridiron. In fact, at one point during his sophomore season, Buggs averaged a touchdown for every five times he touched the ball. He still ranks among the school's all-time leaders in average yards per reception, receiving yards and touchdown receptions.

In 1972, Buggs posted some astounding numbers. He caught 35 passes for 791 yards and eight touchdowns, an average of 22.6 yards per catch. Buggs also averaged 14.2 yards per punt return and ran six punts back for touchdowns. Overall, he scored 84 points in 1972. West Virginia was 8-4 that season and lost to NC State, 49-13, in the Peach Bowl. Following his sophomore campaign, Buggs was named the 1973 West Virginia amateur athlete of the year by the West Virginia Sportswriters Association.

Under head coach Bobby Bowden, Buggs and the Mountaineers compiled an 18-16 three-year record. "Lightning" was selected to play in the 1974 Hula and Senior bowls and caught a 47-yard touchdown pass to help the East top the West 34-25 in the Hula Bowl in Honolulu, Hawaii.

He was picked in the third round of the NFL Draft by the New York Giants and played 10 seasons of professional ball with the Giants and Washington Redskins of the NFL, the Edmonton Eskimos and Montreal Alouettes of the Canadian Football League, and the Tampa Bay Bandits and San Antonio Gunslingers of the USFL. In 1980, Buggs helped Edmonton win the Grey Cup, the CFL's equivalent of the Super Bowl.

The three-year letterman in track for coach Stan Romanoski also held nearly every WVU sprint record until 1992 Olympian James Jett surpassed his times. He once clocked a 9.55 100-yard dash in tennis shoes without warming up.

Born April 22, 1953, at Duluth, Ga., Buggs attended Avondale High School and won All-State honors for coach Crawford Kennedy. He also set state prep track records in the 100-, 220- and 440-yard dashes and the long jump.

He was an inaugural member of WVU's Mountaineer Legends Society in 2016.

Lightning Buggs and Borrowed Tennis Shoes

At the intramural track meet in 1972, Buggs was entered to run the 100-yard dash, the 220 and the long jump. He approached the author, who was running the track meet, and asked if I might be able to find him some tennis shoes to borrow. He was wearing street shoes at the time. I found some for him and he promptly set national intramural records for all three events, ultimately being noted in *Sports Illustrated's* "Faces in the Crowd."

Featured Player: Steve Mike-Mayer, Maryland

Courtesy of Special Collections, University of Maryland Libraries, University of Maryland.

Played West Virginia in 1973
First Team All-American

Mike-Mayer kicked for Maryland from 1973-75, where he received Sporting News All-America honors. He is from a family of place-kickers and soccer players. A native of Budapest, his father was the highest paid professional soccer player in Hungary before the Hungarian Revolution in 1956 forced he and his family to flee to the U.S. via Italy. Steve's older brother, Nick, was a place-kicker for the Temple Owls.

He set multiple records as a sophomore and then proceeded to break them again as a junior and as a senior. He kicked a 54-yard field goal against Villanova. As a sophomore, one of his kickoffs was measured at 87 yards, landing 17 yards beyond the end zone!

Mike-Mayer was a third-round pick in the 1975 NFL Draft by the San Francisco 49ers. He had a six-year career in the NFL, also playing for Detroit, New Orleans and Baltimore.

Featured Player: Randy White, Maryland

Courtesy of Special Collections, University of Maryland Libraries, University of Maryland.

Played WVU in 1973
Consensus All-American
Outland Trophy Winner
Lombardi Award Winner
College Football Hall of Fame

Randy White came to the University of Maryland from Wilmington, Del., and was originally listed as a fullback. Coach Jerry Claiborne moved him to defensive tackle and he was called, in some quarters, "the quickest lineman in the game."

He was a first team All-American in 1973 and was a unanimous selection in 1974. He was 9th in Heisman Trophy balloting that season. Other awards in 1974 included: Outland Trophy—nation's best interior lineman; Lombardi Award—nation's best lineman or linebacker; ACC Player of the Year; State of Delaware Athlete of the Year; Columbus Touchdown Club, Washington Touchdown Club, Pigskin Club—Lineman of the Year; Philadelphia Sports Writers Award-Amateur Athlete of the Year; United Press Lineman of the Year; Liberty Bowl MVP. Maryland later retired his jersey number 94.

Next came 14 years with the Dallas Cowboys. In the Super Bowl following the 1977 season, he was co-winner of the MVP Award. He hit the jackpot in 1994 with election to the College Football Hall of Fame and the Pro Football Hall of Fame.

Featured Player: Paul Vellano, Maryland

Played WVU in 1973
First Team All-American
Maryland Athletics Hall of Fame
Vellano came to Maryland as a high school All-American from Bishop Gibbons HS in Schenectady, N.Y.

At Maryland, he was a two time All-ACC first-team selection and honorable mention All-American as a junior, becoming a first team All-American his senior year. He led the team in tackles, a rare feat for an interior lineman. He was a Kodak All-American first-team pick his senior year when he led the Terp defense to a No. 9 ranking in total defense and a berth in their first bowl since 1955 (Peach Bowl). He was selected by the Chicago Bears in the 1974 NFL Draft.

Courtesy of Special Collections, University of Maryland Libraries, University of Maryland.

Featured Player: Louis Carter, Maryland

Played WVU in 1973

Second Team All-American

Louis Carter of Laurel, Md., was a unique runner/passer/ receiver/return specialist for the Terps. He was selected a second team All American in 1974 by the Football Writers and was MVP of the Coaches All-American college all-star game following the 1974 season. Carter gained 1,056 yards that season in addition to catching 26 passes for 270 yards and a touchdown.

Courtesy of Special Collections, University of Maryland Libraries, University of Maryland.

As a junior, he led the ACC in scoring with 14 touchdowns and threw six TD passes. Named the Best Offensive Player in the 1973 Peach Bowl with 126 yards rushing, he completed 2 of 3 passes for 83 yards, including a 68-yarder. That season, he caught 12 passes for 99 yards and returned 14 kickoffs for 312 yards. All told, he was responsible for 20 touchdowns.

Carter was a third-round pick by the Oakland Raiders in the 1975 NFL Draft and moved to Tampa Bay in the veteran allocation draft. He spent three seasons with the Bucs and threw the first touchdown pass in franchise history when he was stopped at the line of scrimmage and then lobbed the ball across the goal line for an unexpected score.

Game XVI
Maryland 24, West Virginia 3
Maryland leads series 8-6-2

September 18, 1976

Mountaineer Field, Morgantown, W.Va.

Attendance: 35,107

Maryland Head Coach: Jerry Claiborne (5th year)

West Virginia Head Coach: Frank Cignetti (1st year)

Barometer: Maryland finished 11-1 including a loss in the Cotton Bowl and a No. 8 ranking, while West Virginia was 5-6.

Game Notes: Maryland entered the game ranked 10th in the AP poll, fresh off a 31-7 victory over Richmond. They went on to an undefeated regular season and a No. 4 ranking before falling to No. 6 Houston in the Cotton Bowl, 30-21. WVU entered the game unranked following a 28-7 victory over Villanova in their season-opener.

New WVU head coach Frank Cignetti lamented *"they put a pretty good licking on us."*

"Maryland had changed as a team by now. We felt like we could go undefeated this year. West Virginia was one of the games we circled on the calendar that we knew we had to beat. They were pretty good," said Jonathan Claiborne. *"This was a big kick- off game for us."*

WVU grad and former Clemson head coach Tommy Bowden averaged 17.2 yards per catch this season and caught one pass for 12 yards in this game. Said Bowden of the rivalry, *"It's an intense rivalry but not as consistent or as well-known as rivalries like Alabama-Auburn, Florida State-Miami or Florida-Florida State. It doesn't have the sense of hatred that the West Virginia-Pitt game has. But with the players and recruiting, it's intense. It seems to be more of a rivalry for West Virginia than for Maryland, probably due to the conference affiliation that Maryland had with the ACC, while West Virginia was an independent."*

When asked about West Virginia's quest to join the ACC, Bowden said, *"As head coach at Clemson, I didn't really have any input. But when they were considering either Louisville or West Virginia, I thought that surely West Virginia would have a better chance."*

Manges Mangles WVU

MORGANTOWN—Maryland quarterback Mark Manges seemingly did it all as he led his Terrapins to an easy 24-3 victory in front of an overflow crowd at Mountaineer Field.

Manges completed 9 of 13 passes for 119 yards, ran for 68 yards on 15 carries and delivered some devastating blocks along the way.

Sophomore tailback Steve Atkins garnered 133 yards in 23 carries to lighten Manges' load. The Terp defense did their share, limiting the Mountaineers to only one visit inside the 20-yard line all day, resulting in a Bill McKenzie field goal from 29 yards out.

Courtesy of Special Collections, University of Maryland Libraries, University of Maryland.

It was West Virginia's first setback under new coach Frank Cignetti, who said he was proud of his boys despite the one-sided defeat. *"Our young players learned a lot out there today,"* he said, *"and I know we will benefit from it."*

Cignetti praised the Terps, calling them one of the better teams on the WVU schedule—on par with Pitt and Penn State.

Maryland scored on a 78-yard drive in 13 plays in the first quarter, culminating with Manges' 2-yard touchdown plunge. The Terps scored again in the second quarter on a 72-yard drive, beginning with Lumberport, W.Va., native Doug Harbert intercepting a Dan Kendra pass at the Maryland 13 and returning it 36 yards to set up an Atkins TD. A Manges to WR Chuck White 31-yard touchdown pass finished the Terrapin scoring before the half.

The Mountaineer defense stiffened in the second half, holding the Terps to just a 23-yard Mike Sochko field goal.

Maryland rolled up 24 first downs to West Virginia's nine.

Featured Player: Joe Campbell, Maryland

Courtesy of Special Collections, University of Maryland Libraries, University of Maryland.

Played WVU in 1973 and 1976
Consensus All-American
Delaware Sports Hall of Fame

From Salesianum, Del., Campbell went on to earn All-America honors as a defensive tackle at Maryland. He played in five bowl games: Cotton, Peach, Liberty, Hula and Japan. He won University of Maryland's "Sylvester Watts" Award in 1976 as the student typifying the best in intercollegiate athletics.

Campbell was the New Orleans Saints' top draft pick in 1977. Playing at 6-foot-6 and 250 pounds, he was used as a defensive end by the Saints and on special teams with the Raiders and Tampa Bay. He won a Super Bowl ring with the 1981 Oakland Raiders. He played 66 games in his seven-year NFL career, starting 26 games and appeared in all the Raiders' playoff games in that time. Campbell called it a career with the USFL Washington Federals in 1983.

Game XVII
Signature Game #7
West Virginia 24, Maryland 16
Maryland leads series 8-7-2

September 17, 1977
Byrd Stadium, College Park, Md.
Attendance: 45,123
West Virginia Head Coach: Frank Cignetti (2nd year)
Maryland Head Coach: Jerry Claiborne (6th year)
Barometer: Maryland went 8-4 including a win over Minnesota in the Hall of Fame Classic. West Virginia finished 5-6.

Game Notes: Maryland came into this matchup with a 15-game winning streak, ranked No.11 after dropping a place in the AP poll following a lackluster 21-14 win over unranked Clemson in the season-opener. They rebounded with a 7-4 record and an invitation to the Hall of Fame Bowl, where they defeated Minnesota 17-7. After upsetting the Terps, WVU rose to No. 17, but promptly fell out of the rankings with a 28-13 loss at unranked Kentucky. They finished with a 5-6 record.

The Terps wide-tackle-six defense would be tested against WVU's veer offense. *"They have a better home-run threat and they're more versatile,"* said Claiborne. *"Alexander is gonna be one of the greats in the country. There's no doubt about that."* The game lined up to be a battle between Terp running back Steve Atkins and WVU's freshman sensation, running back Robert Alexander.

Mountaineer coach Frank Cignetti said, *"Maryland has a dominating defense. They showed us that last year… their defense will certainly be among the best, if not the best, that we'll see all season."*

The Cumberland Times stated, *"A sellout crowd of 45,000 is expected to jam Byrd Stadium… Over 8,500 tickets were sold in West Virginia, where many of the state's Eastern Panhandle residents live much closer to College Park than they do to Morgantown."*

After the game, Cignetti said, *"We won the game but injuries wiped us out. We lost Steve Lewis, our best receiver, as well as our other receiver for the season. Maryland was very good at this time… Jerry Claiborne had come to Maryland and really turned the program around. He used a unique eight-man defensive front, the 'wide-tackle-six.' We spread out three wide receivers and two backs in order to stretch their line. We were pretty successful running off-tackle. After we won, I was getting calls from everyone to find out what we did!"*

Line Not at Fault
By Larry Yanos
Hagerstown (Md.) Herald-Mail

COLLEGE PARK—They can't blame this one on the offensive line.

The University of Maryland's front five, which has received more than its share of adverse publicity this young football season, performed admirably Saturday afternoon at Byrd Stadium. But the rest of the cast? Well, forget it.

In absorbing a 24-16 defeat to West Virginia, Maryland looked more like a member of the "bottom ten" Saturday than a national title contender and coach Jerry Claiborne has many holes to patch up before Saturday's confrontation with Penn State at University Park, Pa.

To the Terrapins' credit, they hustled back from a 24-0 halftime deficit; but they should never had been behind that far against a team the caliber of the Mountaineers.

"We're just lacking the mental toughness," a disappointed Claiborne said of the upset. "We should not be making these mistakes. West Virginia played an outstanding game, but we gave them too many opportunities. We have to get mentally tough in a hurry or we'll find ourselves with two straight losses."

Maryland's offensive line provided quarterback Larry Dick with more than enough to pass and opened many holes for the running backs. But the Terps had the knack of fumbling away chances in the first half and the secondary was burned on many occasions by West Virginia signal-caller Dan Kendra.

"We had a complete breakdown in the secondary on the third West Virginia touchdown, and we just made some dumb mistakes through-out the afternoon," Claiborne noted. "We'll correct these mistakes in practice because we can't afford a repeat against Penn State."

When Chris Ward fumbled a West Virginia punt in the first quar-ter, setting up the Mountaineer's first touchdown, it set the tone for what was to happen later that afternoon.

West Virginia outplayed Maryland in virtually every department the opening 30 minutes, then had to stave off a dramatic second-half spurt by the Terrapins to hand the College Park gridders their first defeat after 15 straight regular-season victories.

"I don't like losing," Claiborne continues, "We were just outplayed. Our performance in the second half would indicate we could have done that the entire game. We just were not mentally tough enough to get the job done."

Maryland responded to Claiborne's halftime lecture by putting the pressure on West Virginia the second half and narrowed the margin to 24-16 by pinning Mountaineer's punter Bill McKenzie in the end zone following a bad snap.

West Virginia was given a free kick and Maryland's Vince Kin-ney—who turned in a brilliant job—returned the free punt to the 4-yard line of the Mountaineers.

Larry Dick and company tried four straight times to get the ball in the end zone and the West Virginia defense stymied every effort.

The frustrated Maryland quarterback gestured to the press box after the second running play, apparently not in complete agreement with one of the coaches' play-calling, but Claiborne used two more running plays and the Terps were stopped short of the goal line.

Dick did a commendable job filling in for Mark Manges but will probably return to the bench next week if Manges' foot injury responds to treatment.

Chapter 11:

1980-2000:
Nehlen and Ross; Terps Then Lose Way

I became a Terp about this time, moving from Morgantown to College Park for grad school. Having worked in the WVU athletic department and then Maryland's, the old rivalry took on a new meaning for me since I had allegiances to both schools. So, for this "MountainTerp" an old-fashioned tie similar to those in 1944 (6-6) and 1945 (13-13) would make the ideal ending… much better than kissing your sister!

Interestingly, both schools had "Miami Miracles" in this era—the Terps in 1984 and West Virginia in 1993… Coincidence? Hmmm….

Game XVIII
Maryland 14, West Virginia 11
Maryland leads series 9-7-2

September 20, 1980
"New" Mountaineer Field, Morgantown, W.Va.
Attendance: 48,038
Maryland Head Coach: Jerry Claiborne (9th year)
West Virginia Head Coach: Don Nehlen (1st year)
Barometer: Maryland finished 8-4 including a loss to Florida in the Tangerine Bowl (where the author served as the national radio broadcast's color commentator!). West Virginia finished the season with a 6-6 record in Don Nehlen's first year.

Game Notes*:* This was the inaugural season in "new" Mountaineer Stadium. The stadium had been christened two weeks earlier when the Mountaineers defeated Cincinnati in front of a sellout crowd which featured John Denver singing "Country Roads."

"Claiborne made Maryland into a real good team," said Nehlen. "He used that 'wide-tackle-six' defense that everyone thought they could run all over them, but their two middle guys were something.

"The Maryland game was a big rivalry for us," Nehlen recalled. *"It was a big game on our schedule along with Pitt and Penn State every year. Virginia Tech, too. We had to go into Maryland and D.C. to get players in order to be competitive. It's a shame they don't play anymore."*

Former Minnesota Vikings head coach and Terp alumnus Mike Tice, when asked about West Virginia prior to his 1980 start against them said with eyes opened wide and his voice raised an octave, *"Very explosive, that running back they have, Robert Alexander, I think the West Virginia governor declared him a natural resource when the school recruited him. It looks like Alexander is on fire. He sure had a fantastic first game (187 yards in the opening 41-27 win over Cincinnati). It's going to be a tough game. Especially since it's up there. Those people are football-crazy!"*—Baltimore Sun, Sept. 18,1980. Tice was 8-for-15 for 71 yards and rushed for 23 yards.

Maryland's Defense Shines in Stopping Mountaineers

MORGANTOWN—Jerry Claiborne's vaunted defense turned it up a notch as the Terps defeated the Mountaineers, 14-11, holding their top-ranked offense in check. A crowd of 48,038 fans watched from the new Mountaineer Stadium.

West Virginia entered the game first in the nation in total offense, had the top passer in the country in Oliver Luck and the fifth-leading rusher in Robert Alexander. WVU was averaging 549 yards and 46.5 points in their first two games. But this was all stymied by the Terrapins' "wide tackle six" defense.

The Maryland defense bent a bit but never broke until late in the game as West Virginia frantically scored a touchdown and two-point conversion to cut Maryland's lead to 14-11 with just 59 seconds remaining. The threat ended when Chris Havener jumped on Steve Sinclair's onside kick at the Terp 47-yard line. Quarterback Mike Tice ran out the clock, giving the Terps a 3-0 record while dropping the Mountaineers to 2-1.

It looked like the Mounties might break a scoreless tie midway through the second quarter, as they drove to the Maryland 34 with a third-and-1 situation. New WVU coach Don Nehlen put in three fullbacks and two tight ends and sent Walter Easley into the heart of the defense twice for a loss of a yard, giving the Terps noticeable momentum.

With just over five minutes left in the half, Tice engineered a 66-yard, 10-play drive led by the nation's fourth-leading rusher, tailback Charlie Wysocki, who gained 40 yards in seven carries and scored the Terps' first touchdown. Dale Castro added the conversion, giving the Terps a 7-0 lead heading into halftime.

A five-minute drive in the fourth resulted in Maryland's second touchdown, as Wysocki again did the heavy lifting, lugging the ball 45 yards and giving the Terps a 14-3 lead. Wysocki finished with 149 yards on 35 carries, while the Maryland defense limited Alexander to just 70 yards on 13 carries and held the Mountaineer offense to 313 yards, 236 below their average.

Featured Player: Dale Castro, Maryland

Played WVU in 1980

Consensus All-American

Maryland Athletics Hall of Fame

Castro came to Maryland with the intention of earning a scholarship as a baseball pitcher, but contracted mononucleosis during his first semester, causing him to miss tryouts. Afterwards he decided to try out for the football team as a walk-on place-kicker, a position he had played in high school. During his sophomore year, he was offered a scholarship.

In 1979, Castro tied the NCAA record for most field goals in a half with four against

Courtesy of Special Collections, University of Maryland Libraries, University of Maryland.

Mississippi State. In the fourth quarter of that game, he made a fifth field goal. He set a then-NCAA record when he made his first 16 field goal attempts. In total, he made 17 field goals during the season.

Castro was a consensus first team All-American. He concluded his collegiate career in 1980, and he remains among the school's leaders in career punting yards (8,584), field goal percentage (69.2%) and career field goals (27).

Game XIX
West Virginia 17, Maryland 13
Maryland leads series 9-8-2

September 19, 1981
Byrd Stadium, College Park, Md.
Attendance 38,300
West Virginia Coach: Don Nehlen (2nd year)
Maryland Coach: Jerry Claiborne (10th year)
Barometer: West Virginia finished 9-3, including a huge upset win over Florida in the Peach Bowl. Maryland had a 4-6-1 record in Jerry Claiborne's last season before returning to his alma mater Kentucky.

Game Notes: The Terps entered the game as five-point favorites despite being upset at Vanderbilt the previous week, while WVU upset Virginia. It promised to be a shootout between WVU quarterback Oliver Luck and Terps running back Charlie Wysocki, who ran for 149 yards and both Maryland touchdowns the year before. Nobody anticipated this to be a coming-out party for third-string quarterback Boomer Esiason.

"We were down 14-10 with less than five minutes to go. At the fourth down, I called for us to punt the ball and make something happen as soon as their guy caught it. Well, sure enough, their return man fumbled. We managed to score a few plays later to win 17-14."—Don Nehlen.

"Once we beat Maryland at Maryland then it was, okay, we crossed the threshold now we're as good as anybody there is," WVU assistant coach Bill Kirelawich.

Quarterback Oliver Luck commented, *"It was rock-em, sock-em, old-school football. Both teams had big and quality linemen, and they were always close games."*

West Virginia Comes from Behind to Down Injury-Plagued Terps

COLLEGE PARK—Injuries and mistakes were the order of the day as the West Virginia Mountaineers visited Byrd Stadium and came away with an unlikely come-from-behind win. The Terps let this one slip away late in the game with a crucial mistake, giving them their first 0-2 start since 1974.

Maryland had to juggle quarterbacks from the get-go, as first-stringer Brent Dewitz sustained a knee injury the week before at Vanderbilt. Second-teamer Bob Milkovich then re-injured his ribs in the pregame warmup, forcing coach Jerry Claiborne to call on third-stringer Boomer Esiason. Star running back Charlie Wysocki was also injured and missed the game.

Esiason had never played in a varsity game and was greeted by the Mountaineer bull rush with a 15-yard sack. After this baptism, Esiason showed flashes of brilliance, but his overall effort was lacking. His inauspicious start resulted in a 15-for-32 day with 164 yards and two interceptions.

Despite the injuries and mistakes, Maryland seemed to have the game in hand, leading 13-10 with just under five minutes to go and forced a WVU punt from the Maryland 48. Jody McKown hit a 36-yard punt to the Maryland 12, where sophomore Lendell Jones fumbled and the Mountaineer's Rich Hollins covered it.

It took Oliver Luck and company only four plays and some controversy to score, as Luck rolled to right for the score after a superb fake to fullback Dane Cornwell.

In a disputed call on third down, Terrapin defender Jonathon Simmons intercepted Luck's pass to Hollins in the end zone, but was called for pass interference, giving WVU a new set of downs on the Maryland 1.

"I think we threw too much (32 passes)," Claiborne said. *"We should have been running the ball more."*

But Esiason's 32 passes paled to Luck's air show. He was 24-for-51 for 255 yards and one touchdown including many drops and misses.

Featured Player: Boomer Esiason, Maryland

Played West Virginia in 1981, 1982, 1983
Second Team All-American
Maryland Athletics Hall of Fame

Esiason is a state legend and probably the first name that comes to mind when thinking of the greatest Maryland quarterbacks. He last played in a Terps jersey in 1984, but still ranks third in attempts, completions and yards. Esiason went to the pros as Maryland's leader in passing touchdowns, but now sits second to Milanovich. He finished 10th in Heisman balloting in 1993.

Courtesy of Special Collections, University of Maryland Libraries, University of Maryland.

He also had the best NFL career of any ex-Terp quarterback by far, playing 14 seasons, earning four Pro Bowl selections and the 1988 NFL MVP. Esiason is an easily recognizable name to this day. He's been a part of the Super Bowl radio broadcast team since 2000 and, since retiring from playing, he has worked as a football analyst for ABC, HBO and Westwood One. He currently works for CBS Sports on "The NFL Today" and Showtime's "Inside the NFL." He also hosts the morning sports program "Boomer and Gio" on WFAN Radio in New York. In 2019, he was elected to the N.Y. State Broadcasters' Association Hall of Fame.

Game XX
Signature Game #8
West Virginia 19, Maryland 18
Series tied, 9-9-2

September 18, 1982
"New" Mountaineer Field, Morgantown, W.Va.
Attendance: 56,042
West Virginia Head Coach: Don Nehlen (3rd year)
Maryland Head Coach: Bobby Ross (1st year)

Barometer: WVU finished 9-3 including a loss to Florida State and former coach Bobby Bowden in the Gator Bowl. Maryland finished 8-4 under new coach Bobby Ross, including a loss to Washington in the Aloha Bowl.

Game Notes: West Virginia entered this game after one of the biggest wins in school history, a 41-27 win at 9th-ranked Oklahoma. The Terps, meanwhile, were coming off a 39-31 loss at Penn State in front of the biggest crowd ever to witness a Maryland football game.

In a clash of eventual AP Top 20 teams, the Mountaineers outlasted the Terrapins in a nail-biter when Maryland's all-or-nothing bid for a game-winning two-point conversion failed late in the game. WVU's Paul Woodside boomed four field goals, three over 40 yards, and the Terps' Jess Atkinson hit a 49-yarder.

In this clash of titanic quarterbacks, both Maryland's Boomer Esiason and West Virginia's Jeff Hostetler filled the air. Boomer completed 24 of 40 with two interceptions and one touchdown, while Hoss was 19-for-37 with one interception and a TD, and he directed a pair of fourth-quarter scoring drives.

"Any time you play a Bobby Ross team, you know you have a problem," said Nehlen. *"After we beat Oklahoma, our guys were being told they were world-beaters. I told them that beating Oklahoma meant nothing, would go down the drain if we didn't beat Maryland the next week. Maryland went for two and Talley sacked the QB. We won by one."*

"When we lost this game by one point by going for the two-point conversion, it totally changed our mindset," said Maryland center Kevin Glover, later a consensus All-American. *"Coach Ross apologized to us for losing but said that we came here for the win, not the tie. After that game, we were confident of victory wherever we went to play."*

56,042 See WVU Edge Terps 19-18
By Danny Wells
Charleston (W.Va.) Sunday Gazette-Mail

MORGANTOWN—To witness a variety of action building to a dramatic finish, the largest crowd ever to flock to a sporting event in West Virginia, 56,042, came to the right place Saturday afternoon at Mountaineer Field.

For three quarters, the score reflected an outing at the baseball park while the game was being dominated by a young lad, WVU kicker Paul Woodside, who learned his skills on a soccer field.

Throw in a touchdown "bomb" in the fourth quarter followed by a frantic finish and the overflow crowd had a peach of a football game to watch.

The fact that West Virginia University was able to come out with a 19-18 victory over a tough Maryland team made it a perfect afternoon for Mountaineer followers, who have been overflowing the bandwagon ever since West Virginia's grand opening last week in Oklahoma.

If WVU appeared to have left its potent offense in Norman, it may have been cause of some concern in the beginning, but it didn't seem to matter so much when the defense saved the day in the end.

Significant plays cropped up all afternoon, but the most meaning-ful moments boiled to a peak with 1:39 left to play.

Maryland had just driven 75 yards to close within one point of the WVU lead. After a tense timeout, Maryland quarterback Boomer Esiason faded back, looking for a game-winning two-point pass. But a strong rush by Darryl Talley and Ed Hughes caused Esiason to hurry his throw, which sailed out of the end zone.

WVU then took the kickoff and ran out the clock, allowing the Mountaineers to add to their growing stature in the world of football.

When the Mountaineers couldn't move the ball on the ground, and quarterback Jeff Hostetler was dealing with inconsistency in his air game, WVU looked for help from Woodside, who came through with four timely field goals to keep West Virginia in the game.

WVU's lone touchdown was a big one, and probably the most picturesque play of the day. With Maryland holding a 12-9 lead, WVU was on the move at the Terrapins 30. Hostetler suddenly spotted Rich Hollins heading toward the corner of the end zone and the speedy wide receiver made a dandy catch of a perfect throw just before he went out of bounds. The touchdown came with 14:42 left in the game and gave WVU a 16-12 lead.

"The play wasn't called in the huddle," said Hollins. "We have an understanding that if the receivers can get past their defenders, we're supposed to keep running. Jeff has a special talent for picking up the receivers who have their men beat."

Less than three minutes later, Woodside kicked a 20-yard field goal which gave WVU the cushion it needed to survive Maryland's final thrust. West Virginia coach Don Nehlen was a picture of relief in the dressing room after the game.

"I want you to know one thing," he said. "That was a great victory for us. Our kids had a ton of distractions this week and they were able to stick to it and get the job done. Maryland was a darn good team… I don't care if it's one point or a hundred points, it's a great win for us.

"We bent a couple of times but didn't break. Our kicking game was super. Woodie (Woodside) is a beautiful kicker. He kicked off through the end zone and split the uprights all day," Nehlen added.

Woodside, who joined the WVU football scene as a walk-on last season from Falls Church, Va., now has converted 10 consecutive field goal attempts. He made four straight in the Peach Bowl game last year and now has kicked six already this season.

Woodside seemed more nervous answering questions after the game than kicking during the contest. "I don't think a lot about the last one," he said. "I just take each one at a time."

Maryland took a 2-0 lead on a safety in the first quarter when Hostetler was called for intentional grounding the ball from his end zone.

Woodside's first field goal, a 43-yarder, gave WVU a 3-2 lead. Woodside added a 44-yard field goal in the second quarter to make it 6-2.

But Maryland moved to a 9-6 lead halftime lead when Esiason hit Russell Davis on a 10-yard touchdown pass.

In the third quarter, Woodside added a 41-yarder to his field goal collection to tie the score at 9-9 and it still looked like a baseball game on the scoreboard.

Maryland got into the field goal act late in the third quarter when Jess Atkinson kicked a 49-yarder to give the Terps their final lead, setting up the exciting fourth period.

Hostetler finished with 19 completions in 37 attempts for 285 yards. WVU's best runner was Curlin Beck with 35 yards in seven carries. WVU finished with only 46 yards on the ground and didn't get its initial first down rushing until 9:05 left in the third quarter.

Esiason set a Maryland single-game record with 40 pass attempts. He completed 24 for 217 yards. The Terps also had trouble running, gaining only 66 yards.

The crowd spilled over into the grassy section near the scoreboard. The record crowd broke last year's attendance mark of 54,280 for the Pitt game. The stadium seats 50,512.

Featured Player: Jeff Hostetler, West Virginia

Photo by Dale Sparks Photography and Framing.

Played Maryland 1982, 1983
Academic All-American
WVU Sports Hall of Fame

Jeff Hostetler started his college football career as a linebacker at Penn State, but after transferring, became the leader of WVU's 1982 and 1983 teams.

Hostetler's place in Mountaineer lore was established from his very first game at quarterback when he went into Norman, Okla., and emerged with a 41-27 victory over a shocked Oklahoma Sooner squad, throwing for 321 yards and four touchdowns to earn national player of the week honors.

He passed the Mountaineers to the 1982 Gator Bowl and led WVU's come-from-behind 20-16 victory over Kentucky in the 1983 Hall of Fame Bowl. Trailing 10-3 at halftime, Hostetler threw second-half touchdown passes to Rich Hollins and Rob Bennett to defeat the Wildcats.

Hostetler, from Holsopple, Pa., had an 18-6 record as a two-year starter for Coach Don Nehlen and captained the 1983 team. He ranks among WVU's single-season leaders in total offense, passing yards, pass completions, pass attempts, touchdown passes and passing efficiency.

He set WVU's career record for interception avoidance (.0279) and is also among WVU's career leaders in total offense, passing yards, pass attempts, pass completions, touchdown passes, passing efficiency and completion percentage. He was seventh in Heisman balloting in 1983 and also played in the 1984 Hula and Japan bowls.

He was chosen by the New York Giants in the third round of the 1984 NFL Draft and won two Super Bowls with the Giants. Hostetler distinguished himself with his play during the 1990 season, when he took over the starting spot from an injured Phil Simms.

Dispelling critics, Hostetler led the Giants to the NFC title and defeated Buffalo 20-19 in Super Bowl XXV, the closest Super Bowl ever.

His 15-year NFL career included stops with the Giants, Los Angeles/Oakland Raiders and the Washington Redskins. A 1994 Pro Bowl selection for the Raiders, Hostetler finished his pro career with more than 16,000 yards passing and 94 touchdowns.

Hostetler was an exceptional student as well. He was named to the 1984 GTE/CoSIDA Academic All-America team and won a National Football Foundation postgraduate scholarship. He is a member of the WVU Football All-Time Team and was an inaugural member of the Mountaineer Legends Society in 2016.

Boomer and Hoss

Both quarterbacks, Maryland's Boomer Esiason and West Virginia's Jeff Hostetler took circuitous routes to get to the point of facing each other in two classic matchups.

Hostetler originally signed with Penn State and when JoePa turned him into a linebacker, he transferred to West Virginia where he could play quarterback.

Esiason was an afterthought recruit when Terp assistant football coach Tom Groom came to a high school basketball game on Long Island to see one of his recruits and was struck by Boomer's athleticism. Boomer hadn't had a scholarship offer, so he jumped at the chance to visit Maryland and was ecstatic when Jerry Claiborne offered him a scholarship. But Claiborne was a "three yards and a cloud of dust" coach who famously said "three things can happen when you throw the ball and two of them are bad." Boomer languished for a year before Claiborne left and Bobby Ross came to College Park.

The two first faced off in 1982 in Morgantown. This was also the first of five games between vaunted coaches Don Nehlen and Bobby Ross. The mountain air in Morgantown was high in anticipation for this shootout. The 56,000 fans in attendance weren't disappointed. Both Hoss and Boomer threw TD's in this air war. Esiason was 24-for-40 but with two interceptions and 217 yards, while Hostetler was 19-for-37 for 285 yards and one interception. It was a seesaw game as WVU eked out a 19-18 win when Ross courageously went for a two-point conversion to win with less than two minutes left in the game. This evened the series at 9-9-2 in a classic rivalry game.

The 1983 game found WVU ranked 20th while the host Terps were 17th. Boomer led the Terps to an early 10-0 lead. But Hoss roared back with 24 unanswered points and WVU led 24-10 by the end of the third quarter. Boomer mounted a comeback, but it was too little, too late and the Terps fell 31-21.

With these wins, WVU boasts that they were never beaten by Heisman Trophy winner Doug Flutie, nor by future NFL star Boomer Esiason.

Both went on to successful NFL careers. Boomer was the NFL MVP in 1988, while Hoss lead the N.Y. Giants to a victory in Super Bowl XXV over the Buffalo Bills, where he faced off against former Mountaineer teammate, Darryl Talley, and should have been named MVP.

Featured Player: Darryl Talley, West Virginia

Played Maryland 1980, 1981, 1982

Consensus All-American

College Football Hall of Fame

As a linebacker who could play either at the line of scrimmage or on the perimeter, Darryl Talley was a true force on the West Virginia Mountaineer defense. Talley registered 484 career tackles, which was a school record that stood for 21 years. Talley also collected 28 tackles for loss, 19 sacks, and five interceptions in his four seasons in Morgantown. Talley was a unanimous All-American and was the team's Most Valuable Player in 1982 as a senior. He was a second-round selection in the 1983 NFL Draft by the Buffalo Bills and played 12 seasons for the Bills, Atlanta Falcons and Minnesota Vikings, starting 187 of his 216 career games. The two-time Pro Bowler played in four Super Bowls with Buffalo and was selected a first team All-Pro by *The Sporting News* in 1990 and 1993. Talley logged 38.5 career sacks and forced 17 fumbles.

Talley came to WVU in 1978 and spent two seasons playing for Frank Cignetti before Don Nehlen took over the Mountaineer program in 1980. After two building seasons that saw WVU go 5-6 and 6-6, Talley and his teammates jelled to post nine wins, including a 26-6 rout of Florida in the 1981 Peach Bowl.

He went on to stardom in Buffalo as a starter for 12 outstanding seasons at linebacker from 1983-94, never missing a game while playing for the Bills. At the conclusion of his career, Talley was the Bills' all-time leading tackler with 1,137 career takedowns. He also recorded 38-1/2 sacks and 11 interceptions in Buffalo.

Talley played in four Super Bowls and two Pro Bowls as the "heart and soul" of the Buffalo defense where he won the hearts of fans and fellow players alike. *"I like the fact that he's about winning,"* said former San Francisco safety Ronnie Lott. *"He's not about showboating or who's getting the glory or who's making the plays. To me, that's a person giving of himself."*

Talley had a cheering section at Rich Stadium known as the "Talley Whackers," and after the 1990 season he received the Ed Block Courage Award.

He was named to WVU's All-Time Football Team (1980-89). In 2000, he won the Ralph C. Wilson, Jr. Distinguished Service Award.

The native of East Cleveland, Ohio, is a graduate of Shaw High School in Cleveland and earned his bachelor's degree in physical education from WVU. In 2003, Talley became the 20th member of the Wall of Fame in Ralph Wilson Stadium. In 2011, he was elected into the College Football Hall of Fame—the 12th Mountaineer to be honored. He was an inaugural member of WVU's Mountaineer Legends Society in 2016.

Featured Player: Paul Woodside, West Virginia

Photo courtesy of Paul Woodside personal collection.

Played Maryland 1981-84
First Team All-American
WVU Sports Hall of Fame

A look at the kicking section in the West Virginia record book will show that Paul Woodside remains one of the best place-kickers to ever don the Gold and Blue.

He is the only Mountaineer place-kicker to earn first team All-America honors—selected in 1983 when he booted 21 field goals in 25 tries and led WVU in scoring with 100 points. He was also a second team All-American by UPI in 1982 and 1983, and was a third-team pick by the AP in 1982.

A native of Falls Church, Va., Woodside was a four-year letter winner for the Mountaineers from 1981-84. During his four seasons, WVU compiled a 35-13 record and appeared in a bowl game every season, taking home wins in the 1981 Peach, 1983 Hall of Fame and 1984 Bluebonnet bowls.

Originally a walk-on, Woodside will forever be recalled by West Virginia fans for his fourth-quarter field goal that provided the margin of victory in WVU's 17-14 upset of No. 20 Penn State in 1984—the first win for West Virginia over the Nittany Lions in 29 years.

One of the more colorful players of the era, Woodside will also be remembered for the various patterns that he would draw on his shoes with a marker.

Getting the starting nod midway through his freshman season, Woodside went on to re-write the West Virginia kicking record book, setting school records for scoring (323 points), field goals (74) and field goals attempted (93).

At the end of his career, he ranked second all-time in extra points made (101) and attempted (103). He also held the NCAA single-season record for most times kicking two or more field goals in a game with 10 in 1982. Twice that season he had four field goals in a game, against Maryland and Syracuse.

As accurate as he was prolific, Woodside left as the school-record holder for field goal accuracy, connecting on 79.6 percent of his tries, including a school-record 15 straight over the 1981 and 1982 seasons. He also had the two longest boots in Mountaineer history at the time—a 55-yarder against Louisville in 1984 and a 53-yard effort against Syracuse in 1983.

A member of the all-time team from 1980-89, Woodside was drafted in the 12th round by the Buffalo Bills in 1985.

Game XXI
Signature Game #9
West Virginia 31, Maryland 21
West Virginia leads series 10-9-2

September 17, 1983
Byrd Stadium, College Park, Md.
Attendance 54,715
West Virginia Head Coach: Don Nehlen (4th year)
Maryland Head Coach: Bobby Ross (2nd year)
Barometer: WVU was 9-3 including a Hall of Fame Bowl win over former Terp coach Jerry Claiborne at Kentucky. Maryland finished 8-4 including a loss to Tennessee in the Citrus Bowl.

Game Notes: This nationally televised game was one of the largest crowds in Byrd Stadium history. It was the first time in series that both teams were ranked—Maryland 17th and WVU 20th. It was also the first-ever night game at Byrd Stadium, with temporary lights being installed—lighting up the night for a much-ballyhooed matchup of Heisman candidates and future NFL quarterbacks.

"We really went at it last year," said Esiason. *"I don't know him… haven't had the pleasure, except watching him on the field… The big thing is that the two states border each other. West Virginia brings a lot of fans when they play here. And we bring a lot of fans when we play at their place. It's a good rivalry."*

"Maryland's the biggest game of the season," said Hostetler. *"They'll be ready for us more than anybody else."*

West Virginia quarterback Jeff Hostetler threw interceptions which resulted in Maryland taking an early 10-0 lead. A touchdown by Mountaineers running back Ron Wolfley and a field goal by kicker Paul Woodside tied it before halftime. In the second half, Hostetler threw a 42-yard touchdown pass to tight end Rob Bennett to make it 24-10, which put the game out of reach. With the loss, Maryland was dropped from the Associated Press Top 20.

"This was a whale of a football game," said Don Nehlen. *"Maryland ran an all-out blitz and Jeff threw an 8-yard pop pass to tight end Rob Bennett. Bennett was a big guy and not real fast, but I think he took it all the way for a touchdown, almost 50 yards."*

"This was the first night game ever played at Maryland," said Bobby Ross. *"Temporary lights were brought in from Iowa. West Virginia beat our butts because we were so infatuated with the lights!"*

Terps Offense Off in Loss to WVU
By Stan Goldberg
Frederick (Md.) News-Post
COLLEGE PARK—The portable lights worked fine Saturday night as Maryland played West Virginia in the first night game ever at Byrd Stadium. But the Maryland offense performed like it was playing in the dark. The Terps' offensive unit, supposedly the team's strong point,

hardly looked like the same one that averaged 32 points a game last year and gained yardage against such strong defenses as Penn State and Washington. Because of penalties, dropped passes and even the inability to line up on the line of scrimmage properly, the Terps never got their offense going and lost to the Mountaineers, 31-21 before 54,715 fans.

For much of the first half especially, West Virginia's best defense was the Maryland offense. Every time the Terps started to move the ball, they would make a mistake and kill the drive. It was if they were bent on self-destruction.

"We're beating ourselves so much it's ridiculous," said Terp quarterback Boomer Esiason, who went 23-for-42 for 253 yards despite a badly bruised right shoulder. He throws left-handed. "We are killing ourselves. I am not taking anything away from West Virginia, they are a hell of a good football team. But we have to get the kinks out. I don't know why we are making the mistakes. Maybe it is a lack of concentration, but we have to get rid of them "

"We are having the same things plague us this week, that hurt last week," Terp coach Bobby Ross said, referring to Maryland's opening-game 21-14 win over Vanderbilt. "We would complete a pass and a guy would be in the wrong alignment. A back is supposed to go out in a pattern and he stays back and blocks. They are as basic as you get. We have only been running this formation for two years, but yet we line up on the wrong alignment. We would have a drive going and come up with second-and-15. We couldn't get anything going."

And what were some of these mistakes that drove Esiason and Ross crazy? Here is a partial list. A complete list would take too long.

- With the ball at the West Virginia 28 earlier in the first period, Esiason threw to a wide-open Greg Hill at the WVU 4-yard line… Hill dropped the pass.
- On the last play of the half, Hill failed to go out of bounds to stop the clock after catching a 17-yard pass from Esiason at the WVU 28-yard line. Instead, he cut toward the middle, was tackled and time ran out preventing the Terps from trying a field goal. "I thought I was going to go all the way," Hill said later.

- A 19-yard pass from Esiason to Sean Sullivan in the first period that would have put the ball at the West Virginia 12 was nullified when Maryland lined up wrong on the line of scrimmage.
- In that same drive, a 20-yard completion to Hill was nullified by a penalty.
- Esiason had a pass intercepted when his back, who was supposed to go out as a receiver, stayed in the backfield to block, limiting the number of receivers Esiason had available.
- A first-half Maryland series never got going because Esiason bumped into halfback Willie Joyner trying to hand the ball off, resulting in a 5-yard loss. Esiason then overthrew an open receiver two downs later.

"Some of our people did not handle the things they were supposed to handle," said Ross. "I could point a finger at a different person each time."

If Maryland had eliminated the mistakes, it could have led 21-3 at the half instead of settling for a 10-10 tie. The Maryland offense couldn't even take credit for the Terps' first touchdown. An interception by Clarence Baldwin at the WVU 35-yard line set up a 28-yard Esiason-to-Hill touchdown pass with about a minute going in the game.

They added a 43-yard field goal by Jess Atkinson midway in the period to lead 10-0. Maryland stayed with West Virginia in the first half mainly because of a strong defensive line that continually pressured WVU quarterback and All-America candidate Jeff Hosteller. WVU managed a first-period field goal and then tied the game late in the second period on a 2-yard touchdown run by Ron Wolfley.

But in the second half, the defensive line stopped getting to Hosteller and that changed everything. He passed 42 yards to Ron Bennett for a third-period touchdown and 43 yards to Rich Hollins for a fourth-period score. Tom Grey ran 17 yards for a third-period score, but that touchdown was set up on a 34-yard pass from Hosteller to Hollins.

All Maryland could manage in the second half was a 45-yard field goal by Atkinson and a 24-yard touchdown pass from Esiason to Hill with about a minute left in the game. Hosteller finished the day with

11 completions in 22 attempts for 218 yards and two touchdowns. He was 5 of 7 for 163 yards in the second half.

"Hoss had a pretty good game." said WVU coach Don Nehlen. "He got off to a rough start, but was doing an excellent job in the second half. The offense didn't do it early, but the defense held in there when we needed them."

"Defensively, except for about five plays, we played well enough to win," said Ross. "They came up with the big plays and we didn't."

"I really felt bad for Maryland fans," said Esiason. "We are a heck of a better team than we showed tonight. I hope the fans don't shy away."

"I am not going to panic," said Ross. "Last year we were 0-2 at this time. We are one up on last year."

NOTES—The crowd was the second largest at a Maryland game. The largest was 58,973 when the Terps played Penn State in 1975. Esiason said he suffered the bruised shoulder when two West Virginia players landed on him in the first half. "That didn't affect my passing," he said. "West Virginia affected my passing." Maryland hosts Pitt next Saturday. WVU is now 3-0.

Featured Player: Eric Wilson, Maryland

Courtesy of Special Collections, University of Maryland Libraries, University of Maryland.

Played West Virginia 1981, 1982, 1983, 1984
First Team All-American
Maryland Athletics Hall of Fame
Wilson is Maryland's program-record holder for tackles with 481, and no one has sniffed the lead since Jackson left College Park. Wilson played with Chuck Faucette for the 1983 and '84 conference titles, leading the team in tackles and picking up All-ACC nods both seasons. He was also a first team All-American in 1984.

Wilson was picked in the seventh round of the 1985 NFL Draft by the Green Bay Packers. He played for the Buffalo Bills in 1985 and was a replacement player with the Washington Redskins during the 1987 strike, receiving a Super Bowl ring with the Redskins.

Featured Player: Kevin Glover, Maryland

Played WVU in 1981, 1982, 1983 and 1984

First Team All-American

Maryland Athletics Hall of Fame

Glover played for a pair of ACC championship teams and was a first team All-American in 1984. He followed that by going in the second round of the 1985 NFL Draft. He played 15 years in the NFL, 13 years with the Detroit Lions, where he started at center in every game for nine years. His final two years were with the Seattle Seahawks. He was selected to three Pro Bowls—in 1995, 1996 and 1997.

Courtesy of Special Collections, University of Maryland Libraries, University of Maryland.

"We viewed the rivalry as very competitive," said Glover. "We shared borders and were only a few hours away. Their crowd was very into it, it was always a tough, physical game. Ironically, West Virginia recruited me and was the first school to offer me a scholarship. The first photo in my high school scrapbook is of the WV helmet! But I started going to Maryland for Lefty's basketball camp when I was in junior high, so when Maryland made me an offer, I decided to stay home."

Game XXII

Signature Game #10

Maryland 20, West Virginia 17

Series tied, 10-10-2

September 22, 1984

Mountaineer Stadium, Morgantown, W.Va.

Attendance: 58,353

Maryland Head Coach: Bobby Ross (3rd year)

West Virginia Head Coach: Don Nehlen (5th year)

Barometer: The Terps went 9-3 including a victory over Tennessee in the Sun Bowl. WVU went 8-4 including a win over TCU in the Bluebonnet Bowl.

Game Notes: The Terps came to Morgantown 0-2 to face the 18th-ranked Mountaineers (3-0) and prepared for a barrage of abuse from the WVU faithful. *"Their fans are loud, nasty and, I hate to say this, obnoxious,"* said Terp kicker Jess Atkinson.

"They won and they were still throwing beer bottles at the team bus when we were leaving," said Maryland defensive tackle Scott Tye of the previous time Maryland ventured to Mountaineer Stadium. *"We'd like nothing more than to beat them, just because it's West Virginia... It's somewhat comparable to Death Valley at Clemson. You've got to wear your helmets on the sidelines all the time."*

"Maryland turned the tables on us the next year (1984) ... almost the same scenario," said Don Nehlen. *"They had a big kid from Pennsylvania at quarterback (Frank Reich), but instead of hitting the tight end, he hit the wide receiver on a slant. We had a blitz called but our daggone corners didn't move and the wide receiver took it in for a score."*

Future Maryland All-American J.D. Maarleveld said, *"My first start was against West Virginia in 1984. I was scared and nervous. Coach Friedgen sat next to me on the bus to Morgantown and drilled me the entire way with plays and assignments... They played smash-mouth football and you knew you were in a game after that! Jozwiak was a great player for them.*

"I remember leaving on the bus after the game and we drove through a section with a bunch of old homes. We passed one house and an old lady on the front porch smiled at us and gave us the finger!"

Terps Bring WVU Down to Earth
By Bob Parasiliti, Martinsburg (W.Va.) Journal
MORGANTOWN—Thud.

That was the sound that the ball made when West Virginia quarterback Kevin White dropped the final snap of the game Saturday at Mountaineer Field.

Thud. It was the same sound that the ball made when Maryland's Jess Atkinson connected on a 20-yard field goal just 21 seconds earlier.

And thud. That was the sound of the hearts of 58,353 Mountaineer fans falling as the high expectations for WVU got knocked down a peg in the 20-17 loss to the Terrapins.

The 18th-ranked Mountaineers entered the game with a 3-0 record and were a decisive 12-point favorite over the 0-2 Terps. But the records seemed to be the only thing oddsmakers seemed to take into account.

Maryland's rebuilt offense shredded the WVU defense with a slashing running game for 195 yards and 369 yards of total offense while the specialty teams provided good position for the Terps and sewed the Mountaineers up in the shadow of their own goalpost.

The Mountaineers became human. And in some cases, the less-than-supernatural state wasn't good enough.

"I've been telling people we need to improve, and now people can see that I've been telling the truth." said WVU coach Don Nehlen. "I think anytime you play a team and neither turns the ball over, it's whoever wants the win the most."

"I have to give Maryland credit—they didn't have any turnovers. I kept waiting for Maryland to do all those dumb things I'd heard of so often. When there are no turnovers, it's who has the ball last and kicks the field goal."

And that is about what it came down to.

The Terrapins were a team which had fumbled away scoring opportunities inside the 10 with losses to Syracuse and Vanderbilt, while the offensive line failed to keep the rush away from quarterback Frank Reich, who had been sacked for 96 yards in losses in the first two games.

But Maryland made some changes in the offensive line and everything fell together.

Maryland took WVU's final kickoff after a Paul Woodside 32-yard field goal knotted the score at 17-all. With 6:46 remaining in the game, the Terps began what was a make-or-break drive on their own 13, in the shadow of their goalpost.

Reich's passing and the determined running of backs Alvin Blount and Rick Badanjek moved the ball downfield on the time-consuming 15-play, 84-yard scoring drive.

Reich hit of 3 of 4 passes on the drive for 46 yards, including a critical third-and-7 aerial to Greg Hill for 12 yards.

Blount did most of the rest of the work with his runs, bouncing off would-be tacklers for extra yardage.

After having a 2-yard touchdown by Badanjek nullified on a motion penalty, Maryland settled for Atkins' 20-yard boot for the winning score.

"I thought offensively we did a super job," said Maryland's relieved head coach Bobby Ross. "We didn't do anything to stop ourselves. Today we had it all together. I thought we did a good job of running the football and didn't do anything to stop ourselves."

"The crucial third-down call was called by Joe Krivak from the press box. It was a great call and a great catch. We were expecting pressure and it worked on that play."

The Terp running game was able to find some chinks in the Mountaineers defensive armor.

WVU has been one of the top defenses in the nation by allowing only 13 points in its first three games while forcing turnovers to set up good field position for the offense.

The defense was unable to stop Maryland from scoring, nor was it able to coax a turnover.

Maryland ran the ball to the outside of the WVU defense and stretched it away from the strength in the middle of the defensive secondary, which had made most of the stops the first three games.

"They're big plus was that they had a lot of speed at the wide-outs," said WVU defensive back Mike Scott. "That spread us out on the defense and made the secondary play man-to-man instead of zone most of the time."

"We would be covering our men and then they would run the ball. You'd look up and there would be a back right in front of you. Then when we tackled 33 (Blount), we wouldn't wrap him up and he'd bounce away."

Maryland set the tone for the game early as Keeta Covington took Steve Superick's first punt from the Maryland 36 and returned it to the WVU 14 early in the first period.

The Terps cashed in three plays later as Blount squirted in from the 5 for the score. Atkinson added the extra point to give Maryland an early 7-0 lead.

The lead held for the first quarter as Atkinson and Woodside each missed field goals. Atkinson was wide on a 28-yard attempt, while Woodside missed his from 33 yards.

Atkinson atoned for his earlier miss early in the second quarter by connecting on a 34-yard kick to give Maryland a 10-0 lead.

WVU countered on the ensuing kickoff with an 80-yard drive, highlighting the running of Pat Randolph and Ron Wolfley. The Mountaineers got on the board when quarterback Kevin White connected with Randolph for a 1-yard strike for the score. Woodside added the kick to cut the halftime deficit to three.

The Mountaineers took the lead in the second half when White scrambled out of the pocket at the 7:41 mark of the third quarter and scampered 28 yards for a touchdown to finish off a 75-yard drive. Woodside's 69th consecutive extra point gave WVU a 14-10 lead.

WVU was in poor field position all game as they began each of its drives inside their own 25.

Maryland put together a 68-yard drive which began at the end of the third quarter but paid off in the fourth when Badanjek went around WVU's end for a TD against the Mountaineer's goal-line unit.

Woodside knotted the score with a 32-yarder with 6:53 left in the game to set the stage for Maryland and Atkinson.

WVU rolled up 362 yards of offense including 219 yards on the ground. Wolfley topped the output with 88 yards on 19 carries. Blount had 88 yards on 20 tries for Maryland.

Maryland's Miami Miracle

On Nov. 10, 1984, at the Orange Bowl, Maryland backup quarterback Frank Reich threw six touchdown passes against the University of Miami in the second half, completing the greatest comeback in college football history. The Terrapins, losing 31-0 at the half, ended up winning the game 42-40. "In the first half, everything that could possibly go wrong, went wrong," one of Reich's teammates said. "In the second half, everything that could possibly go right, went right."

In the first two quarters of the game, Miami out-gained the Terps 328 yards to 57 and ran up their 31-point lead, but they didn't do it graciously.

"The comeback never would've happened if it had not been for the attitude of the Miami Hurricanes," one Maryland player remembered. "No question about it. Those guys were the biggest cheap-shot, trash-talking, classless outfit of football players I've ever seen in my life."

He added: "You can almost take getting beat if a team is kicking your butts and they're doing it cleanly. And there was no question that they were kicking our butts in the first half. But that team made us mad, and it gave us a little extra incentive." And the Terps dug in their heels.

For the second half, Coach Bobby Ross replaced first-string quarterback Stan Gelbaugh with Reich, who had a steady, consistent arm. The new QB completed 12 of 15 passes and gained 260 yards. In the third quarter, he threw two touchdown passes and ran a third in himself to cut Miami's lead to 34-21.

In the fourth, he drove 55 yards in nine plays and his teammate Tommy Neal scored a 14-yard touchdown to make the score 34-28. Then, with about 9-1/2 minutes left to play, Reich threw a long pass that glanced off Miami safety Darrell Fullington's hands and landed in Maryland player Greg Hill's, who ran it in for another touchdown, putting the Terps ahead 35-34.

Miami fumbled the ensuing kickoff, Terp Rick Badanjek grabbed the ball and scored again. Now the Terrapins were up 42-34. For a minute, it looked like Reich's luck had run out. Miami got the ball after a bad punt snap and scored a quick touchdown, making the score 42-40. But Keeta Covington prevented the two-point conversion and preserved Maryland's miraculous victory.

To many, this 1984 game in the Orange Bowl was college football's greatest and most exciting comeback. Reich went on to become Jim Kelly's (a Miami grad who had finished his college career two years earlier) backup for the Buffalo Bills, where he was responsible for the greatest comeback in *pro* football history... In 1993, he threw four second-half touchdown passes for the Bills, who came from a 35-3 deficit to beat Houston 41-38.

Game XXIII
Maryland 28, West Virginia 0
Maryland leads series 11-10-2

September 21, 1985
Byrd Stadium, College Park, Md.
Maryland Head Coach: Bobby Ross (4th year)
West Virginia Head Coach: Don Nehlen (6th year)
Attendance: 51,250
Barometer: The Terps finished 9-3 including a win over Syracuse in the Cherry Bowl. WVU finished 7-3-1 and went bowl-less.

Game Notes: The Brawl at Byrd promised to be a physical, trash-talking game. *"We're not a team of talkers, we're a team of hitters, like Coach Ross says. Believe me, this is a big rivalry for us. A big rivalry. We're not going to be playing patty-cake with them,"* said Terp running back Rick Badanjek.

Ross and Nehlen downplayed any talk of bad blood. *"I think it's intensified over the last couple of years, but I think that's due to competitiveness of the games,"* Ross said. *"Which is good, that's what you want."*

"The games with Maryland since I've been here have been very hard-fought," said Nehlen.

The 17th-ranked Terps still remembered the 19-18 heartbreaking loss in Morgantown three years earlier when fans pelted Maryland players with oranges on the sideline.

"If you're not up for this one, you don't have a heart in your body," offensive tackle Tony Edwards said.

"There's no love between Maryland and West Virginia," defensive guard Neal Samson said. *"You're going to hear shoulder pads crack!"*

Another sellout crowd was expected for this version of the Battle of the Potomac. The No. 17 Terps came into the game 1-1 after a heart-breaking loss to No. 10 Penn State, 20-18, while WVU boasted a perfect 2-0 record.

Gelbaugh Comes of Age; Terps Blank West Virginia
COLLEGE PARK—This was supposed to be a physical, in-the-trenches, rock-em, sock-em game under the lights at Byrd Stadium. It wasn't even close as 17th-ranked Maryland scored on its first three possessions and shut out the Mountaineers for the first time since 1950 in front of 51,250 raucous fans.

Maryland improved to 2-1 after a heartbreaking opening-day loss to Penn State. It was West Virginia's first loss of the season (2-1).

"I thought it was, overall, a pretty good performance," said coach Bobby Ross whose team had its first shutout since 1982. *"We came out shooting hard. We got an early break on the first exchange of punts and played pretty well from there on in."*

After struggling offensively in their first two games, the Maryland offense put on a show for the Mountaineers, gaining 518 total yards. It also proved to be the coming-out party for quarterback Stan Gelbaugh, who was 15-for-23 for 263 yards and two touchdowns.

"I was extremely happy to see Stan have that kind of game," Ross said. *"We felt he was coming around. Tonight, we saw Stan Gelbaugh be the Stan we knew he could be."*

This was Maryland's first home win over the Mountaineers since 1966 and their first shutout of a D-I team in five years, when the Terps beat Virginia 31-0. The Mountaineers hadn't been shut out since 1982.

Maryland dominated both sides of the ball, recording six sacks, grabbing one interception and limiting the Mountaineer running attack to just 84 yards. Maryland spread the ball around with Tommy Neal gaining 90 yards and two touchdowns, Alvin Blount adding 89 yards and Rick Badanjek finishing with 47.

The Mountaineer quarterback duo of Tony Reda and John Talley were just 16-for-28 for 188 yards and an interception.

West Virginia coach Don Nehlen said, *"we can't stop the run anymore. When you can't stop the run, you can't stop anything. We can't force anyone to do what we want them to do anymore. It was a mess."*

Maryland's Miracle Man

Courtesy of Special Collections, University of Maryland Libraries, University of Maryland.

J.D. Maarleveld, a native of Jersey City, N.J., enrolled at the University of Notre Dame after graduating from Saint Joseph of the Palisades High School, where he played offensive tackle. Shortly after his sophomore year in 1982, he was diagnosed with Hodgkin's lymphoma, one of the more curable types of cancer when discovered in its early stages.

Notre Dame head coach Gerry Faust assured him that he had a position on the team after he recovered. Maarleveld forced himself to eat and maintained a vigorous workout routine throughout the duration of his chemotherapy, and he lost only 35 pounds as a result.

A year later, doctors assessed that he was free of cancer. However, Faust informed his parents that there was no longer a place for him on the Notre Dame team and was unsure whether he was still in football condition. Faust recommended that Maarleveld transfer to a Division II school.

A high school coach Maarleveld knew in New Jersey, connected him with Maryland, Pitt, Delaware and Clemson. Bobby Ross arranged for him to go to NIH to make sure he was okay to play. Ross subsequently sent him the paperwork to come to Maryland, but J.D. didn't respond until Ross called to inquire. Maarleveld told him, he didn't know you (Ross) really wanted me! After a laugh, he transferred to Maryland to play under offensive line coach Ralph Friedgen. In 1984, he was the recipient of the Brian Piccolo Award, the Atlantic Coast Conference (ACC) award for overcoming adversity. In 1985, he was named a consensus first team All-American. He is a member of the Maryland Athletics Hall of Fame.

Game XXIV
Maryland 24, West Virginia 3
Maryland leads series 12-10-2

September 20, 1986
Mountaineer Stadium, Morgantown, W.Va.
Attendance: 63,500
Maryland Head Coach: Bobby Ross (5ᵗʰ year)
West Virginia Head Coach: Don Nehlen (7ᵗʰ year)
Barometer: Maryland finished 5-5-1, while WVU finished 4-7.

   Game Notes: Both teams came into this game with identical 2-0 records, hoping to break into the Top 20, in what turned out to be Bobby Ross's last year at Maryland.

   "Playing West Virginia, you know it's going to be physical. They're tough, especially in their stadium. With their fans it's comparable to Death Valley in Clemson," said wide receiver Azizuddin Abdur-Ra'oof.

   "For the coaches and players, this is one of our biggest games," said WVU linebacker Matt Smith. *"Last year they just blew us out, and our coaches said they are saying that West Virginia will never beat Maryland again!"*

   Of course, there's the recruiting angle. West Virginia had eight current players from the D.C. area on their roster with another from Baltimore. *"The rivalry has gotten pretty intense, and it's usually a physical, smack-em-up game,"* said QB Mike Timko. *"Part of it was as soon as Coach Nehlen came here, Maryland was the team he wanted to catch. That's the yardstick our staff like to measure our program by."*

   Maryland coach Bobby Ross said that the recruiting battles have *"intensified the rivalry. We're constantly going against one another, and it sure helps to beat the other team when it comes to recruiting players that winter."*

   "I really enjoy it myself," Ross said of playing in Morgantown. *"To me it exemplifies what college football is all about with the enthusiastic crowd and the beautiful stadium."*

   "The thing about playing in the 'Big House,' which is what we call Mountaineer Stadium," said Timko, *"is that we're not the home-town team, we're the home-state team.*

Don't Look a Gift Horse in the Mouth; Terps win 24-3

MORGANTOWN—The undefeated Maryland Terrapins took advantage of nearly every Mountaineer miscue to hand West Virginia its first loss of the season in front of 63,500 at Mountaineer Field.

Maryland coach Bobby Ross said after the Terps got off to their best start since 1980, *"The fumble was a very big play for us, probably the biggest of the game."*

The fumble happened late in the third quarter with the Terps nursing a 10-3 lead when they were forced to punt. West Virginia's Harvey Smith muffed the fair catch and Maryland's Scott Saylor recovered it at the WVU 23. After retreating to the 34 due to a holding penalty, Terp quarterback Dan Henning hit Ferrell Edmunds at the 15 and he tiptoed down the sideline for his second touchdown of the game. He had snagged a 3-yard touchdown in the first quarter.

Maryland tried to give the game to West Virginia a few times, but the Mountaineers seemingly didn't want it and kept returning the gifts back to the Terps.

Three times in the first half, West Virginia had the ball inside the Maryland 30-yard line but only mustered three points, partially because two untried kickers missed makeable field goals. The Terps scored their first touchdown after the first missed field goal.

Maryland threatened again late in the first half but had to settle for a Dan Plocki 26-yard field goal, giving the Terps a 10-0 halftime lead.

The Terps had their way with the Mountaineers the rest of the way. The muffed punt swung the momentum, as the Terps turned it into a 17-3 lead. Late in the game, as the Terps attempted to run out the clock, Alvin Blount broke out on a fourth-and-1 for a 24-yard touchdown run with 27 seconds remaining.

Featured Player: Brian Jozwiak, West Virginia

Played Maryland 1982, 1983, 1984, 1985
Consensus All-American
WVU Sports Hall of Fame

Brian Jozwiak will forever be known as one of the most dominating offensive linemen in school history. In 1985 alone, Jozwiak was tabbed as an All-American by five different sources.

He became the fourth consensus All-American in school history and the sixth Mountaineer to be selected in the first

Coach Nehlen with Jaws, photo by Dale Sparks Photography and Framing.

round of the NFL Draft. He was also a second team All-American by the Associated Press in 1983.

During his tenure on the offensive line, No. 77 guided the Mountaineers to a 33-13-1 record and three bowl appearances. The Catonsville, Md., native was originally recruited as a defensive lineman, but made the switch in 1983. A member of WVU's 1980-89 all-time team, Jozwiak was taken with the seventh pick in the first round of the 1986 NFL Draft by the Kansas City Chiefs and played for three seasons before injury forced him to retire.

Off the field, Jozwiak was heavily involved in community service in Morgantown during his days as a Mountaineer. Among the charities he was involved with were Special Olympics, March of Dimes, Easter Seals and the WVU Children's Hospital.

He was an inaugural member of WVU's Mountaineer Legends Society in 2016.

Game XXV
Maryland 25, West Virginia 20
Maryland leads series: 13-10-2

September 19, 1987
Byrd Stadium, College Park, Md.
Attendance: 40,125

Maryland Head Coach: Joe Krivak (1ˢᵗ year)
West Virginia Head Coach: Don Nehlen (8ᵗʰ year)
Barometer: WVU finished 6-6 including a loss to Oklahoma State in the Sun Bowl, while the Terps were 4-7.

Game Notes: Both teams entered with 1-1 records. Maryland owned three consecutive wins over the Mountaineers, and WVU was coming off a disappointing 4-6 season.

"We want the bragging rights back," WVU nose guard David Grant said. *"They beat us last year, but our place-kicker was hurt and missed four field goals… All we know is every time in the past when we've beaten them, we've gone to a bowl game."*

As usual, West Virginia came into the game talking smash-mouth football. *"West Virginia is tough and physical, and the one thing that they do as well as anybody is to try to intimidate you. They talk, they taunt, they jump up and down when they make a good play. It's crazy,"* said Terp WR Abdur-Ra'oof.

"This is a big rivalry," Terp center Bill Hughes said. *"One of the better ones in football and everyone on the line is a little hot. There's nothing cute and fancy about them. It'll be ugly. It always is."*

"This was always a special game for us, especially those years we went to Morgantown, because we still had a lot of friends in West Virginia from our time in Weirton," remembered Mrs. Jeanine Krivak.

Terps Spot WVU Two TD's but Still Win

COLLEGE PARK—West Virginia's Eugene Napoleon ran back the opening kickoff 94 yards for a touchdown. On the first play from scrimmage, linebacker Robert Pickett picked off Dan Henning's first pass and charged 26 yards into the end zone to give West Virginia a 14-0 lead just 30 seconds into the game—before many of the 40,125 sun-drenched fans had even gotten seated.

But the Terrapins came back for a 25-20 victory over the rivaled Mountaineers in a game laced with turnovers, comebacks and emotion.

The Maryland defense created six Mountaineer turnovers—three fumbles and three interceptions. The Terp running game opened lanes for Henning's passes, rushing for 116 yards and keeping the West Virginia "D" honest. Henning went 22-for-37 for 216 yards and made the audible call of his career. And don't overlook the emotional lift that sophomore running back Mike Anderson provided as he entered the game after being diagnosed with leukemia the previous summer.

Maryland's defense dominated the game, holding quarterbacks Major Harris and Mike Timko to just five pass completions combined. The offense did their part, chinking away at the WVU lead with a 39-yard Dan Plocki field goal and fullback Dennis Spinelli's 1-yard touchdown dive cutting the West Virginia lead to 14-10.

The Terps took a 19-14 lead in the third quarter on a 37-yard Plocki field goal and a 3-yard touchdown pass from Henning to Bren Lowery.

West Virginia's "A.B." Brown, who carried the Mountaineer offense with 168 yards, aided an 88-yard scoring drive that put the Mounties ahead 20-19 with 8:48 left in the game.

Three minutes later, Maryland regained the edge. Two plays before the score, the Terps had a first down on their own 47 and Maryland coach Joe Krivak sent in a running play. But Henning, reading a defensive shift, called the audible and instead passed to the 6-foot-6 Edmunds, who drew single coverage from an undersized Terry White (5-foot-8). Edmunds lugged it to the West Virginia 13. Lowery then sewed it up with a 13-yard sweep around left end for the game-winner with 5:49 to play.

Quarterback U

Generally, not known for its quarterbacks, there was a time during the Bobby Ross and Joe Krivak eras, that the Terps were indeed "Quarterback U!" Between 1991 and 1996, the Terps boasted a string of NFL quarterbacks, with six of them… yes, SIX, all starting on the same Sunday afternoon in 1992.

Boomer Esiason (Terp Class of 1984) started the string in 1984 with the Cincinnati Bengals. Boomer played for four teams in his 14 years in the NFL, taking the Bengals to the 1989 Super

Bowl, losing to the Joe Montana-led 49ers. He was the NFL MVP in 1988. Boomer's now a CBS sports anchor.

Following Boomer was **Frank Reich (Class of '85)**. Reich, famously generaled the greatest comeback in college football history against Miami in 1984, as he came off the bench at halftime to replace Stan Gelbaugh with the score 31-0. He led the Terps to a 42-40 win over Bernie Kosar's Hurricanes. Reich repeated the feat nine years later, backing up the injured Jim Kelly for the Buffalo Bills in the 1993 Wild-Card Game against Warren Moon's Houston Oilers. The Bills were losing 35-3 shortly after the start of the second half, but Reich rebounded the team to a 41-38 overtime win. He spent 14 years in the NFL and is now the head coach of the Indianapolis Colts.

Stan Gelbaugh (Class of '86) followed Reich and had leapfrogged back and forth as a starter with Reich. He played nine years in the NFL and started 12 games, mainly with the Seattle Seahawks. **Dan Henning, Jr. (Class of '88)** set the Terps single-season passing record of 2,775 yards in 1985. He played sparingly for the New England Patriots.

Neal O'Donnell (Class of '90) was the next in line. He played 14 years in the NFL starting with the Pittsburgh Steelers, leading them to the 1995 AFC Championship Game. He finished his career with the Jets, Bengals and Titans. **Scott Zolak (Class of '91)** finishes the string. He played for the Patriots for all but one of his nine years in the league, starting seven games.

But as former Terp assistant coach Lou Corso says, "not so fast my friends." There is one more in the Terp quarterback line! **Mike Tice (Class of '81)** preceded Boomer, serving as the Terps' QB in the 1979 and 1980 seasons. He played 15 seasons in the NFL, starting most of those games as a tight end for the Seattle Seahawks and Minnesota Vikings!

So, on one Sunday afternoon in 1992, six former Terp QB's were starters in the NFL!

Shortly thereafter, **Scott Milanovich (Class of 1996)** broke passing records for the losing Terps, and a decade later, **Scott McBrien (Class of 2004)** led the Terps to three of the most successful consecutive seasons in Maryland football history.

Now, the Mountaineers were no slouch in this quarterback category either, with Heisman candidates **Major Harris, Pat White,** and **Will Grier,** along with Super Bowl Champion **Jeff Hostetler**; and future NFL stars **Oliver Luck** (Houston Oilers), **Mark Bulger** (St. Louis Rams) and **Geno Smith** (NY Jets).

Shoot, in the late 80's I even got two Brittany bird dog pups and named them "Boomer" and "Major!"

Game XXVI
West Virginia 55, Maryland 24
Maryland Leads Series: 13-11-2

September 17, 1988
Mountaineer Stadium, Morgantown, W.Va.
Attendance: 60,128
West Virginia Head Coach: Don Nehlen (9th year)
Maryland Head Coach: Joe Krivak (2nd year)
Barometer: WVU finished with an undefeated 11-0 season but lost the national championship to Notre Dame in the Fiesta Bowl. Maryland finished 5-6.

Game Notes: I-68 from Morgantown to the Maryland line ought to be called "*The Gov. Arch Moore Highway.*" Arch Moore pushed hard to get the W.Va. portion opened in time for the 1988 "*Battle of the Potomac*" in Morgantown, so despondent Maryland fans could get out of the state quicker after losing the game. The ribbon was cut just in time for the Terps to limp back to College Park after a 55-24 loss to the Major Harris-led Mountaineers. What a year that was!

The undefeated and 12th-ranked Mountaineers, led by quarterback sensation Major Harris, welcomed the 1-0 Terps to Morgantown. The Terps' primary focus was to stop Harris, much like they did the previous year. But Las Vegas didn't think they could and pegged the Mounties as 23-point favorites.

"The third game was against Maryland, who was always a tussle against us, whether at home or away. We got behind Maryland early in the game (14-0) but managed to pull ahead by halftime and we won handily, 55-24. I knew then, because we won by so much, that I had a really tough and solid football team," said Don Nehlen.

Terrapins Go Up Early, Fall to WVU in Blowout
MORGANTOWN—Reversal of fortune. Last year, West Virginia led the Terps 14-0 just 30 seconds into the game but the Terps went onto win.

In a mirror of that, the Terps went up 14-0 in the first four minutes, before the 12th-ranked Mountaineers woke up and trounced the Marylanders 55-24 in front of 60,128 rain-soaked fans at Mountaineer Field.

The Mountaineers dug themselves a hole when "A.B." Brown fumbled on the first play to set up a Mike Beasley 11-yard touchdown run two plays later. A series later, Beasley scored again on a 74-yard option play, putting the Terps ahead 14-0.

"Man, they must have our number," WVU coach Don Nehlen said later.

This seemed to wake up the Mounties, as they scored 17 unanswered points.

But in the final minute of the half, Maryland completed an 80-yard drive, culminating with Neal O'Donnell's 7-yard quarterback draw, putting the Terps ahead, 21-17.

Led by sophomore phenom Major Harris, the Mountaineers roared back. Harris took his team 80 yards in five plays, finishing with a 3-yard bootleg to put West Virginia ahead for good, 24-21, with three seconds left in the half. On the day, Harris threw for 150 yards and rushed for 46.

Charlie Baumann kicked a 41-yard field goal on the first possession of the second half following a Parker interception of an O'Donnell pass. On the ensuing kickoff, Maryland's Beasley separated his shoulder, ending his day as well as the Terps' running game.

The Mountaineers went on to score 28 unanswered points, highlighted by a 55-yard pass from Harris to Reggie Rembert and a Bo Orlando 56-yard interception for a touchdown. The 55 points allowed by Maryland were the most they'd given up since Penn State scored 63 in 1971.

"We all have got to get better. We have work to do," Nehlen said, *'Our kids will think they lost the game when I get done with them tomorrow."*

"I'm disappointed how we played, but not discouraged," said Maryland coach Joe Krivak. *"We just weren't good enough in the second half."*

Featured Player: Major Harris, West Virginia

Played Maryland in 1987, 1988, 1989

First Team All-American

College Football Hall of Fame

Major Harris was one of college football's most exciting performers in the mid-1980s. Coming to Morgantown at a time when West Virginia was coming off consecutive bowl-less seasons, the Pittsburgh, Pa., native ignited a flame in the West Virginia football program.

Photo by Dale Sparks Photography and Framing.

After struggling through the early part of his redshirt freshman season, the elusive signal-caller had a breakout game against East Carolina in 1987 and never looked back. He produced 1,200 yards passing and 615 rushing yards in helping WVU to a John Hancock Sun Bowl berth against Oklahoma State.

The following season, he was nearly perfect in directing West Virginia to the school's first-ever undefeated, untied regular season and a matchup against No. 1-ranked Notre Dame in the Fiesta Bowl for the national championship.

In getting the Mountaineers there, Harris baffled opponents all season with his daring, unpredictable, wide-open style. That was never more evident than in West Virginia's 51-30 dismantling of long-time nemesis Penn State. Harris outgained the entire Penn State team,

301-292, and produced the school's most exciting run ever in the first quarter of that game.

As the play clock wound down, Harris forgot the play he had called in the huddle. As soon as the ball was snapped, the entire West Virginia team went in one direction and Harris went the other.

He faked out the entire Penn State team, leaving no less than seven tacklers grabbing air on the way to the most gorgeous touchdown run in school history—a mere 26 yards forever embedded in the memories of West Virginia football fans.

Coach Don Nehlen said of the run, "*I had called 37 and he ran 36. Everybody else on our offense went one way, and Major went the other. He literally ran through the Penn State defense for a touchdown of about 30 yards. After he scored, Major came to the sideline and apologized. He said, 'My fault, Coach.' People still ask me about that play all of the time... If there was a contest for most exciting player, Major would win it hands down.*"

That run and several more like it helped him finish fifth in the Heisman Trophy race that year and earn ECAC Player of the Year honors.

As a junior, Harris was equally spectacular despite not having as strong a supporting cast. He passed for 2,058 yards and rushed for 936 yards to finish third in the 1989 Heisman Trophy balloting. He earned first team Kodak All-America honors and was a second team AP and Football News All-American. Like 1988, Harris was again voted ECAC Player of the Year.

He established a WVU record with 7,334 total yards and became one of just two quarterbacks in Division I history to pass for more than 5,000 yards and rush for more than 2,000 yards. His 2,161 rushing yards ranked eighth at the time on the school's all-time rushing list.

After the completion of his junior year, Harris was convinced to leave school early and was drafted in the 12th round by the Los Angeles Raiders, though he would never play a down in the NFL. Instead, Harris played one season in the Canadian Football League with the British Columbia Lions before spending parts of the next five years in the Arena Football League.

He was inducted into the College Football Hall of Fame in 2009, and in 2010, he was named The Legend of the Sun Bowl. He was also an inaugural member of the Mountaineer Legends Society in 2016.

"Harris was the best football player I've ever seen… He was ahead of his time. If he'd have just been born 10 years later, he would have been all-world in the NFL," said Bill Kirelawich, WVU assistant coach.

Game XXVII
West Virginia 14, Maryland 10
Maryland leads the series 13-12-2

September 9, 1989
Byrd Stadium, College Park, Md.
Attendance: 45,000
West Virginia Head Coach Don Nehlen (10th year)
Maryland Head Coach Joe Krivak (3rd year)
Barometer: WVU finished 8-3-1 including a loss to Clemson in the Gator Bowl, while the Terps finished 3-7.

Game Notes: West Virginia entered the game with a 1-0 record and ranked 17th, while the Terps lost their opener to NC State.

Maryland's secondary would be sorely tested, as WVU wide receiver Reggie Rembert will get Maryland's attention. Terp coach Joe Krivak said they'll throw to him five or six times a game, and he can run the reverse. *"You can never leave him. He goes into the locker room or into the stands, you have to go with him, because they may throw him the ball!"* Along with the 6-foot-6 Rembert, WVU used 6-foot-5 tight end Adrian Moss as well as a speedster freshman James Jett.

All are on the receiving end of Heisman candidate and master innovator quarterback Major Harris's long ball.

"We don't worry about (Harris) when he drops straight back in the pocket," said Terp cornerback Scott Rosen. *"It's when he's running around that he beats you on the long ball."*

Maryland Melts Down to Mountaineers
COLLEGE PARK—Maryland keyed on Mountaineer superstar Major Harris and held him in check most of the day, but still succumbed to

the 17th-ranked Mountaineers on a hot and humid afternoon at sold-out Byrd Stadium.

The Terp defense held Harris in check the first half, limiting him to just 21 yards rushing on seven attempts and 99 yards on 7-of-12 passing. Speedster wide receiver Reggie Rembert was also kept silent in the Maryland heat.

Maryland broke the steamy tie late in the first quarter with a 49-yard run by tailback Ricky Thompson, giving the Terps a 7-0 lead. The Terps scored again late in the first half on a 28-yard Danny DeArmas field goal. It could have been more, but the sophomore kicker hit the crossbar on a 37-yard attempt halfway through the second quarter. Maryland led 10-0 at the half.

That's when West Virginia stripped down, many players chucking pads and braces due to the heat, and came out to turn the game around in the second half. On their first possession, Harris completed a nine-play, 65-yard drive by going eight yards into the right corner of the end zone. Brad Carroll's kick made it 10-7 with nine minutes left in the third.

With 9:34 remaining in the game, West Virginia completed a 10-play, 89-yard drive with a 1-yard dive by tailback Garrett Ford, Jr., making it 14-10.

Maryland had chances but didn't have the killer mentality. On the ensuing drive the Terps Neil O'Donnell connected with Barry Johnson on a 52-yard pass and run, but was stripped from behind and WVU's Darrell Whitmore recovered at the Mountaineer 11.

The Terps had one more chance. After a fumbled punt by WVU's Tim Williams, Maryland's Dean Green recovered it at the WVU 19 with 6:44 left in the game. The Terps pushed it to a first-and-goal from the 8, but were stuffed on fourth down by the Mountaineer defense.

"We knew Maryland was a top-notch team," said Harris. *"We knew it would be a dogfight. But we also had the confidence of knowing it was just a matter of time before we would score and come back."*

Terrapin coach Joe Krivak lamented, *"We're having key people making mistakes. I don't know what we're going to do differently. We had the chance to put it in, but we didn't do it. When you have first-and-goal from the 5, there has to be some excitement. You have to come out ripping and snorting all over the ball."*

Game XXVIII
Maryland 14, West Virginia 10
Maryland leads series 14-12-2

September 8, 1990
Mountaineer Stadium, Morgantown, W.Va.
Attendance: 64,950
Maryland Head Coach Joe Krivak (4th year)
West Virginia Head Coach Don Nehlen (11th year)
Barometer: The Terps finished 6-5-1 including a tie with Louisiana Tech in the Independence Bowl, while WVU finished 4-7

Game Notes: New Mountaineer quarterback Greg Jones finally got his chance to start the previous week, defeating Kent State 35-24 when he went 12-for-25 for 174 yards. A transfer from Miami, he backed up Vinny Testaverde and Steve Walsh, and at West Virginia, Major Harris.

Talk about tough schedules… the Terps played SIX ranked teams in 1990, defeating No. 25 West Virginia and No. 8 Virginia. They fell to No. 16 Clemson, No. 6 Michigan, No. 23 Georgia Tech (eventual national champion, coached by former Terp Bobby Ross), and No. 21 Penn State. They finished 6-5 and tied Louisiana Tech in the Independence Bowl.

"I was the Acting AD at this time and this was my first away game," said Dr. Suzanne Tyler. *"Maryland was sitting in the end zone and I remember a Maryland guy catching a long pass for the winning touchdown (Gene Thomas from Scott Zolak). We were dressed in red in a sea of blue and gold. The West Virginia fans began pointing at us after the catch yelling 'You, You, You!' They weren't threatening, but we still felt like we needed to leave quickly!"*

Zolak-to-Thomas Gives Terps Another Comeback Win
MORGANTOWN—For the second week in a row, the combination of quarterback Scott Zolak and wide receiver Gene Thomas lit up the

Terps' scoreboard in the waning minutes of the game. 64,950 stunned Mountaineer fans watched their No. 25 Mountaineers fall to unranked Maryland in Mountaineer Stadium.

With 2:27 remaining, Zolak hit Thomas on a 59-yard strike to give the Terps an unlikely 14-10 win. It came on a third-and-10 play from the Terps' 41-yard line, as Zolak hit Thomas in stride as he streaked untouched across the middle of the field.

The week prior, the two combined for a 51-yard TD to give the Terps another 14-10 victory against Virginia Tech.

The Terps opened the game with a long drive but running back Troy Jackson fumbled on the WVU 22. Both teams missed field goals in the first half.

This was a defensive battle, with Maryland breaking the scoreless tie just 73 seconds before halftime when Zolak hit Barry Johnson on a 42-yarder to the Mountaineer 9. Two plays later, he hit Johnson again for an 8-yard touchdown, making the score 7-0 at the half.

Redshirt quarterback Darren Studstill took over the WVU offense in the second half after a Greg Jones concussion. He started slowly, but led West Virginia to two late scores. The first was a 39-yard Brad Carroll field goal that narrowed Maryland's lead to 7-3.

With 4:21 remaining, Studstill struck again, leading the Mounties on a 13-play, 80-yard drive that ended with a 2-yard pass to running back Jon Jones, giving WVU their first lead of the day, 10-7.

The Terrapins then made another 80-yard drive, this time in eight plays, setting up the game-winning Zolak-to Thomas combination. The drive was aided by a crucial WVU holding call after the Mountaineers sacked Zolak on third-and-10 at the Terps' 20.

Game XXIX
West Virginia 37, Maryland 7
Maryland leads series 14-13-2

September 21, 1991
Byrd Stadium, College Park, Md.
Attendance: 40,442

West Virginia Head Coach Don Nehlen (12ᵗʰ year)
Maryland Head Coach Joe Krivak (5ᵗʰ year)
Barometer: West Virginia finished 6-5, while Maryland finished 2-9.

Game Notes: Mike Beasley returned to Byrd Stadium for the first time in three years. This time, however, he wore the Gold and Blue of the Mountaineers (2-1) after transferring from Maryland (1-1) following the 1988 season and having to sit out the previous year. He was switched from running back at Maryland to wide receiver in the West Virginia offense.

Backup quarterback John Kaelo started for the Terps, as first stringer Jim Sandwisch is out with a shoulder injury.

"It's going to be a traditional West Virginia game," said Krivak. *"West Virginia uses this as a barometer to their season. If they beat us, they have a good year. If they don't, they usually have a mediocre one."*

Krivak was right. The teams have played in each of the last 11 years. In the last five years that WVU beat Maryland, they went to five bowl games and were 46-13-1. In the other six years, they were 35-33-1 and went to two bowl games.

Maryland offensive tackle David DeBruin said, *"It's a big game. I don't like West Virginia."*

This was West Virginia's first season in the Big East. Maryland was favored by 3-1/2 points.

West Virginia Stomps Terps
COLLEGE PARK—Maryland drew first blood as they punched the Mountaineers in the nose before 40,442 at Byrd Stadium. Unfortunately for the Terps, it simply served to wake up the Mountaineers.

The Terrapins scored on their first possession, going 62 yards in eight plays to set up a 35-yard touchdown pass from backup quarterback John Kaelo to Richie Harris. Everything went downhill after that.

The Mountaineers shrugged it off and *"smacked us in the face,"* said Terp linebacker Mike Jarmolowich.

Maryland couldn't stop the Mountaineer option, quarterback Darrin Studstill or running back Adrian Murrell, who had 93 yards rushing with two minutes left in the first quarter. He finished the game with 141 on 20 carries.

Murrell took center stage after the Terps' early score, sparking a 72-yard drive with a 44-yard scamper to the Terp 28. Not to be outdone, Studstill then got 11 yards after being forced out of the pocket on fourth-and-10. He then hit Murrell on a 13-yard touchdown to tie the score with 6:15 left in the first.

The Mountaineers came right back with another 72-yard drive, led by Murrell and Studstill. Studstill scored on a 3-yard run around the left end to make it 14-7.

Maryland coach Joe Krivak then pulled Kaleo for injured Jim Sandwisch, who could do no better. Yes, the Terps came into the game with some key injuries. But it wouldn't have mattered, as the Mountaineers battered the Terps.

The Mounties later mounted a 63-yard drive in 12 plays, with fullback Rodney Woodard plowing untouched into the end zone from six yards out, giving WVU a 21-7 lead.

West Virginia held the Terps to just 99 yards in total offense at the half, while gaining 229 yards on the ground alone. The second half was much the same, with WVU shredding the Terrapins with two more touchdowns and a field goal while keeping the Terrapin offense impotent.

"We couldn't stop their trap. We couldn't stop their belly option. We couldn't stop their sprint draw, we couldn't stop anything," Krivak said.

Game XXX
West Virginia 34, Maryland 33
Series Tied, 14-14-2

September 19, 1992
Mountaineer Stadium, Morgantown, W.Va.
Attendance: 56,727
West Virginia Head Coach Don Nehlen (13th year)
Maryland Head Coach Mark Duffner (1st year)
Barometer: West Virginia finished 5-4-2, another bowl-less season. Maryland was 3-8.

Game Notes: Maryland came into the game with an 0-2 record, while the Mounties were 1-0-1, having beaten Pitt but tying Miami… of Ohio! This was Terps' new head coach Mark Duffner's first game at Mountaineer Stadium, having coached previously at Holy Cross.

But the Mountaineers may have been distracted, as the natives had become restless with Mountaineer coach Don Nehlen. Four years after playing Notre Dame for the national championship, Mountaineer fans were expecting another run after consecutive bowl-less seasons, despite Nehlen's 87-51-2 record. Nehlen, naturally defensive, responded to the firestorm: "*I'm the most loyal football coach West Virginia's ever had. Every other good coach who was ever here started to build something and ran out on them. I've stayed… and I've had a lot of opportunities to leave.*"

"*If they had lost Saturday against Pitt, there probably wouldn't have been 20,000 fans at the stadium for Maryland,*" said Albie Scudiere a Morgantown businessman and past president of the Mountaineer Touchdown Club. "*Now it'll probably be just about sold out.*"

Mountaineers Spot Terps 19, Win 34-33

MORGANTOWN—There was no joy in MoTown as the fourth quarter of the game began. The score was 33-14 with but 14:48 to play. The Terrapins had silenced the crowd of 56,727 with three unanswered touchdowns in the second half. But then the magic happened.

Backup quarterback Darren Studstill tossed three fourth-quarter touchdowns to lead WVU to a 34-33 victory, erasing the big deficit. Studstill replaced starter Jake Kelchner to a chorus of boos as the second half began, following an elbow injury to Kelchner.

It took Studstill the third quarter to get loosened up, as he was just 2-for-4 for 12 yards. By the start of the fourth quarter, Maryland had extended their lead to a comfortable 19 points after a 12-yard touchdown pass from John Kaleo to Marcus Badgett, aided by the recovery of an onside kick following a David DeArmas 33-yard field goal.

Studstill, an option quarterback, began to roll out of the pocket and scramble, confusing the Terp defense as he peppered them with short passes. He finally hit running back Adrian Murrell with a 10-yard touchdown with about 10 minutes remaining, tightening the score to a dozen.

Six minutes later, Studstill hit running back Ed Hill with a 6-yard score.

Finally, with just 1:20 left, Studstill found Murrell for a 20-yard touchdown, giving West Virginia the lead by one as the two-point try failed.

The Terps had one last gasp as they drove to the West Virginia 35. But Kaleo's pass fell incomplete on fourth-and-8 as Maryland coach Mark Duffner inexplicably shunned a field-goal attempt.

Murrell rushed for 115 yards on 21 carries and one touchdown. Studstill was 14-for-21 with 166 yards and three touchdowns.

Maryland's Kaleo finished 22-of-41 for 254 yards and two interceptions.

Featured Player: Mike Compton, West Virginia

Played Maryland in 1990, 1991, 1992
Consensus All-American
WVU Sports Hall of Fame

Mike Compton was a consensus All-American for Mountaineer football, starting at center from 1990-92 and earning four varsity letters. A finalist for the Lombardi Award, he earned first team All-America honors from *The Sporting News*, *Playboy*,

Courtesy of Blue and Gold News.

Football News, Kodak, Walter Camp, AP and UPI. He also was a first team All-Big East selection the first two years of that league's existence. He served as team captain as a senior and played in the East-West Shrine and Hula Bowl all-star games.

A native of Richlands, Va., Compton was decorated off the field as well for his academic and service achievements. A CoSIDA Academic All-American as a junior and senior, the honors student in physical education received the NCAA Top Six award and was selected to speak to the 1993 NCAA Convention in Dallas representing all student-athletes.

Selected in the third round of the NFL Draft by the Detroit Lions, Compton played there eight years, serving as a starter on offensive lines that produced Barry Sanders' record-setting seasons. From 2001-03, he was a member of the New England Patriots, earning two Super Bowl rings. Having played every offensive-line position during his professional career, he spent the 2004 season with the Jacksonville Jaguars.

He was an inaugural member of WVU's Mountaineer Legends Society in 2016.

Game XXXI
West Virginia 42, Maryland 37
West Virginia leads the series 15-14-2

September 18, 1993
Byrd Stadium, College Park, Md.
Attendance: 42,008
West Virginia Head Coach: Don Nehlen (14th year)
Maryland Head Coach: Mark Duffner (2nd year)
Barometer: West Virginia went on to an 11-0 regular season before losing to Florida in the Sugar Bowl. Maryland finished 2-9.

Game Notes: After three straight years of no bowls, the Mountaineer players and fans were getting restless. WVU (1-0) seemingly took this frustration out on Eastern Michigan in their opener, 48-6 and had an extra week to prepare for this rivalry game.

Maryland came into the game 0-2, after a loss at 14th-ranked North Carolina, 59-42. They rank last among D-I schools in points allowed and yards allowed. The Terps lost to Virginia in their opener, 43-29.

"Maryland (0-2) has a high-scoring offense that seems to score at will," said Don Nehlen. *"I just hope and pray they don't find the secret to their defense."*

"We're hungry for this win. This is a game we've got to have," said Terp coach Mark Duffner.

"In 1993, the two teams were locked in an exciting shootout which ultimately ended in a win for the Mountaineers on their way to an unexpected undefeated regular season," said Chris Boyer, an administrator at

both WVU and Maryland. *"But, what most sticks in my mind was, after a score by one of the teams, an unruly Terps fan made his way on to the field during the ensuing kickoff to taunt the 'Eers. Unfortunately, the fellow got a little too close to a WVU special-teamer (Keith Taparausky) who dropped him with a fierce lowered shoulder to the (not particularly muscular) mid-section. Judging by the collective gasp, I think most of the crowd may have assumed the worst for the deviant, but fortunately the police ultimately escorted him off the field and allowed the entertaining game to go on."*

Mountaineers Hold on to Defeat Terps, 42-37

COLLEGE PARK—In a marathon 3-hour and 43-minute game, West Virginia held on to defeat Maryland 42-37 in Byrd Stadium in front of 42,008. Both quarterbacks were made to look like All-Americans by the defenses.

West Virginia's Jake Kelchner was 15-of-19 for 270 yards and two touchdowns, while Maryland's Scott Milanovich broke his week-old Maryland record with 35 completions and five touchdowns. He threw for 451 yards, bettering John Kaleo's mark from a year ago.

The Mountaineers scored four touchdowns in the first 24 minutes, but only led 28-17 due to three lost fumbles.

On West Virginia's first possession, they drove 77 yards with Robert Walker taking it in from the 6. But the Terps answered in just 17 seconds, as Milanovich heaved an 80-yard bomb to his favorite receiver Jermaine Lewis.

Walker fumbled on the next Mountaineer possession, resulting in the Terps' Ken Lytle making his first college field goal of 25 yards to give the Terps a 10-7 edge.

It was short-lived, as West Virginia then rolled for three straight touchdowns on drives of 65, 82 and 80 yards.

Maryland closed the game somewhat when they recovered another Walker fumble in the shadow of the end zone. Milanovich hit Lewis for a 3-yard touchdown, making it 28-17 at the half.

The teams exchanged touchdowns in the third quarter, with Maryland's Geroy Simon catching a 12-yarder from Milanovich after a 63-yard drive. The two-point conversion failed. Two minutes later, Kelchner responded with a 40-yard touchdown pass to Mike Baker after a five-play, 65-yard drive.

Following a Mountie interception, the game appeared over when Jimmy Gary scored another WVU touchdown, making it a 19-point lead with less than nine minutes to go.

Milanovich engineered two late touchdowns. In a four-play, 68-yard drive, Milanovich hit Lewis for another touchdown, closing the gap to 42-30. After another WVU turnover, Maryland needed only 29 seconds to cover 30 yards with a Milanovich-to-Jason Kremus touchdown pass covering five yards.

With 2:47 left in the game, the Terps trailing 42-37, and all three of their timeouts remaining, Duffner opted for an onside kick. West Virginia recovered and ran out the clock for the win.

Featured Player: Rich Braham, West Virginia

Photo courtesy of Dale Sparks Photography and Framing.

Played Maryland 1990, 1991, 1992, 1993
First Team All-American
WVU Sports Hall of Fame

Former walk-on turned All-America offensive lineman Rich Braham made 37 starts at left tackle for West Virginia from 1990-93.

Braham started every game as a senior captain in 1993 and anchored a line that paved the way for Robert Walker to rush for a then-school record 1,250 yards. The All-Big East selection was the team's most valuable player and recognized on the Kodak, UPI and the AP All-America teams after helping lead the Mountaineers to their second undefeated regular season (11-0) in school history. Braham was also the recipient of WVU's Ira E. Rodgers Award for outstanding leadership, academic and football achievement.

The Morgantown, W.Va., native started each game of the 1992 season and garnered the Whitey Gwynne Award as the Mountaineers' unsung hero on offense. Braham's sophomore season was his first as a full-time starter after starting the last three games of the 1990 season as a freshman.

Braham, who received a bachelor's degree in finance at WVU, was picked in the third round of the 1994 NFL Draft by the Arizona Cardinals before later being traded to the Cincinnati Bengals that season. He appeared in 146 games and made 142 starts during his 13-year career in Cincinnati. He played the early part of his career at left guard and then switched to center full-time in 1999, where he made his last 98 starts.

Cincinnati coaches raved how the former University High standout made such a smooth transition to center, as a new era began of giant defensive tackles manning the middle of NFL defenses.

At the time, Braham was only the seventh man to play at least 13 seasons in a Cincinnati uniform. During his tenure in Cincinnati, he blocked for Pro Bowl running backs Corey Dillon and Rudi Johnson, and protected quarterbacks Boomer Esiason, Jeff Blake and Carson Palmer.

He was an inaugural member of WVU's Mountaineer Legends Society in 2016.

The Miracle in the Mountains

November 20, 1993—the date the once-dominant Miami Hurricanes were brought down to size by a surging group of West Virginia Mountaineers. The undefeated and 8th-ranked Mountaineers posted a 17-14 upset of the 4th-ranked Hurricanes, putting West Virginia into the national championship discussion for the second time in five years.

The largest crowd in WVU history, 70,222 jammed into Mountaineer Stadium to watch history in the making and perhaps the greatest win in West Virginia history. The Mountaineers came into this nationally televised game having run the table, beating Maryland, Missouri and Virginia Tech before breaking into the Top 25. A week later they defeated No. 17 Louisville and began their climb to the top 5.

Miami was winding down a decade of dominance but fought back into the top 5 after an early season loss to Bobby Bowden's FSU Seminoles. Miami had never lost a Big East game; the bowl coalition was in its first year and West Virginia was eyeing a national championship under Don Nehlen.

Electricity was in the air. Snow was a possibility. The 'Canes had ordered kerosene heaters for the sidelines, but mysteriously their order had been misplaced. But prepared for chicanery, Miami officials brought electric warming benches with them. A telling and lasting image shows Miami linemen huddling around their bench heaters, while across the field, the Mountaineer line unflinchingly stared at them clad in their blue short-sleeved jerseys.

West Virginia's defense stuffed the Hurricanes from the opening gun. The 'Eers held the 'Canes to just 14 first downs and 223 yards (only 111 on the ground) on this brisk November evening. Miami was held scoreless in the first half for the first time since 1984.

In the first half, the WVU offense sputtered and tripped, moving inside the Miami 30 four times in the first quarter yet coming away with only a Tom Mazzone field goal, closing the half with a 3-0 Mountaineer lead.

The Hurricanes scored the first two times they touched the ball in the second half. First, driving 80 yards after the second-half kickoff, giving them a 7-3 lead. However, the Mountaineers stormed back, going 66 yards in 13 plays, closing with a 1-yard Jake Kelchner pass to Rodney Woodard, making the score 10-7 with 1:19 left in the third quarter.

Miami responded with an eight-play, 80-yard drive to retake the lead, 14-10, with 12:21 left in the game.

Mike Baker returned a Miami punt to the Miami 30, setting up West Virginia's final score. WVU took a 17-14 lead with six minutes left, as Robert Walker scored on a 19-yard run around left end. The Mountaineers got back to the Miami 9 in the final seconds, but Kelchner took a knee twice to run out the clock.

The Miracle realized.

Game XXXII
Maryland 24, West Virginia 13
Series Tied, 15-15-2

September 17, 1994
Mountaineer Stadium, Morgantown, W.Va.
Attendance: 62,852
Maryland Head Coach: Mark Duffner (3ʳᵈ year)
West Virginia Head Coach: Don Nehlen (15ᵗʰ year)
Barometer: West Virginia finished 7-6 including a loss to South Carolina in the Carquest Bowl. Maryland finished 4-7.

Game Notes: Maryland (0-2) came to Morgantown seeking their first September win in coach Mark Duffner's third season. West Virginia (1-2) had beaten only Ball State at the last minute and lost to Rutgers and Florida.

Maryland had lost to defending national champion Florida State, despite being the first ACC team to own a lead over FSU at halftime (20-17). But the 'Noles scored five unanswered touchdowns in the second half. The Terps also fell to Duke.

The Terps boasted a pass-happy run-and-shoot offense which suited the WVU defense. But the Mountaineer offense was certainly suspect.

West Virginia was slated as two-touchdown favorites, much to the surprise of coach Don Nehlen, who was surprised about the eight points WVU received in the AP polling. *"We got votes in the AP poll?"* Nehlen asked incredulously. *"Did my wife vote?"*

The Terps were 0-2 to start the season for the third straight year. They'd been outscored an average of 50.5-18 to begin the season. West Virginia started the season 1-4, but rallied to finish 7-5, culminating with a loss in the Carquest Bowl to South Carolina, 24-21. Maryland finished the season 4-7.

Foley's Arm, Williams' Legs Beat Mountaineers
MORGANTOWN—Maryland handed the Mountaineers a 10-spot in the first quarter but dominated the rest of the game in front of 62,852 soggy fans at Mountaineer Stadium.

West Virginia had their chances but didn't seem to want to score, as their first two drives ended on mental mistakes and the third died at the Maryland 4 on a Jim Freeman fumble. However, Maryland made up for the WVU miscues with Scott Milanovich's second fumble on his own 15-yard line, setting up Bryan Baumann's 34-yard field goal to finally break the scoreless tie.

Just two minutes later, a Milanovich interception set up West Virginia for a 59-yard drive, culminating with a Jim Freeman 1-yard touchdown dive to give the Mountaineers a 10-point lead at the end of the first quarter.

Backup quarterback Kevin Foley replaced Milanovich to start the second quarter.

With the help of transfer Allen Williams' 163-yard effort, Foley engineered three drives in the second quarter to give Maryland a 17-10 lead and the Terps never looked back.

Foley's first was an eight-play, 80-yard drive ending with a 12-yard touchdown pass to Geroy Simon that cut the lead to 10-7. A 58-yard drive followed with third-string option quarterback Brian Cummings coming into the game, and he took it in from the 3, giving the Terps the lead for good.

Two minutes later, the Terps closed the half with a 68-yard drive and a 29-yard field goal by Joe O'Donnell.

The Mountaineers finally got back on the board late in the third quarter, sparked by Robert Walker's 25-yard run, setting up another Baumann field goal of 29 yards that closed the gap to 17-13.

After the Maryland defense forced West Virginia's seventh punt of the game, Williams had a key 25-yard run of his own to make the final 24-13.

Featured Player: Todd Sauerbrun, West Virginia

Played Maryland 1991, 1992, 1993, 1994
Consensus All-American
WVU Sports Hall of Fame

Todd Sauerbrun was a first team All-Big East Conference selection in 1992, 1993, and 1994, and an honorable mention All-American in 1992 and 1993. As a senior in 1994, he set an NCAA record with a 48.4-yard punting average and was recognized as a consensus first team All-American.

He was drafted by the Chicago Bears 56th overall in the 1995 NFL Draft, playing five seasons with the Bears, and is ranked second on the team in all-time punting average. He spent the 2000 season with the Kansas City Chiefs and was signed by the Carolina Panthers before the 2001 season.

Sauerbrun achieved both his greatest success and biggest problems while with Carolina. He was picked for the Pro Bowl to represent the NFC in the 2002, 2003, and 2004 seasons. Sauerbrun also became the first player from either conference since the AFL-NFL Merger in 1970 to lead his conference in gross punting average for three consecutive seasons (2001–03).

Game XXXIII
Maryland 31, West Virginia 17
Maryland leads series 16-15-2

September 16, 1995
Byrd Stadium, College Park, Md.
Attendance: 48,055
Maryland Head Coach Mark Duffner (4th year)
West Virginia Head Coach Don Nehlen (16th year)
Barometer: Maryland finished 6-5, while WVU was 5-6.

Game Notes: The Terps entered the game 2-0 for the first time in five years. It was anticipated the game would draw the largest crowd at

Byrd Stadium in the decade. The Mounties were three-point favorites despite having lost to Purdue and defeating Temple in prior weeks.

"On a rainy night in 1995, the Terps were off to their best start in years and we sold out Byrd (with its new upper deck) for the first time," said Chris Boyer, an athletic administrator at each school. *"While the ultimate 31-17 Maryland victory came over what would be a down WVU squad that year, the fact that it came against the archrival Mountaineers seemed to validate in our minds that the Terps were, indeed, back that year. Alas, the remainder of that season for the Terps is the story for another book."*

Terps Force Seven Turnovers, Give Up Four, Win 31-17

COLLEGE PARK—The Maryland Terrapins improved to 3-0 for the first time in 10 years after defeating its second consecutive ranked team at sold-out Byrd Stadium. The largest crowd since 1985, 48,005, braved the weather to celebrate the Terps' surprising rise.

On a rainy night, the Terps forced seven WVU turnovers while giving up four of their own.

The Mountaineers took the initial lead on a Bryan Baumann 35-yard field goal. Only 45 seconds later, sophomore running back Buddy Rogers, who had 112 yards on 21 carries, took the Terps on his back and scored on a 54-yard touchdown run, giving the Terps a 7-3 lead.

West Virginia's top running back Robert Walker, who shredded the Terrapin defense the past two years, was held out with an ankle injury. And the Mountaineers mustered only 211 yards in total offense.

West Virginia fumbled the ensuing kickoff at their own 23. Four plays later, sophomore quarterback Brian Cummings ran around the right side for an 11-yard touchdown, giving Maryland a 14-3 lead at the end of the first quarter.

Midway through the second, the Mountaineers' Aaron Beasley intercepted a Cummings pass and took it 49 yards into the end zone, closing the deficit to 14-10 at the half.

The Terps outscored the Mounties 17-7 in the third quarter.

After another turnover, Cummings hit Mancel Johnson on a 24-yard touchdown pass. Joe O'Donnell followed it with a 47-yard field goal, giving the Terps a 24-10 lead.

Mountaineer quarterback Chad Johnson hit Lovett Purnell with a 16-yard strike in the corner of the end zone on a third-and-12 play, narrowing the score to 24-17 with 4:57 left in the third.

But senior wide receiver Jermaine Lewis broke Maryland's career touchdown reception record with an 11-yard catch from Cummings, closing the third quarter with a 31-17 lead and turning the lights out on the Mountaineers.

Featured Player: Aaron Beasley, West Virginia

Courtesy of Special Collections, University of Maryland Libraries, University of Maryland.

Played Maryland 1992, 1993, 1994, 1995
Consensus All-American
WVU Sports Hall of Fame

One of the greatest defensive players in Mountaineer football history, Aaron Beasley was a three-year starter and a first team All-America cornerback at WVU from 1992-95.

A Pottstown, Pa., native, Beasley was a consensus All-American in 1995 after leading the nation with a then-school record 10 interceptions. He was a first team All-American by *Football News*, Walter Camp, American Football Coaches' Association, UPI and College Sports. A unanimous All-Big East first-team selection, Beasley was a Jim Thorpe semifinalist and one of 15 semifinalists for the *Football News'* Defensive Player of the Year award.

For his career, Beasley tallied 19 interceptions. Three of those picks were returned for touchdowns. He had 38 pass breakups, including a then-school record 18 his senior season.

He appeared in 43 career games, making 36 consecutive starts and tallying 143 tackles, including 97 solo. A sociology and anthropology major and member of WVU's Athletic Director's Academic Honor Roll, Beasley was a member of the 1994 Sugar Bowl and 1995 Carquest Bowl teams.

Beasley was drafted by the Jacksonville Jaguars in the 1996 NFL Draft with the 63rd overall pick and played for the squad until 2001.

He then spent two seasons with the New York Jets and played the 2004 season with the Atlanta Falcons.

For his professional career, Beasley played in 121 games, 105 as a starter, and recorded 362 tackles and 24 interceptions.

He was an inaugural member of WVU's Mountaineer Legends Society in 2016.

Game XXXIV
West Virginia 13, Maryland 0
Series tied, 16-16-2

September 28, 1996
Mountaineer Stadium, Morgantown, W.Va.
Attendance: 54,542
West Virginia Head Coach: Don Nehlen (17th year)
Maryland Head Coach: Mark Duffner (5th year)
Barometer: West Virginia finished 8-4 including a loss to North Carolina in the Gator Bowl. Maryland finished 5-6

Game Notes: This Thursday-night ESPN game had 23rd-ranked and 3-0 West Virginia hosting the 2-1 Terps. With an unsettled quarterback situation, Maryland came to Morgantown as big underdogs (12.5 points). But WVU coach Don Nehlen wasn't happy. *"Heavens to Betsy… Maryland told us when the schedule was made that they were playing last week, when I found out they didn't have a game, I wasn't going to play them on a Thursday. We got home (from Purdue) at 3 a.m. Sunday!"*

Both defenses so far, had been outstanding. WVU was ranked 7th in the nation in total defense, while the Terps were 14th. The Terps were 5th and the Mounties tied for 6th in turnover margin. Maryland's challenge would be to stop redshirt freshman running back Amos Zereoue, the first back in WVU history to rush for 100+ yards in three straight games.

Surprisingly, Maryland had won five of eight games played in Morgantown since Don Nehlen became WVU coach.

The game appeared eerily similar to the last time the Terps came to MoTown in 1994. The Terps were big underdogs, which the ranked WVU didn't take too seriously, ending with a 24-13 upset. Déjà vu?

Mountaineers Shut Out Terps

MORGANTOWN—In their first shutout since this rivalry began in 1919, 23rd-ranked West Virginia held the Maryland Terrapins scoreless at Mountaineer Stadium to improve their record to 5-0. The Mountaineers entered the game ranked fifth nationally in scoring defense and undoubtedly improved that ranking after shutting out Maryland 13-0. West Virginia blanked Pitt in their season-opener, 34-0 in Pittsburgh.

"Last year it took us until November to get five (wins)," said WVU coach Don Nehlen. *"And now we have five and we're not even out of September, so that's nice."*

The West Virginia defense resembled that of the Sam Huff-era as they held the Terps to just five first downs and 62 yards of total offense. They also intercepted four Maryland passes as the Terp offense struggled throughout the day.

The Terrapin defense did its part in holding the Mountie offense to just 250 yards in total offense and a dozen first downs. But they couldn't stop redshirt freshman phenom, "Famous Amos" Zereoue, who gained 145 of those yards on 31 carries.

Jay Taylor opened the scoring with a 33-yard field goal late in the first quarter.

About four minutes into the second, Zereoue ran a draw play on third-and-41. He went right up the middle for 42 yards and a Mountie first down. Six plays later he went into the end zone from the 1, giving West Virginia a 10-0 lead with 9:18 left in the half.

Three of WVU's four interceptions came on the Terps' first three possessions of the second half, giving the offense the ball at the Terp 44, 30 and 28. But the Mountaineer offense could only collect on a 38-yard field goal by Taylor.

"This was our best overall performance since I've been here," said West Virginia defensive lineman Canute Curtis, a senior. *"We created turnovers and applied constant pressure."*

Maryland running back Buddy Rogers, who rushed for 112 yards against the Mountaineers last season, had 10 yards on four carries before leaving with an injury in the third quarter.

Featured Player: Canute Curtis, West Virginia

Played Maryland 1993, 1994, 1995, 1996
Consensus All-American
WVU Sports Hall of Fame

One of West Virginia's most decorated defenders, Canute Curtis was a three-year starter at rush linebacker, appearing in 43 games with 36 career starts from 1993-96.

A native of Amityville, N.Y., Curtis earned consensus All-America honors in 1996 after anchoring the nation's No. 1-rated defense. The 1996 Big East Defensive Player of the Year, he ranked first in the WVU record books in career sacks (34.5) and single-season sacks (16.5). As a senior, he was second in the nation with 16.5 sacks for 121 yards. A finalist for the Dick Butkus and Bronko Nagurski awards, he made 67 tackles in 1996, while leading the Mountaineers to an 8-4 record and a Gator Bowl appearance.

Playing for coach Don Nehlen, Curtis made 192 tackles (126 solo), six forced fumbles, five fumble recoveries and 15 career pass breakups. In four years, he helped WVU to a 31-17 record and three bowl appearances. In his career, he made 35 consecutive starts.

During his senior season, Curtis paced the 1996 defense that ranked first nationally in total defense (217.5), second in rush defense (61.5), fourth in scoring defense (12.4) and fifth in pass efficiency defense (86.8).

Curtis was a unanimous selection to the All-Big East first team as a senior and earned second-team honors as a junior. In 1996, he was named as the Big East Defensive Player of the Week three times.

A 1997 graduate of WVU, Curtis was selected by the Cincinnati Bengals in the sixth round of the NFL Draft. In six years with the Bengals, he appeared in 70 games and started at linebacker in 15 contests.

The 2002 season was his last, and it may have been his best campaign in the NFL. He played in all 16 games for coach Dick LeBeau and started at outside linebacker 11 times. He finished ninth on the team with 51 tackles.

In his career with the Bengals, he made 101 tackles and had three quarterback sacks.

He was an inaugural member of WVU's Mountaineer Legends Society in 2016.

Game XXXV
West Virginia 31, Maryland 14
West Virginia leads series 17-16-2

October 11, 1997
Byrd Stadium, College Park, Md.
Attendance: 31,210
West Virginia Head Coach: Don Nehlen (18th year)
Maryland Head Coach: Ron Vanderlinden (1st year)
Barometer: West Virginia finished 7-5 including a loss to Georgia Tech in the Carquest Bowl, while Maryland finished 2-9

Game Notes: West Virginia's "Famous Amos" Zereoue entered the game as the nation's second-leading rusher, averaging 150.2 yards per game (6.5 yards/carry). Future NFL star, quarterback Marc Bulger had become the starter as a sophomore.

West Virginia had won six of the last nine meetings between these rivals to tie the series at 16-16-2. West Virginia came into the game as a 9.5-point favorite.

Maryland's new coach Ron Vanderlinden said, *"We can't let Zereoue run wild, but that's easier said than done. He can make you miss in a phone booth! He's the complete package. He has a fullback's size and power combined with a tailback's speed and quickness."*

WVU Coach Don Nehlen said, *"Maryland is getting better all the time. Their defense is of the multiple type, and they seem to understand their defensive package better. Up front they've got enough big guys to bounce you around. Their ends are great big guys."*

Terp quarterback Brian Cummings said, *"You talk about rivalries at Maryland, you talk about Virginia and then West Virginia. It's the ACC against the Big East, and there are a lot of implications… We're both always jockeying for position to go to a bowl game, but they've made it and we haven't."*

Zereoue, Bulger Combine for Another Mountaineer Win

COLLEGE PARK—On a rare October meeting of these border rivals, the West Virginia Mountaineers alternated their poisons on the Maryland defense.

For a half, the Terps focused on the nation's second-leading rusher, "Famous Amos" Zereoue, while future NFL star quarterback Mark Bulger led the charge. When they focused on Bulger, Zereoue wielded the hammer. Only 31,210 came to Byrd Stadium on this fall afternoon to see Maryland coach Ron Vanderlinden's debut against Don Nehlen and this sometimes-bitter rival.

On the Mountaineers' second possession, Bulger burned a Maryland blitz, hitting tight end Chris Wable on a 27-yarder on third-and-3. Wable caught another crucial third-down pass three plays later. Then, reminiscent of last year, Zereoue opened the scoring with a 16-yard draw play with one-minute left in the first quarter.

Zereoue finished with 145 yards on 30 carries, while Bulger was 18-for-28 for 193 yards and two touchdowns. Zereoue was held to just 36 yards in the first half.

As the second quarter began, senior quarterback Brian Cummings attempted a flare pass to freshman LaMont Jordan but threw behind him and into the arms of strong safety Barrett Green, who took it 49 yards to the house, giving WVU a 14-0 lead.

It looked like the Mounties were on the verge of a blowout when a personal foul was called against the Mountaineers on an ill-advised hit on Terp punt returner Tony Jackson, giving Maryland the ball on the Mountaineer 41 with 5:45 remaining in the half. Eight plays later, Terp running back Buddy Rogers bulled in from the 2, making it 14-7 at the half.

It was all West Virginia in the second half. Bulger engineered a 76-yard drive in the third quarter, connecting with Shawn Foreman for an 8-yard touchdown with 8:54 left. Taylor hit a 19-yarder with two seconds left in the quarter to give WVU a 24-7 lead.

Maryland had a last-gasp effort early in the fourth quarter when Cummings ended a 75-yard drive as he rolled left and threw back to tight end Mike Hull for an 8-yard touchdown, closing the Mountaineer advantage to 10 points.

Bulger led a 78-yard drive to close the Mountaineer scoring, hitting wide out Jerry Porter on a 6-yard score, making the final 31-14.

Game XXXVI
West Virginia 42, Maryland 20
West Virginia leads series 18-16-2

September 19, 1998
Mountaineer Stadium, Morgantown, W.Va.
Attendance: 52,297
West Virginia Head Coach: Don Nehlen (19th year)
Maryland Head Coach: Ron Vanderlinden (2nd year)
Barometer: West Virginia finished 8-4 including a loss to Missouri in the Insight.com Bowl, while Maryland finished 3-8.

Game Notes: The 19th-ranked Mountaineers (0-1) entered the game as the only winless team in the Top 25, losing their opener to Ohio State. WVU came into the game as 20-point favorites. Maryland (1-1) was coming off a 31-19 loss to No. 10 Virginia.

"We're expected to win. If we lose focus, I don't think we have what it takes to achieve our goal," said Mountaineer quarterback Marc Bulger. The key, clearly, for the Terrapins was to stop Heisman candidate Amos Zereoue, who was held to just 77 yards against Ohio State but rolled up 145 yards against the Terps in each of the last two meetings.

In coach Don Nehlen's 19 years at the WVU helm, West Virginia had beaten Maryland 10 times. In those seasons, they were 82-32-3 and went to eight bowl games. When Maryland won, WVU is a pedestrian 47-45-1 with just three bowl appearances.

"I'm impressed the way our players have come together. The attitude of this team is completely different from a year ago," said second-year coach Ron Vanderlinden.

Bulger, Zereoue Master Terps… Again
MORGANTOWN—The combo of "Famous Amos" Zereoue and Marc Bulger shredded the Terps in front of 52,297 rowdy Mountaineer

fans in Morgantown. After an opening-game loss to top-ranked Ohio State and a bye week, the 19th-ranked Mountaineers and their fans were ready to rumble, and rumble they did to a 42-20 shellacking of the visiting Terrapins

In what has become a recurring theme, quarterback Bulger and running back Zereoue dominated the Maryland defense. Bulger passed for 283 yards and three touchdowns, while Zereoue ran for 135 yards and two touchdowns.

Bulger led West Virginia to their first three touchdowns. The first came at the end of a scoreless first quarter as he directed a 92-yard drive in 10 plays, finishing it with a 9-yard touchdown toss to Khori Ivy as the quarter expired.

Maryland had their chances, but couldn't capitalize on fumbles by Bulger and Zereoue, gaining just 20 yards on both possessions while being flagged for 30 yards in penalties.

The Terps finally responded with a 51-yard drive and a 43-yard Brian Kopka field goal.

West Virginia roared back with three touchdowns to finish the half with an insurmountable 28-3 lead. Zereoue finished an 89-yard drive with a 5-yard touchdown. On their next possession, Bulger hit Shawn Foreman on a 14-yard fade for another touchdown after a 53-yard drive.

The Mountaineers ended their first-half juggernaut with a blocked punt by David Carter at the Maryland 5. Carter recovered it for a touchdown in the end zone.

Zereoue had 91 yards rushing by halftime, while Bulger was 18-for-21 for 274 yards.

The Mountaineers extended their lead with 11:03 left in the third quarter when Bulger hit Pat Green on a 10-yard score.

At this point, the Terps switched quarterbacks but to no avail. Starting quarterback Ken Mastrole was just 3-of-9 passing for 27 yards. New quarterback Randall Jones fumbled on his second play on the Maryland 13. Three plays later, Zereoue took it in from the 3, making the score 42-3 with 9:23 left in the third quarter.

Adding to their reputation of poor sportsmanship, WVU was flagged twice as golf balls and a whiskey bottle were thrown onto the field.

Game XXXVII
Maryland 33, West Virginia 0
West Virginia leads series 18-17-2

September 18, 1999
Byrd Stadium, College Park, Md.
Attendance: 33,169
Maryland Head Coach: Ron Vanderlinden (3ʳᵈ year)
West Virginia Head Coach: Don Nehlen (20ᵗʰ year)
Barometer: Maryland finished 5-6, while West Virginia finished 4-7.

Game Notes: The Terps entered this game with a 2-0 record and hopes for a postseason bowl. The Mountaineers were 1-1 and, unlike recent years, have struggled running the ball and have had trouble stopping the run.

"If I were Maryland, I'd be foaming at the mouth," said WV coach Don Nehlen. *"We've given up about 9 million yards (actually 479 in two games) and we're ranked 111th out of 114 teams against the run.* Maryland's star running back LaMont Jordan scorched Western Carolina the previous week for 158 yards and three touchdowns.

"In years past, it was just talk," said Terp cornerback Lewis Sanders of a bowl bid. *"People didn't believe it. It was just a thought in the back of their minds and they said it out loud. We feel we can talk seriously about it now."* Sanders came into the matchup as the ACC's Special Teams Player of the week after returning a kickoff 98 yards. He led the nation in average kickoff return yards with 48.7.

"West Virginia had their way with us the last three years," said Terp coach Ron Vanderlinden. *"They have a stable program and an outstanding coaching staff. Plus, they have a super quarterback in Marc Bulger. He's an NFL-type quarterback throwing in an offense that gives you all kinds of looks."*

"It's the only team on our schedule that we play every single year," said Nehlen of the rivalry that has been played 20 consecutive years.

Terps Rout Mountaineers 33-Zip

COLLEGE PARK—Sweet revenge. In a shocking turn of events, the woebegone Maryland Terrapins won their biggest game of coach Ron Vanderlinden's shaky tenure against their greatest rival. After losing three straight games to the Mountaineers by a combined score of 86-34, the Terps manhandled West Virginia, shutting them out for the first time since 1985.

Potential All-America quarterback Marc Bulger was held without a touchdown pass for the first time in his career, threw four interceptions and lost a fumble. On the Terp side of the ball, potential All-America running back LaMont Jordan made up for last year's fiasco and broke out for 164 yards and a touchdown.

"I was the most surprised guy in Byrd Stadium today that we shut out West Virginia," said Vanderlinden, who went 5-17 in his first two years. *"To see all those fans come out on the field after the game is what college football is all about. It's the greatest feeling in the world to win where people aren't spoiled and just want a win of any kind. There is no winning ugly here."*

Both teams seemed sluggish coming out of the box, each committing turnovers in the scoreless first quarter. WVU also missed a 44-yard field-goal attempt.

West Virginia failed to convert a fake punt early in the second quarter and the Terps quickly took advantage, as quarterback Calvin McCall hit Jermaine Arrington on a 62-yard juggling catch, falling out of bounds at the West Virginia 9-yard line. Jordan took it in from the 7 for the first score of the game.

Brian Kopka added two field goals to make the score 13-0 at halftime.

Maryland padded their lead in the third when McCall ended an 83-yard drive with a 1-yard touchdown pass to Eric James.

Lewis Sanders grabbed an errant pitchout by Bulger and returned the fumble 28 yards for a touchdown, expanding the score to 26-zip.

McCall closed the scoring following Bulger's fourth interception with a 42-yard drive, finishing with an 8-yard touchdown pass to fullback Matt Kalapinski.

Featured Player: LaMont Jordan, Maryland

Played West Virginia in 1997, 1998, 1999, 2000

Second Team All-American

Maryland Sports Hall of Fame

Homegrown LaMont Jordan, from nearby Suitland, Md., came to College Park as a highly recruited athlete. He made an immediate impact as a freshman starter at tailback, gaining 689 yards and being named runner-up for ACC Rookie of the Year.

He began to break out in 1998, his sophomore year, with 906 yards rushing and three touchdowns. In 1999, he had one of Maryland's best seasons ever. He broke Charlie Wysocki's single-season rushing record with 1,632 yards and 16 touchdowns. He added 285 pass receiving yards and another TD. As a senior, he gained 920 rushing yards along with 11 touchdowns.

Courtesy of Special Collections, University of Maryland Libraries, University of Maryland.

He finished his Terp career as No. 1 in career yards (4,147), single-season yards (1632), most rushing yards in a game (306) and touchdowns in a season (16). He also holds the record for most 100+ rushing yards in a season (16) and was named to the ACC's All-Decade Team.

Jordan was a second team All-American by *Football News*. He was inducted into the Maryland Sports Hall of Fame in 2019. In 2020, he became the color commentator for Terp radio broadcasts with play-by-play legend Johnny Holliday.

Game XXXVIII
West Virginia 30, Maryland 17
West Virginia leads the series 19-17-2

September 16, 2000
Mountaineer Stadium, Morgantown, W.Va.
Attendance: 53,007
West Virginia Head Coach: Don Nehlen (21st year)
Maryland Head Coach: Ron Vanderlinden (4th year)

Barometer: West Virginia finished 7-5 including a win over Ole Miss in the Music City Bowl. Maryland finished 5-6.

Game Notes: Following an awful season last year, WVU's Don Nehlen said coming into the Maryland game, *"There were several games (including Maryland) I wanted to leave early, but I couldn't find a way out of the place without getting seen!"*

Both teams entered this game with 1-0 records, with West Virginia defeating Big East-foe Boston College 34-14 and the Terps with an unimpressive 17-10 win over Temple. The Terps seemed lost with a rebuilt offensive line and a backup quarterback.

The Mountaineer faithful would be there. *"There is no way you can prepare for a game like this,* said Terp wide receiver Guilian Gary *"because you can't blast that kind of noise into a practice field."*

"This game will be a big challenge for us," said Terp coach Ron Vanderlinden. "It's an ESPN game, our first big road game of the season before a sellout crowd, in a very tough place to play, and we're going against a quality team."

As usual, Terps running back and Heisman hopeful, Lamont Jordan would be the most-watched player on the field, having gained 164 yards against the Mounties last year, but was held to just 62 yards against Temple in the opener.

"Jordan looked awfully good to me," said Nehlen. *"On one play he went left, right and forward at the same time!"*

WVU's Goal-Line Stand Stops Terps
MORGANTOWN—Typical of this border rivalry, this game was not without controversy as West Virginia held on to beat the visiting Terrapins 30-17 before 53,007 fans in Mountaineer Stadium.

With the Mountaineers holding the lead 23-17, the Terrapins drove 76 yards to the West Virginia 4 with under seven minutes left in the game. All-American LaMont Jordan blasted off the right side for what the Terps thought was a touchdown, only to be ruled that he was down just inches short. On the next play, quarterback Calvin McCall tried to sneak it in, but after a long huddle the officials ruled that he, too, was just inches short.

Even Mountaineer coach Don Nehlen thought McCall was in. *"All I kept looking for was an official with his hands up, and when I didn't see it, I said 'Thank the Lord."* A touchdown and the likely extra point would have put Maryland ahead 24-23.

Instead, West Virginia mounted a 99-yard drive in 4:57, with Cooper Rego going the final two yards to make the score 30-17. The drive was highlighted by a 39-yard pass from quarterback Brad Lewis to Rawlings, Md., native, fullback Wes Ours. Ours was not recruited by Maryland.

West Virginia led 20-3 at halftime, but the Terps valiantly attempted a comeback. McCall engineered a 77-yard drive and dove in for a 1-yard score, making it 20-10.

Late in the third quarter, West Virginia botched a punt that Leon Joe turned into a 54-yard touchdown, cutting the score to 20-17.

A Jon Ohliger field goal of 26 yards giving WVU a 23-17 lead set up the controversial goal-line stand by the West Virginia defense.

But this lead was not without some drama. WVU muffed a punt at their own 9 and it was recovered by the Terps' Moises Cruz. The Terps failed to capitalize and came away with no points.

The Mountaineers held Jordan to only 38 yards on 18 carries, but he still became the Terps' all-time rushing leader, breaking Charlie Wysocki's record of 3,369 yards from 1978-81.

West Virginia's Cooper Rego replaced an injured Avon Cobourne in the second half. Rego gained a career-high 114 yards, while Cobourne had 97 before injuring his ankle.

Chapter 12

2001-2010:
Returning Home: The Fridge and Rich Rod

2001 was a sea-change year for West Virginia and Maryland. Former Mountaineer Rich Rodriguez "came home" after making a name for himself as an offensive genius and innovator. He began experimenting with Glenville State, then refined and improved his offense at Tulane, where he joined Tommy Bowden, and followed Bowden to Clemson where his skills were on the national stage.

Ralph Friedgen returned home after making a similar name for himself as an offensive guru. He teamed with his mentor, Bobby Ross, at Maryland, Georgia Tech, San Diego Chargers, and back to Georgia Tech before coming to College Park. Both coaches were alumni of their respective schools and secured their first Division I head coaching job in 2001.

This one had the makings of memories of Woody and Bo, The Fridge and Rich Rod…

Fridge told *The Baltimore Sun*: *"I can remember it (WVU) being a rivalry when I played and that was a long time ago. I just think that we don't have really any rivalries. Virginia's getting to be a rivalry now. We're going to play Navy next year and that was always a rivalry when I played. Those are good to have… Anytime you're able to play a team year-in and year-out, especially a team from a border state, it takes on tremendous meaning, not only with fans but with recruiting."*

As the teams prepared to meet in 2007, *The Washington Post* wrote: *"Friedgen won his first four meetings against West Virginia, a streak capped by a 41-7 thrashing of the Mountaineers in the Gator Bowl after the 2003 season.*

"We just got killed, [they] beat us every which way they could beat us," Rodriguez said after that game. *"They were dominant. What was disappointing for us was that, even though they were clearly the better team, I don't think we were playing our best or giving our best against them."*

That changed in 2004, when West Virginia beat Maryland in overtime, the first of three straight victories over the Terrapins.

Despite the swings, Friedgen and Rodriguez had compiled the exact same record, 52-24, as head coaches of their respective programs to that point.

"It's been a long, competitive rivalry for many, many years," Rodriguez said. *"I think the two teams have been very close."*

"West Virginia was able to get kids that we couldn't get in school. Maryland's policies were tougher than Virginia's, UNC's, Penn State's and Ohio State's. Until Maryland gets a president who recognizes the value of big-time athletics, they'll struggle. We had a kid who wanted to transfer from Penn State, and Maryland would only accept six of his 39 hours from Penn State," said Friedgen.

Alas, all good things must come to an end. Fridge and Rich Rod each finished 4-4 against each other. During the seven years of this coaching rivalry, Rodriguez was 60-26, while Fridge was 56-31. Fridge "owned" Rich Rod, winning their first four games, including two blowout victories in 2003 and the subsequent Gator Bowl. In a dramatic turnaround and signature game in the series, Rich Rod's Mountaineers bounced back by winning the 2004 contest in overtime and going on to win in each of the next three years.

Rodriguez dismayed all Mountaineer fans by being upset in his last game at his alma mater against archrival Pitt, costing WVU a shot at the national championship and shortly thereafter leaving for Michigan. Fridge lasted until 2010, but after challenges with athletic directors Debbie Yow and Kevin Anderson, despite winning ACC Coach of the year, he was fired for not filling the stands.

But those eight games were something to behold!

Game XXXIX
Maryland 32, West Virginia 20
West Virginia leads series 19-18-2

September 29, 2001
Byrd Stadium, College Park, Md.
Attendance: 40,166
Maryland Head Coach Ralph Friedgen (1ˢᵗ year)
West Virginia Head Coach Rich Rodriguez (1ˢᵗ year)
Barometer: Maryland finished 10-2 including a loss to Florida in the Orange Bowl. West Virginia finished 3-8.

Game Notes: The game was a makeup of the September 15th game that was postponed in the aftermath of the 9/11 terrorist attacks on Washington, New York and Pennsylvania. On top of that, earlier in the week, Maryland's campus was hit by a tornado!

The Terps came into the game with a 3-0 record, while the Mountaineers were 2-1. Maryland sought to start the season 4-0 for only the third time since 1978. WVU had won four of the last five meetings between the border rivals.

"They're going to make us throw the ball to beat them," first-year coach Ralph Friedgen said. *"They're not going to let Bruce run for 100 yards, would you?"*

Bruce Perry had run for at least 100 yards in each of the previous three games, including a whopping 276 against Wake Forest the previous week. Perry, for his part, led the nation with a 175-yard average. Conversely, West Virginia gave up an average of 214 rushing yards per game, including 325 in a season-opening loss to BC.

"If we can't stop them from running the football, it's going to be a long afternoon," said first-year WVU coach Rich Rodriguez.

This game legitimized Maryland's 3-0 record and allowed them to break into the AP Top 25 for the first time in years, catapulting them to a 10-1 regular-season record and a ticket to the Orange Bowl.

Terps' Perry Gives Fridge First Rivalry Win

COLLEGE PARK—New coaches roamed both sidelines as 40,166 fans came to Byrd Stadium to see an unbeaten Maryland team face a rebuilding Mountaineer squad.

The Terps have had just one winning season since 1990, so the excitement was guarded. When it was over, Ralph Friedgen joined Curly Byrd as the only two coaches to begin their Maryland tenures with four straight wins.

Bruce Perry was again the workhorse, going 153 yards on 31 carries and a touchdown. Quarterback Shaun Hill threw for a touchdown and ran in another while passing for 192 yards.

But the Mountaineers were very generous with their hosts, giving away four interceptions and two fumbles.

West Virginia drove into Terrapin territory on its first drive, but it ended with a Tony Jackson interception in the end zone.

Late in the first quarter, Maryland's Marc Riley scored a 3-yard touchdown, set up by Perry's 27-yard ramble, giving the Terps a 7-0 lead.

Assisted by three 15-yard penalties, West Virginia drove into field-goal range, with Brenden Rauh hitting a 27-yard field goal to start the second quarter, shaving the score to 7-3.

The Terrapins came right back on an 80-yard drive, capped by a 6-yard Perry touchdown. With Nick Novak's missed kick, the score was 13-3.

West Virginia came right back with a 54-yard drive of their own but had to settle for another Rauh field goal of 34 yards with 9 1/2 minutes left in the half.

The Mountaineers forced a Maryland punt and drove 74 yards as quarterback Brad Lewis scrambled for 21 yards on a fourth-and-2. He then hit Phil Braxton on an 8-yard dart to tie the score at 13.

With just 2:15 remaining in the half, Matt Whaley scooped up a Lewis fumble and raced 52 yards for a Terrapin touchdown. A Vedad Siljkovic kick failed giving them a 19-13 halftime lead.

Late in the third quarter, Maryland's Randall Jones intercepted Lewis and returned it 29 yards, setting up a 29-yard touchdown pass from Hill to Guilian Gary, giving the Terps a 25-13 with 41 seconds left in the third quarter.

But WVU's Shawn Terry responded immediately, running back the ensuing kickoff for a 100-yard touchdown, the fourth of his career, to make it 25-20 at the end of the quarter.

The Terrapins responded with a nine-play, 81-yard drive, with Hill taking it in from the 1, giving the Terps their final margin of victory, 32-20, after finally converting an extra point.

Game XL
Signature Game #11
Maryland 48, West Virginia 17
Series tied, 19-19-2

October 5, 2002
Mountaineer Stadium, Morgantown, W.Va.
Attendance: 55,146
Maryland Head Coach Ralph Friedgen (2nd year)
West Virginia Head Coach Rich Rodriguez (2nd year)
Barometer: Maryland finished 11-2 including a win over Tennessee in the Peach Bowl. West Virginia finished 9-4 including a loss to Virginia in the Continental Tire Bowl.

Game Notes: Maryland entered the game with a 3-2 record and an unknown future, having been obliterated by Florida State and Notre Dame, while beating no-names Wofford, Akron and Eastern Michigan. West Virginia boasted a 3-1 record with similar wins against overmatched Cincinnati, Chattanooga and East Carolina and a loss at Wisconsin. WVU was slated as a 3-point favorite.

Quarterbacking the Terps was WVU transfer Scott McBrien, who came to Maryland after a nasty divorce with West Virginia coach Rich Rodriguez. McBrien commented on his return to Morgantown, "*It will be crazy. It will be a different atmosphere. They've got great fans. I'm sure they won't boo me. Yeah, right!*"

West Virginia topped the nation in rushing with a 345.5 average behind Avon Cobourne, who individually led the nation (159 yards/

game). But the Mountaineers were close to the bottom in passing, having only 33 passing yards in a win over East Carolina the previous week.

"Our front seven has to stop the run and make them one-dimensional," said Maryland's All-America linebacker E.J. Henderson.

"I always wanted border rivals—Virginia, West Virginia and Penn State were good ones. I always tried to get Navy, as it was an in-state rival, and we finally did (in 2005)." said Ralph Friedgen.

In Even Series, Terps Build an Edge
By Mike Burke
Cumberland (Md.) Times-News

MORGANTOWN—Last Saturday at Mountaineer Field, the reality played out. Maryland was bigger, stronger and faster than West Virginia was. Not only that, Maryland puts better football players on the field than WVU does. The most telling signs of this came in the form of the missed WVU tackles that led to big plays for the Terps in their 48-17 win. It was also evident when West Virginia had the ball, as Maryland grounded what was the leading statistical ground game in the nation entering the game.

Maryland won the game up front, in the middle, on the perimeter and on special teams, and when that happens it's usually because of talent. But don't overlook the edge Maryland also had on the sidelines.

West Virginia's Rich Rodriguez and the coaching staff he assembled is essentially getting on-the-job training at college football's highest level. Of the nine WVU assistants, only three have at least three years of Division I-A and/or professional coaching experience. Rodriguez had never been a head coach at the Division I-A level. But then neither had Maryland's Ralph Friedgen when he returned to College Park. Friedgen, however, 16 years Rodriguez's senior, had been offensive coordinator for Maryland teams that went to bowl games every year, a national-champion Georgia Tech team, and the San Diego Chargers team that went to the Super Bowl.

Friedgen's first hires at Maryland were offensive coordinator Charlie Taaffe and defensive coordinator Gary Blackney, who were head coaches collegiately and professionally. Friedgen, Taaffe and Blackney now form the fifth-most experienced triumvirate in college football today, with 85 years of combined full-time experience at the college and/or pro levels. That total includes five coaches (excluding Friedgen, Taaffe and Blackney) who have been at it 18 years or more, and the 206 years means an average of almost 21 years of experience per coach on this year's staff.

Experience isn't always the complete answer, but when it comes to two programs such as Maryland and WVU that are again making new starts for themselves, coaching experience gets a team a lot closer to that answer.

Maryland and West Virginia share a true football rivalry, as the overall record of 19-19-2 indicates. Forget what both teams call their respective series with Penn State—neither Maryland (1-35-1 against the Lions), nor West Virginia (9-48-2) were rivals of Penn State. They were homecoming dates.

Rodriguez said last year that Virginia Tech (20-26-1 vs. WVU), Pitt (58-33-1), and Syracuse (30-19-1), are the Mountaineers' true rivals, and as far as proximity to Pitt and the Big East ties to all four schools, that's true. But it seems that the Maryland-WVU rivalry has been more of a true rivalry in that both sides enter each season feeling they have a chance to win that particular game. Both teams annually call the Maryland-WVU game their "barometer game."

As we've come to find, the best way to measure a team is to measure it against its closest rival. In terms of history, Maryland and West Virginia are each other's closest rivals. And from the looks of things on Saturday, and now for three of the last four seasons, Maryland holds the advantage on the measuring stick.

Featured Player: E.J. Henderson, Maryland

Courtesy of Special Collections, University of Maryland Libraries, University of Maryland.

Played WVU 1999, 2000, 2001, 2002
Consensus All-American,
Bednarik Award Winner
Butkus Award Winner
Maryland Athletic Hall of Fame
College Football Hall of Fame
E.J. Henderson graduated from Aberdeen HS in Aberdeen, Md.

He held three NCAA records: career total tackles per game (12.5), season unassisted tackles with 135 in 2002, and career unassisted tackles per game (8.8). He was recognized twice as a first team All-ACC selection (2001, 2002), twice as the ACC Defensive Player of the Year (2001, 2002), and twice as a consensus first team All-American (2000, 2001). As a junior in 2001, he was honored as the ACC Player of the Year. As a senior in 2002, he was the recipient of the Chuck Bednarik Award and Butkus Award, recognizing him as America's best college defensive player and best college linebacker, respectively. He was also selected as the Defensive MVP in the Terrapins' 30–3 victory over the Tennessee Volunteers in the 2002 Chick-fil-A Peach Bowl.

Game XLI
Maryland 34, West Virginia 7
Maryland leads series 20-19-2

September 20, 2003
Byrd Stadium, College Park, Md.
Attendance: 51,073
Maryland Coach Ralph Friedgen (3rd year)
West Virginia Coach Rich Rodriguez (3rd year)
Barometer: Maryland finished 10-3, while West Virginia was 8-5. The two teams met in the Gator Bowl.

Game Notes: *"This game had become a real rivalry by now!"* said radio commentator and former Terp player Jonathan Claiborne. *"It* *was always exciting and had great coaches and programs. It was a lot of fun for the fans and the players. And the unexpected always seemed to happen."*

This would be the 41st meeting between the two schools, which have played every year since 1980. WVU had won seven of the last 13, while the Terps have won two in a row.

Both teams entered this game with 1-2 records. Maryland lost to Northern Illinois in overtime and lost to No. 13 Florida State before beating I-AA Citadel. West Virginia had lost both its home games to Wisconsin and Cincinnati while defeating East Carolina.

WVU transfer Scott McBrien cast off the monkey on his back in last year's 48-17 shellacking of the Mountaineers in Morgantown, so WVU came to Byrd Stadium as *"just another opponent."*

Terps Dominate Mountaineers… Again
COLLEGE PARK—Scott McBrien did it again as he led his Terrapin team to another rout of his former school, West Virginia, in front of 51,073 black-clad fans. With the help of running back Bruce Perry and a tough Maryland defense, the Mountaineers were never in the game as the Terps cruised to a 34-7 win under the lights at Byrd Stadium.

Maryland opened a 20-0 lead in the first half, outgaining the Mountaineers 279-58.

Under heavy pressure, McBrien rolled out of the pocket, ducked a charging defender and fired a 34-yard strike to Latrez Harrison at the 5-yard line. Two plays later, Perry dove in to make the score 7-0.

On the Terps' next series, McBrien hit Jo Jo Walker for a 24-yard gain on third-and-24 to set up a 41-yard Nick Novak field goal.

Maryland had two more drives in the second quarter resulting in a 2-yard Josh Allen TD and a 32-yard Novak field goal.

Late in the third quarter, Perry scored again, this time on a 12-yard run, putting the Terps ahead 27-0. Adding insult to injury, McBrien connected with Harrison again for a 25-yard TD, making it 34-0.

McBrien left the game early in the fourth quarter, having gone 14-for-25 for 220 yards and a touchdown. He also had a 43-yard run to set up another.

WVU quarterback Rasheed Marshall was 2-for-7 for 25 yards before being pulled late in the game. Defensively, the Mounties gave up 411 yards before forcing Maryland's first punt with 11 minutes left in the game.

When most of the second-teamers were on the field, the Mountaineers avoided a shutout as Kay-Jay Harris scored on a 13-yard rush.

Featured Player: Grant Wiley, West Virginia

Played Maryland 2000, 2001, 2002, 2003
Consensus All-American
WVU Sports Hall of Fame

Grant Wiley, one of only 11 consensus first team All-Americans in Mountaineer football history, finished his career as WVU's all-time leader in tackles (492), tackles for loss (47.5) and solo tackles (288).

A four-year starter at linebacker from 2000-03, Wiley was one of five finalists for the Bronko Nagurski Award in 2003, signifying the top defensive player in the nation. A unanimous All-Big East first team selection in 2003, Wiley led the nation in forced fumbles (7), was third in tackles per game (12.85) and 11th in solo tackles (7.6). He finished the year with 167 tackles, 14 tackles for losses and two interceptions.

Courtesy Blue and Gold News.

For his career, Wiley finished with eight interceptions, 17 pass breakups, nine forced fumbles, two fumble recoveries and 29 double-figure tackle performances.

The Trappe, Pa., native was a vital cog in the West Virginia defense, helping the Mountaineers finish with a 7-5 record and victory in the Music City Bowl as a freshman, a 9-4 record and berth in the Continental Tire Bowl as a junior, and an 8-5 mark, the Big East Championship and an appearance in the Gator Bowl as a senior.

As a senior in 2003, Wiley earned first team All-America honors from the Football Writers Association of America, *The Sporting News,*

Associated Press, SI.com, Rivals.com, CSTV and *Southern Football Weekly.* He earned All-Big East first team honors as a junior and was the 2000 Big East Rookie of the Year. Wiley had a career-high 18 tackles against Miami.

He was an inaugural member of WVU's Mountaineer Legends Society in 2016.

Game XLII
Signature Game #12
Maryland 41, West Virginia 7
Maryland leads series 21-19-2

January 1, 2004
Gator Bowl, Jacksonville, Fla.
Attendance: 78,892
Maryland Coach Ralph Friedgen (3rd year)
West Virginia Coach Rich Rodriguez (3rd year)

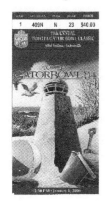

2004 Gator Bowl ticket. Courtesy of Special Collections, University of Maryland Libraries, University of Maryland.

Barometer: This was the only time the teams met each other in a bowl game.

Game Notes: *"I had to talk my way into the Gator Bowl,"* said Maryland coach Ralph Friedgen. *"Debbie (Yow) had me handle all the bowl negotiations, and Rick Catlett, executive director of the bowl wanted to take NC State instead of us. I told him that Maryland would never come to another Gator Bowl if he didn't take us. He asked, can you bring 35,000 fans? I told him we could play West Virginia three times a week and fill the stadium every time. I think it was the last time the Gator Bowl sold out!"*

For the first time ever, the No. 20 Mountaineers (9-2) met the No. 23 Terps (9-3) in a bowl game. This game, a rematch of the regular-season game between the two, promised fireworks. Maryland had beaten the Mountaineers 34-7 in September, and the Mountaineers were seeking revenge.

In the regular season, WVU transfer QB Scott McBrien threw for three touchdowns and ran for one. Maryland's explosive specialist Steve Suter returned a punt 76 yards for a touchdown, while all-time scoring leader Nick Novak kicked two field goals.

After that humiliation, WVU won seven of its next eight games, including wins over No. 3 Virginia Tech and No. 20 Pitt, with a 22-20 loss at 2nd-ranked Miami. Maryland also won seven of eight after defeating WVU, none against ranked opponents.

The rematch would gauge how far the Mountaineers have come following the Terp blowout. On the other hand, Maryland viewed this rematch as one where they had nothing to gain and everything to lose. *"Maryland-West Virginia is a tremendous rivalry,"* said Friedgen, *"and I have tremendous respect for them. If we played each other 11 times a year, it would still be a good football game!"*

Maryland Bowls Over WVU
By Ryan Young
Frederick (Md.) News-Post

JACKSONVILLE—West Virginia had more than a month to prepare for a rematch with Maryland after receiving its Gator Bowl invitation. The Mountaineers had three months to reflect on the defeat they received at the Terps' Byrd Stadium in September, their most lopsided of the season. They also had the momentum of a seven-game winning streak. None of that mattered Thursday, as Maryland routed West Virginia, 41-7, before 78,892 at Alltel Stadium in what has become a one-sided matchup.

The Terps (10-3) scored the game's first 31 points en route to their fourth straight win against the Mountaineers (8-5)—the last three by at least 27 points. "Our team was determined today to come out and prove a point to the nation that we're one of the elite teams," said Maryland senior receiver Jafar Williams, who caught two touchdown passes.

By winning the Gator Bowl and earning its third straight double-digit win season, Maryland (10-3) joined an exclusive club that includes Texas, Oklahoma, Miami and Washington State. To achieve the feat, the Terps won 10 of their final 11 games following an 0-2 start. That was the goal Maryland coach Ralph Friedgen preached to the team this past week. "How many times has Maryland been in the same breath as those teams?" Friedgen asked rhetorically. "That's how much it means."

On the eve of the Gator Bowl, West Virginia coach Rich Rodriguez said Maryland was the best opponent his team had played all season.

Led by quarterback Scott McBrien, the Terps did what they could to uphold the compliment. McBrien, the former Mountaineer who transferred to Maryland before the 2001 season, closed his collegiate career with what he called a "storybook ending." The senior threw for a career-high 381 yards and three touchdowns, completing 21 of 33 passes. He also ran for a touchdown, and set Maryland bowl records in passing yards, passing touchdowns and offensive yards.

"You couldn't write a better script, really," McBrien said. "It's hard to believe it ended like this." McBrien said he didn't think he'd ever play football again after leaving West Virginia. Yesterday he ran off the field carrying his Gator Bowl MVP trophy, which he can put next to his Peach Bowl Offensive Player of the Game trophy from last season.

"He's meant a lot to this program the last two years," Friedgen said. "I think he's not really appreciated by other people around the country. Here's a guy who's won 21 games the past two years. How many quarterbacks do you know that have done that? I don't know if he's the leading passer, or the leading this or the leading that. I know what: I like a guy who wins football games. He has a special place in my heart."

The Gator Bowl also proved to be a special ending for Williams, who had a rough senior season. He started the year as one of the Terps' main receiving targets, but dropped passes early in the season slipped him further and further down the depth chart. He caught only 10 passes, one for a touchdown, in eight regular-season games. Against the Mountaineers, he caught four balls for 65 yards and the two scores.

"I was really happy for Jafar Williams, to see him make some plays," Friedgen said. "Here's a guy who a few weeks ago was struggling mentally and emotionally."

Maryland had 522 offensive yards to West Virginia's 241. Mountaineer quarterback Rasheed Marshall threw for 87 yards. The team's top running back, Quincy Wilson, rushed for 49 yards and Kay Jay Harris had 56.

"We got our tails kicked today," West Virginia coach Rich Rodriguez said. "Maryland played well and made plays. We played hard, just not well in any phase."

Senior Bruce Perry led the Terps on the ground with 70 rushing yards. Steve Suter led all receivers with 84 yards on four catches, including the play of the game. Running a deep route down the left sideline early in the third quarter, Suter tipped McBnen's pass up in the air away from the defender and, while falling to the ground, caught the ball with one hand for a 43-yard reception, which set up McBrien's touchdown run.

McBrien, who has several close friends on West Virginia's team, said he's just glad the game is over. As for his future, the quarterback said he is going to pursue playing at the next level. "I'm going to give it a shot. What do I have to lose?' What are they going to say, 'No?'" McBrien said.

"That wasn't one of my main goals going into college. I was here to be competitive, have fun and play the game that I love, and if I ever had the opportunity, I was going to go for it. I might have the opportunity, I might not, but I'm going to give it a shot. If it doesn't work out, I'll move on."

NOTES—The 41 points are the most Maryland has ever scored in a bowl game. The Terps have now outscored West Virginia 45-0 in the first quarter and 79-0 in the first half of the last three meetings between the teams.

Featured Player: Steve Suter, Maryland

Played West Virginia: 2002, 2003, 2004

Second Team All-American

Suter had an outstanding high school career at North Carroll HS in Hampstead, Md., and came to College Park and was redshirted in 2000. He played in four games in 2001, returning one punt for 3 yards, an inauspicious beginning to what was to come.

He had a breakout year in 2002 when he tied the NCAA record with four punt-return touchdowns. He set the NCAA record for punt (56) and kickoff returns (78). He had a 91-yard touchdown reception, the second-longest in Terp history. He was named second team All-American by *The Sporting News*.

Courtesy of Special Collections, University of Maryland Libraries, University of Maryland.

Against West Virginia in the 2004 Gator Bowl, he had four receptions for 84 yards and returned a punt 76 yards for a touchdown.

Only 5-foot-9 and 194 pounds, Suter was the fastest player on the team as well as the strongest, pound for pound!

Game XLIII

Signature Game #13
West Virginia 19, Maryland 16
Maryland leads series 21-20-2

September 18, 2004

Mountaineer Field at Mylan Puskar Stadium, Morgantown, W.Va.

Attendance: 60,358

West Virginia Head Coach: Rich Rodriguez (4th year)

Maryland Head Coach: Ralph Friedgen (4th year)

Barometer: West Virginia finished 8-4 including a loss to Florida State and former head coach Bobby Bowden in the Gator Bowl. Maryland finished 5-6.

Game Notes: This edition was in Morgantown at high noon on September 18. The Mountaineers entered the game ranked seventh in the country with a 2-0 record, looking for revenge from two embarrassing losses to the Terps in 2003. The Terps, on the other hand, came across I-68 sporting a similar 2-0 record and a No. 21 ranking.

Maryland was West Virginia's only ranked team on the schedule. Maryland still was to host No. 5 Florida State and traveled to No. 13 Virginia and No. 15 Virginia Tech.

This was viewed as a "make-or-break" game for RichRod. After three humiliating losses to Maryland, his system and program were beginning to be questioned. He needed a big win in Morgantown to justify his philosophy.

Joel Statham replaced Scott McBrien as the Terps' signal-caller, and threw for 268 yards and two touchdowns over the over-matched Temple Owls the previous week. Though not untested, he was still green. WVU's quarterback Rasheed Marshall was 0-3 against Maryland and had averaged only eight completions and 72 yards passing. *"It's a new year,"* Marshall said. *"We've just got to stay positive. Erase the past."*

Mountaineers End Terrapins Torments
By Todd Murray
Morgantown (W.Va.) Dominion Post
MORGANTOWN—Sleep did not come easy for West Virginia football teammates Kay-Jay Harris and Rasheed Marshall on Friday night.

The two seniors sat up most of the night in their hotel room as they awaited the Mountaineers' much-anticipated matchup with Maryland's 21st-ranked Terrapins.

All night, it would be quiet in the room, and then there would be an outburst, Harris said.

Oh, I feel good!

Oh, we're going to win!

"We sat in our room and visualized the plays we were going to make," Harris said. "It felt good."

Harris couldn't have known how good until Marshall hit receiver Chris Henry on a 7-yard slant pattern for a touchdown on WVU's first overtime possession, giving the seventh-ranked Mountaineers a dramatic 19-16 victory Saturday before 60,538 at Milan Puskar Stadium.

As soon as Henry came down with the football, he hurled it into the air as the Mountaineers' sideline erupted in pandemonium. The players mobbed Henry in the end zone. WVU coach Rich Rodriguez jumped around on the field with his arms raised in triumph.

"This wasn't a monkey we got off our back, it was more like a gorilla," said a drained Rodriguez, whose team improved to 3-0.

The victory snapped a frustrating string of four losses to the Terrapins, who had outscored the Mountaineers, 155-51, during that stretch.

The Mountaineers could finally say they had defeated the Terrapins and coach Ralph Friedgen. "I think my heart stopped for a little bit," Marshall said. "I saw Coach Rod run out on the field. I saw the fans going crazy. Right then and there I knew it was signed and sealed West Virginia came out on top."

Harris, the Mountaineers' senior tailback, didn't see Henry's catch. He was on the ground after executing a block. "I ended up looking between a guy's legs," he said. "I saw Chris holding the ball, and I took off to Section 110."

That would be the student section.

"I think I was out of breath by the time I got there," Harris said. "They pulled me up the stairs. I celebrated with the students, and it felt good."

Friedgen was quick to credit the Mountaineers. "They are a good program with good players," Friedgen said. "They did a really good job today. This is a great rivalry, and I am looking forward to a good game next year. It's good for college football, the universities and the fans from each school."

On WVU's game-winning play—a third-and-3 situation—the Mountaineers came to the line without a play call. Marshall scanned the defense and called for a slant.

"We weren't executing our deep balls," Rodriguez said. "We were starting to hit some slants in the second half. That's what we called on that play."

Fittingly enough, the decisive matchup featured Henry, WVU's most dangerous receiver, against Maryland's best cornerback Dominique Foxworth. It was a matchup that did not always work in WVU's favor Saturday.

"They won a lot of those battles, but we won one at the end," Rodriguez said. "I thought Rasheed made a big throw."

Marshall said the play developed perfectly. "It was a simple play," he said. "We run it all the time in practice. All it was was two slant routes. I looked the safety to the left and tried to get the linebacker to flow left. I saw them take the jump left, and I just came back right and there 'Slim' was."

Rodriguez awarded two game balls Saturday. The first ball went to a WVU defense that limited Maryland (2-1) to one touchdown and three field goals. The Terrapins threw for only 108 yards and rushed for 187.

WVU cornerback Adam "Pac-Man" Jones intercepted two passes and recorded a team-high eight tackles. Fellow cornerback Anthony Mims tallied the first interception of his career in the second quarter.

"We played really well on defense," WVU defensive coordinator Jeff Casteel said. "All of the credit goes to the kids. They hung in there. We asked them to be able to take their best shot and be able to play the next two or three snaps. That's what we haven't been able to do in the previous games. Maryland's a great football team, powerful, down-hill physical football, and our guys answered the bell today."

The second game ball went to the oft-maligned Marshall, who battled back from a 3-for-9 first-half performance and completed 7 of 11 passes for 92 yards and the game-winning touchdown. Marshall also ran for 47 yards.

Harris, who had been receiving treatment on his sore hamstring all week, helped out by rushing for 142 yards and one touchdown. That score on a 6-yard burst in the opening quarter was set up by the first of Jones' two interceptions.

The Mountaineers intercepted two passes and recovered a fumble in the first quarter, but the offense could capitalize only once. Meanwhile, Maryland pulled to 7-3 on Nick Novak's 31-yard field goal with 11:48 left in the second quarter.

Brad Cooper missed a field-goal attempt with 26 seconds left in the half, and the Mountaineers settled for a 7-3 lead.

Cooper's 45-yard field goal gave WVU a 10-3 advantage before the Terrapins rallied. Joel Statham connected with Derrick Fenner on a 27-yard scoring pass that knotted the score at 10 with 1:21 left in the quarter.

The battle of the field goals continued in the final quarter. Novak hit a 46-yarder that made it 13-10, Maryland, with 9:23 to play. Cooper responded with a 37-yarder that tied matters at 13 at the 6:24 mark.

Each kicker had a chance to win the game in the final 1:15, but Novak was wide on his 49-yarder, and Cooper's 39-yarder was blocked with just 5.6 seconds to play.

"They blocked a kick and guys' heads just dropped," Marshall said. "I said, 'Pick your head up! We get a shot.' If we want to win the game, we have to believe in it. I think they believe in it."

The Mountaineers won the overtime coin flip and elected to begin on defense. WVU held Maryland to a 33-yard Novak field goal. Two Marshall runs and two Harris carries brought the Mountaineers to the 7, where WVU ended the game in dramatic fashion with the slant pass to Henry.

"I'm really proud of our guys," Rodriguez said. "I thought they fought all the way to the end. I thought Maryland did the same thing. They've got a great ballclub. They're very well coached.

"I really like the chemistry and leadership of our team. The whole preseason camp and all summer, all they were asked about was the Maryland game. It was hard to keep them focused. This week, I knew they were ready to play. We didn't play our best game, but part of that was due to them. We fought, we scratched, we hung in there and made the plays in the end to win it."

Postscript: For 24 consecutive years, I've hoped for a tie. In Saturday's rendition of the Battle of the Potomac, I almost got it, as both the Maryland Terrapins and West Virginia Mountaineers tried hard to give the game to each other. Despite the raucous sellout crowd in MoTown, the Mountaineers did not look like a 7th-ranked team; but neither did the Terps appear to be an 18th-ranked power. This became the Fridge's first losing season.

Featured Player: D'Qwell Jackson, Maryland

Played WVU 2002, 2003, 2004
Consensus All-American

As a freshman in 2002, Jackson saw action in all 14 games and led all freshmen in tackles with 51, including 38 solo stops. As a sophomore, he started all 13 games at middle linebacker and led the team with 136 tackles (90 solo). Jackson earned second team All-ACC honors that year.

Having established himself as the leader of the Terrapin defense, Jackson started all 11 games in 2004 and led the ACC with 123 tackles. He was a first team All-American by Collegefootballnews.com and second team by Rivals.com,

Courtesy of Special Collections, University of Maryland Libraries, University of Maryland.

also receiving All-America honorable mention by *Pro Football Weekly*.

Jackson entered his senior year on the preseason watch list for the Bednarik, Lombardi, Nagurski and Lott Awards. He became a three-time All-ACC performer after finishing the season with 137 tackles, 6.5 for loss, four sacks and two interceptions. Jackson was also named ACC Defensive Player of the Year, joining E.J. Henderson as the only Terps to earn this honor.

Jackson became only the seventh player in school history to record over 400 tackles in a career. His 447 tackles rank fourth on Maryland's all-time record list behind linebackers Eric Wilson (481, 1981-84), E.J. Henderson (473, 1999-2002) and Chuck Faucette (466, 1983-86). He also joined Ratcliff Thomas (1993–95) and Henderson (2000–02) as the only Maryland players to lead the team in tackles over three consecutive seasons.

Featured Player: Adam Jones, West Virginia

Played Maryland 2003, 2004, 2005

First Team All-American

A graduate of Westlake HS in Atlanta, Ga., Adam Jones was named to collegefootballnews.com's All-America first team and was an honorable mention All-American at kick returner. Jones was also named Big East Special Teams Player of the Year. His 76-yard punt return against East Carolina was his season-long return and the only punt return for a touchdown in Jones' career. He ended his college career in the 2005 Gator Bowl.

Photo by Randy Litzinger.

Jones is second on West Virginia's career kickoff return yardage list with 1,475 yards. He is 11th on the school's career punt return yardage list with 404 yards, while his 10.92 yards per punt return is the sixth most in school history.

As a junior in 2004, he was the secondary captain and led the team in tackles and interceptions. Jones also played briefly on offense, as well as returning punts and kickoffs for the second season. He was named first team All-Big East as a defensive back and honorable mention All-American by several sources.

Game XLIV
West Virginia 31, Maryland 19
Series tied at 21-21-2

September 17, 2005
Byrd Stadium, College Park, Md.
Attendance: 52,413
West Virginia Head Coach: Rich Rodriguez (5th year)
Maryland Head Coach: Ralph Friedgen (5th year)
Barometer: Maryland went on to a 5-6 record, and West Virginia went 11-1 with a Sugar Bowl victory over Georgia and No. 5 final rating.

    Game Notes: The Terps (1-1) came into this game as a three-point favorite, seeking a measure of revenge after having lost to WVU last year

19-16 in overtime. It would be a tough row to hoe, as West Virginia (2-0) led the nation in total defense by allowing an average of only 128.5 yards per game. The Mounties were also third in the nation in pass defense, allowing just 80.5 yards per game. The Terps' offense started eight players who began their college career a mere two weeks ago.

Maryland coach Ralph Friedgen said of his youngsters, *"I know we're going to be very, very good, I just don't know when."*

The matchup had been dead-even the last 16 years (8-8) and Maryland led this close rivalry 21-20-2. *"I played here in the early '80's and it was a rivalry then,"* said WVU coach Rich Rodriguez. *"They've had a good team with some good players and they've beat us pretty good."*

West Virginia had some burgeoning stars in QB Pat White, fullback Owen Schmitt and tailback Steve Slaton. The latter two had planned on playing for Maryland but were spurned by Friedgen.

White Leads Mountaineers to 31-19 Win Over Terps

COLLEGE PARK—In this annual barometer game, West Virginia came to Byrd Stadium armed and ready, while the Terps fumbled, stumbled and struggled. Maryland was held to just 50 yards rushing— the entire game—by a domineering Mountie defense coupled with an inept Terp ground game. The seventh-largest crowd in Byrd Stadium history, 52,413 witnessed the Maryland collapse, as Mountaineer running backs racked up 301 yards on the ground.

In a glimpse of things to come, redshirt freshman quarterback Pat White entered the game late in the third quarter with West Virginia leading 7-6. He proceeded to lead three WVU touchdown drives, breaking the game wide open. He only passed for 29 yards (3-for-5) but led the Mounties to 24 points and 144 yards in the fourth quarter and gained 62 yards on the ground.

The scoring began six minutes into the second quarter when Jason Gwaltney scored on a 1-yard dive following a 97-yard drive, putting WVU up 7-0.

Maryland responded with a 33-yard Dan Ennis field goal at the end of the first half, closing the gap to 7-3. He hit another field goal— this one 34 yards—toward the end of the third quarter.

This is when WVU starting quarterback Adam Bednarik went down, and White began his generalship beginning at his own 47. Darius Reynaud gained 27 yards on a flanker reverse and fullback Owen Schmitt capped it off with a 3-yard dive, giving the Mountaineers a 14-6 lead with 14:52 left in the game.

Four minutes later, Pernell Williams finished a 57-yard drive with a 1-yard run, raising the score to 21-6. The drive featured Schmitt runs of 20 and 34 yards.

It took Maryland just 19 seconds to respond as quarterback Sam Hollenbach hit tight end Vernon Davis with a 73-yard pass and run for a touchdown. The Mounties fumbled away the ensuing kickoff and Hollenbach made the Mountaineers pay, as he hit Jo Jo Walker with a 12-yard touchdown to close the score to 21-19 with 8:24 left in the game.

The West Virginia defense stiffened as WVU locked up the game with a 3-1/2-minute drive, with Gwaltney posting his second TD of the day on a 15-yard score. WVU's Pat McAfee closed the scoring with a 40-yard field goal.

Hollenbach finished 20-for-31 for 291 yards and two TD's.

Featured Player: Vernon Davis, Maryland

Played West Virginia 2003, 2004, 2005
Consensus All-American

Vernon Davis attended nearby Dunbar High School in Washington, D.C., and was one of the most highly recruited players his senior year. As a freshman in 2003, Davis saw the most consistent action of any true freshman, playing in all 13 contests. He had five receptions for 87 yards (11.8 avg) and led the kickoff-coverage unit with eight solo tackles.

Photo by Randy Litzinger.

In 2005, Davis was a consensus All-American and All-Atlantic Coast Conference first-team selection. He was a finalist for the Mackey Award, given to the nation's top tight end. He started every game, leading the team with 51 receptions and the ACC with 871 receiving yards (17.1 avg). His six touchdown catches rank tenth on the school's season-record list. His 51 receptions also rank 10th on Maryland's season chart while his 871 yards rank fifth.

Davis seemingly lived in the weight room, setting Terp records for a tight end in the bench press (460 pounds), power-clean (380 pounds), index (824 pounds) and squat (685 pounds). He finished his college career with 1,371 yards on 83 receptions for 16.5 yards per catch, the best average of any tight end drafted in the first round to that time.

Game XLV
West Virginia 45, Maryland 24
West Virginia leads series 22-21-2

September 14, 2006
Mountaineer Field at Mylan Puskar Stadium, Morgantown, W.Va.
Attendance: 60,513
West Virginia Coach Rich Rodriguez (6th year)
Maryland Coach: Ralph Friedgen (6th year)
Barometer: West Virginia finished 11-2 including a Gator Bowl victory over Georgia Tech and a No. 10 ranking. Maryland finished 9-4 including a victory in the Champs Sports Bowl over Purdue.

Game Notes: This was a Thursday night game. *"I did a stupid thing," said Ralph Friedgen. The head of ESPN begged me to play West Virginia on a Thursday night. All my coaches said not to do it, but I thought the exposure would be good for us. It wasn't a good idea."*

West Virginia (2-0) hosted Maryland (2-0) in this Thursday night showcase. The showcase was not only for the 5th-ranked Mountaineers, but their tailback Steve Slaton, who was eager to play for Maryland until The Fridge withdrew his scholarship offer. Slaton went up the road to Morgantown and now faced his expected coach. Slaton was fifth in the nation in rushing, averaging 154 yards per game.

Owen Schmitt joined Slaton as a spurned Terp in the Mountaineer backfield and broke out in last year's game for 80 yards against the Terps. The key might have been the continued growth and maturity of quarterback Pat White. White came into the game last year when the starting quarterback was injured and hadn't looked back. He led three fourth-quarter TD drives as the Mounties rolled 31-19.

Slaton, White Roll Over Terps

MORGANTOWN—The game was over almost as soon as it began, as the West Virginia Mountaineers rolled up 28 unanswered points and 230 yards of total offense in the first quarter. Much of WVU's early success can be attributed to tailback Steve Slaton, who was spurned by Maryland before coming to Morgantown.

A national television audience, along with 60,513 raucous fans, watched the dismantling of the Terps on this Thursday night game.

Slaton gained 145 yards and two touchdowns on eight carries and West Virginia scored on all four possessions in the first quarter. Just 3:07 into the game, Slaton scored on a 38-yard sweep after a 69-yard drive to start the onslaught.

Maryland attempted a reverse on the ensuing kickoff but fumbled the ball on their own 11. Three plays later, quarterback Pat White hit Darius Reynaud for a 5-yard touchdown.

On their next possession, Slaton scored on a 37-yard sweep, making the score 21-0.

West Virginia intercepted a Sam Hollenbach pass and Slaton promptly took off for a 52-yard gain, being taken down at the 2. He tried to punch it in but fumbled into the end zone where Mountaineer tight end Brad Palmer dove on it for another WVU score.

Maryland finally broke the ice with a 15-play, 80-yard drive for their first score on a Hollenbach-to-Joey Haynos 6-yard TD.

West Virginia's Pat McAfee and Maryland's Dan Ennis exchanged field goals before Reynaud returned the Terps' kickoff 96 yards for another Mountaineer touchdown, making the score 38-10 at the half.

Maryland actually "won" the second half 14-10, but it was too little, too late for a Terp comeback.

Slaton wound up with 195 yards rushing and two touchdowns. Fullback Owen Schmitt, also spurned by the Terps, added 55 yards, while White chipped in 85 of his own along with a TD. He also was 6-for-9 for 46 yards and another touchdown.

Maryland's Hollenbach was 24-for-45 for 211 yards with two touchdowns and two interceptions.

Featured Player: Dan Mozes, West Virginia

Played Maryland 2003, 2004, 2005, 2006
Consensus All-American
Dave Rimington Trophy Winner
WVU Sports Hall of Fame

Dan Mozes, a four-year starter from 2003-06, was one of the best offensive linemen ever at WVU and helped lead the Mountaineers to one of the greatest periods in WVU football history.

A native of Washington, Pa., Mozes was one of the main cogs of an offensive line that led WVU to a 38-12 overall record, 22-5 mark

Photo by Randy Litzinger.

in the Big East, three conference championships, four bowl appearances, including the first BCS bowl appearance and win in the school's history (38-35 win over Georgia in the Sugar Bowl).

As a senior in 2006, Mozes won the Rimington Trophy, signifying the nation's best center, and became the first player in school history to win a national player of the year honor. He earned consensus All-America honors, one of 11 Mountaineers in school history to do so. Mozes earned All-America first-team honors from the AFCA, FWAA, Walter Camp, *Sporting News*, AP, ESPN, Rivals and Scout.

In 2005, Mozes helped lead the Mountaineers to an 11-1 record and a 7-0 mark in the Big East. WVU participated and won its first BCS game in school history, defeating Georgia in the Sugar Bowl in Atlanta. Mozes started the first three games at guard that season before moving to center. He earned Associated Press All-America second-team honors, All-Big East first-team honors and was a Rimington Trophy finalist.

Mozes played in the Senior Bowl and signed as a free agent with the Minnesota Vikings in 2007. He sustained a season-ending knee injury in August and missed the entire 2007 season. Mozes returned for training camp in Minnesota the next summer before retiring from the game in 2008.

Game XLVI
West Virginia 31, Maryland 14
West Virginia leads series 23-21-2

September 13, 2007
Byrd Stadium, College Park, Md.
Attendance: 53,107
West Virginia Head Coach: Rich Rodriguez (7th year)
Maryland Head Coach: Ralph Friedgen (7th year)
Barometer: Maryland finished 6-7 with a loss in the Emerald Bowl. West Virginia finished 11-2 including a Fiesta Bowl victory and a No. 6 ranking.

Game Notes: Maryland seemed to be reeling after the embarrassment on national TV to the Mountaineers last year. They fell behind by 28-0 in the first quarter and never recovered. It even overflowed into the Terps' bowl victory over Purdue, but they still hadn't gotten over the stigma from last year's game in Morgantown. The rematch was another Thursday night game, as the Terps hosted No. 4 West Virginia in hopes of shedding the Mountaineer albatross.

The teams wouldn't meet again until 2010, Maryland bumping WVU in favor of a questionable home-and-home series with California. So, this would be the last time in this decade to get even with WVU, as the series stood at 22-21-2 in favor of the Mountaineers.

The Terp defense was ranked 7th in the nation, giving up only 175 yards per game. But they needed to be on their toes to stop Mountaineer star running back Steve Slaton, who was supposed to go to Maryland. Teamed with roommate Patrick White, the pair formed one of the few Heisman candidate teammates. West Virginia, on the other hand, was ranked 7th nationally in total offense, 2nd in rushing and 4th in scoring. Slaton was the nation's leader in career touchdowns (43), rushing yards per game (125.1), points per game (10.3) and yards per carry (6.34).

Postscript: Rodriguez quit after losing to Pitt in regular-season finale. Bill Stewart coached the upcoming Fiesta Bowl and led West Virginia to a 48-28 victory over Oklahoma.

Slaton Scores 3 TDs to Lead West Virginia past Maryland

COLLEGE PARK—The setting was near perfect for this "final" contest: a gloriously clear night sky in the low 70's, a national television audience on ESPN's Thursday Night Football, and the fifth-largest crowd ever (53,107) to squeeze into Chevy Chase Bank Field at Byrd Stadium.

The stadium was electric. The Terps had promoted it as a "black-out" and the entire student section wore black to match the Terps' jerseys. Anticipation was high, as the Terps were poised to upset the 4th-ranked Mountaineers.

From the opening gun, the Terps were playing with reckless abandon. Emotion and the hostile home crowd can get a team fired up. But eventually, talent trumps emotion, and it did in College Park this night as the Mounties righted their ship and prevailed 31-14.

Hoping to avoid another slow start like last year, the Terps were determined to start strong. However, they experienced déjà vu, as Terp quarterback Jordan Steffy fumbled the first snap of the game, recovered by Johnny Dingle at the Terp 22. Two plays later, Mountaineer quarterback Pat White opened the scoring with a 20-yard scamper. Just 40 seconds had elapsed.

Unlike last year, though, the Terps didn't fold up their tent. Maryland engineered a 75-yard drive, featuring a 33-yard pass from Steffy to Darrius Heyward-Bey on third-and-10 from the West Virginia 49. Keon Lattimore ran in from the 4 to tie the game at 7-7.

The Terps battled evenly with the Mountaineers for the first quarter and a half, but WVU's duo of running backs—All-American Steve Slaton and freshman Noel Devine—eventually broke loose and combined for 280 rushing yards, spelling the end of the Terps' dream of an upset.

Slaton scored again in the second quarter on a 22-yard rush to go into the half with a 14-7 Mountaineer lead.

It was all West Virginia from then on. Slaton scored twice more, set up by gains of 31 and 76 yards from his backup Devine. Pat McAfee added a 32-yard field goal before the Terps were able to muster another score when Danny Oquendo caught a 22-yard Steffy pass to make the final 31-14.

WVU outrushed the Terps 353-89.

Featured Player: Steve Slaton, West Virginia

Played Maryland 2005, 2006, 2007

Consensus All-American

WVU Sports Hall of Fame

Steve Slaton was one of the top playmaking running backs in the nation from 2005-07, earning consensus All-America honors in 2006.

The Levittown, Pa., native rewrote the WVU and Big East record books during his three-year career as a Mountaineer, helping West Virginia to bowl wins in the 2005 Sugar Bowl, 2006 Gator Bowl and 2007 Fiesta Bowl.

Photo by Randy Litzinger.

For his WVU career, he ranks first in rushing touchdowns (50), total touchdowns (55) and total points by a non-kicker (330); ranks second in total 100-yard rushing games (21), all-purpose yards (4,775), all-time receiving yards by a running back (805) and second in Big East history in total touchdowns with 53. Slaton left WVU third all-time in rushing yards with 3,923 for his career. He and Pat White became the third duo in FBS history to rush for 1,000 yards in consecutive seasons.

In the WVU single-season list, Slaton posted the most rushing with 1,744, most all-purpose yards with 2,104, tied for the most consecutive 100-yard rushing games with six and most rushing yards in Big East history by a true freshman with 1,128 yards. He ranks first (19) and third (18) for most touchdowns (rushing and receiving) in a season and ranks second for most receiving yards by a running back with 360.

In 2005, Slaton emerged as WVU's lead tailback as a true freshman, rushing for 1,128 yards in 10 games and scoring 19 touchdowns. He was the 2005 Big East Rookie of the Year, while earning first team freshman All-America honors by Rivals and second-team honors by *The*

Sporting News, CollegeFootballNews and Scout. He was one-point shy of setting the school record for points in a game when he posted 36 against Louisville. WVU finished the regular season 10-1 and 7-0 in the Big East. Slaton ended the season as the Sugar Bowl MVP with 204 yards rushing in the win over Georgia, highlighted by a pair of 52-yard touchdown runs. His 204 yards were not only a Sugar Bowl record, but the second-most rushing yards ever in a BCS game.

As a sophomore, Slaton earned consensus All-America honors when he set a WVU record with 1,744 yards rushing in a season and ranked fourth in NCAA rushing. He was one of three Doak Walker Award finalists, finished fourth in the Heisman Trophy balloting and was a Maxwell Award semifinalist. Slaton earned first team All-America honors by the AFCA, FWAA, Walter Camp, *The Sporting News, AP* and Scout. His season rushing total was a WVU record for a season, breaking Avon Cobourne›s record of 1,710 yards. Slaton and White combined for 2,963 yards and 34 rushing touchdowns. They also combined for 4,978 total yards and 49 total touchdowns.

In his final season as a Mountaineer, Slaton accumulated 1,051 yards and scored 17 touchdowns, posting his third straight year of 1,000 or more yards rushing. He led WVU to another Big East title and a Fiesta Bowl win over Oklahoma. Slaton broke Ira Rodgers' WVU record in career rushing touchdowns with 50. He left WVU as the top active points per game leader (9.4), first in touchdowns (50), fifth in yards per game (109.0) and third in rushing yards (3,923).

Slaton entered the 2008 NFL Draft after his junior season and was selected in the third round by the Houston Texans. He played four years for the Texans (2008-11), one for the Miami Dolphins (2011) and finished his career in the Canadian Football League with the Toronto Argonauts (2014).

Featured Player: Pat White, West Virginia

Played Maryland 2005, 2006, 2007. 2008
First Team All-American
WVU Sports Hall of Fame

Pat White was the nation's most versatile threat at quarterback, becoming the first college quarterback to start and win four consecutive bowl games from 2005-08.

The Daphne, Ala., native set 19 WVU, Big East and national records during his illustrious

Photo by Randy Litzinger.

career, including finishing as the all-time rushing quarterback in NCAA history with 4,480 yards (now ranks second).

West Virginia was 35-8 with White as the starting quarterback. He led the Mountaineers to bowl wins in the 2006 Sugar, 2007 Gator, 2008 Fiesta and 2008 Meineke Car Care. White set Big East records in touchdowns responsible for (103), total offense (10,529) and became the first player in Big East history to pass for more than 10,000 yards. He posted a 7-2 record against Top-25 opponents during his career.

As a freshman in 2005, he ranked second in WVU all-time freshman rushing with 952 yards and seven touchdowns. That season, he set a Big East and WVU quarterback rushing record with 220 yards against Pitt, breaking the Big East mark of 210 yards set by Michael Vick of Virginia Tech. The season culminated with White leading the Mountaineers to a win over No. 8 Georgia in the Sugar Bowl.

White was the Big East Offensive Player of the Year in 2006 and was a semifinalist for the Davey O'Brien Award. White broke his own school and Big East record for rushing yards by a quarterback when he ran for 247 yards against Syracuse, the fourth-best single game rushing effort in WVU history. Against Pitt, he rushed for 220 yards and threw for 204, becoming one of only eight players in NCAA history to rush and pass for 200 yards in the same game. His 424 yards of total offense tied Marc Bulger's school record. White directed the Mountaineers to a Gator Bowl win over Georgia Tech and earned Gator Bowl MVP honors.

As a junior in 2007, White was named Big East Offensive Player of the Year for the second straight year, as well as earning All-Big East first-team honors for the second consecutive year after leading WVU to another Big East title. He was a semifinalist for the O'Brien and Walter Camp Player of the Year awards, finishing sixth in the Heisman Trophy balloting. White led the Mountaineers in rushing with 1,335 yards, threw for 1,724 yards and accumulated 3,059 yards of total offense with 28 touchdowns. The season ended with WVU's second BCS victory in three years with a Fiesta Bowl win over No. 3 Oklahoma, and he earned Fiesta Bowl Offensive MVP honors.

In White's final season, he eclipsed the 4,000-yard rushing, 6,000-yard passing, 10,000-yard total offense and 4,000-yard all-purpose yardage marks. He finished his career fourth on the school's all-time all-purpose yardage list with 4,480 yards. For the season, White ran for 974 yards and eight touchdowns and passed for 1,842 yards and 21 touchdowns. He threw for a career-best and bowl-best 332 yards on 26-of-32 passing and three touchdowns in the win against North Carolina in the Meineke Car Care Bowl. That season, he threw for five touchdowns against Villanova, setting a Milan Puskar Stadium record (the second-most in a game in school history). White was named All-Big East first team for the third straight year and was a finalist for the Johnny Unitas Golden Arm Senior Award. He was seventh in Heisman balloting this year.

White was picked in the second round of the NFL Draft by the Miami Dolphins, playing the 2009 season with the Dolphins. He signed with the Washington Redskins in 2013 and then played one season for the Edmonton Eskimos of the Canadian Football League in 2014. He announced his retirement from professional football in 2015. Also, a standout on the diamond, White was selected by the Anaheim Angels in the fourth round of the 2004 Major League Baseball draft.

Bowden's Farewell

In the 2010 Gator Bowl between Florida State and West Virginia, Florida State coach Bobby Bowden, who previously coached at West Virginia, coached the final game of his legendary career. Bowden had been the head coach at Florida State since 1976 and had won two national championships, 13

Bill Stewart greets Bobby Bowden following Bowden's final game, a 33-21 victory over WVU in the 2010 Gator Bowl. Photo by Dale Sparks Photography and Framing.

ACC championships and had a 14-year streak of top-five finishes during that time. A record crowd of over 84,000 witnessed Bowden being carried off the field after a 33-21 Florida State victory on January 1, 2010.

The Flame-Out

"Veni Vidi Vici," may have been the mantra for the homecoming and soaring success that both Ralph Friedgen and Rich Rodriguez brought to their respective alma maters at the turn of the century. Like a comet, they took each program to heights rarely attained previously. Sadly, their comets flamed out much too soon.

Rodriguez started slowly, totally revamping predecessor Don Nehlen's offense, and finished the first year with a 3-8 record. But that followed with seasons of 9, 8 and 9 wins before ending with three 11-win seasons. He had won the hearts of Mountaineer faithful by turning down the Alabama job (really!) which subsequently went to Nick Saban (a native West Virginian) after the 2006 season. But, RichRod's tenure abruptly ended after the upset loss against massive underdog and archrival Pitt in 2007's Backyard Brawl. The

No. 2 Mountaineers were on their way to an undefeated season and a place in the BCS National Championship game in New Orleans.

Rumors abounded and egos soared. Rodriguez ultimately spurned his home state by announcing that he was leaving to become the head coach at Michigan. Mountaineer Nation was incensed and wounded. Like a jilted lover, their favorite son had fled to "greener pastures."

But in his seven years, he not only led West Virginia to three consecutive 11-win seasons, but also to three Top-10 rankings and three bowl victories (Sugar, Gator, and Fiesta—the last of which Bill Stewart coached).

The Ralph Friedgen saga at Maryland is different, but no less intriguing. Like Rodriguez, Fridge was one of the top assistant coaches in the nation, winning the Frank Broyles Award in 1999 when he decided to leave Georgia Tech and return home to Terp-land. His success took off even quicker than did Rodriguez's.

He started with 10, 11, and 10-win seasons with trips to the Orange, Peach and Gator bowls. He brought enthusiasm back to autumn Saturdays in College Park. The students were energized, as The Fridge led his team to their section to sing the fight song after each victory. During his run, Maryland won five of Fridge's seven bowl games.

However, the Terps then came back to earth and averaged only about six wins per season over the next six years. The excitement was gone, as were the crowds. His relationship with athletic director Debbie Yow had soured. He rebounded with nine wins in 2010 with a victory at the Military Bowl, a No. 23 ranking and ACC Coach of the Year honors. Alas, that wasn't enough as new athletic director Kevin Anderson showed Fridge the door.

Like a Shakespearian tragedy, Rodriguez and Friedgen left their programs in turmoil—Rodriguez by quitting on West Virginia and Friedgen for Maryland quitting on him. Oh, what might have been…

Chapter 13:

2010-2018
The Misfits

After RichRod and the Fridge left their respective schools, the athletic directors and presidents had a difficult decision to make. Who could they get to continue the success of Rodriguez and Friedgen? Both schools whiffed.

In College Park, rumors had it that Mike Leach, most recently from Texas Tech, had the inside track. But he was a loose cannon and, after a disastrous interview, the Terps turned to UConn coach Randy Edsall to take the football program from "good to great," said athletic director Kevin Anderson, as Edsall was announced in early 2011. A strict disciplinarian, Edsall was 2-4 when he was fired in the midst of the 2015 season (he was 22-34 during his 4-1/2 years).

Maryland then promoted offensive coordinator Mike Locksley as interim head coach—someone who had a 2-26 record as head coach at New Mexico. He was let go at the end of the 2015 season with a 1-5 record in College Park.

Next, Maryland turned to Michigan and hired defensive coordinator D.J. Durkin, primarily due to his pedigree with Urban Meyer and Jim Harbaugh, and his obvious knowledge of the Big Ten. It's said that Durkin's "fire and passion" were a big part of his landing the job, along with his recruiting prowess. The "fire and passion" caught up with him a year later with the death of Jordan McNair.

Durkin was suspended over McNair's death, three weeks prior to the opening of the 2018 season. Matt Canada was promoted from offensive coordinator to the interim head coach and went 5-7 that season. During the investigation, Durkin was on full pay and was reinstated as head coach on October 31 by the Maryland Board of Regents. But Durkin was fired the next day by university president Wallace Loh, who at the same time announced his pending retirement (which he later rescinded).

Now Locksley, who was passed over in favor of Durkin, assumed the reins in 2019. Can he bring stability and success to the program much like Friedgen, Ross, Claiborne and Tatum before him?

In Morgantown, Bill Stewart was promoted from interim to full-time head coach following an emotional Fiesta Bowl win over Oklahoma. He loved West Virginia and bled blue and gold. Stew was 9-4 in each of his three seasons, giving him a respectable 28-12 record, including the Fiesta Bowl win. But despite these nine-win seasons there was a notable drop off from Rodriguez's tenure.

New athletic director Oliver Luck wasn't convinced that Stewart was the right guy for the job. So, in 2011, he brought in Dana Holgorsen, the offensive coordinator from Oklahoma State, to help guide WVU into the Big 12—essentially making he and Stewart co-coaches until Holgorsen took over a year later. An unhappy Stewart added to the drama by creating a smear campaign to undermine Holgorsen. This skullduggery was the final straw and Holgorsen became head coach for the 2011 season.

Holgorsen was never a good fit. Loyalty is huge in West Virginia. He didn't like West Virginia or its fans. He didn't like the media. He wore a silver and black shirt at all games, thumbing his nose to the torrents of blue and gold that enveloped Mountaineer Stadium. It has been reported that he also had off-the-field problems. But he won football games.

In his eight-year tenure, he was 61-41 with seven bowl games, two postseason victories and three top-17 rankings. Most West Virginians sighed in relief when Holgorsen announced he was leaving to become the head coach at the University of Houston. Eight years on edge—wondering if and when Holgorsen would blow himself up—was finally over.

So, during this period of "Misfits," the Terps hadn't been able to find the right coach in five tries after firing Friedgen following the 2010 season. They accumulated a record of 38-61 (almost the opposite of Holgorsen's). Meanwhile, the "Mountaineer Misfits" had an 89-53 record after Rodriguez's departure. But despite WVU's success on the field, there was trouble in MoTown.

Now, Neal Brown, former head coach at Troy State, is captain of the Mountaineer ship—his first foray into the Power 5. The drama has ended but will the "W's" come? Nehlen, Bowden and Pappy are watching!

Game XLVII
West Virginia 31, Maryland 17
West Virginia leads series 24-21-2

September 18, 2010
Mountaineer Field at Milan Puskar Stadium, Morgantown, W.Va.
Attendance 60,122
West Virginia Head Coach: Bill Stewart (4th year)
Maryland Head Coach: Ralph Friedgen (10th year)
Barometer: West Virginia finished 9-4 including a loss in the Champs Sports Bowl. Maryland finished 9-4 with a win in the Military Bowl.
Game Notes: "*I feel like the 2010 MD-WVU game was a big game,*" said Blaine Stewart, son of the late Bill Stewart. "*Especially for my dad, because it was the first time WVU & Maryland played during his tenure (since 2007). Both teams being 2-0 and WVU coming off a tough win at Marshall the week before, it was a great test to see how WVU could respond. Geno, Tavon, and Stedman exploded onto the scene that day as young guys, and WVU was able to hold on to the commanding win.*"

The 2-0 Terps came into Mountaineer Stadium's raucous, sellout crowd with an eye for revenge. But they'd have to stop wide receiver Tavon Austin, a product of Baltimore's Dunbar High School. He had 14 catches for 175 yards coming into the game. The Terps were a bit untested with a close win over Navy, followed by a blowout over Morgan State.

"We're the neatest, tidiest, most courteous fans out there," WVU coach Bill Stewart said, tongue firmly placed in his cheek. *"Our fans will not get rambunctious, will not rock the bus like the old days, and they will be very cordial. It's a great place to play when you're from here, and a tough place to play when you're not."*

In prepping for the noise levels, Terp coach Ralph Friedgen piped in loud music during practices, including many renditions of "Country Roads."

"This is a very big game for us," Friedgen commented. *"We will learn a lot about who we are after this."*

"They're awesome fans (in Morgantown)," said Terp linebacker Alex Wujciak, *"loud, obnoxious—everything you'd want."*

"I think it's something that should happen every year," senior Terp safety Antwine Perez opined.

Smith Leads Mountaineers to 31-17 Win Over Terps

MORGANTOWN—In what seems to be the norm in these games, one team jumps way ahead of the other and holds on to win. This year's version was no different as West Virginia jumped to a 28-0 lead on the arm of sophomore quarterback Geno Smith, who tossed four touchdown passes in front of a raucous crowd of 60,122 in Morgantown.

Smith finished 19-for-29 with 268 yards, four touchdowns and no interceptions. Running back Noel Devine kept the Terp defense on its heels, as he rushed for 131 yards.

Only three minutes into the game, the Mountaineers struck. Smith hit Tavon Austin on a 6-yard strike, set up by a Devine 50-yard dash. Four minutes later, Smith hit Austin again, this time on a wide-open 5-yard pass.

Fellow wide receiver Stedman Bailey took over from there, making an acrobatic grab for a 26-yard touchdown late in the second quarter and catching a 5-yard touchdown early in the third.

The Mountaineers then gave up 17 unanswered points, as the Terps attempted a comeback.

Terrapin quarterback Jamarr Robinson had an awful first half but came out after halftime and threw two third-quarter TD bombs to

Torrey Smith, of 60 and 80 yards, making the score 28-14 with four minutes left in the third quarter.

Five minutes later Maryland threatened again, as Smith dropped a potential touchdown pass in the end zone against double coverage. The Terps settled for a 35-yard Travis Blitz field goal just as the fourth quarter started.

West Virginia "took the air out of the ball" and focused on the running game. Fullback Ryan Clarke carried eight straight times on the ensuing 16-play drive that ate up nearly nine minutes of clock and ended with when Tyler Bitancurt hit a 23-yard field goal to make the final score West Virginia 31, Maryland 17.

Austin had a big day against his home-state team, with seven catches for 106 yards and the two touchdowns.

Game XLVIII
West Virginia 37, Maryland 31
West Virginia Leads Series 25-21-2

September 17, 2011
Byrd Stadium, College Park, Md.
Attendance: 53,627
West Virginia Coach Dana Holgorsen (1st year)
Maryland Coach Randy Edsall (1st year)
Barometer: West Virginia soared to a 10-3 record including an astonishing 70-33 victory over #14 Clemson in the Orange Bowl. Maryland finished 2-10.

Game Notes: This rendition of the rivalry brought two new coaches to the game, Dana Holgorsen from Oklahoma State and Randy Edsall, the former head coach at Connecticut. The Mountaineers (2-0) came to College Park as the 18th-ranked team in the nation, while the Terps (1-0) were coming of a huge opening-game victory over Miami, where they unveiled their new Under Armor uniforms and helmets. The Terps are 1.5-point favorites.

The Baltimore Sun said, *"Maryland's outfits look like someone tore up the state flag and glued the pieces on a practice uniform."* But the players loved them.

"Much of this is dictated toward recruiting, and the other thing is the revenue generation and the opportunity to merchandise things that represent the University of Maryland and the athletic department," said new athletic director Kevin Anderson.

"I can remember when I was here being introduced as the head coach," said Edsall. *"That day I had people telling me 'You've got to beat West Virginia.'" I understand the importance, them being from a neighboring state, the rivalry that builds."*

Holgorsen apparently didn't study up on the rivalry and simply stated the obvious, pulling out tried-and-true clichés.

After starting sluggishly against Norfolk State, the previous week, Holgorsen commented on his first road game, *"We've got to learn to be on the road. They'll be rowdy and will have a good crowd, and that's a tough place to play. It's hard to get the home crowd out of it. But by starting fast is the only chance you've got."*

"It's definitely a rivalry game," said Maryland quarterback Danny O'Brien, *"It's very intense, a lot of electricity in the room."*

Maryland had switched to an up-tempo offense, similar to that of West Virginia.

Mountaineers Score Early, Hang on for Win Over Terrapins

COLLEGE PARK—West Virginia quarterback Geno Smith threw for a career high 388 yards to lead the 18th-ranked Mountaineers to a 37-31 victory at Byrd Stadium.

Another sellout crowd of 53,627 attended this border rivalry.

As has been their norm as of late, the Mountaineers jumped to a big lead and had to stave off a furious Terrapin comeback.

Maryland broke the ice, taking a 3-0 lead on a 25-yard Nick Ferrara field goal after a 77-yard drive. It was all West Virginia for the next 20 minutes as they stacked up three unanswered touchdowns and a field goal to lead 24-3. With 2:32 left in the half, the Terps finally scored again on a Danny O'Brien 18-yard touchdown pass to Kevin Dorsey.

The Mountaineers marched right back to hit a 34-yard Tyler Bitancurt field goal as the first half ended, making the score 27-10.

Smith engineered a 77-yard WVU drive following the second half kickoff, with Stedman Bailey snagging a 34-yard TD pass from Smith, swelling the score to 34-10.

Following an exchange of possessions, the Terrapins drove 61 yards as Davin Meggett ran it in from 20 yards out. The two-point conversion failed, so Maryland was within 34-16.

After a Smith interception, Maryland drove 44 yards in seven plays with D.J. Adams scoring the first of his two touchdowns on a 6-yard score. The score then stood at 34-23.

The Terp defense forced a Mountaineer punt, followed by a 12-play, 66-yard drive with Adams taking it in from the 2 to make the score 34-31 with 10:29 still left in the game.

Smith then led a 14-play, 65-yard drive ending with another Bitancurt field goal, giving the Mounties a little breathing room and forcing the Terps to go for a TD with the score 37-31.

O'Brien nearly did it, marching the Terps to the Mountaineer 35 before tossing an interception, ending the game.

West Virginia gained 480 yards in total offense while the Terps had 477. O'Brien had 289 yards passing with two touchdowns and three interceptions; Meggett gained 113 on the ground. Tavon Austin caught 11 passes for 122 yards to lead the Mountaineers.

Game XLIX
West Virginia 31, Maryland 21
West Virginia Leads Series 26-21-2

September 22, 2012
Milan Puskar Field at Mountaineer Stadium, Morgantown, WV
Attendance: 58,504
West Virginia Coach Dana Holgorsen (2nd year)
Maryland Coach Randy Edsall (2nd year)
Barometer: West Virginia finished 7-6 including a loss to Syracuse in the Pinstripe Bowl; Maryland finished 4-8.

Game Notes: Eighth-ranked West Virginia (2-0) came into this game as a whopping 27-point favorite in Morgantown. This was the first season that WVU competed in the Big 12 Conference. West Virginia was averaging a gaudy 55.5 points and 612 yards per game, third in the nation. WVU was led once again by quarterback Geno Smith and wide receiver and former Baltimore Dunbar star Tavon Austin.

In their most recent game in Morgantown, Maryland appeared flustered by the noise level, committing three delay-of-game penalties in their first offensive series, which only encouraged the crowd to yell louder.

Maryland's defensive coordinator Brian Stewart had coached against Dana Holgorsen's no-huddle offense before, so the Terp defense should be ready this time.

Smith and Austin Outlast Maryland

MORGANTOWN—Tavon Austin, plucked from under the nose of the Terps, loves playing Maryland. He caught three touchdown passes for the 8th-ranked Mountaineers, leading them to a 31-21 win in front of 58,504 at Milan Puskar Stadium.

Austin, from Baltimore's Dunbar High School, caught 13 passes for 179 yards, setting a school record in career receptions (208). He had 31 catches and 407 yards in his three games against the Terrapins.

West Virginia scored two early touchdowns and held on to win, which seemed to be the script of this rivalry game of late.

Despite the hype of this being a matchup of offensive talent, the Mountie defense scored the first points. On Maryland's second series, Mountaineer safety Darwin Cook broke through the line and caused freshman Perry Hills to fumble. Linebacker Doug Rigg scooped up the ball and rambled 51 yards for the first score of the game.

With 4:24 left in the first quarter, Austin caught a Geno Smith pass in the middle and went 44 yards up the right sideline to put the WVU ahead 14-0.

Despite these early scores, the Mounties often looked flat and the Terps came right back to score on a Hills 42-yarder to Stefon Diggs with under two minutes left in the opening stanza.

Early in the second, the Terrapins scored again to tie the game at 14. This time Hills hit Marcus Leak on a 12-yard touchdown, capping a nine play, 64-yard drive.

West Virginia scored 10 unanswered points to close the half with a 24-14 lead, including another Smith touchdown to Austin for 24 yards.

After a scoreless third, Smith hit Austin again for a 34-yard touchdown, making the score 31-14 with eight minutes left.

Fifty-three seconds later, Hills hit Diggs on a 56-yard touchdown to finish the scoring at 31-21.

Diggs caught three passes for 113 yards and added 63 yards on kick returns and 25 on punt returns.

Hills was 20-of-29 for 305 yards, three touchdowns and one interception, while Smith was 30-for-43 for 388 yards and three touchdowns.

The Mountaineer Miracle Man

Stedman Bailey, the Mountaineer Miracle Man. Photo by Randy Litzinger.

Stedman Bailey came to WVU from Miramar HS in Florida and was a high school teammate of WVU's Geno Smith. He started nine games as a freshman in 2010 and earned All-Big East freshman honors. He had two touchdown receptions against Maryland.

As a sophomore in 2011, he set the WVU single-season record for receiving yards (1,279) and tied the school record for most TD receptions (12) in a season. He had five consecutive 100-yard receiving games, setting another WVU record. In the Orange Bowl, he had five receptions and a touchdown.

His final season in Morgantown, Bailey gathered 114 receptions for 1,622 yards and 25 touchdowns. He earned three first team All-America selections.

He was a third-round pick by the St. Louis Rams in 2013. He played three years for the Rams and had 59 catches for 843 yards and two touchdowns, as well as a punt return for a 90-yard touchdown in 2014.

All this pales when compared to what Bailey endured next. In November 2015, Bailey was in a rented SUV with his cousin, his 10-year-old son and 6-year-old daughter waiting for a family friend to emerge from his house. They were getting ready to go to dinner before leaving Miami for Atlanta to spend Thanksgiving with Bailey's mother. In an apparent case of mistaken identity, an unknown car pulled up behind Bailey's SUV and opened fire. Bailey, who was in the passenger seat, took two bullets to the head. His cousin was hit three times before he was able to dive on top of his kids to protect them, taking eight more bullets.

The family friend ran to the car and sped to the nearest hospital, breaking 100 miles per hour on the way. It was a miracle… divine intervention that he lived. Doctors thought he'd never walk again, but Bailey ignored them.

Two and a half years later, he not only returned to WVU for classes and joined Dana Holgorsen's staff as a student assistant but has worked out to the point that he attended the NFL Combine to prove he could still play. Watching his daily workouts, one would never know that he has an implant in his head and a scar from ear to ear.

He continues to have faith that an NFL team will give him a chance, already matching workout numbers he had before the shooting. That included a 4.43 40-yard dash, good enough for sixth among the 37 wide receivers at the combine.

He's already planned his touchdown celebration following his first NFL touchdown after the accident, culminated by ripping off his helmet for the world to see his scar. In the meantime, he may be under consideration by head coach Neal Brown to become WVU's wide receivers' coach in 2020. He's ready for the miracle to happen—after all, he already is a miracle.

Featured Player: Tavon Austin, West Virginia

Played Maryland 2010, 2011, 2012
Consensus All-American
Johnny Rodgers Award Winner
A native of Baltimore, Md., Austin attended Dunbar High, a hotbed for football talent.

Austin (5-foot-8, 174 pounds) caught 215 balls for 2,475 yards (11.5 yards per catch) and 20 touchdowns over his final two college seasons, also rushing 88 times for 825 yards (9.4 per carry) and four more scores. He scored five career return touchdowns, four on

Photo by Randy Litzinger.

kickoffs and one on a punt.

As a junior in 2011, Austin had 100 receptions for 1,180 yards and eight touchdowns. He added 189 rushing yards on 18 carries and another touchdown. He also returned two kicks for touchdowns. He was a first team All-American by CBS Sports.

During the Mountaineers' 70-33 win in the 2012 Orange Bowl, he set an Orange Bowl record with four touchdown receptions. As a senior in 2012, he finished with 114 receptions for 1,289 receiving yards and 12 receiving touchdowns to go along with 643 rushing yards and three rushing touchdowns. In addition, he had 32 kick returns for 813 yards and a kick-return touchdown, and 15 punt returns for 165 yards and a punt-return touchdown. He was the 2012 All-Purpose Performer of the Year as announced by the College Football Performance Awards association. He was also eighth in Heisman balloting.

The Rams selected West Virginia WR Tavon Austin with the No. 8 overall pick in the 2013 NFL Draft.

Game L
Maryland 37, West Virginia 0
West Virginia Leads Series 26-22-2

September 21, 2013
M&T Bank Stadium, Baltimore, Md.

Attendance: 55,677
Maryland Head Coach Randy Edsall (3ʳᵈ year)
West Virginia Head Coach Dana Holgorsen (3ʳᵈ year)
Barometer: The Terps went 7-6 including a loss to Marshall in the Military Bowl, while the Mountaineers finished 4-8.

GAME NOTES: West Virginia (2-1) had won seven straight games in this border battle. But Maryland (3-0) entered this game as a five-point favorite in this, the first-ever matchup at M&T Bank Stadium in Baltimore. Maryland was making a concerted effort to woo Baltimore-area recruits and fans alike, particularly after losing Dunbar star Tavon Austin to West Virginia.

"The big thing is they (WVU defense) create pressure with their front," said Maryland offensive coordinator and future head coach Mike Locksley.

The Terps led the nation in sacks, averaging 4.67 per game. Maryland's challenge would be slowing down West Virginia's spread offense without two starting cornerbacks.

The Terps were hoping that it would feel like a home game and that red, white, black and gold-clad fans would outnumber the blue and gold Mountaineers. Traditionally, the Mountaineers bring tens of thousands of fans to road games. With Maryland's 3-0 start, things looked promising!

Maryland Rolls Over West Virginia

BALTIMORE—In a reversal of roles, it was the Maryland Terrapins who jumped out to a big lead. But unlike past years, they didn't need to hold on for the win. Instead, they put the hammer down and rolled to a 37-0 victory over the Mountaineers at Baltimore's M&T Bank Stadium in front of 55,677.

It was Maryland's most lopsided win in this border rivalry since the Jack Scarbath-led 54-7 blowout in 1951.

Late in the first quarter, WVU muffed a Maryland punt and A.J. Hendy recovered it at the WVU 24. Three plays later, quarterback C.J. Brown hit tight end Dave Stinebaugh on a 6-yard tipped pass to open the onslaught.

Less than a minute later, Hendy intercepted a Ford Childress sideline pass and took it 28 yards to the house to make it 14-0 at the end of the first.

Three Brad Craddock field goals of 50, 36 and 30 yards gave the Terps a comfortable 23-0 lead with 1:35 left in the half.

The Terrapins weren't finished. With rain beginning to fall, Yannik Cudjoe-Virgil tipped and intercepted a pass at the line of scrimmage, and the Terps took over at the WVU 6-yard line. Brown snuck in from the 1 to make it 30-0 at halftime.

It rained hard throughout the third quarter, chasing many fans home. But a few were still on hand to see Brandon Ross score the final touchdown from the 3 late in the fourth quarter.

The Maryland defense were the stars of the show. The defense, led by Hendy's "pick-six" and two recovered fumbles, forced three more turnovers. In the first half, West Virginia was limited to only 65 yards in offense, yet accrued 61 yards in penalties.

Maryland broke a seven-game losing streak in the series with this win.

Featured Player: Brad Craddock, Maryland

Played West Virginia 2012, 2013, 2014
First Team All-American,
Lou Groza Award Winner
Brad Craddock was recruited by Maryland while he was playing soccer and Australian Rules Football at Tabor Christian College in Adelaide, Australia.

At 6-feet tall, Craddock was initially supposed to be a punter with the Terps.

Photo by Randy Litzinger.

Instead, he was moved to place-kicker. He finished the first season with only 10 of 16 field goals made, posting a 62.5 success rate. He also handled kickoff duties for the Terrapins.

Under the tutelage of former Pro Bowl and Baltimore Ravens kicker Matt Stover, Craddock's stats improved greatly in his second season with the Terrapins. In one of his career highlights, Craddock converted three field goals, including one from 50 yards, helping the Terrapins to a 37–0 win over West Virginia in the 2013 match.

In a game against Penn State, Craddock kicked a 43-yard field goal with less than a minute to go, allowing the Terrapins to take the lead. The Terps won 20-19 and became bowl-eligible. He finished the year having made 18 of 19 field goals for a 94.7 percent success rate. He posted a long of 57 yards, and his lone miss came on the last kick of the season from 54 yards out.

Craddock earned national recognition as a second team All-American. He received the Lou Groza Award, awarded annually to the country's top collegiate place-kicker.

In his three years at Maryland, Craddock accrued several records. When he finished at Maryland in 2014, he had booted the most consecutive field goals in the history of the Maryland Terrapins and the entire Big Ten Conference (24), as well as the longest field goal in Terrapin history (57 yards against Ohio State).

Heartbreak Hotel

These teams have had some classic battles that were decided in the last minutes of the game, sometimes on the last play! Unfortunately for the Terps, most have been chalked up as Mountaineer wins. Here's a look at the classic nail-biters…

1945—The Tie. In Morgantown, the Mountaineers made a furious comeback in the waning moments, driving from their 44-yard line to the Terrapin 1. Harold McKibben passed to Vic Bonfili for the Mountaineers' second touchdown, making the score 13-12. Tom Jochum kicked the extra point to earn a 13-13 tie.

1973—The Buggs Run. WVU All-American Danny Buggs returned a Maryland punt 69 yards with just eight seconds on the clock for a 20-13 win in College Park.

1977—The Goal-Line Stand. West Virginia nearly squandered a 24-0 lead to the 11th-ranked Terps but held on with a tremendous goal-line stand to win 24-16 in College Park. Led by Fran Gleason and Harold Woods, West Virginia stopped Maryland three times inside the 4-yard line, topping it off with a stop of Terp quarterback Larry Dick on a 4th-down keeper.

1980—The Onside Kick. West Virginia drove frantically down the field for a touchdown and a two-point conversion, cutting the Maryland lead to 14-11 with 59 seconds left. But Maryland's Chris Havener dove on an onside kick on the 47-yard line, preserving the Terrapin victory in Morgantown. Quarterback Mike Tice iced the cake and the last 57 seconds by falling on the ball three times to end the game.

1981—The Fumble. With about 4-1/2 minutes to go and leading 13-10 at Byrd Stadium, Maryland forced a West Virginia punt. Lendell Jones muffed it and West Virginia's Rich Hollins recovered on the Terps' 12-yard line. Four plays later, Mountaineer quarterback Oliver Luck rolled around right end for a Mountaineer touchdown and a 17-13 win.

1982—The Gutsy Call. In Morgantown, Maryland drove 76 yards in 16 plays to cut West Virginia's lead to 19-18 with 1:39 remaining. Instead of going for the tie, Coach Bobby Ross gambled for all the marbles. Quarterback Boomer Esiason rolled right, but All-America linebacker Darryl Talley broke through the Terp line and rushed Boomer into an errant throw. West Virginia held on for the win.

1984—The Kick. Maryland started their game-winning drive on their own 13-yard line with about two minutes to play. They drove to the West Virginia 3 with the score tied at 17. On fourth and goal, All-American Jess Atkinson was called on to kick the game-winning field goal with 21 seconds remaining to give the Terps a 20-17 upset victory over the 18th-ranked Mountaineers in Morgantown.

1992—The Comeback. Backup Darren Studstill threw three touchdown passes in the fourth quarter to rally West Virginia from a 19-point deficit for a 34-33 victory in Morgantown. The game-winner came on a 20-yard TD pass to Adrian Murrell with 1:20 left.

2004—The OT TD. In Morgantown, the 8th-ranked Mountaineers needed overtime to put away the Terps 19-16. On third down in the first overtime, Rasheed Marshall threw a dart to wideout Chris Henry for a 7-yard touchdown catch and a Mountaineer victory.

2014—The Kick II. West Virginia gave away a 22-point lead in College Park to set up Lou Groza finalist Josh Lambert's game-ending heroics. QB Clint Trickett directed a 65-yard drive to turn the game over to Lambert at the 37-yard line for a game-winning field goal as time expired, giving West Virginia a 40-37 victory.

Game LI
West Virginia 40, Maryland 37
West Virginia Leads Series 27-22-2

September 13, 2014
Capital One Field at Maryland Stadium, College Park, Md.
Attendance: 48,154
West Virginia Coach Dana Holgorsen (4th year)
Maryland Coach Randy Edsall (4th year)
Barometer: WVU finished 7-6 including a loss to Texas A&M in the Liberty Bowl, while Maryland also finished 7-6 including a loss to Stanford in the Foster Farms Bowl

Game Notes: This was the first year that Maryland (2-0) competed in the Big Ten after 61 years in the ACC and entered the game as three-point favorites. This came after a 37-0 shellacking of the Mountaineers (1-1) last year, the most-lopsided win by Maryland in this series since 1951. But this was a different and better West Virginia team.

Quarterback Clint Trickett had taken the reins of the Mountaineer offense and kept the game against No. 2 Alabama close. He threw for

365 yards and no interceptions against the Tide in the Georgia Dome. He then led WVU past FCS-power Towson, 54-0. Maryland was 2-0 with wins over James Madison and South Florida.

Terp quarterback C.J. Brown was a threat with his arm and his legs. He ran for 60 yards and three touchdowns against JMU, but threw for just 111 yards against the Dukes and threw two interceptions week against South Florida. Maryland trailed lowly South Florida entering the fourth quarter and had six turnovers against them.

Lambert Kicks West Virginia over Maryland, 40-37

COLLEGE PARK—"Here we go again" could have been the theme of this 51st edition of this border rivalry before 48,154 at recently re-named Capital One Field at Byrd Stadium. West Virginia rolled to a 28-6 lead into the third quarter but staved off the Terrapins' comeback when Josh Lambert hit a 47-yard field goal at the buzzer to break a 37-37 tie.

This offensive highlight reel featured Mountaineer quarterback and Florida State transfer Clint Trickett passing for 511 yards and four touchdowns. He was 37-for-49 in the game. WVU finished with 694 yards in total offense to the Terps' 447. Maryland quarterback Wes Brown ran for a TD and threw for one, gaining 161 yards on the ground and throwing for 241 more.

The fireworks began on the first play from scrimmage as Wendell Smallwood pulled in a 50-yard pass from Trickett, setting up Rushel Shell's 1-yard scoring dive.

There were many more touchdowns to come.

Trickett hit wide receiver Mario Alford with a 43-yard scoring pass late in the first quarter to make it 14-0. Maryland answered with a 46-yard Brad Craddock field goal.

But less than a minute later, Trickett connected on a short pass to Kevin White who turned it into a 44-yard touchdown.

Craddock responded again, this time with a 41-yarder, making the score 21-6 midway through the second quarter.

WVU responded as well, with Mario Alford making a tough catch in the back corner of the end zone for a 36-yard score and a 28-6 lead with six minutes still left in the first half.

On the next play, Brown hit Stefon Diggs for a 77-yard touchdown. On the ensuing series, Brown was knocked out of the game, but replacement Caleb Rowe hit Jacquille Veii for a 26-yard touchdown to close the gap to 28-20 at halftime.

Brown returned with a bang, taking the first snap of the second half for a 75-yard touchdown jaunt, bringing the Terps within one point.

The Mountaineers blocked a Terrapin punt late in the third quarter. It rolled out of the end zone for a safety and a Mountaineer lead of 30-27.

On their ensuing possession, Trickett led the Mounties on a 56-yard drive, with Daikel Shorts catching a 11-yard TD pass from Trickett, giving WVU some breathing room with a 10-point lead.

West Virginia mistakes allowed Maryland to roar back. A fumbled punt return set up another Craddock field goal. The Terrapin defense forced a Mountaineer punt and punt return specialist William Likely took it 69 yards for the score, tying the game at 37 with under 10 minutes left.

Trickett directed a 13-play, 65-yard drive to give Lambert a chance to win the game with a 47-yard field goal in one of the most exciting games in this series' history.

Featured Player: Kevin White, West Virginia

Played Maryland in 2013, 2014

Consensus All-American

Kevin White was a junior college transfer from Lackawanna College in Scranton Pa. In 2014, White was an All-America wide receiver. He caught 109 passes for 1,447 yards and 10 touchdowns.

He ranked third in the country in catches that year (first in the Big 12), sixth in receiving yards (second in the Big 12) and

Photo by David Flowers/ ICON Sportswire

had the fifth-most touchdowns in the conference with 10. Not many expected this type of leap in production from White, as he only posted

35 catches, 507 yards and five touchdowns his first season on campus. Let's take a gander at just how White arrived in Morgantown.

White's best single-game totals came at Maryland in 2014. He caught 13 passes for 216 yards and a score in WVU's 40-37 win.

He would top those 13 catches weeks later against Texas, when he hauled in 16 passes for 132 yards. He didn't score in that contest and WVU lost, 33-16.

In seven of the 10 career games White didn't score a touchdown, his team lost.

White did it every way imaginable for a wide receiver, too. He turned screens into 60-yard gains, he'd blow past defenders with his amazing speed, he'd even high-point the ball in the end zone versus a double team to come down with the catch. Many players have played wide receiver at West Virginia, but very few did it the way White did. His brothers Ka'Raun and Kyzir, a wide receiver and a safety, followed their older brother's footsteps and played on the West Virginia Mountaineers football team. He was the seventh overall pick in the 2015 NFL Draft.

Featured Player: Mario Alford, West Virginia

Played Maryland in 2013 and 2014
First Team All-American

Mario Alford is a 5-foot-8 wide receiver from Greenville, Ga., and played for WVU in the 2013 and 2014 seasons. During the 2014 season, he accumulated 65 receptions for 945 yards and 11 touchdowns. He also led the nation by returning 26 kickoffs for 743 yards and two touchdowns. He was voted a first team All-American by two groups as a kick returner.

Photo by John Rivera/ ICON Sportswire

He was a seventh-round pick by the Cincinnati Bengals in the 2015 NFL Draft. He played for four NFL teams before moving to Canada, where he played the 2018 season with the Toronto Argonauts. He is currently playing for the Montreal Alouettes.

Game LII
West Virginia 45, Maryland 6
West Virginia Leads Series 28-22-2

September 26, 2015
Mylan Puskar Field at Mountaineer Stadium, Morgantown, W.Va.
Attendance: 61,174
West Virginia Coach Dana Holgorsen (5th year)
Maryland Coach Randy Edsall (5th year)
Barometer: West Virginia finished 8-5 including a victory over Arizona State in the Cactus Bowl, Maryland finished 3-9.

Game Notes: West Virginia native Brad Paisley made a surprise visit to Mountaineer Field for the pregame show. Working in conjunction with the Mountaineer Marching Band, he raised the roof with his rendition of "Country Roads."

Kickers Josh Lambert (WVU) and Brad Craddock (UM) became fast friends last year at the Lou Groza Award ceremony. Craddock won and Lambert was a finalist. Now they faced each other in this rivalry renewal. Last year, Craddock kicked three field goals, but Lambert kicked the game-winning 47-yarder as time expired.

After losing a back-and-forth rain-soaked battle with West Virginia last year, the Terrapins were hoping to exact some revenge.

Revenge goes both ways, as WVU coach Dana Holgorsen reminded his team of another rain-soaked border battle with the Terps two years ago, when Maryland shellacked the Mountaineers 37-0.

Postscript: After a 2-4 start, Maryland head coach Randy Edsall was relieved of his duties and was replaced by Mike Locksley.

West Virginia Rolls Terrapins, 45-6
MORGANTOWN—West Virginia dominated the visiting Terrapins on a sunny day in Morgantown as West Virginia's favorite son, Brad Paisley, made a surprise visit to sing "Country Roads," while 61,174 fans lustily sang along. It proved to be a bad omen for the Terps.

Mountaineer quarterback Skyler Howard threw for 294 yards and four touchdowns and Wendell Smallwood rushed for a career-high 147 yards, leading the Mounties to a 45-0 lead before Maryland got on the scoreboard in the fourth quarter.

West Virginia dominated both sides of the ball, as the offense rang up 601 yards while the defense forced five interceptions.

This was the ninth WVU win in the last 10 meetings of these border rivals.

West Virginia held Maryland on downs on a fourth-and-1 play at the WVU 39 on their opening drive. Howard then led the Mounties on a 61-yard drive, with Elijah Wellman catching a 7-yard touchdown.

Later in the quarter, the Mountaineers pinned the Terps deep in their own territory, forcing two punts that didn't get out of the Maryland side of the field. Both led to West Virginia touchdowns, making the score 21-0 at the end of the first quarter.

Howard led a five-play, 80-yard drive culminating with a 41-yard touchdown pass to Sheldon Gibson, making it 28-0.

If that wasn't bad enough for Maryland, the interceptions came in the second quarter and, when the dust settled, Caleb Rowe had tossed three and the Terps had also lost a fumble. WVU led at the half by a 38-0 score.

Rowe was replaced by Oklahoma State transfer quarterback Daxx Garman late in the third quarter. Garman threw a 46-yard touchdown to Jarvis Davenport midway in the fourth quarter to end the Terps' scoring drought. He also tossed an interception.

Brandon Ross was Maryland's lone bright spot, as he gained 130 yards on the ground, including a 55-yard run late in the second quarter that he fumbled through the end zone.

A national television audience watched this "final" version of this river rivalry. Scheduling discussions continued, though, and a two-game series was originally scheduled for 2020 in Morgantown, but ultimately cancelled due to the Corona Virus. The 2021 contest is scheduled for College Park.

Featured Player: William Likely, Maryland

Played West Virginia 2013, 2014, 2015
First Team All-American

William Likely was a three-year starter at Maryland, where he earned All-America honors as a kick returner. He was also the only player in D-I college football to start on both sides of the ball during his junior and senior years and was named one of the most versatile in the country by NFL.com.

Photo by Randy Litzinger.

He finished his collegiate career with eight touchdowns, the last of which came on a 100-yard kick return against Iowa in 2015. He is tied for first in school history with two interceptions returned for a touchdown and ranks 11th all-time in all-purpose yards.

The former Maryland jack-of-all-trades made his debut for the Canadian Football League's Hamilton Tiger-Cats in 2019, returning a kickoff for a 110-yard touchdown. The score proved to be the difference in a 30-23 win over the defending-champion Calgary Stampeders, which had beaten the Tiger-Cats 15 consecutive times.

He tore his ACL against Minnesota as a senior at Maryland in 2016. The injury prevented Likely from hearing his name called during the 2016 NFL Draft, and he was signed by the New England Patriots as an undrafted free agent that summer.

4th Quarter

The Future Is Bright… Right?
2019-??

Chapter 14:

The New Kids on the Block

"Prepare for the unknown by studying how others in the past have coped with the unforeseeable and the unpredictable."

George S. Patton

Both institutions' goal is to hire a head coach who will win games, fill the stands and stay for 15-20 years, all while staying out of trouble. This is obviously a tall order, and only WVU's Don Nehlen has achieved this gold standard in the last 75 years.

So how do we know if new coaches Neal Brown or Mike Locksley will stick? Is there a formula? Conventional wisdom suggests that the coach should be an alumnus and should have D-I head coaching experience. Really? Let's take a look at the hires each school has made since WWII.

"Insanity is doing the same thing and expecting a different result."

Albert Einstein

Maryland's winningest coaches since WWII:
- **Jerry Claiborne** (1972-81), 77-37-3 (.671). Left the head coaching position at Virginia Tech to come to Maryland. Left Maryland to be head coach at his alma mater (Kentucky).
- **Ralph Friedgen**, (2001-10), 75-50-0 (.600). Maryland alumnus. Had no head coaching experience, left Georgia Tech's OC

position prior to coming to Maryland. Fired from Maryland for not filling stands.

- **Jim Tatum** (1947-55), 73-15-4 (.815). Left the head coaching position at Oklahoma to come to Maryland. Left Maryland to be head coach at his alma mater (UNC).
- **Bobby Ross** (1982-86), 39-19-1 (.669). Was previous head coach at VMI but left the KC Chiefs QB coach position to come to Maryland. Left Maryland in wake of Len Bias death to be head coach at Georgia Tech.
- **Tom Nugent** (1959-65), 36-34-0 (.514). Left the head coaching position at Florida State to come to Maryland. "Retired" from Maryland to go into broadcasting.

Maryland has seemingly preferred coaches who had successful head-coaching experience whether with major or smaller programs. They have not necessarily preferred coaches with ties to Maryland.

While West Virginia's winningest coaches since WWII have been:

- **Don Nehlen** (1980-2000), 149-93-4 (.616). Had previously been the head coach at Bowling Green but came to WVU from the OC position at Michigan. Retired after 21 seasons in Morgantown.
- **Dana Holgorsen** (2011-18), 61-41 (.598). Came to WVU from the OC position at Oklahoma State. Left WVU to be head coach at Houston
- **Rich Rodriguez**, (2001-07), 60-26 (.698). WVU alumnus. Had previously been the head coach at Glenville State, but came to WVU from OC position at Clemson. Left WVU to be head coach at Michigan
- **Pappy Lewis** (1950-59), 58-38-2 (.604). Had previously been head coach at Washington and Lee but came to WVU from an assistant coach position at Mississippi State. Left WVU for the NFL.
- **Bobby Bowden** (1970-75), 42-26 (.618). Had previously been head coach at Howard (Ala.), but was promoted from OC at West Virginia to become WVU's head coach. Left WVU to be head coach at Florida State.

WVU has come from a different angle. None of their top five coaches came to WVU from a head-coaching position. All came from top assistant positions, primarily on the offensive side of the ball. Only Rodriguez is a WVU alumnus. They do, however, seem to have a legitimate concern that they are only a notch in a coach's resume.

"Those who cannot remember the past are condemned to repeat it."
George Santayana

The ongoing issue for both schools has been whether this is a "stepping-stone" job or a destination. Neither wants a "stepping-stone," so what criteria have been used to find "the one"? Here are some criteria that are often used and how it worked out for each school (those **bolded** are among the top-five winningest coaches at each school).

1. Do we hire an up-and-coming coach with virtually no head coaching experience?
   a. i.e., Maryland's Durkin, **Friedgen**, Vanderlinden, Krivak, Ward, Bryant
   b. i.e., West Virginia's **Holgorsen**, Stewart, **Rodriguez**, **Nehlen**, Cignetti, **Bowden**, Carlen
2. Do we hire a head coach with non-Power Five head coaching experience?
   c. i.e., Maryland's Locksley (New Mexico), Duffner (Holy Cross), **Ross (VMI)**, **Nugent (Florida State, at the time)**
   d. i.e., West Virginia's Brown (Troy), **Nehlen (Bowling Green)**, **Lewis (Washington and Lee)**, Kern (Carnegie Tech)
3. Do we hire a coach from the pros?
   e. i.e., Maryland's **Ross (K.C.)**, Saban (Buffalo), Mont (Washington)
   f. i.e., West Virginia's DeGroot (L.A.)
4. Do we hire a coach with big-time head coaching experience?
   g. i.e., Maryland's Edsall (Connecticut), **Claiborne (Virginia Tech)**, **Tatum (Oklahoma)**, Shaughnessy (Stanford)
   h. None from West Virginia

5. Do we hire a highly successful high-school coach?
    i. i.e., Maryland's Lester
    j. i.e., West Virginia's Corum
6. Do we hire an alumnus?
    k. i.e., Maryland's **Friedgen**, Ward, Mont
    l. i.e., West Virginia's **Rodriguez**, Corum

Historically, Maryland has made questionable choices when selecting a head football coach. Only one coach in Terrapin history has coached for more than a decade in College Park. To find him, one has to go all the way back to Curley Byrd, who coached for 23 years nearly a century ago. Since WWII, Maryland has had 18 coaches. Jerry Claiborne coached 10 years (1972-81); as did Ralph Friedgen (2001-10); Jim Tatum coached for 9 years (1947-55); Tom Nugent, 7 years (1959-65); Bobby Ross, 5 years (1982-86); Joe Krivak, 5 years (1987-91); and Mark Duffner, 5 years (1992-96). The other 10 coaches coached 23 years, or an average of 2.3 years each!

Obviously, longevity provides stability, loyalty and success. Why then, has Maryland gone through so many coaches? It doesn't seem to be a "stepping-stone" but more an issue of bad luck and bad choices. Former Maryland assistant athletic director Gothard Lane said, *"Maryland shoots themselves in the foot more frequently and more accurately than any other school!"* Tatum and Claiborne both left for their alma maters. Bobby Ross left in the wake of the Len Bias death and the rest were essentially fired. Friedgen is the only Maryland alumnus to prowl the sidelines since Bob Ward some 50 years ago. Fridge was fired, not because he didn't win, but allegedly because he didn't fill the stands.

Mike Locksley stands as the newest Head Terp. He is a native of D.C. and played at Towson, so he's as close as you can get to a native Terp. He's said to be a great recruiter, but his head coaching record was an abysmal 3-31 at New Mexico and as the interim head coach at Maryland. He's well-traveled with stops at Illinois, Florida and Alabama, but the question remains whether he can win as the head man. If he's successful, will this be a stop along the way for him or will he embrace the Terrapins, return them to their glory years and lead them for the next 15 or 20 years?

"Maryland's a different deal," said former Terp head coach Ralph Friedgen. *"It's not like every other school, and when they hire coaches that have no association with Maryland, they go about three or four years and then find out it's different… Mike understands what the whole deal is and how to do it. It's not going to be easy because of the tragedy. This is where Mike wanted to be, this has been… a lifelong goal of his."*

West Virginia has had more success in their coaching selections, albeit with some stumbles along the way. Conversely, the Mountaineers have had just 12 coaches since WWII. Don Nehlen led the way with a 21-year stint (1980-2000). Pappy Lewis coached 10 years (1950-59); Dana Holgorsen, 8 years (2011-18); Rich Rodriguez, 7 years (2001-07); Bobby Bowden, 6 years (1970-75); and Gene Corum, 6 years (1960-65).

WVU has had issues with the "stepping-stone" conundrum. Gene Corum and short-timers Frank Cignetti and Bill Stewart were reassigned. Pappy Lewis left for the NFL, Nehlen retired, Holgorsen left for the head coaching job at Houston, Rodriguez left for the top job at Michigan, Bowden for Florida State, Carlen for Texas Tech and DeGroot for New Mexico State.

Like Locksley, Neal Brown also is new in 2019. He's from nearby Kentucky and played at Kentucky and UMass. He's been head coach at Troy (Ala.) for four years, winning 35 games and three bowls. He's said and done all the right things to embrace Mountaineer Nation. He seems like the real deal. We do wonder whether, if he's successful, will he stay in Morgantown and build a legacy of longevity and success like Don Nehlen?

"Neal Brown was on my radar," said WVU alumnus Tommy Bowden. *"He is one of the top, up-and-coming young coaches in the country… They need some more talent, but he'll bring them around."*

So where will Brown and Locksley fit among the Mountaineer and Terrapin head coaches? Neither are alumni but are from adjoining areas. Can Locksley heal the program, win and fill Maryland Stadium?

While Brown had great success at Troy for four years. Granted it's not Alabama, but can he follow Lewis' and Nehlen's lead and succeed on the big stage?

Both schools need a shot in the arm laced with a large dose of integrity. West Virginia has been much more successful, but former coach Holgorsen never embraced West Virginia, its fans or its culture and had some questionable behavioral issues during his tenure. Maryland's recent history has been abysmal, on and off the field… most recently under the oppressive tenure of Durkin and the death of Jordan McNair.

Can these two "saviors" right their respective ships and return their programs to the level of respect and envy of their peers and their starving fans? Hopefully, the stars are aligned for them both. Locksley will reportedly make $15.6 million over the next six years, while Brown's six-year contract tops $19 million! The gamble on success doesn't come cheap!

Time will tell…

"Grading WVU Football Coach Neal Brown: WOW!"
By Chip Zimmer, Martinsburg (W.Va.) Journal

Photo by Scott Winters/ ICON Sportswire

Did WVU Athletic Director Shane Lyons and President Gordon Gee hit a home run with their hire of Troy head coach Neal Brown? From watching his introductory press conference, it sure looks like it! Wow! Time will tell, but let's look at some key areas to see if, indeed, Brown can check all the boxes, he signed a 6-year deal for $19 million last week.

First of all, where is Troy? If you're like me, you had to look it up to find it! It's in rural southeastern Alabama, 50 miles southeast of Montgomery; about 75 miles north of the Florida panhandle and about 60 miles west of the Georgia border. Troy has been an NCAA Division I Football Bowl Subdivision (Group of 5) program since 2001. Prior to that they were NCAA Division II (like Shepherd) where they won National Championships in

1984 and 1987. Their Veteran's Memorial Stadium holds 30,402. The largest crowd to see a Troy football game there was 29,612 on September 1, 2018, when the Trojans lost to Boise State 59-20.

Neal Brown became Troy's head coach for the 2015 season. He went 4-8 in a rebuilding year and followed that with a 31-8 record the ensuing three seasons, including three 10+ victory seasons and bowl victories. Brown is from Danville, KY and played at Kentucky and UMASS. He served as an assistant coach at UMASS, Sacred Heart and Delaware before becoming wide receiver coach and offensive coordinator at Troy for 3 years. He left Troy to become offensive coordinator first at Texas Tech and then at Kentucky before taking over the helm at Troy.

So how does this prepare him for the Mountaineers?

Almost Heaven, Character/Integrity: This is a critical area for success in West Virginia; something we've been lacking for quite some time with our football program. By all indications, Coach Brown is a winner here. He's a family man with three children. He treats his players and coaches and their families like…family and seemingly truly cares about them as people and students. This should be like manna from Heaven for returning and incoming players and their parents. My daughter experienced a similar coaching change at a different university and it was an abject nightmare.

"First and foremost, what I wanted in a coach was a person with character," Lyons explained. "I wanted somebody who is going to follow the NCAA rules, do it the right way as far as institutional policies go…. I wanted somebody intelligent and somebody with energy, and then it expanded to are they a winner? Do they have head coaching experience? That was really important to me."

Larry Blakeney, retired AD at Troy, who first hired Brown commented "His wife, she understands the coaching business, and they've got beautiful kids. They're a primo family to lead the program. They're good folks and West Virginia couldn't do any better."

GRADE: A+

Driving Down the Road, Experience: He has served as a head coach at a NCAA Division I school, albeit, a Group of 5 program, like Marshall, Cincinnati, Houston and Navy. He was offensive coordinator at two Power 5 schools (Texas Tech and Kentucky). He has a great record (35-16), but playing in front of 29,000 fans at Troy is a far cry from 60,000 screaming Mountaineers when the Texas Longhorns stampede into Mountaineer Field!
GRADE: B+

Take Me Home Country Roads, WV Ties: None, but he grew up in Eastern Kentucky and has lived in rural Alabama for four years. He is comfortable with Appalachian heritage. This is not a mandatory requirement, but it certainly helps to have a coach who has an inherent love of the people and the state of West Virginia. His Kentucky roots imply that a comfort level between the coach and state will continue to grow. Unlike Holgorsen; Carlen, Bowden and Nehlen successfully nurtured relations with the Mountaineer Nation in the beginnings of their tenures in MoTown. Hopefully, Brown will as well.
GRADE: B

All My Memories, Coaching Philosophy: Brown advocates a no huddle, wide open offensive style, reminiscent of Rich Rod's spread offense. He's a "air raid" disciple, having played for Hal Mumme at Kentucky and coached under Mike Leach at Texas Tech. His entire career has been on the offensive side of the ball, which will be a huge plus as WVU maneuvers through the Big12 minefield. He advocates a balanced attack, running nearly as often as he throws. Troy averaged 30.6 points per game last year. He'll need to find another 10-15 points per game to compete in the Big 12. On Defense, he's moving to a 4-2 and is no slouch, ranking in the top 25 in a variety of defensive categories. During his 4 years at Troy, his teams won at Death Valley (LSU and almost at Clemson's) as well as at Nebraska's Sea of Red. As offensive coordinator at Texas Tech, he engineered an upset over #3 Oklahoma. He's bringing in some outstanding coordinators who will ratchet it up even more.
Grade: A-

As Neal Brown moves to West "by God" Virginia, we welcome him with open hearts and arms. We've longed for a coach who embraces the heart and spirit of the Mountain State, and it seems, we've found one in Neal Brown. This Mountaineer hopes that he brings us the classiness of Jim Carlen, the integrity of Bobby Bowden, the inner strength of Frank Cignetti, the longevity of Don Nehlen, the enthusiasm of Rich Rodriguez, and the love of Bill Stewart. LET'S GOOOOO MOUNTAINEERS!

Postscript: In 2019 West Virginia won three of their first four games before losing 5 in a row including losses to the #11, #5 and #12 teams. They then won at #24 Kansas State before losing to #21 Oklahoma State, finishing with a 5-7 record. Despite not being bowl-eligible, there was comfort and hope for 2020 that the Mountaineers were in the game until the end in 4 of their losses.

In virus ravaged 2020, WVU finished 6-4 with a Liberty Bowl victory over Army. The Oklahoma game was first rescheduled and two weeks later, cancelled due to COVID.

Maryland hires Mike Locksley… Again

Courtesy of Special Collections, University of Maryland Libraries, University of Maryland.

The Maryand Terrapins brought Mike Locksley back home. The Terps hired Alabama's offensive coordinator to lead them back to respectability following three turbulent years under D.J. Durkin, who was fired under pressure following the death of Jordan McNair in the summer of 2018.

Locksley described Maryland as his "dream job," something Terp fans haven't heard in a long time.

ESPN's Scott Van Pelt, a Maryland grad, tweeted: *"People outside the DMV won't get it, but people from there absolutely will. Especially his former Terp players. Unrivaled local respect among local HS coaches, he can help heal & unite the factions like no other. Welcome home, Lox!"*

Ironically, Locksley returns to Maryland after being passed over for the head coaching position three years ago, which went to Durkin. In the meantime, he served as an analyst as well as the offensive coordinator at Alabama and just won the Broyles Award which goes to the best assistant coach in the country. He served as Maryland's interim head coach following the firing of Randy Edsall in 2015.

Locksley's first chore will be to heal the program. It was a culture of fear and mistrust. From all indications, Locksley is the right man to do this. He's well respected among his current and former players and their parents, as well as boosters and high school coaches.

Next, he'll need to change the culture of losing. Maryland has had only four glimpses of national notice in its century plus of football.

- Jim Tatum (Four 9-win seasons in nine years)
- Jerry Claiborne (Three 9-win seasons in 10 years)
- Bobby Ross (Two 9-win seasons in five years)
- Ralph Friedgen (Five 9-win seasons in 10 years)

They haven't had a winning season since 2014 and have had only two winning seasons—both just 7-6—since Friedgen left a decade ago.

This will not be an easy task. First, he'll have to answer some questions about his abysmal record at New Mexico. But Locksley's knowledge of the DMV, coupled with his recruiting acumen, seems to make him perfectly suited for the job. This is critical if he is to bring the Terps into a competitive level in the Big Ten East.

That means distancing themselves every year from Rutgers and Indiana. If these are Maryland's peers on the gridiron, then the Terps will go through this process all over again in four or five years.

It also means being competitive on an annual basis with Penn State, Michigan State, Ohio State and Michigan. Being competitive with these Big Four Horsemen means beating a couple of them every year! No, that's not a typo: BEATING some of them EVERY YEAR!

Then there's the arms race for facilities. With Under Armour's help, they've opened a state-of-the-art indoor facility in Cole Field House to go along with the Gossett Center at the stadium. So, it seems that they're able to check off that box.

Locksley said all the things Terrapin Nation needed to hear. He didn't guarantee wins, titles, championships or bowl victories. "I'm not here to just build a winning football team. I'm here to build a winning football family," he said.

If he can heal the program, build a culture of trust and keep the DMV's blue-chip players at home, then Locksley could be the next Terp coach to join the legends of Byrd, Tatum, Claiborne, Ross and Friedgen. It'll take time and patience, but turtles are known for that!

Postscript: The Terps started out with a bang under Locksley in 2019, scoring 142 points in their first two games, including a 63-20 win over No. 21 Syracuse. Things pretty much went south from there, beating only Rutgers the rest of the way to finish with a 3-9 record. There may be growing concern as, except for close losses at Temple and Michigan State and a home loss to Indiana, the Terps were never in the games—giving up 52 to Minnesota, 54 to Nebraska, 59 to Penn State and 73 to Ohio State.

In the 2020 COVID shortened Big 10 season, Maryland finished 2-3 including a win over Penn State. Games with Ohio State, Michigan and Michigan State were cancelled.

In Memoriam

As I put the finishing touches on this book on Veteran's Day, 2020, I am reminded of those valiant sailors who served on the USS West Virginia and the USS Maryland, both of which were severely damaged on Dec. 7, 1941 at Pearl Harbor. Special mention to a late family friend Garth Summers, who survived Pearl Harbor on the Maryland.

Comrades in arms, these two battleships were moored on "Battleship Row" on that fateful day.

The Maryland was toward the front, moored near the Ford Island Naval Air Station, inboard and somewhat protected by the ill-fated Oklahoma, which capsized as a result of the bombings. The USS Maryland, on the other hand, was able to open fire against the enemy and send teams of its sailors on rescue missions to retrieve those stranded on the other battleships. The ship was eventually struck by two bombs, one of which exploded in the ship's hull and caused serious flooding. She was credited for shooting down four Japanese planes and sustained four deaths and 13 wounded in the attack.

She went to Puget Sound for repairs and, two months later, was back in action, playing significant roles in the South Pacific battles of Marshall Islands, Saipan, Leyte Gulf and Okinawa, among others.

The West Virginia was moored right behind the Oklahoma, outboard of the Tennessee, and sustained serious damage from nine torpedo hits, ultimately sinking in the 40-foot-deep harbor. Had it not been so shallow, it would have been a total loss. She sustained 106 deaths and an unknown number of wounded in the attack. Three sailors survived in sunken air pockets for 16 days until they finally succumbed.

But, she too, was raised and taken to Puget Sound for extensive repairs. Two years later, she returned to Pearl Harbor and on to the Admiralty Islands, where she re-joined the Maryland in Battleship Division 4 and played significant roles in the invasion of the Philippines, as well as the battles of Surigao Straits, Leyte Gulf, Okinawa and Iwo Jima.

West Virginia and Maryland:

Naval Heroes… Friendly Rivals… Great Football…

Fair Winds and Following Seas!

Resources

1st Quarter: The Rivalry

Chapter 1: The Path to the Rivalry

- www.sports-reference.com
- www.espn.com/college-football/columns/story?columnist=schlabach_mark&id=2926329
- https://thesportsarsenal.com/tag/seven-sinners
- *"Maryland, Clemson can't play in SC: Terps, Tigers on year probation". Asheville Citizen. December 15, 1951. Archived from the original on April 30, 2019. Retrieved April 18, 2019.*
- *"Seven schools quit SC to form own conference: Tebell says Virginia might join; No state schools in new lineup". Newport News Daily Press. May 9, 1953. Archived from the original on April 30, 2019. Retrieved April 17, 2019.*
- *"Atlantic Coast Conference brings Virginia into fold: Plan to admit West Virginia is turned down; Conference decides to operate as eight-school organization for indefinite period". Petersburg Progress Index.* Archived from *the original on April 30, 2019. Retrieved April 17, 2019.*

Chapter 4: The Future of the Rivalry

- Zimmer, Chip. Charleston Gazette-Mail, September 4, 2015

2nd Quarter: A Look Behind the Curtains

Chapter 5: The Tradition

- www.roadsideamerica.com/story/11456
- https://umdarchives.wordpress.com/tag/mascot/

- www.espn.com/college-football/story/_/id/11735028/under-armour-maryland-terps-perfect-match
- www.nytimes.com/2015/08/26/sports/ncaafootball/under-armour-seeks-to-do-for-maryland-what-nike-did-for-oregon.html
- www.baltimoresun.com/sports/terps/tracking-the-terps/bs-sp-cole-field-house-maryland-0802-story.html
- www.espn.com/espn/commentary/story/_/page/wilbon-110907/university-maryland-new-football-uniforms-making-terrapins-relevant
- www.theintelligencer.net/x-old-sections/wvu-150th/2017/09/wvus-mascot%e2%80%88bring-on-the-boom/
- https://mountaineerweek.wvu.edu/about
- Zeise, Paul. Sunday, January 07, 2001, Post-Gazette Sports Writer, Copyright ©1997-2019 PG Publishing Co., Inc. All Rights Reserved.
- www.msnsportsnet.com/jackfleming/ Jack Fleming Tribute
- Steinburg, Dan. The Washington Post, October 1, 2013
- WV metronews.com
- https://espnpressroom.com/us/bios/patrick_mike/
- Ungrady, Dave. Tales from the Maryland Terrapins
- Umterps.com
- Collegegridirons.com
- Washington Post, March 13, 2019

Chapter 6: The Characters
- Fairman, Gail. The Daily Athenaeum, 1973
- Baltimore Sun, 8/29/2005

Chapter 7: The Fans
- https://chapspitbeef.com/the-history-of-maryland-bbq-and-pit-beef/

Chapter 8: The Coaches
- Attner, Paul. "The Terrapins."
- http://insider.espn.com/college-football/insider/columns/story?columnist=davie&id=2457483
- Johnson, Jim. http://www.hoyafootball.com/history/byrd.htm
- www.orlandosentinel.com/news/os-xpm-1986-12-28-0280290240-story.html

- University of Maryland Sports Hall of Fame
- WVU Sports Hall of Fame
- College Football Hall of Fame
- Browning, Al. *I Remember Paul "Bear" Bryant*. Cumberland House Publishing. pp. 100–101. ISBN 1-58182-159-X.
- Phillips, B. J. (September 29, 1980). "Football's Supercoach". *Time*. Retrieved April 2, 2016.
- Florida Sports Hall of Fame
- www.washingtonpost.com/wp-dyn/articles/A54031-2004Jan27_2.html
- www.buffalosportshallfame.com/member/lou-saban/
- Washington DC Touchdown Club
- Ungrady, Dave. "Tales of the Maryland Terrapins" Page 210-220
- Georgia Tech Sports Hall of Fame
- Virginia Hall of Fame
- washingtonpost.com/wp-srv/sports/longterm/memories/bias/launch/bias19.htm
- https://everipedia.org/wiki/lang_en/Joe_Krivak/
- Syracuse Sports Hall of Fame
- www.baltimoresun.com/topic/sports/football/ralph-friedgen-PESPT008511-topic.html
- www.sbnation.com/college-football/2016/12/28/14100818/randy-edsall-hired-uconn-coach
- https://collegefootballtalk.nbcsports.com/2018/10/31/reports-maryland-fires-head-coach-d-j-durkin/
- http://blackathlete.net/2008/10/the-story-of-dick-leftridge/
- University of South Carolina Athletic Hall of Fame
- https://smartfootball.com/grab-bag/the-throwin-game-is-like-a-disease
- Texas Tech Hall of Honor
- Pownell, Don. Blue and Gold News
- "Bobby Bowden wins last game, but can't beat NCAA". *Jacksonville.com*.
- The Times-Union. "Movie opens old wounds for Bowden—Jacksonville.com".
- "A Tenure Longer Than Expected and Shorter Than Desired" *The New York Times*, August 31, 2010.
- Crawford, Brad, August 19, 2017. 24/7Sports

- www.timeswv.com/sports/hertzel-column-o-toole-joins-long-list-of-eccentric-wvu/article_fdb09fc5-fa19-5050-9483-302f53b70771.html
- www.flickr.com/photos/digitalcollectionsum/albums/72157689777663656
- www.usatoday.com/story/sports/ncaaf/2015/09/24/maryland-wvu-features-2-of-college-footballs-best-kickers/72748338/
- Glenville State Athletics Hall of Fame
- Wetzel County Hall of Fame
- https://mountaineersports.com/dana-holgorsen-vs-neal-brown/

3rd Quarter: The Games

- Abpriddy Apr 3, 2014, 11:00am EDT in The Smoking Musket:
- www.reddit.com/r/CFB/comments/6sikqr/forgotten_teams_1993_west_virginia_mountaineers/

Chapter 9: 1919-1960

- Pittsburgh Daily Post, October 19, 1919
- Baltimore Sun, October 17, 1943, AP
- The Raleigh Register (Beckley, W.Va.), October 15, 1944
- Baltimore Sun, October 28, 1945, AP
- The Terrapins, Maryland Football; Baltimore Sun
- The Raleigh Register (Beckley, W.Va.), November 2, 1947
- The Raleigh Register (Beckley, W.Va.), November 28, 1948
- Maryland Tips West Virginia, *Daytona Beach Morning Journal*, November 25, 1949
- The Raleigh Register (Beckley, W.Va.), November 25, 1949
- Cumberland (Md.) Sunday Times, November 19, 1950, AP
- Beaver County (Pa.) Sports Hall of Fame.
- Maryland Whips West Virginia; Mo Modzelewski Outgains Opponent, *Toledo Blade*, November 24, 1951.
- Cumberland Sunday Times (Md.), Sunday, November 25, 1951, AP, George Bowen
- Associated Press, November 25, 1951
- https://umdarchives.wordpress.com/2017/10/19/queens-game-60-years/
- Cumberland (Md.) Sunday Times, September 20, 1959, UPI

- www.baltimoresun.com/bs-mtblog-2011-12-catching_up_with_gary_collins-story.html
- Beckley (W.Va.) Post-Herald/Raleigh Register, September 18, 1960, AP

Chapter 10: 1966-1979
- Charleston (W.Va.) Sunday Gazette-Mail, October 16, 1966, by A. L. "Shorty" Hardman
- The Daily Times (Salisbury, Md.), September 21, 1969, AP
- https://news.lib.wvu.edu/2015/06/23/muhammad-ali-visits-wvu-in-1969/
- Salisbury (Md.) Daily Times, November 29, 1970
- Beckley Post-Herald (W.Va.), September 16, 1973, AP by Gordon Beard
- Sunday Gazette-Mail (W.Va.), September 19, 1976, by A.L. Hardman
- https://bleacherreport.com/articles/222744-what-a-long-strange-trip-its-been-wvu-football-before-1980
- Delaware Sports Hall of Fame
- West Virginia Surprises Maryland, *Pittsburgh Post-Gazette*, September 19, 1977.
- The Daily Times, Salisbury, Md., September 18, 1977.

Chapter 11: 1980-2000
- Baltimore Sun, September 18,1980
- Baltimore Sun, September 21, 1980 by Bill Free
- Baltimore Sun, September 20, 1981 by Bill Free
- www.testudotimes.com/maryland-terps-football/2017/6/6/15743774/best-quarterback-in-history-poll
- Ungrady, Dave. "Tales of the Maryland Terrapins," Page 201
- Baltimore Evening Sun and Salisbury Daily Times, September 19, 1982.
- Baltimore Sun, September 18,1983, by Bill Free
- The Salisbury Daily Times, September 23 1984
- www.history.com/this-day-in-history/maryland-gets-a-miracle-in-miami
- Baltimore Sun September 22, 1985
- Baltimore Sun, September 21, 1986
- Baltimore Sun, September 20, 1987

- Salisbury Daily Times, September 18, 1988
- The Daily Times, Salisbury, Md., September 10, 1989
- The Star-Democrat, Easton, Md., September 9, 1990
- Baltimore Sun, September 22, 1991
- Salisbury Daily Times, September 20, 1992
- Baltimore Sun, September 19, 1993
- www.smokingmusket.com/2014/4/3/5556430/west-virginia-mountaineers-miami-hurricanes-football-1993
- The Star-Democrat (Easton, Md.), September 18, 1994
- Salisbury Daily Times, September 17, 1995
- The Star Democrat, Easton, Md., September 29, 1996
- Salisbury Daily Times, October 12, 1997
- Annapolis Capital, September 20, 1998
- Baltimore Sun, September 19, 1999
- Associated Press, September 17, 2000

Chapter 12: 2001-2010

- www.washingtonpost.com/wp-dyn/content/article/2007/09/12/AR2007091202685.html
- The Star Democrat, Easton, Md., September 30, 2001
- The Star Democrat, October 6, 2002
- Associated Press, 2004
- www.espn.com.au/college-football/undefined September 19, 2004
- Dull, Doug, Creese, Greg and O'Connor, Sean, 2004 *Toyota Gator Bowl Guide*, Maryland Football Media Information, December 2003.
- Pells, Eddie Terps Trounce Mountaineers in Gator Bowl, University of Maryland Terrapins Football official website, Associated Press Sports, 1 January 2004.
- www.espn.com/college-football/undefined September 17, 2005
- Parasiliti, Bob. Hagerstown Herald Mail, September 15, 2006.
- www.espn.com/college-football/game/_/gameId/272560120 September 13, 2007
- www.espn.com/college-football/undefined, September 18, Associated Press
- ESPN, September 18, 2010

Chapter 13: 2011-2018

- Hawley, Aaron. https://pittsburgh.sbnation.com/west-virginia-mountaineers/2011/9/17/2431608/west-virginia-vs-maryland-mountaineers-intercept-obrien-3-times-hold
- www.espn.com/college-football/recap?gameId=322660277 September 22, 2012
- www.rotoworld.com/college-football/nfl-draft/player/41209/tavon-austin 2013
- www.espn.com/college-football/recap?gameId=332640120 2014
- www.espn.com/college-football/undefined
- www.foxsports.com/college-football/story/wvu-football-do-you-remember-when-kevin-white-112216
- ESPN, September 26, 2015

4th Quarter: The Future is Bright… Right?

Chapter 14: New Kids

- Zimmer, Chip. Martinsburg Journal, January 12, 2019.
- Alex Kirshner@alex_kirshner Updated Dec 4, 2018, 8:25pm EST https://www.sbnation.com/college-football/2018/12/4/18104885/mike-locksley-maryland-coach-hired

Back Cover Image: Courtesy of Special Collections, University of Maryland Libraries.

ABOUT THE AUTHOR

Chip Zimmer received his B.S. and M.S. degrees from West Virginia University and his Ph.D. from the University of Maryland, College Park. He has worked for both athletic departments, the Washington Capitals, Sport for Understanding and DelWilber Sports Marketing. He also served as the Athletic Director (interim) at George Washington University. He is the only person to have honorary memberships with both Maryland's and West Virginia's letterman clubs. He retired as chairman of Shepherd University's MBA program and lives with his wife, Barbara, splitting time between homes in Williamsburg, Va., and Swanton, Md. Their daughter, Kate Gonzalez, is a graduate of Maryland and the William and Mary School of Law. He has been a health care and sports marketing consultant for over 20 years and is a monthly columnist with the *Martinsburg (W.Va.) Journal*.

"If there were a Mt. Rushmore of sports marketing's founding fathers it would surely include the likenesses of Bob Savod of North Carolina, Don Canham of Michigan, Russ Potts and Chip Zimmer of Maryland. These men moved the decimal point in today's salaries and overall budgets to the point that would have been unthinkable 20 years ago. They didn't draw attention to themselves, but brought the world to college athletics!"

Walt Atkins

Made in the USA
Las Vegas, NV
22 August 2021

28682731R00216